dealing with the devil

East Germany,
Détente, and
Ostpolitik,
1969–1973

M. E. SAROTTE

The University of

North Carolina Press

Chapel Hill & London

dealing
with the
devil

© 2001 The University of North Carolina Press
Manufactured in the United States of America
This book was set in Aldus by Keystone Typesetting, Inc.
Book design by April Leidig-Higgins

The paper in this book meets the guidelines for permanence and durability of the Committee on Production Guidelines for Book Longevity of the Council on Library Resources.

Library of Congress Cataloging-in-Publication Data
Sarotte, M. E.
Dealing with the devil : East Germany, détente, and Ostpolitik, 1969–1973 / M.E. Sarotte.
p. cm.—(The new Cold War history)
Includes bibliographical references and index.
ISBN 0-8078-2599-9 (cloth: alk. paper)
ISBN 0-8078-4915-4 (pbk.: alk. paper)
1. Germany (East)—Politics and government.
2. Detente. 3. Germany (West)—Foreign relations—Europe, Eastern. 4. Europe, Eastern—Foreign relations—Germany (West) I. Title. II. Series.
DD288.S27 2001 327.43′1′009047—dc21 00-046690

A portion of this work appears, in somewhat different form, as "A Small Town in (East) Germany," *Diplomatic History* 25, no. 1 (January/February 2001) and is reprinted here with the permission of Blackwell Publishers.

05 04 03 02 01 5 4 3 2 1

For Frank and Gail Sarotte

Contents

Maps and Illustrations

Preface

Forty-eight hours after leaving the United States for the first time, I found myself stranded under an East Berlin guard tower. Compared to the suffering experienced by others at the East German border, it was an event of no importance, but it made me start to question. It happened during the Reagan era of the Cold War in 1986, when I was a still a teenager. I had flown to West Germany to visit an exchange student who had lived with my family. We decided to go together for a sightseeing drive in East Berlin, unaware that American and West German citizens had to use different crossing points to enter. We were forced to separate but agreed to rendezvous at the nearest visual landmark just over the border, a guard tower on the East German side. I crossed on foot without problem, but my German friend was not so lucky. We had bought postcards of the Berlin Wall and the sight of this Western propaganda on the rear seat of his car inspired the border guards to demand a complete auto search.

Waiting for my ride, I found myself sitting alone for hours at the base of the tower. I had never seen weaponry at close range before. I began to wonder how the guard above me had got there, how the Wall had got there, how the dictatorship survived and created fear. As the time dragged on, my self-centered questions (would I ever see home again?) became more philosophical. My mother, a social worker, had spent her life trying to prevent conflict on an individual level. I thought about conflict prevention on an international level. Was it possible to deal with dictators? At what cost?

As it turned out, I was on my way within a couple of hours, and on my way home within a couple of weeks; but the questions stayed with me. At the time I thought that the chances of finding answers to them were slim. Then the unexpected events of 1989 followed just three years later. The protesters who brought about a revolution in East Germany opened archives as well as border crossings. So I was able to look for answers to my questions after all.

I conducted the majority of the research for this book in the quietly chaotic atmosphere of post-unification German archives. Staff members were still, years later, in the process of sifting through the unexpected windfall. During my research, document collections were variously renumbered, relocated, recatalogued, and deemed lost and completely unobtainable, until suddenly obtained. Whole archives moved altogether in the course of my investigation. The inconveniences of working in newly opened collections, however, were outweighed by the drama of reading files retrieved from Stasi shredders; of interviewing men who, for most of the Cold War, had no faces that Westerners could see; of unfolding maps showing what points on the border should be sealed on 13 August 1961; of piecing together deadly plans to further fortify that border (and to build the kind of guard towers under which I had found myself stranded).

Perhaps the most moving aspect of the research was the manner in which many archival staff members, often former East Germans themselves, went above and beyond the call of duty to help me conduct my research and uncover secrets that had been hidden for most of their lifetimes. For this reason I am indebted to the staff of the former Socialist Unity Party (SED) archive, the former GDR state archive, and the former Stasi archive.

Most official Western materials were closed at the time of my research (often indefinitely), but enough significant materials were accessible in private collections to establish a credible outline of the Western view of events. For their help in tracking down these documents and photos, I am grateful to the staff members of the Bundesarchiv in Koblenz, the Egon Bahr Depositorium and Willy Brandt Archiv of the Friedrich Ebert Stiftung in Bonn, and the National Security Archive in Washington, D.C.

Moreover, the following participants in events enriched my analysis by allowing me to speak with them personally and in some cases giving me permission to view private papers as well: Egon Bahr, Hans-Otto Bräutigam, Horst Ehmke, Antonius Eitel, Valentin Falin, Günter Gaus, Gunter Görner, Ulrich Sahm, Helmut Schmidt, Karl Seidel, and Markus Wolf. These conversations proved to be an enormous help in evaluating written documents.

In addition to these professional debts of gratitude, I have accrued many personal debts as well. This project would not have been possible without the remarkable generosity of several institutions that provided me with the financial wherewithal to research and to write. A consistent source of support was the International Security Studies Program of Yale University, which provided not only funding but also unmatched camaraderie. The major support for research expenses came through the Bundeskanzler Scholarship Program of the Alexander von Humboldt Foundation, which made me feel like a cherished part of an international Humboldt family. Further funding came from the German Academic Exchange Service (DAAD) and the Bernadotte Schmitt Grant of the American Historical Association. During my longest research stay in Germany, both the Max-Planck-Gesellschaft (AG/TRAP-Berlin) and the Institut für Geschichtswissenschaften at the Humboldt-Universität provided collegial context and contacts.

Funding for writing during term times came from the John M. Olin Institute, where I was an Olin Fellow, and the Belfer Center for Science and International Affairs. These two institutions, both part of Harvard University, provided excellent working environments. A Josephine DeKarman Scholarship and a Myrna Bernath Prize Fellowship from the Society for Historians of American

Foreign Relations funded writing during summers as well. To all of these institutions, I am grateful.

Finally, I would like to express my gratitude to a number of individuals. The temptation is great to list extensively after every single name the myriad ways each person has helped me; in the interest of brevity, I will resist. For advice in the planning stages of this project and help in securing the funding, archival access, and interviews needed to make it possible, I am indebted to Professor Paul Bushkovitch, Professor Sir Michael Howard, Dr. Kurt-Jürgen Maaß, Dr. Heide Radlanski, Dr. Christian Raskob, Professor Jeffrey Sammons, Dr. Bernie Stein, Dr. Constanze Stelzenmüller, and Professor Heinrich August Winkler. For their support, friendship, and, in many cases, hospitality, I am extremely grateful to Carola Aehlich, Professor William and Mary Lee Bossert, Dr. Andrew and Jacalyn Blume, Professor Daniel Drezner, Ulrike Fleischer, Karin Göpel, Sylvia Gräfe, Dr. Ina Hadshiew, Jim and Linda Jackson, Ruth Kirchner, Hilde Kroll, Volker Lange, Professor Mark Lawrence, Anneliese Müller, John Logan Nichols, Professor Kate O'Neill, Ernst-Georg Richter, Dr. Jeffrey Richter, Steven Sarotte, Marc Scheffler, Dr. Jennifer Siegel, Claus and Rita Wulf, and Jonathan Zatlin.

The following hardy individuals edited most or all of the manuscript in its initial stages and thereby improved it greatly. To Professor Catherine Epstein, Dr. Hans-Hermann Hertle, Dr. Douglas Selvage, and Dr. Patrick Whelan I extend my thanks. I am further grateful to Peter Jukes, Kathy Malin, Professor A. James McAdams, Dr. Timothy Snyder, and an anonymous reviewer for their help in finalizing the book manuscript.

I received my training as a historian at Yale University, where I submitted an earlier version of this manuscript as my dissertation. My gratitude to the members of this department, both faculty and staff, is enormous. I was honored to be part of this institution and particularly honored to receive one of its prizes for my thesis. The members of my committee deserve special thanks. Professor John Lewis Gaddis repeatedly provided needed reminders to keep the big picture in view. Professors Paul Kennedy and Henry Ashby Turner encouraged both this project and its author with equal measures of knowledge and patience.

Finally, I dedicate this work to my parents, Frank and Gail Sarotte—but not, as my mother wondered, because they remind me of East German dictators. Rather, they have always served as examples of wisdom and courage, at no time more so than in the summer of 1999 when my mother was diagnosed with metastasized cancer. I offer this book to them in admiration of the way they combine *so viel Güte bei so viel Festigkeit*—so much kindness with so much strength.

Note on Usage

Terminology

Writing about divided Germany in the Cold War poses a host of linguistic conundrums. For starters, one has to be careful with the seemingly standard adjectives "international" and "national." Neither West nor East Germany transcended statehood during the Cold War and became a nation wholly separate from the other (East German proclamations notwithstanding). Indeed, how to describe the status of the two Germanies in the international Cold War political system—not independent nation-states, but clearly more than colonies—remains an open challenge. Henry Kissinger called West Germany "an economy in search of a political purpose," while historian Charles Maier similarly suggested that "both Germanys have been more economic polities than nation-states."[1]

As a result, the words "national" and "foreign" do not appear in this study's discussion of the two Germanies' relations to each other. Indeed, precisely when and in what way the words "nation" and "national" could be used was an extremely contentious topic of negotiation between East and West Germany. To use these terms uncritically would mean to ignore a key aspect of German-German rivalry. Battles over phrasing were a central feature of German-talks—in fact, the two sides even fought over what to call the negotiations themselves. The East Germans claimed that their bilateral contacts represented "foreign relations," while the West Germans insisted that they were not. This study avoids using either the East German term for the negotiations—namely, international relations—or West German—namely, inner-German relations. Instead, it simply refers to them as German-German contacts. This attempt to use neutral terminology is intended to prevent implying via semantics that the two Germanies were states like any other, establishing the usual forms of international relations. They were not.

Even the English terms "East and West Germany" are problematic. They were almost never used by German speakers at the time. "East Germany" would literally have translated as "Ostdeutschland," but instead that state referred to itself as the German Democratic Republic, or GDR; while "West Germany" preferred "Federal Republic of Germany," or FRG, to "Westdeutschland." In other words, German speakers avoided names that reflected the partition of their country, while English speakers preferred them. However, since "East Germany" and "West Germany" are common usage in English, they have been employed here.

Another terminological pitfall is the discrepancy between the Socialist Unity Party, or SED, as the ruling East German party was commonly known, and East Germany itself, the GDR. In writing about the Warsaw Pact, it is necessary to avoid conflating the communist regimes with their peoples. Hence I have tried to refer to the ruling party, the SED (or, for variety, using "East Berlin" as a synonym) *as distinct from the GDR.* The distinction is obviously tricky, since the SED did speak for the GDR and act (illegitimately) in the name of its citizens. I use the term GDR when discussing the international commitments made in its name. I avoid using GDR when discussing preferences; generally preferences and perceptions were those of the SED leadership, not the people of the GDR. Clearly this is a difficult distinction to make, and often I have simply made a judgment call on which was more appropriate.

Finally, some of the specialized vocabulary requires explanation. Scholarly literature has ascribed a range of meanings to the terms Ostpolitik (Eastern policy) and Deutschlandpolitik (German policy). Confusingly, some scholars use Ostpolitik to refer to the pre-1969 period (in which case the policies of the new chancellor, Willy Brandt, are called the "new Ostpolitik") while others use the term for the years 1969–1974, that is, Brandt's time in office. To complicate matters, Deutschlandpolitik is sometimes treated as a synonym to Ostpolitik, sometimes as a separate policy. Neither approach is entirely accurate; though Deutschlandpolitik and Ostpolitik are hardly synonyms, treating them as separate entities has the unfortunate effect of decoupling German-German relations from their international context.

Hence the usage in this book requires clarification. On the following pages, the term Ostpolitik refers to the broad range of West German initiatives—toward the German Democratic Republic, Eastern Europe, and the Soviet Union—that took place a during the narrow time period of Brandt's chancellorship, that is, 1969–1974. The term Deutschlandpolitik is not used. This usage is purposely chosen to emphasize the interconnected nature of Brandt's policies toward both the other half of Germany and the Warsaw Pact.

Translation Technicalities

Further challenges arise when summarizing in one language the research that was done in four: English, German, Russian, and, in rare instances, French. As a result, a word needs to be said about the issue of translation. The entire main text of this book is in English. Translations are my own.[2] Emphases shown are present in the original source unless otherwise noted. The few times it seemed desirable to have a foreign-language word appear in the main text, such as when there was no exact translation, an explanation of the word follows immediately.

The spelling of proper names is maintained, unless a common English spelling exists (such as Munich instead of München and Politburo instead of Politbüro). Following usage during the time period under discussion, Beijing is referred to as Peking throughout.

In contrast to the text, however, the endnotes employ the original languages of the sources, in order to enable specialists to identify them precisely and find them easily. (English translations or summaries accompany the more significant original quotations, however, to allow nonspecialists to understand the footnotes as well.) Given the advances in word-processing technology, it was possible to use the original Cyrillic characters for Russian terms, thus obviating the need for either transliterating or transcribing the Russian in the notes. As a consequence of this linguistic division between text and endnotes, proper Russian names occasionally have different spellings in the two places. In the text they have been transliterated into English; in the corresponding endnotes, they are given in the original language of the source. Hence, since the memoirs of "Dobrynin" are available in English, this same spelling appears in both the main text and the citation; however, since the memoirs of "Kevorkov" have been published only in German, under the name "Keworkow," the former spelling appears in the text and the latter appears in the notes, while the Russian-language writings of "Abrasimov" are cited under "Абрасимов." I have applied this guideline to foreign-language documents that refer to Russians by proper names as well, not least because there were not consistent SED spellings for these names. For example, while in the main text I consistently employ the spelling "Brezhnev," the East and West German documents cited in the notes vary between "Breshnew," "Breschnew," and "Breschnjew." The instances where different spellings occur are few, and it is hoped that they may be forgiven in the interest of maintaining consistent spellings in the main text.

Abbreviations

ABM	Anti-Ballistic Missile (usually an adjective, as in "ABM systems" or "ABM treaty")
CDU	Christlich-Demokratische Union (Christian-Democratic Union, West German)
CPSU	Communist Party of the Soviet Union
CSCE	Conference on Security and Cooperation in Europe
CSSR	Czechoslovak Socialist Republic
CSU	Christlich-Soziale Union (Christian-Social Union, West German)
DM	deutsche mark (West German currency)
GDR	German Democratic Republic (East Germany)
FBS	Forward-Based Systems (arms control term)
FDJ	Freie Deutsche Jugend (Free German Youth, East German)
FDP	Freie Demokratische Partei (Free Democratic Party, West German)
FRG	Federal Republic of Germany (West Germany)
HM	Hauptamtlicher Mitarbeiter ("official coworker" of the Stasi)
IM	Inoffizieller Mitarbeiter ("unofficial coworker" of the Stasi)
KGB	Soviet secret police
MBFR	Mutual Balanced Force Reduction (Talks)
MfS	Ministerium für Staatssicherheit (Ministry for State Security, i.e., Stasi; see Bibliography for list of departments)
MIRV	Multiple Independently Targetable Reentry Vehicle
NATO	North Atlantic Treaty Organization
NÖS	Neues Ökonomisches System (New Economic System, East German)
NSDM	National Security Decision Memorandum (U.S.)
NVA	Nationale Volksarmee (National People's Army, East German)
RIAS	Radio im amerikanischen Sektor (West Berlin radio station, "Radio in the American Sector")
PRC	People's Republic of China
SALT	Strategic Arms Limitation Talks
SED	Sozialistische Einheitspartei Deutschlands (Socialist Unity Party of Germany, i.e., the ruling party in the GDR)
SPD	Sozialdemokratische Partei Deutschlands (Social Democratic Party of Germany)
UN	United Nations

dealing with the devil

Introduction: Opposing Devils

Von Zeit zu Zeit seh ich den Alten gern
Und hüte mich, mit ihm zu brechen.
Es ist gar hübsch von einem großen Herrn,
So menschlich mit dem Teufel selbst zu sprechen.

From time to time I see the fond Old Man
And hold myself back from breaking with Him.
How nice it is to see his greatness decline
To dealing with the devil like a human.
—Goethe, *Faust*

After decades of confrontation, leaders of the two Cold War German states met for the first time in 1970. One gave the other a ceremonial gift copy of *Faust*, Goethe's magnificent poetical play about the dangers of bargaining with the devil. It so happened that the gift came from the representatives of the German Democratic Republic (GDR) under the leadership of Willi Stoph, and was given to West German Chancellor Willy Brandt.[1] The book was presumably a not-so-subtle reminder from the East German ruling regime—the Socialist Unity Party, or SED in German—that it controlled both Goethe's final resting place and, by extension, the cultivation of his legacy.[2] The SED venerated Goethe in ways verging on the bizarre. Acting on party orders in the fall of 1970, a secret team exhumed Goethe's bones in the dead of night, cleaned them thoroughly—and then re-buried them. The party seems to have hoped to stave off decay.[3] It was for much the same reason—to stave off decay—that party leaders found themselves sitting opposite their capitalist counterparts at a negotiating table.

The gift of *Faust* was a surprisingly appropriate choice. It could just as well have been given by the West Germans to the Easterners, for both sides found themselves facing a Faustian challenge. After decades of cold-shoulder hostility, each began to speak civilly with the devil next door. Both sides had no doubt about the evil intentions of the other, but they hoped that by entering into a conversation they could achieve gains not winnable via confrontation. The extent to which they each succeeded in dealing with the devil is the story at the heart of this book.

This story is told primarily from the perspective that we have known the least about until now: namely, that of East Germany and the Soviet Union. This account uses new documents and interviews to explore their reaction to détente. Put more precisely, this book provides the first analytical narrative of the response of the Politburo of the SED, under the guidance of the Communist Party of the Soviet Union (CPSU), to both détente and its West German contemporary, Ostpolitik, in the years 1969–1973.[4] This narrative provides a behind-the-scenes look at how a Warsaw Pact dictatorship dealt with both its friends and its enemies. It disassembles the cynical artifices constructed by negotiators and reveals how the East German dictatorship made its own citizens into bargaining chips. It also explains a great deal of superpower maneuvering in the détente era, since German concerns were ever-present on the minds of leaders in Washington and Moscow. This study reveals the complicated relationship between the contemporaneous but not always coordinated policies of détente and Ostpolitik. More generally, this book provides a case study of how the relationship between center and periphery functioned in the Cold War Soviet empire. It is a particularly informative case because it is one in which East German and Soviet interests diverged. Finally, this book highlights one of the defining characteristics of the Cold War: namely, the tight interconnection of local and global politics.

At this point, the reader might rightly say, hold on, why bother with East Germany? After all, wasn't it just a Soviet puppet state, and a gray and dreary one at that, renowned only for producing highly dubious Olympic athletes? Since it did not enjoy full political autonomy, what is the point of examining its politics and diplomacy at all? If one must study the GDR, why not focus instead on a topic independent of the international impotence of its political leadership—say, domestic daily life and disciplinary technology in a dictatorship? And why just the years 1969, 1970, 1971, 1972 and 1973?

These are fair questions. They represent the concerns of the political scientist, who wants to know why *East German* politics and diplomacy should be interesting either empirically or theoretically. They represent the concerns of the social historian who wants to know why East German *politics and diplomacy* should be interesting methodologically. They represent the concerns of the devoted reader of political history as well, who wants to know why this particular bit of history is worthwhile. All these would-be readers raise their voices in a chorus with the layman and student: Why bother?

There are several reasons to bother. First, this history shows that the term "puppet state" is not an entirely accurate way to describe the GDR. It is accurate to say that, when Moscow and East Berlin's interests diverged (and this study shows where), Moscow prevailed. The East German tail did *not* wag the Soviet dog.[5] However, the Soviets feared East Germany's potential *to start wagging* as a result of its contacts with the West. The GDR could do so either intentionally, or unintentionally, perhaps by provoking unwanted outbursts of German nationalism. The SED managed to unnerve the Soviet leadership repeatedly in the détente era because of such fears, despite Moscow's micromanagement of nearly every significant decision. In other words, while the Soviets knew they were in charge, they feared the possibility that Ostpolitik could bring unwelcome and potentially uncontrollable change. Historical and theoretical literature about power politics in earlier time periods has shown that a great power's fears and perceptions about what might happen in the future often carry as much weight as current reality.[6] As John Lewis Gaddis put it, "because perceptions rivaled reality in shaping world events, even the appearances of changes in the existing order could, in their effects, approximate real ones."[7] This book shows that such political prolepsis maintained its significance for decision-makers in the Cold War as well.

Secondly, this book shows that the lack of full political autonomy did not prevent the GDR from functioning as an actor on the world stage. As political scientists Alexander Wendt and Daniel Friedheim have pointed out, there existed an ongoing tension between the nominal "sovereignty" of the GDR and its de facto inequality in comparison to other states on the international level.[8] The analysis provided here explains how the SED resolved this tension and navigated rough diplomatic waters without the ballast of either full sovereignty or domestic legitimacy. The SED's increasingly effective efforts to gain recognition from West Germany and other states helped to distract attention from the missing ballast (until the ship of state ran undeniably aground in the 1980s). To borrow terms originated in the work of the political scientists Robert Jackson and Carl Rosberg, the SED used external juridical sovereignty to compensate for missing empirical sovereignty.[9]

Moreover, the East German archives illuminate more than just the diplomacy of the GDR; they serendipitously explain many aspects of Warsaw pact and superpower relations in the Cold War as well. The former East German files are more accessible than those of any other former Warsaw Pact state; and since these states had very similar party structures, a look into the GDR's relatively accessible files can help us understand those states whose files are not similarly open (particularly the Soviet Union). Moreover, given that the archives are open with no time restrictions (in contrast to Western materials, which, ironically, are now more difficult to obtain than Eastern files), the GDR documents provide some of the first accessible evidence from a number of key Cold War events and relationships. These include, to name just a few examples, the U.S.-Soviet summit of 1972, Moscow-Hanoi contacts, and Soviet-Chinese clashes.

These new sources reveal, among other things, the startling extent to which relations with China influenced European politics at this time. Henry Kissinger's relations with China turned out to be a productive policy for Europe, because Western negotiators could use the Sino-Soviet rivalry to extract concessions from Moscow over Europe. In his 1993 bestseller, British scholar Timothy Garton Ash argued that Bonn coordinated its dealings with Moscow and East Berlin to extract maximum results; he termed this process "working the triangle" between the three cities.[10] The findings presented here show that the triangle must be stretched into a square to incorporate a fourth crucial city: Beijing.

More importantly, East German sources yield new information about not just the narrative but also the nature of international détente. They show how détente closely linked international diplomacy to domestic politics in disparate corners of the globe. They reveal the unexpected consequences of détente negotiations, such as the ouster of the SED leader Walter Ulbricht. They detail how the states involved in negotiations began to evaluate their interests differently than they would have were confrontation still the order of the day.

They also explain some of the measures the East German ruling regime took against its own people, the citizens of the GDR. The dichotomy between a history of politics and a history of daily life is a false one when studying the GDR. One of the tragic aspects of daily life in an authoritarian state is the extent to which political leaders can constrain their citizens' range of actions and manipulate the disciplinary mechanisms of power.[11] As the historian Charles Maier has explained, the SED and its secret police maintained a kind of *"arcana imperii,* the power of mystification and secrecy," which enabled them to "corrupt independent action, stifle dissent, and preclude the emergence of a public realm."[12] This study shows how the Cold War forged links between decisions made on the international level by the SED and Soviets and the restrictions on individuals in the states they controlled. To cite examples, which are explored in detail later: the rise in contacts with the West led the SED Politburo to increase both the size of the secret police and the deadly fortifications on its border. Or another: the status of Sino-Soviet relations—truly a global issue—sealed the individual fate of a few hundred children seeking visas to reunite with their families on the other side of the Berlin Wall. Or another: as strange as it may seem, the SED's high-level international relations determined whether or not a bus in transit to the West could stop to let its passengers use toilets.

Caution is needed at this point; this study is not a social history; it focuses on a political elite. The impact of détente and Ostpolitik on the population of the GDR is a subject of great moment and deserves a book of its own.[13] However, on the pages that follow, the GDR's population appears only when it influences the thinking of the political elite, which is to say that, sadly, it is mostly absent. This absence should not be understood to mean that the citizens of the GDR were unimportant, or that the SED controlled all aspects of their private lives. Rather, it confirms the dictatorial nature of the regime by showing that the SED ruled without regard for the people. Ordinary citizens were often casualties of Cold War tensions: they were driven from their homes near the border to make way for a larger deathstrip or used as bargaining chips in negotiations. As leading GDR scholar James McAdams has rightly pointed out, "the only reasonable hope that the East German government might be convinced to alter its policies" at this time lay not with the people of the GDR but rather "with the inclinations of the SED's leader or with those among his closest circle of confidantes"—and, of course, with the Soviets.[14]

Finally, the eventful years 1969–1973 are the focus because they represent a fundamental shift in Cold War politics. Short time periods of dramatic change always appeal to historians; the old order, in breaking down, reveals its secrets, and the new order is still too young to have any. The early years of détente and Ostpolitik represent just such a time of change. From the Berlin Blockade and Airlift of 1948–49 onward, the question of how to deal with the German division had long enmeshed both sides in confrontation. As Peter Merkl has pointed out, an "air of unreality and hopeless entanglement" came to surround the relationship between Bonn and the East by 1970. "Twenty-five years after the end of World War II, the tensions in Europe were still unrelieved, with nearly one-third of a million American troops and half a million Soviet troops stationed in various Western and Eastern European countries."[15] A sense of perpetual crisis prevailed. The SED Politburo observed in 1970 that "the question of the ordering of the relations between our two states is not some second-rate issue, but rather a cardinal problem of peace in Europe."[16]

Détente and Ostpolitik represented dramatic changes because they employed engagement and negotiation rather than confrontation. In Europe, this required a profound shift in the thinking of the Warsaw Pact, the Soviet-led counterpart to NATO. The division of Germany, until then considered a cornerstone of the Warsaw Pact, was suddenly transformed into an object of bargaining.[17] Moreover, Ostpolitik coincided with a significant transition in superpower relations, thanks to Vietnam and rising Sino-Soviet tensions. And the years of its implementation saw the societal upheavals of the late 1960s and early 1970s as well. Student revolutionaries filled the capitals of Western Europe, often finding themselves in violent confrontations with police. Protests against the Vietnam War undermined trust in U.S. leadership and brought its allies into difficulties. Small wonder that the historian Peter Pulzer found that these years, the time of Brandt's chancellorship, "brought about a greater change in the FRG's status and structure than any other five-year span" in the Cold War.[18] It is easy to agree with the historian Tony Judt when he argues that "the years 1968–1975 were the hinge on which the second half of our century turned."[19]

So these years, as short a time as they may seem, were a dramatic turning point, when two antagonists entered into a new dialogue and into what became—increasingly—a Faustian pact. This term has been used before to describe how the West felt about the Soviets.[20] This book shows that détente forced both sides in the Cold War—not just the West—to deal with the opposing devil. For differing reasons, both sides sought the prize of learning how to coexist more peacefully; both had to make concessions in pursuit of this prize. For all these reasons, understanding the language and the drama of negotiation in the era of Ostpolitik is most definitely worth the bother.

A word need be said about what this study does not do, to avoid raising false expectations in readers. This book examines the East German interaction with both the West Germans and the Soviets. It does not provide the mirror image, that is, the West German view of interactions with East Germany and with the United States. Topics such as the debate over Ostpolitik within Brandt's party, the SPD, or the tensions between the SPD and its governing coalition partners, or the changing Western popular opinion of Brandt's policies, or the attacks of the conservative West German press on Ostpolitik have been discussed by other authors and are beyond the scope of the present study. (Books that provide information on these topics, along with many others, are described in the Note on Sources and listed in the Bibliography.) In general, this study addresses the internal debate in West Germany over Ostpolitik only in relation to its impact on the SED.[21] This study does not cover the events of 1989; readers looking for a more extensive history of the German division should turn to James McAdams's *Germany Divided*, or H. A. Turner's *Germany from Partition to Unification*, or W. R. Smyser's *From Yalta to Berlin*. Finally, this book does not conclusively settle the question of whether Ostpolitik hindered or helped reunification. It does, however, clarify a key aspect of this debate. Those who would vilify détente and Ostpolitik often claim that they fulfilled the wish of the SED leaders to be treated like international statesmen and increased the economic security of the GDR. Those who would defend Ostpolitik claim that the SED regime was afraid of the long-term consequences. This study shows that both claims have merit.

What this book does do is answer the following questions, both in detail in the narrative and in summary fashion in the conclusion: What did the SED, and its Soviet backers, hope to gain by entering into the German-German conversation? What did they expect to concede in return? How did they go about pursuing their aims, and were those aims ever divergent? What degree of success did they obtain? Most importantly, why do these details matter? What larger insights do these findings yield for our understanding of the Cold War?

Setting the Stage in 1969:

Old Worries and New Initiatives

in the Era of Nixon and Brandt

Old Worries: Historical Prologue to 1969

Understanding détente and Ostpolitik, and the East German and Soviet response to them, requires an understanding of the historical context from which they arose. Hence some stage-setting is necessary before introducing the main political actors and events of the détente era. In the German context, one way to view West German Ostpolitik and East Berlin's response to it is to recognize both as the results of "lessons" learned during the first half of the Cold War. As political scientist Alexander George has shown, political leaders often follow a personal operational code, or a "set of assumptions about the world, formed early in one's career, that tend to govern without much subsequent variation the way one responds to crises afterwards."[1] George's colleague Jack Snyder has applied this concept to the détente and Ostpolitik negotiations over Germany, arguing that these talks can be seen as the result of "rational learning about the objective constraints and incentives of the international system."[2] As a result, an overview of the historical events that shaped the behavioral codes of the rulers involved, and the learning that resulted, helps to make later events more understandable.[3]

Although many more could be added, there seem to have been six major historical concerns that shaped these leaders' codes: (1) the desire to prevent future conflict in the wake of World War II; (2) the wish to avoid Soviet intervention during the prolonged division of Germany; (3) the hope that negotiations about small, specific matters could succeed, as they did in the 1960s in Berlin; (4) the worry about the implications of the Prague invasion of 1968; (5) the desire of the SED regime to make itself a model of economic success; and (6) the importance of the growing Sino-Soviet rivalry at the end of the 1960s.

In the Wake of World War II

All leading politicians of the détente era had shared the devastating experience of at least one and usually two world wars. Obviously, the impact of the experience of war is a profound one in more ways than it is possible to describe, but there seem to have been a few aspects that particularly influenced the thinking of German leaders and the formation of Ostpolitik. First, as author Timothy Garton Ash has pointed out, the shared experience of wartime devastation produced a kind of "commandment" for the West Germans that nothing was more important than peace.[4] Garton Ash mentioned this commandment in order to take exception to it, implying that there may in fact have been causes more noble than promoting peace for the West to pursue, such as supporting East European dissidents. As will be discussed, at least some of the East Germans involved in negotiations considered prevention of a third world war as their main goal.

Second, developments in the late 1940s unintentionally created two antithetical halves out of what had been a unified German nation.[5] At war's end, the United States, France, Britain, and the Soviet Union had established provisional zones of occupation. Because these zones were supposed to be temporary, durability was not one of the criteria used in their demarcation. Clearly, a divided Berlin well inside the Soviet zone was hardly an ideal long-term arrangement for either side. However, the realities of post–World War II politics soon hardened the provisional demarcation lines into fortified borders.

The division was political and economic as well as geographic. Politically, the three Western zones soon adopted a common democratic constitution called the Basic Law, while the Eastern zone increasingly fell under the authoritarian control of Moscow and its hand-picked German affiliates from the German Communist Party. In 1946 these affiliates, headed by Walter Ulbricht, oversaw the forced merger of those portions of the German Social Democratic Party and the German Communist Party active in the Soviet zone into one so-called "Socialist Unity Party" (or SED). The old rivalry between socialists and com-

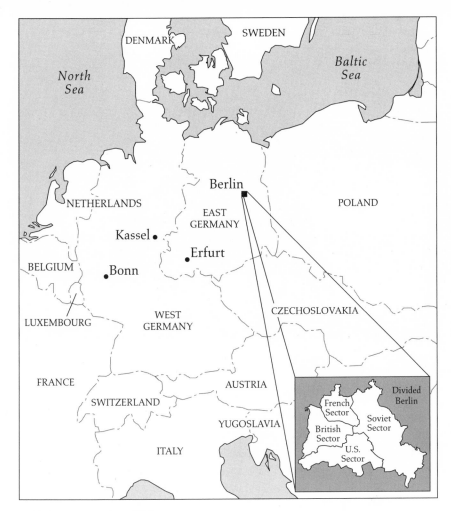

Divided Germany in the Cold War

munists for the mantle of German socialism thereby took on a new twist.[6] Western Social Democrats were incensed at the treatment to which their colleagues in the East were treated. Economically, the Western zones benefited from the Marshall Plan, while the Eastern zone endured Soviet expropriation of its industrial plant and collectivization of its agriculture. Moreover, the establishment of a separate economy in the Soviet zone, which had previously been closely integrated into a united German economy, required extensive investment in heavy industry, to the deficit of consumers.[7] Hence the Eastern zone was truly at a disadvantage compared to the West. On top of this, the SED regime had to contend with a paucity of raw materials, massive emigration, and discontent on the part of its workforce.

Walter Ulbricht, leader of the SED, delivers his New Year's greetings for the year 1969. (Signatur G 1230/13/1, Bundesarchiv Koblenz)

The most significant expression of such discontent occurred on 17 June 1953, when a protest on the part of East German workers dissatisfied with changes in work requirements and pay levels turned into a political challenge to the authority of the SED. Soviet tanks rolled in to end the protest.[8] Paradoxically, it seems that this event actually strengthened Walter Ulbricht's grip on power. There had been signs that Moscow was considering replacing him, since he had been the main source of resistance to Soviet pressure to modify the harsh policies adopted by the SED in 1952. Ulbricht failed to show decisive leadership during the crisis. After the revolt was crushed, however, any kind of dramatic change seemed inherently too risky, and Ulbricht was allowed to remain in his post.

Avoiding Soviet Intervention

The importance of 17 June 1953 for Ostpolitik and détente lay primarily in its impact on the mindset of Eastern and Western policymakers. The events of that day showed both sides the risks of popular movements. The Easterners learned that even small protests could quickly spiral out of control. SED policymakers were reminded that they faced domestic constraints on their freedom of action, even if those constraints were not as apparent as those in the West. For its part, the West saw that popular protest in a Soviet satellite ended in brutal repression, a pattern repeated again in Hungary in 1956 and in Prague in 1968. Politicians like Egon Bahr became convinced that mass public airings of grievances were to be averted, because they invariably would end in Soviet intervention.[9]

Despite the uprising, the SED after 1953 still chose to shift its economic priorities toward rapid industrialization at the expense of consumers. Farmers were pressured to enter agricultural collectives. Independent tradesmen found themselves losing work unless they joined cooperatives sponsored by the regime. Attacks on churches intensified.[10] As a result, the number of people fleeing into West Germany increased. Between the beginning of 1961 and the second week of August that year, 155,000 residents of the GDR had registered in the West as refugees. The total number of those who had fled Communist rule between the end of World War II and 1961 was roughly equal to one out of every six inhabitants of the regions of Germany occupied by the USSR.[11]

To staunch the flow of refugees, the SED sealed off East Berlin from West Berlin by beginning construction of the Berlin Wall on 13 August 1961.[12] The fortifications along it increased daily; soon there were guard-dog runs, mines, and watchtowers. In essence, the SED and the Soviets had claimed absolute authority over East Berlin, a claim that the three Western powers refused to recognize de jure but did not challenge de facto. Altercations on the border led to a grim situation in late 1961, when Soviet and American tanks faced each other across only a few dozen yards of pavement at Checkpoint Charlie. The Wall also became the site of numerous escape attempts, often ending in tragedy. The Wall's construction revealed that the leadership of the GDR, in order to keep its own people, had to imprison them.[13] By the end of the 1960s, the SED regime had planted more than a million mines along the German-German border. Before the Wall would come down in 1989, nearly 700 people would die in escape attempts.[14]

The mayor of Berlin at the time of the Wall's construction was Willy Brandt.[15] In his memoirs, Brandt wrote that he learned a bitter lesson on that fateful 13 August 1961, not only about his neighbors to the East but also about his allies to the West. He saw that reliance on cooperation with the West alone would not solve the problems of the German division. As he remembered, he began to search for answers to the following questions: "If we had to live with the Wall for any length of time, how could it be made less impenetrable? How could we find a modus vivendi . . . between the two parts of Germany?"[16] In other words, Brandt felt that it was incumbent upon him as the policymaker-on-site to find new ways to deal with what was clearly going to be a prolonged division. Those policies should not be so drastic, however, as to inspire a massive popular response which would in turn provoke Soviet intervention.

Within the scope of their authority, Brandt and his chief aide Egon Bahr worked to achieve small agreements with the East, such as issuing special passes to enable West Berliners to visit East Berlin on certain holidays. The first of these agreements (the so-called "Passierschein Abkommen," or Pass-Agreement) went into effect for the Christmas holidays in 1963 and represented the first trans-Wall traffic since its construction.[17] It was clear that Brandt hoped even then to widen the scope of his authority and to apply his ideas on a larger scale. As Soviet Foreign Minister Gromyko recalled in his memoirs, during talks at this time with Soviet diplomats in Berlin ostensibly over minor issues, Brandt would find ways to discuss FRG-Soviet relations as a whole.[18]

In response to ongoing West German attempts to negotiate more such agreements, SED chief Walter Ulbricht set up a state secretariat that was responsible for this issue and reported solely to him. One of the leading figures involved in negotiating the Pass-Agreements was the East German legal scholar Michael Kohl. He would later become Egon Bahr's sparring partner in the German-German negotiations.[19]

Hoping West Germany Could Make a Difference

The success of the Pass-Agreement of 1963 convinced Brandt and Bahr that worthwhile results could emerge from negotiations with the East.[20] The two men felt vindicated in their belief that such contacts could yield real, if admittedly meager, results.[21] They also realized that playing an active part in managing relations with the GDR was in the self-interest of the West Germans, because the construction of the Wall showed them that their allies would not necessarily act on their behalf. Wits have remarked that the two greatest fears of West European statesmen in the Cold War were that the United States would not defend them from the Soviets, and that the United States would (meaning that Europe would once again become a battlefield). The experience of watching the Wall go up made the former seem more likely.

Out of this realization emerged the July 1963 speech of Egon Bahr in Tutzing. Originally written as a speech for Brandt, until its content was deemed too controversial, it suggested that the best way to create change (*Wandel*) might be through a process of closer political cooperation or rapprochement (*Annäherung*) with East Germany.[22] Brandt and Bahr wanted to go beyond the existing German-German contacts, which were limited to the Pass-Agreements, some forms of trade, and clandestine deals to secure the release of prisoners.[23]

At this time Brandt and Bahr could implement their ideas only in West Berlin. However, there were signs that Bonn as well was rethinking its stance toward the East.[24] Foreign minister Gerhard Schröder had put a chink in the armor of the West German Hallstein Doctrine, according to which the FRG would not maintain diplomatic relations with states that had relations with the GDR. Schröder found that "the East European communist regimes were 'born' with diplomatic relations to the GDR. They had no choice in the matter and so could not be expected to honor the Hallstein Doctrine."[25] In 1966, the West German government sent so-called "Peace Notes" (that is, letters in which the FRG indicated a willingness to negotiate treaties barring the use of force) to all the states with which it had diplomatic relations and to the entirety of the Eastern Bloc except for the GDR.[26] The Eastern Bloc rejected these overtures.[27] This approach was preordained to fail because it sought to bypass both Moscow and East Berlin in extending a "bridge" directly to the states of East Central and South-Eastern Europe.[28]

Chancellor Kurt-Georg Kiesinger tried again in January 1967 by announcing that he intended to pursue a "new Ostpolitik."[29] In a break with the tradition of returning all correspondence from the SED regime unopened, Kiesinger responded to a letter from Stoph suggesting that the two Germanies engage in talks.[30] Disagreement over what preconditions there should be to such talks meant that they did not actually come about during the Kiesinger administration, but the fact that letters could even be exchanged was, as historian Rudolf Morsey put it, "new in Bonn."[31]

The Soviet bloc, for its part, repeated in July 1966 and again at the Budapest meeting of the Warsaw Pact in March 1969 a previously expressed desire for a collective conference on European security.[32] Contacts between West Germany and the Soviet Union at the ministerial level resumed in April 1969, the first such talks since 1958. A West German delegation comprised of the leading FDP politicians—Walter Scheel, Wolfgang Mischnick, and Hans-Dietrich Genscher—visited Moscow in July 1969, and an SPD delegation comprised of Helmut Schmidt, Alex Möller, and Egon Franke followed in August.[33]

These hints of a thaw in relations were not helped by Ulbricht's attempt in February 1967 to increase the sovereign identity of the GDR by abolishing the old German citizenship law of 1913 as the basis for determining citizenship, thereby cutting yet another thread that linked the two Germanies. A revision of the GDR penal code in January 1968 effectively "put an end to what remained of legal unity between the two Germanies."[34] A new constitution, which went into force in April 1968, clearly defined Ulbricht's party, the SED, as the ruling force in East German state and society.

The entry of Brandt's party, the SPD, into a ruling coalition with the Christian Democrats in 1966 provided a hopeful sign for the cause of German-German rapprochement. This coalition was due in no small measure to the negotiating skill of the SPD politician Herbert Wehner, who had broken with the Communist Party during the war. The CDU/SPD Grand Coalition had the effect, as Kissinger put it, of resolving "the issue of whether in fact the Social Democrats were fit to govern."[35] Brandt took charge of the foreign ministry and placed Bahr at the head of an internal planning staff, which began working on various models for engaging the East.[36] Kissinger noted in his memoirs that,

Original members of NATO

Later members of NATO

Warsaw Pact members

ICELAND

SWEDEN

NORWAY

Baltic
Sea

GREAT
BRITAIN

DENMARK

IRELAND

NETHERLANDS

EAST
GERMANY

POLAND

BELGIUM

WEST
GERMANY

CZECHOSLOVAKIA

Atlantic
Ocean

LUXEMBOURG

SWITZERLAND

AUSTRIA

HUNGARY

FRANCE

ITALY

YUGOSLAVIA

ALBAN

PORTUGAL

SPAIN

GRE

Mediterranean Sea

TUNISIA

ALGERIA

MOROCCO

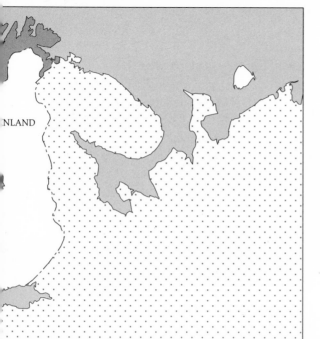

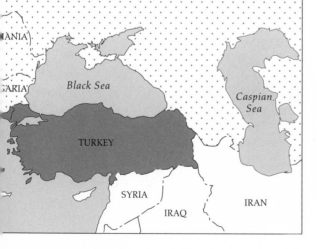

even though Foreign Minister Brandt was only the number-two person in the government headed by Kurt-Georg Kiesinger, Brandt's behavior "suggested in no sense that he considered himself a subordinate of the Chancellor."[37] It was clear that he hoped one day to fill the number-one slot himself.[38]

Further hopeful signs for the cause of engagement appeared in the international sphere by early 1968 as well. The NATO member governments issued the Harmel Report in December 1967, which called for NATO to pursue détente with the Warsaw Pact while continuing its traditional security role. In March 1968, American president Lyndon Johnson made the momentous decision to change course in Vietnam, turning down General William Westmoreland's request for more reinforcements and halting most U.S. bombing in North Vietnam.[39] On 1 July 1968, the United States, Russia, and Britain signed the Nuclear Non-Proliferation Treaty.[40] Charles de Gaulle called for "détente, entente, coopération."[41] Closer to Germany, the reformer Alexander Dubček replaced the Stalinist leader of Czechoslovakia, Anatol Novotný, and the heady days of the Prague Spring of 1968 followed.

Worries about Prague

Events in Prague soon reinforced the worries of 1953, however. The forceful intervention in August 1968 by the Soviet tanks reminded the world both where authority in the Eastern bloc ultimately rested and how it could and would be used. Six days after the invasion, the Czechoslovak leaders were flown to Moscow for a dressing-down by Soviet leader Leonid Brezhnev. What participant Zdeněk Mlynář recalled from Brezhnev's tirade bore a striking resemblance to comments Brezhnev would later make about East Germany as well. According to Mlynář, Brezhnev justified the Prague invasion in the following way: "In the name of our dead in the Second World War, who sacrificed their lives for your freedom as well, we are completely justified in sending our soldiers to you."[42]

In West Germany, the experience of witnessing Soviet tanks rolling through the streets of Prague reconfirmed the sense on the part of Brandt, Bahr, and others that any resolution to the German question must go through Moscow.[43] It also confirmed the worry, as Bahr recalled, that free expressions of popular will in the East would only cause a crackdown. Having seen the same pattern in East Berlin in 1953 and Hungary in 1956, and now again in Prague in 1968, the two men were determined that there should not be a repeat performance.[44] As Werner Link has explained, the sense arose that "massive changes to the system endanger the evolutionary process. . . . [T]he careful path to stabilization via a reduction of tensions in Europe was regarded as a precondition for European peace and order." This, he pointed out, gave efforts at détente "a strongly governmental-statist touch."[45]

In the Warsaw Pact, historian of Soviet politics Christopher Andrew found that "the shock of the Prague Spring influenced the policy of the Kremlin and the KGB to Eastern Europe for the next twenty years." It led to the enunciation of the Brezhnev Doctrine of September 1968, which formally spelled out the restricted sovereignty of the Warsaw Pact states. As Andrew explained, while each state "had the right to take its 'own separate road to socialism,' the policies adopted by them 'must damage neither socialism in their own country nor the fundamental interests of the other socialist countries.' " Were such "damage" to occur, the doctrine clearly implied that "the other socialist states, led by the Soviet Union, had, as in Czechoslovakia, an 'internationalist duty' to 'act in resolute opposition to the antisocialist forces.' "[46]

SED Desire to Make Itself a Model

The danger of self-assertiveness on the part of Soviet satellite states seems to have made rather less of an impact on Walter Ulbricht than it should have. In 1967 and 1968 he displayed ideological daring by claiming that socialism could be a "long-lasting social formation in its own right" and not just a step on the way to Communism. This claim threatened Soviet dominance on at least three counts. It implied that the *Socialist* Unity Party of the GDR might in fact be on a developmental par with the *Communist* Party of the USSR, both having created a long-lasting formation.[47] It suggested that the SED might believe in a different interpretation of Marxism than Moscow, namely a less predetermined version in which history might not necessarily culminate in communism. Finally, it carried with it the risky implication that the communist Soviet Union might not be the ultimate model for the socialist GDR; the GDR might in fact be a model in its own right.[48]

A contradiction emerges: while Ulbricht felt free to show ideological daring himself, he condemned the heretical deviations occurring in Prague. SED documents contain critical remarks from Ulbricht about Prague throughout 1968. Ulbricht's main objection seems to have been that the Prague reformers' actions produced risks not just for themselves but also for the entire Warsaw pact. For example, at a socialist block leaders' meeting on 23 March 1968 in Dresden, Ulbricht called for "some kind of agreement on how we can prevent newly appearing problems in this or that socialist country from being used as weapons in psychological war against us by imperialism."[49] He repeated this concern in discussions about Czechoslovakia in Moscow on 8 May and Warsaw on 14–15 July 1968. "We are dealing with a broad front, which is against Marxism-Leninism and indeed against everything," he claimed.[50] Finally, as recent scholarship has shown, the East German National People's Army (NVA) was actively involved in all preparations for the invasion and was scheduled to be part of the invading force.[51]

In her political biography of Ulbricht, former SED party archivist Monika Kaiser has attempted to explain this contradiction by suggesting that it did not in fact exist. She argues that Ulbricht did not condemn the Czechoslovak reformers at all—rather, that he was very much in favor of the new leadership in Prague.[52] In her opinion, he agreed to an invasion only "at the very end," by which she seems to mean the days immediately preceding the invasion.[53] According to Kaiser, the SED's negative attitude toward Prague in the media of the GDR was the work of Erich Honecker and party ideologue Kurt Hager. However, it is difficult to reconcile Kaiser's interpretation with many statements made by Ulbricht well in advance of the invasion. For example, at the Moscow meeting of 8 May—nearly four months before troops rolled in—he said: "I see no other way. The military exercise must be carried out as quickly, but also as thoroughly, as possible."[54] Ulbricht's actions speak even louder than his words. Under his political leadership, the East German NVA was actively involved in all Soviet-led preparations. The military historian Rüdiger Wenzke, an expert on the Prague invasion, found that Soviet invasion plans "met with opposition neither in the SED nor in the NVA."[55] Only a last-minute order, presumably from Moscow, kept most East Germans on their own side of the border (although a handful did set foot on Czechoslovak territory).[56] Both Wenzke and Jan Pauer, another specialist on the Prague Spring, classify Ulbricht as one "of the fiercest critics of Czechoslovak reforms in 1968."[57]

The contradiction remains: how can Ulbricht's own willfulness in the late 1960s be reconciled with his simultaneous hard-line stance against daring reform in Czechoslovakia? The answer lies in Ulbricht's own perception of events. He himself saw no contradiction between his condemnation of Prague's experiments and his enthusiasm for his own. Ulbricht, having met Lenin personally and spent decades in office, felt entitled on the basis of his seniority to call for independent initiatives. Other party leaders (such as those in Czechoslovakia) were not similarly entitled. In understanding this thinking, the findings of James McAdams and of Wenzke are once again useful. McAdams has argued that one of Ulbricht's goals was to show "that the GDR really was building a viable and humane alternative to western capitalist society."[58] In particular, he wanted it to be more successful than its allies. Wenzke found that Ulbricht repeatedly praised the SED as a "model" to the rest of the Warsaw Pact.[59]

Ulbricht's desire to make the GDR some kind of a model is key to understanding not only his reaction to Prague but also the ways in which he would react to the initial Ostpolitik overtures of the Brandt government as well. Ulbricht felt keenly the need to live up to the West German economic example. He seems to have hoped throughout the 1960s to turn the GDR into a model of economic success.[60] The most important attempt to do so was the so-called "New Economic System" (NÖS) introduced in 1963.[61] It maintained the preeminence of central state planning but, as political scientist Hans-Hermann Hertle has described it, contained "elements of an orientation to profit and return as criteria of economic affairs, a reform of the price system, and the reduction of subsidies."[62] It allowed factories greater legal and economic independence.

The challenge to centralized planning inherent in NÖS inspired controversy within the SED. Its primary opponents were Politburo members Honecker, Willi Stoph, Hermann Axen, and even Stasi chief Erich Mielke.[63] It was controversial because it implied that greater economic cooperation with the West was necessary. As Hertle put it, "only through the import of the most modern Western technologies did the NÖS-organizers have a chance to close the gap of labor productivity [between the GDR] and . . . capitalistic countries."[64]

As the 1960s progressed, Ulbricht increasingly hoped that a combination of Western technology, Soviet raw materials, and socialist labor would help the GDR to pull even with and perhaps surpass FRG economic indicators. In other words, he hoped to achieve success by importing both Soviet raw goods at prices below those of market level—such as cheap oil—and modern Western industrial technology—such as refining equipment.[65] Combining the two via the superior method of socialist work would then produce desirable goods for export (which in the case of oil could earn hard currency on the world market).[66] He even seems to have seen central planning as an advantage in this regard: it could be used to focus all resources on whatever was considered to be the key task at any given time.[67]

Getting the Soviets and the West to play their assigned roles in the scheme proved to be problematic, however. In the East, dealings with the USSR were hardly straightforward. The Soviet Union seems not to have been enamored of the idea of playing the role of cheap raw goods supplier, presumably because it would prefer to sell marketable goods at market prices, rather than at the discounted prices common within the socialist bloc. One particularly awkward confrontation occurred during a meeting in Moscow in July 1969, at which a delegation sent by Ulbricht sought to increase the amount of promised oil deliveries from the Soviet Union for 1975 from 3 million to 17.5 million tons. In response to the East German request, Brezhnev disingenuously protested, "Whatever do you need so much raw oil for? I don't entirely understand it. It's a product that smells, it has not got a nice scent, and if you spill it and stain something, it is not easy to get the stains out."[68] Nor was Brezhnev thrilled with the idea of East Germany as a model from which the USSR should learn. The Soviet leader reportedly remarked to Ulbricht's deputy Erich Honecker in July 1970, "[P]eople say that the best model of socialism either has been or is being developed in the GDR. Everything is done better in the GDR, everyone should learn from the GDR, [the] GDR shines socialism out to other countries, does everything right."[69]

Soviet leader Leonid Brezhnev with Erich Honecker. (Signatur R 0819/29 N, Bundesarchiv Koblenz)

On top of the dubious ideological implications, importing Western machinery and goods cost hard money. By 1970 the GDR was roughly 2 billion "Valuta-Mark" in debt to various Western countries. (A Valuta-Mark was the GDR's foreign trade bookkeeping unit and equal to one West German Mark, or "DM"; keeping accounts in DM outright was politically unpalatable.)[70] The GDR had to overcome numerous internal hurdles as well. The infrastructure was in a sorry state. Aging train lines, rolling stock, and transport trucks that had been in service since World War II were all in need of attention. The shortcomings of the construction industry were numerous. An unresponsive pricing system—in which prices depended neither on the costs of the materials or wages involved but rather on central decree—hampered reform. In December 1965, the head of the state planning commission, Erich Apel, had committed suicide, reportedly in despair over the chances of successful modernization.[71] Efforts to modernize in the last two decades of the GDR's existence led to enormous indebtedness and became one of the significant factors in the collapse of the GDR.[72]

While Ulbricht presumably did not foresee collapse, he did clearly see the need for reform in the planned central economy of the GDR to stave off decay. It therefore seems likely that his hope of accruing rapid benefit through closer economic cooperation with the West (specifically via technological imports) strongly shaped his response to Brandt's initial overtures. As will be discussed shortly, his attitude toward these initiatives was more welcoming than Cold War scholarship has reported it to be.[73] In other words, hope of economic gain made him more willing to engage, rather than rebuff, West Germany. This dynamic does not seem to have been in operation with regard to Czechoslovakia. No economic hopes mitigated Ulbricht's hard-line stance toward his socialist neighbor. Hence it is perhaps not as inconsistent as it may seem that he was on the side of hard-liners on the issue of Prague reforms but, as shall be discussed, on the side of reformers in dealings with the FRG.

The Impact of the Growing Sino-Soviet Rivalry

The Prague crisis illuminated not only the threshold of Warsaw Pact tolerance for deviation but also the widening Sino-Soviet rift. It seems as if the communist regime that took the lesson of Prague most profoundly to heart (other than, of course, Czechoslovakia) was China. Recent scholarship suggests that the shock of the extreme Soviet reaction to a deviant communist state registered strongly with the Chinese Communist leaders and fueled their hostility toward Russia. The Chinese seem to have felt particularly nervous about the Soviet claim, demonstrated clearly in Prague, that the USSR could justifiably intervene in any socialist state where they found socialism to be in danger. The Chinese leadership apparently worried that this definition could conceivably be applied to the People's Republic of China (PRC) as well, and this worry played a part in the October 1968 decision of PRC defense minister Lin Biao to put the PRC on a war footing.[74] Rising Chinese hostility had a significant impact on the German situation, since it made the Russians more willing to compromise in Europe, in hopes of avoiding difficulties on two "fronts." This dynamic was hardly a mystery to policymakers of the time.[75] The topic came up when an SPD delegation under Helmut Schmidt visited Moscow during the midst of the Prague crisis (20–23 August 1968). The Soviet summary of the visit, sent to the SED, remarked curtly that "the speculation of some circles in the FRG as to how the Soviet-Chinese differences of opinion might be used for their own political goals was completely unwarranted."[76] It may have been unpleasant, but it was certainly not unwarranted; as this book will show, Soviet fears about China were one of the main reasons Moscow was willing to negotiate détente with West Germany.

Sino-Soviet tensions turned into actual fighting with a border skirmish on 2 March 1969. SED files shed new light on this important event. According to a Soviet summary of events passed on to East Berlin, a group of thirty Chinese soldiers had intentionally tried to provoke a reaction by trespassing on what the USSR felt to be its territory—tiny Damansky Island in the Ussuri River. When Soviet border guards approached them, they opened fire. The Soviet contingent

The Soviet Union and China

eventually repulsed the Chinese, but the battle resulted in dead and wounded on both sides. The Soviet report added that the Chinese had acted with shocking brutality, killing the wounded by either shooting them at close range or stabbing them.[77] A subsequent report from Moscow to East Berlin complained that the Chinese were hindering weapons and munitions transports for North Vietnam, which needed to travel across Chinese territory.[78] On 21 March, the Chinese reportedly refused to accept a call from Prime Minister Kosygin to discuss these matters.[79] The Chinese Communist Party's Ninth Congress, held in April 1969, forecast a dual confrontation with both the United States and the Soviet Union.[80]

Although the initial Sino-Soviet clash seems to have been provoked by the Chinese, the clashes that followed probably originated with the Soviets.[81] Frighteningly, in the 28 August 1969 issue of *Pravda*, the Soviet leadership raised the specter that Soviet-Chinese border conflicts could widen into a larger confrontation. An article accused the Chinese of supporting the "antisocialist forces" in Czechoslovakia and warned that the "dangerous, reckless and adventurous position" of the current leadership in Peking could affect "the fate of the peoples of the whole planet."[82] Kissinger found *Pravda*'s references to modern lethal weapons and their means of delivery particularly threatening.[83] Suddenly the notion of nuclear conflict between the Chinese and the Soviets expressed by Harrison Salisbury's 1969 book *War between Russia and China* seemed frighteningly realistic.[84] In the summer of 1969, Kissinger and President Richard Nixon were worried that the Soviets might in fact be preparing for a massive and perhaps nuclear attack on China. As a result, "Nixon took perhaps the most daring step of his presidency by warning the Soviet Union that the United States would not remain indifferent if it were to attack China." Kissinger later argued that the true significance of Nixon's readiness "to support a country with which the United States had had no diplomatic relations for twenty years, with which his own Administration had as yet had *no* contact whatsoever on any level" was that it "marked America's return to the world of *Realpolitik*."[85]

Nonetheless, the border clashes continued into September 1969. Only after the Soviets more or less surprised the Chinese with talks that month—after accepting a Chinese invitation to negotiate which had been phrased and timed so as to make it almost impossible to accept—did relations improve marginally.[86] A summary of the meeting, given later to the SED by the Soviets, stated that a Sino-Soviet meeting on 11 September "did produce some progress in the normalization of state relations . . . our trade has increased somewhat. . . . We are of the opinion that further efforts at normalizing the Soviet-Chinese relations must be undertaken."[87]

New Actors and New Initiatives

New Governments in Both the United States and the Federal Republic in 1969

It was against this backdrop in 1969 that two new governments entered office, in Washington in January and in Bonn in October. The key statesmen—Nixon, Kissinger, Brandt, and Bahr—all shared two important traits. They were new to their jobs, and they were willing to use their new authority to take risks. For Brandt, the risk-taking took the form of public offers to negotiate with the SED regime and the Soviet Union as well as other Warsaw Pact members; in the United States, it was the less publicly trumpeted but equally important private contacts with the Soviets and Chinese. In some ways the new Nixon administration had no choice, in part because by the end of the 1960s, "the Soviet Union had acquired strategic intercontinental military forces approaching those of the United States in numbers, if not yet in capability."[88] Kissinger emphasized this parity in his very first conversation with Bahr, pointing out that it necessitated a global approach to questions of security.[89]

If these global strategic realities dictated the necessity, it was nonetheless the individuals in charge who determined the methods and pacing of détente. Nixon had been such a staunch anti-Communist in the past that he was impervious to criticism of being "soft on reds." He could both move quickly and argue convincingly that he was negotiating from strength.[90] Nixon provided the will; his national security adviser, Henry Kissinger, provided the way. Along with Nixon, Kissinger's personality strongly shaped U.S. foreign policy. His personal set of beliefs about how best to manage international politics dominated decision-making, since he and Nixon excluded the normal legislative and foreign policy bureaucracy as much as possible from shaping policy. As Kissinger describes them, his keys in dealing with the Soviets were the principles of concreteness (that is, trying to deal in specifics), restraint, and, most importantly, linkage (that is, tying together a variety of issues when negotiating).[91]

It was due to Kissinger's principle of linkage—and to the inherent interrelatedness of the problems—that superpower maneuvering would continuously affect the situation in divided Germany. One of the first examples of this occurred shortly after Nixon assumed office. The FRG decided to hold the formal election of its president in West Berlin. Because it refused to view West Berlin as part of the FRG, the Warsaw Pact leadership saw this as a provocation. As a result, the East Germans and Soviets increased harassment of traffic to Berlin as a means of expressing their displeasure. In return, Nixon, who visited West Berlin in February 1969, ordered a step-up in U.S. military traffic between West Berlin and West Germany.[92] However, the Soviet harassment suddenly stopped after the initial Sino-Soviet border clash, since Moscow thought that the West Berlin provocation and Chinese skirmish were *planned to coincide*. A Soviet report about the Chinese attack, shared with East Berlin, noted that it was in no way a coincidence that the skirmish took place "just at the same time as Bonn started its provocation [by holding its] presidential election in West Berlin."[93] In other words, the Soviets felt that they were the victims of coordinated actions and did not want to be involved in even small skirmishes on two "fronts" at once. Not for the last time, events in the Far East had direct consequences for the German situation.[94]

Just as the Soviets' biggest day-to-day worry at this time was China, the central preoccupation of the Nixon administration was the war in Vietnam and U.S. efforts to bring an end to the conflict or, failing that, to terminate American involvement therein. To this end, the first U.S. troop withdrawal occurred in July 1969, and years of fitful secret negotiations with the North Vietnamese began the following month.[95] In the same month, the American president also made the first statement of what would be called the "Nixon Doctrine." This doctrine implied that the United States would, in the future, be reticent to send soldiers abroad and would instead delegate the raising of manpower to the threatened region.[96] Finally, Kissinger's policy of linkage meant that one part of his attempts to enable the United States to exit Vietnam were his efforts to establish some kind of détente in Europe.[97]

Hence, various issues became interrelated. This interconnectedness was encouraged by the tendency of all of the main actors—Brezhnev and Ulbricht, Nixon and his confidante Kissinger, Brandt and his confidante Bahr—to conduct key diplomacy personally, usually through "back channels," and hence become

On his first visit to West Germany as president in 1969, Richard Nixon (right) speaks with the West German chancellor Willy Brandt (center) and trade minister Karl Schiller. (Signatur H 0410/201/17 N, Bundesarchiv Koblenz)

individually involved in policymaking toward several different regions.[98] Kissinger recalled in his memoirs that one of the first things he did upon taking office was to establish a personal, private link to the Soviet ambassador, Anatoly Dobrynin. Kissinger recounted that "the most sensitive business in US-Soviet relations came to be handled between Dobrynin and me."[99] He found Dobrynin's "unquestioning support of the Soviet line an asset" because "it enabled us to measure the policies of his masters with precision and buttressed his own influence at home."[100] Bahr and Kissinger also had a direct channel to one another, established on 13 October 1969 before Brandt even officially took office.[101] This channel made use of U.S. Marines as go-betweens because Kissinger "didn't consider the CIA to be secure enough."[102] Kissinger also relied heavily on Kenneth Rush, the U.S. ambassador to Germany. Kissinger found Rush to be the right man for the job at hand—namely, shutting Rush's employer, the State Department, out of any negotiations of importance.[103] Bahr also established a behind-the-scenes link to Brezhnev for Brandt.[104] As a result, a very small number of individuals, communicating in overlapping circuits, made the key decisions. Information that Bahr received over, say, the Soviet channel, would then naturally influence how he perceived information from

Although he did not become secretary of state until 1973, Henry Kissinger exercised a decisive influence on U.S. foreign policy from the beginning of the Nixon presidency. (Signatur R 0428/301 N, Bundesarchiv Koblenz)

the American channel. Occasionally allies would find out from their "enemies," via a back channel, information they did not know about each other.[105]

Brandt Becomes Chancellor

Just as the strong personality of Henry Kissinger influenced both the style and substance of foreign policymaking in Washington, so too did the self-confidence of Willy Brandt enable a shift in West German policies. That the SPD would take over the chancellorship was by no means a foregone conclusion after the voting in the West German national election on 28 September 1969.[106] The CDU/CSU received a plurality of the vote and a congratulatory telephone call from Richard Nixon. Brandt, however, did not lack for courage. As a man who had spent World War II in exile organizing resistance to the Nazis, he trusted his own intuition in tricky political situations. He decided that the ability to lead a coalition government with the liberal FDP was preferable to making the compromises needed to be part of another Grand Coalition with center-right parties. By 21 October he had assembled a working SPD-FDP coalition, and on 28 October he gave his equivalent of an inaugural speech.[107]

With his assumption of office, political power passed into the hands of a center-left coalition for the first time in postwar West Germany.

The chancellorship gave Brandt the opportunity to put into practice policies he had been considering since his days as mayor of Berlin.[108] Without altering the strategy of Western integration established by his predecessors from the opposing conservative Christian Democratic Union (CDU), he decided to augment it with a daring new approach: direct talks with Moscow, Warsaw, Prague, and—most controversially—East Berlin. Brandt felt that the interests of West Germany would be better served by a policy of "change through rapprochement" than by cold-shoulder confrontation.

Brandt's efforts to use his chancellorship to normalize relations to the East began with his inaugural speech of 28 October 1969.[109] In it, the new chancellor made clear that he intended to distinguish himself from his predecessors by trying to negotiate with the East in the interest of preventing further alienation between the two Germanies. He showed that, while he was unwilling to view the GDR as a foreign country, he could regard it as something else—another state on German soil. As he put it, "even if two states exist in Germany, they cannot regard each other as foreign countries." He also emphasized the importance, not only for West Germany but indeed for all the Western allies, of talking with the Soviet Union, especially about the status of Berlin.[110] A series of small but significant actions helped convey the seriousness of his intentions. Brandt renamed the "All-German Ministry" the "Ministry for Inner-German Relations."[111] At Wehner's behest, he closed the controversial "eastern office" of the SPD, which had maintained clandestine contact with former Soviet zone SPD members.[112] He also signed the Nuclear Non-Proliferation Treaty on 18 November 1969.

The conservatives in Germany, headed by the CDU, saw Brandt's initiatives as a threat to West Germany's ties to its Western allies, as a morally unjustified act of recognition of an unsavory regime, and as a confirmation of controversial borders, which might hinder eventual unification. Ironically, as historian Heinrich August Winkler has pointed out, the CDU thereby switched political fronts.[113] In the first half of the Cold War the CDU had promoted integration with the West in preference to reunification with the East. At that time, it was the SPD that worried about hindrances to a possible reunification.

Brandt's loyal aide Bahr helped the chancellor to survive this CDU and media criticism by serving often as a lightning rod. Bahr, who had actually been in the Wehrmacht during the war until discovery of a half-Jewish ancestry caused him to leave the army, had begun his postwar career as a reporter with RIAS (radio in the American sector).[114] His journalism experience helped him to defend Brandt's policies from media representatives opposed to engaging the

Egon Bahr in 1964, after he left journalism to work for Willy Brandt as head of press relations for the West Berlin Senate. (Signatur C 0210/40/ 1 N, Bundesarchiv Koblenz)

Eastern Bloc, particularly the various newspapers owned by the publisher Axel Springer.[115] In fact, Brandt relied on Bahr not only to defend but also to formulate and implement Ostpolitik. Under the title of state secretary, Bahr essentially functioned as Brandt's personal emissary to the Soviet Union and the GDR from 1969 onward.

Brandt and Bahr's experiences in office mirrored those of Nixon and Kissinger (although West German policymaking was not burdened by the strains of a foreign war). Like Nixon, Brandt assigned execution of foreign policy to a trusted subordinate outside of the institutionalized policymaking structure. Like Kissinger, Bahr attained de facto control over the key elements of foreign policymaking, thanks to the patronage of the top officeholder.[116] Kissinger and Bahr shared a further similarity: they both had been forced to leave their German hometowns. As a result of his German origins, Kissinger remained particularly interested in policymaking involving Germany throughout his career.[117] Seymour Hersh, author of a critical biography of Kissinger, found that the U.S.

national security adviser "viewed himself as the ultimate authority on Berlin and the overall German question" and intensely disliked competition from Brandt's initiatives.[118] Kissinger's dislike notwithstanding, there was no denying that he and Nixon were thinking along lines similar to those of Bahr and Brandt. Both pairs of leaders, although from parties at the opposite ends of the political spectrum, were willing to wager that they could redefine the conduct of the Cold War via unprecedented talks with their Communist equivalents.

Eastern Counterparts

It is especially important to understand the personalities of the Eastern rulers with whom the Western leaders were dealing, because in systems that concentrate authority at the top and suppress the political voice of the population, the preferences of individual rulers determine policy.[119] The Soviet leader during the era of negotiations, Leonid Brezhnev, was by Communist standards a relative newcomer to top office, having attained the position of party leader after ousting Nikita Khrushchev in October 1964. His newness did not imply new thinking; in fact, a kind of Brezhnevian neo-Stalinism emerged. As one history of Russia described him, Brezhnev positively "encouraged fawning and toadying." He also suffered from many illness throughout his time in office. In the 1970s and 1980s, he "gradually deteriorated into a breathing mummy."[120]

Brezhnev's rule seems not to have been as absolute in nature at first as it was later in the Cold War. It seems that he was, in the first years of his rule, less a dictator than head of a "consensus-driven leadership," pulled between the relatively more dovish views of the prime minister, Andrei Kosygin, and those of the hawkish head of the KGB, Yuri Andropov. Indeed, Andropov played quite a significant role in foreign policy formulation, along with foreign minister Andrei Gromyko.[121] It appears that one of the main challenges Brezhnev was to face during the era of détente with the United States and West Germany was reconciling the views of Andropov and Gromyko. Both wanted to influence the making of policy, but while Andropov worked to establish a back channel to Bonn, Gromyko saw the key to German negotiations in Washington.[122] However, the existence of disagreement among senior party figures in Moscow does not seem to have altered the willingness of that regime to intervene in the affairs of its neighbors, as witnessed by events in Prague and Poland.

In contrast to the Western and Soviet top leaders, the head of the SED, Walter Ulbricht, had been "on the job" throughout the Cold War.[123] As mentioned before, Ulbricht had become the de facto head of East Germany even before its inception in 1949, having been sent back from exile in Moscow in 1945 by the Soviet Union to manage its occupied German territories.[124] Ulbricht would frequently refer to his decades at the top of Communist politics as a means of asserting his own authority, to the annoyance of his colleagues not only in East

Berlin but also in Moscow. He would, as previously noted, play up the fact that he had met Lenin personally, implying that his status as one of the original disciples gave his analysis of any situation added insight.[125] Ulbricht believed his seniority and the experience of having weathered many storms in office entitled him to show ideological daring. It also, he thought, entitled him to advise Brezhnev, rather than the other way around. According to political scientist James McAdams, Ulbricht particularly refused "to give ground on his state's claims to a leading role in any settlement of the national question [so that] he could at least hold open the possibility that Germany might someday be reunified under socialism."[126] This sense that he should play a leading role in relations with West Germany would increasingly earn him the Soviet leader's animosity.[127]

Other key figures on the East German side of negotiations could draw on decades of ruling experience at the top level before 1969 as well. Honecker, Ulbricht's protégé, had held the influential position of head of the Free German Youth (FDJ) from 1946 to 1955, which enabled him to establish a network of contacts and allies early on in his career.[128] He was already a candidate-member of the Politburo by 1950. The two most important figures at the Ministry for State Security for the negotiations, Erich Mielke and Markus Wolf, had both been in charge since the 1950s.[129] The stunning personal continuity in East German politics was unmatched in any of the other key countries involved in Ostpolitik and détente, namely the FRG, the United States, and the Soviet Union. The challenge of Brandt's initiatives would soon reveal that both Ulbricht and Honecker believed that, on the basis of their extensive personal knowledge and experience, they knew how to respond in the manner best fitting the interests of the GDR. These two responses stood in conflict to one another and would ultimately result in Ulbricht's downfall.

Good Cop, Bad Cop: The Opening Act of the West German–Soviet Bloc Dialogue

Because of their decades-long experience of confrontation with the West, the SED leaders at first doubted Brandt's sincerity in offering a policy of engagement. In his memoirs, Markus Wolf, the head of Stasi espionage outside of the GDR, recollected that it was not clear at the time that Brandt really was prepared to break with the past. As Wolf put it, he and his colleagues did not see that "with the new social-liberal government, new independent national politics had begun in the Federal Republic of Germany."[130]

More importantly, Wolf recollected in his memoirs that he sensed ambivalence in the Soviet reaction to Brandt. In an interview with the author in 1996,

Wolf claimed that "Brezhnev was playing both sides."[131] On the one hand, Brezhnev wanted to promote closer Soviet–West German relations. He was particularly interested in opportunities to weaken West Germany's cooperation with its nuclear power protector, the United States, and to prevent nuclear proliferation.[132] On the other hand, Wolf recalled Brezhnev telling the SED to follow the exact opposite course.

Documents from the Stasi archive support Wolf's assertions. The files show that KGB chief Andropov, presumably acting on Brezhnev's instructions, did in fact advise Mielke and Wolf to hold back from dealing with West Germany. Andropov told them that Brandt's approach did not amount to "a decisive change" in the policy of the FRG.[133] Even though Brandt was "throwing Kiesinger's tactical line overboard," it was clear that his initiatives promoted "the interests of West Germany, its monopolists and not our interests."[134] Andropov took care to point out that, while he could speak only in his own name, he was also "familiar with the opinion of our leading comrades."[135] These comrades, he reported, recognized "the intent to liquidate the GDR" in Brandt's inaugural speech.[136] Above and beyond that, Brandt's policies served, in their opinion, to strengthen the alliance with the United States and NATO.[137] In responding to Brandt, the Soviets told the SED to act only in consultation with "all socialist countries" because "a unified front is of great importance."[138]

Rapprochement with the West Causes the First Cracks in the Facade of Communist Unity

Clearly, Moscow was worried about the potential that the GDR might respond to the FRG on its own. These worries had merit: Ulbricht was indeed hoping to test Brandt by sending the West German government a draft of a German-German treaty of basic relations. Ulbricht suggested that he and Brezhnev speak privately in November to discuss the matter.[139] Instead of a private little chat, Brezhnev insisted that a large multilateral meeting involving all of the Eastern Bloc should take place before Ulbricht sent his draft treaty, presumably to impose peer pressure on the GDR to toe the line. Furthermore, Brezhnev showed who was boss by calling this meeting for the first days of December, despite the fact that this time conflicted with a long-planned SED Central Committee meeting.[140] When the conflict was pointed out to him, Brezhnev made clear that the date of the Central Committee meeting should be changed (a highly unusual event), saying that he hoped that Ulbricht and the "Communists of the GDR correctly understood and appreciated the importance of the preparation of an agreed-upon political line."[141] As a result, a meeting of the Warsaw Pact leadership assembled in Moscow in early December. For good measure, a rare joint session of the Politburos of the Communist Party of the Soviet Union (CPSU) and the SED took place as well, on 2 December 1969.[142]

According to a document that appears to contain remarks from the joint session, Brezhnev announced that Willy Brandt's entry into office was a result of the Warsaw Pact's "common, strong politics."[143] However, Brezhnev added, there was little cause for celebration, because Brandt's change in approach was only superficial; in fact, Brandt wanted "to devour the GDR."[144] The key was to reveal the true intent of Brandt's demagoguery to the population of the GDR.[145]

A quarrel between Brezhnev and Ulbricht over the text of the latter's draft treaty is highly revealing. In comments made at the joint session, Brezhnev complained extensively about the lenient wording of the draft treaty. Brezhnev was upset that it called only for the exchange of "missions," not formal embassies, between the two Germanies.[146] Brezhnev also disliked using the word "progress" in referring to the change in the West German government.[147] According to notes handwritten by Honecker, Ulbricht had used this very term at a special Politburo meeting on 30 October 1969 in referring to the new Brandt government.[148] Yet another key failing of the draft treaty, according to Brezhnev, was the fact that it neglected to address what would later become a key concept in negotiations: "*völkerrechtliche Anerkennung*," or full legal recognition of the GDR as a sovereign state. Instead, the draft asked only for "the taking up of normal, equal (*gleichberechtigter*) relations."[149] Brezhnev made clear before the assembled meeting of all Warsaw Pact leaders on 3–4 December 1969 that he would prefer a treaty that specified full legal recognition.[150] Brezhnev's complaints seem to have made more of an impact on Erich Honecker than on Ulbricht. In a speech afterwards, at the postponed Central Committee meeting on 12–13 December 1969, Honecker echoed Brezhnev's skepticism about the new Brandt initiatives. He complained that even though Brandt had managed to pronounce "the three letters G-D-R" in his inaugural speech, he still had not made the necessary offer of relations between sovereign states on the basis of "*Völkerrecht*," or international law.[151]

In short, Ulbricht was not the one demanding full legal recognition—Brezhnev was. This would imply that Ulbricht was *more* willing to cooperate with the West, *not less*, than Brezhnev. In other words, Brezhnev was playing the role of the hawk by setting the threshold to cooperation impossibly high.[152] This disagreement between Moscow and East Berlin was the first of many to be caused by Willy Brandt's initiatives. Then, as later, Moscow prevailed. The final versions of the cover letter and the draft treaty incorporated all of the Soviet leader's concerns. The word "progress" was nowhere to be found. The draft did insist on recognition in accord with the "norms of international law" and called for the establishment of embassies.[153]

The SED forwarded the final version to the West German president, Gustav Heineman, on 17 December 1969.[154] Heinemann answered by saying that he would pass it on to Brandt for reply.[155] To the surprise of the East Germans, the

West German government also made clear its intent to publicize the exchange of letters, which it did; the Politburo then called a special meeting that drafted a matching article for publication in *Neues Deutschland*.[156] The extreme demands, such as immediate full recognition of the sovereignty of East Germany, made the draft treaty unworkable in any real sense. Brandt chose to ignore it in his reply and instead suggested that talks should commence between the two Germanies.[157]

Brezhnev Plays Both Sides: Soviet Attitudes toward German-German Rapprochement

Yet even as Brezhnev criticized Ulbricht, he forged ahead with the Soviet Union's own bilateral relations with West Germany behind closed doors. As Wolf put it, "Brezhnev would change his stripes when he changed conversation partners and say what he considered to be opportune."[158] It was crucial for Brezhnev to "control the opening to the West himself." According to Wolf, "Nothing would be more inconvenient for him than independent contacts between East and West Germany which would be hard to oversee."[159]

Although Brandt could not have known these internal details of GDR-Soviet tension at the time, he nonetheless displayed awareness that advances in German-German relations depended heavily on the attitude of Moscow. Brandt therefore strove to keep Moscow involved in his efforts to reconfigure relations with the East. Practically as soon as he entered office, Brandt's foreign minister Walter Scheel voiced interest in talks with the Soviets. The goal was to produce some kind of agreement on mutual renunciation of the use of force.[160] Furthermore, in February 1970, trade agreements were signed in Essen, providing for an exchange of Soviet natural gas for German-made pipeline and other equipment, to be financed by a consortium of seventeen West German banks, led by Deutsche Bank.[161]

The most significant aspect of the West German approach to the Soviet Union was the emphasis placed by Brandt and Bahr on establishing direct, top-level communication to the Soviet leader (which, as in the case of the United States, would often bypass the State Department). The way in which the FRG-Soviet back channel came to exist and the modalities of communication between Bonn and Moscow merit consideration because they help to shed light on Soviet attitudes toward German-German rapprochement. On 19 November 1969—only two days after the United States and the USSR began the opening rounds of what would become the Strategic Arms Limitation Talks (SALT)—Brandt wrote directly to the chair of the Soviet Council of Ministers, Kosygin.[162] In his letter, Brandt used a metaphor of Gromyko's: "If you want to dig a tunnel, you have to drill into the mountain from both sides, and you have to make sure that the drills will meet in the middle."[163]

Only Brandt, Bahr, and Scheel, as well as the typist, Bahr's secretary Elisabeth Kirsch, knew of the existence of this letter. Bahr was therefore astonished when a Soviet "journalist" who turned up on Christmas Eve 1969 began discussing this letter with him.[164] Bahr sought to determine whether he was dealing with an emissary from the top by asking the "journalist," Valeri Lednev, if the person who had sent him carried enough weight to matter in the formulation of global policy issues. The Soviet emissary reportedly replied, "Absolutely, because it's Brezhnev."[165] Bahr was pleased with this response and, as a result, established a secret, direct channel to Brezhnev via Lednev and his KGB colleague V. Kevorkov.[166] Bahr's files show that this channel conveyed not only practical messages related to organizing meetings but also interpretations of issues of great importance to both sides. For example, a communication in January 1970 emphasized the Soviet worry about the Chinese. Moscow assumed that the only reason the Chinese continued to conduct rather desultory talks with Soviets at all was to avoid being accused of ending them; there was in fact little hope of reaching any accord.[167]

Bahr was convinced from the level of details the go-betweens knew that they were connected directly to Brezhnev. He felt could rely on their assessment of how far the FRG could go in making requests for rapprochement with Moscow.[168] Bahr came to rely on this channel as an important source of honest advice about what could and could not be expected from Moscow.[169] One of the specific issues on which the Soviet back channel was most helpful, Bahr remembered, was in assessing Ulbricht. He claimed that the channel helped ease disappointment in Bonn over the uncompromising tone of the letter and draft treaty that the FRG had received from Ulbricht on 17 December.[170]

However, if the above reconstruction of events leading to the production of the Ulbricht draft treaty is correct—that is, that the Soviets insisted on the insertion of more hard-line language—then *Brezhnev* was actually responsible for making the tone more uncompromising. In other words, Brezhnev forced Ulbricht to take a more hard-line stance, then sent a KGB emissary to Bonn who essentially told Brandt and Bahr that they need not worry about Ulbricht's hard-line stance because they could rely on Moscow to be more accommodating. In other words, Brezhnev had a kind of good-cop/bad-cop routine in operation, with Ulbricht set up as the bad cop. Such tactics would be consistent with Brezhnev's main goal: to concentrate control of the conduct of the German-German rapprochement in his own hands. These tactics also imply that Bahr's confidence in his Soviet back channel as a reliable, honest indicator of Eastern Bloc politics was misplaced, since this channel had told him not to worry about "Ulbricht's" hard line.

Brezhnev was clearly telling different people different stories. Even as he cautioned East Berlin against rapprochement, he allowed his foreign minister to begin talks with the FRG. The West German ambassador in Moscow, Helmut Allardt, began exploratory conversations with Gromyko on the subject of what would become the Moscow Treaty.[171] Brezhnev also pursed rapprochement on the superpower level. Preliminary bilateral talks on arms control with the Americans had begun in November 1969. On top of this, maneuvering was already underway to commence quadripartite talks on Berlin.[172] Brezhnev's interest in negotiation did have its limits, however; he still viewed confrontation as a useful tool. For example, one of his ambassadors raised the specter of global warfare in conversation with the United States. The Soviet ambassador in East Berlin, Pjotr Abrasimov, warned the American ambassador in Bonn, Kenneth Rush, that everything possible needed to be done to avoid complications regarding West Berlin.[173] Abrasimov told Rush that it was crucial to prevent West Germany from causing "a clash of the Soviet Union and the GDR with the USA and the other powers because of West Berlin, despite the fact that the FRG had absolutely no rights to this city."[174] The Soviets also decided in December 1969 that joint Warsaw Pact military exercises should be held on GDR territory in February and March 1970.[175]

Brezhnev's response to Brandt's initiatives was, in short, to institute a kind of double game. On the one hand, he told Ulbricht to make his treaty demands more stringent; on the other, he implied to Bahr that the FRG should not worry about an obstinate Ulbricht and should instead deal directly with Moscow. He agreed to talks over Berlin with the three other occupying powers in Germany but also used threats and showy military exercises as well. Clearly, the path ahead would be a tricky one for all involved.

The opening act of the FRG-GDR dialogue showed how much the personal experience of the leaders involved mattered to the conduct of international politics. New leaders in the West evinced a clear desire to try fresh approaches in dealing with the GDR under Ulbricht and the Soviet Union under Brezhnev. However, participants on both sides had to master the difficult task of reconciling the worries of the past with the present interests of the many parties involved in Berlin and in Germany. Brezhnev's concern that his German satellite would show too much policymaking independence complicated matters by leading him to play his relations with one Germany off those with the other.

Ironically, the United States and its allies seemed to share similar anxiety about an overly independent German ally. The United States worried that closer cooperation between the FRG and the Warsaw Pact would cause a corresponding decrease in West Germany's cooperation with NATO. Documents challenge this assumption. In his initial letter to Kosygin of November 1969, Brandt had in fact said outright that he thought it would be not only illusory but also dangerous "if one would proceed from any basis other than the existing alliances and systems of security."[176] The memoirs of the Soviet emissary involved in the Brandt-Brezhnev channel also record Brandt's emphasis that the West Germans, "if a critical situation arose, would without doubt stand on the side of the United States."[177] But U.S. policymakers did not seem to share Soviet confidence on this point.[178] Worry on the part of both superpowers that their respective German ally would show too much initiative would be a constant factor as German-German rapprochement moved from its opening act to actual negotiations.

Speaking Civilly Face-to-Face
in the First Half of 1970:
Meetings in Moscow, Erfurt,
Berlin, and Kassel

two

The winter of 1969–70 was a bitter one in northern Europe. The month of December, the coldest in Berlin since 1893, had forced the Politburo to make various unplanned allotments of energy to insure there would be enough heat. In the GDR, frigid conditions lasted well into March, when heavy snow closed streets and forced trains to stop running.[1] Even worse, the cheap grade of brown coal commonly used in the GDR contained a good deal of water. When temperatures remained below freezing for a long period of time, the coal would freeze into the transport trucks and could be removed only with heavy machinery, which was in short supply.

The frigid climatic conditions contrasted with the beginnings of a thaw in international relations at this time. Building on the initial contacts of late 1969, a variety of odd couples arranged to meet face-to-face in the first half of 1970. In January, Egon Bahr headed to Moscow to begin negotiations with Foreign Minister Andrei Gromyko. Bahr thereby began his personal participation in bilateral West German-Soviet relations, one-half of Brezhnev's "double-game."

The game's other half comprised Soviet-GDR bilateral relations. These were severely strained by the dramatic events accompanying the first face-to-face meeting between Willy Brandt and his East German equivalent Willi Stoph. Originally scheduled for Berlin, the Brandt-Stoph meeting took place in Erfurt in March. The unexpectedly emotional welcome that Brandt received from the locals there inspired significant superpower worries and shaped the subsequent development of Ostpolitik to a greater extent than ever suspected. For this reason, the events in Erfurt in March 1970 and their aftermath merit closer scrutiny than they have yet received in scholarly literature.

Similarly, the beginnings of the quadripartite talks merit a fresh look as well. Through these "Berlin talks," the four occupying authorities in divided Cold War Germany attempted to formalize the status of Cold War Berlin. Henry Kissinger characterized the quadripartite talks as being of "almost theological complexity" and called them the most complicated in which he was ever involved.[2] This is no small "compliment," considering what other delicate negotiations Kissinger was conducting at or around this time: secret meetings with the North Vietnamese in Paris and clandestine contacts with China via Pakistan.

Finally, a fruitless follow-up meeting to Erfurt took place in Kassel in May. Despite the lack of immediate results, these four conversations—Moscow, Erfurt, Berlin, and Kassel—had a significant impact in the longer term. They not only ruptured SED unity but also added up to a fundamental reshaping of the conduct of the Cold War.[3]

Moscow

The First Round, 30 January–17 February 1970

Via the secret back-channel contacts with Moscow, described in Chapter 1, Bonn and Moscow agreed to begin talks about a non-aggression pact. Egon Bahr flew to the Soviet capital at the end of January 1970 to lead an eight-member delegation in negotiating what would become the Moscow Treaty.[4] The Soviets did not allow East Germany any role in these talks, although the division of Germany was a constant topic. Instead, Bahr dealt directly with Gromyko, who was advised by the foreign ministry's German expert Valentin Falin, and with the emissaries of the secret channel, who were under the direction of Andropov and Brezhnev.[5]

In terms of diplomatic etiquette, giving Bahr the job of head negotiator was technically a breach of protocol, since he was not foreign minister and hence not Gromyko's equal. In fact, he was not affiliated with the West German foreign affairs ministry at all; officially he was only a state secretary in the West German chancellery. Bahr could have had a more exalted position, had he wished; at the time of the election, Brandt had offered Bahr a choice of titles. Bahr had refused. He did so, in a move reminiscent of Kissinger's style, so as to have a free hand in structuring policy toward the East, unencumbered by institutional affiliations.[6] Both he and Brandt viewed the foreign ministry in particular as a stronghold of career bureaucrats from rival domestic political camps, and they preferred to deal directly with hostile governments themselves.[7] The fact that Bahr enjoyed Brandt's full confidence and support gave him the de facto authority he needed. In addition, as historian Arnulf Baring has shown, Brandt felt that sending the West German foreign minister (that is, Walter Scheel) would have raised expectations too much, and Brandt trusted Bahr more in any case.[8]

Hence, the decision was made to send Bahr. His papers contain summaries of the negotiations he conducted in Moscow, which correspond well with similar Soviet summaries forwarded to East Berlin.[9] According to Bahr's papers, his mandate was to obtain not only some kind of non-aggression accord but also more general Soviet signals that would indicate that serious German-German talks could proceed. He and Brandt had long felt that Moscow's tolerance would be crucial to success in German-German negotiations, and they wanted to begin securing it as quickly as possible.[10] The West Germans also realized that the Soviets would not be moved by words alone; on 1 February 1970, an agreement was reached to exchange Soviet natural gas for West German pipeline, favorably financed by a consortium of West German banks.[11]

Bahr first met with his Soviet counterparts on 30 January 1970. He immediately addressed what Moscow considered to be a core issue: European borders. Bahr made clear that the FRG under Brandt would be willing to recognize formally all existing 1970 borders. According to Bahr's papers, Gromyko commented that this offer was merely a recognition of reality, not a concession.[12] Bahr emphasized that a large exception was the border between the two Germanies. Recognizing that border, he said, would be tantamount to "giving up on the unification of Germany." This was out of the question, because West Germany's constitution-like Basic Law required the government to avoid any steps that could impede an eventual unification.[13] Furthermore, there could be no mention of "full legal recognition for the GDR from the FRG."[14]

For their part, the Soviets reported to East Berlin that they had rejected the West German notion of relations between the two Germanies having a "special character." Such a designation could lead to a "*de facto* denial of the sovereign rights" of the GDR, were the FRG to treat its neighbor differently than other foreign states.[15] At the next meeting, on 3 February, the Soviet side also made clear that they wanted FRG recognition of *all* existing Cold War borders, that is, including the German-German border—seemingly an ultimatum that Bahr could not fulfill.[16] Immediately thereafter, however, Moscow offered a way out. The Soviet delegation reportedly told Bahr that "no one could forbid the FRG to have its own interests," implying that one-sided expressions of desire for uni-fication might be acceptable.[17] Bahr returned the favor by suggesting that it might be possible to find formulations that would be compatible with West Germany's legal obligations.[18] He also noted that it would be possible to negoti-ate with the GDR according to the norms of international law, a goal that the GDR and the USSR both desired, because it implied that GDR-FRG relations might be "international." Bahr reiterated, however, that there would need to be an awareness of the "special character" of relations between the two.[19] At a meeting with the chair of the Soviet Council of Ministers, Andrei Kosygin, on 13 February, Bahr further pointed out that realists in the West German govern-ment did not see the existence of the GDR as a hindrance to the development of relations with the Soviet Union. After all, unification was a matter for the future to decide. Bahr was quick to emphasize, however, that "no one in Bonn intended to suggest that the Soviets or the GDR should change allies."[20] Indeed, the Soviet report of Bahr's comments explicitly stated that the FRG "considered its 'Ostpolitik' subordinate to its NATO obligations."[21]

Bahr was less categorical about the longer term, according to the Soviet summary. He reportedly observed that it would be "extremely dangerous to set a goal of dissolving the existing Bloc alliances . . . as long as a European system of security had not yet been created."[22] While convoluted, this statement im-plied that dissolution, or perhaps some other kind of loosening of ties, would be possible if a European system could be established. Kosygin, in his response, seized the moment to suggest just such a loosening. According to East German records of the meeting, Kosygin "pointed out the necessity of the FRG conduct-ing a more independent policy, and of not constantly looking back to the West" and seconded Bahr's interest in a European security conference.[23] In other words, Kosygin held out a temptation that West Germany's allies feared would prove irresistible to the FRG: that of becoming a more independent, neutral factor, balancing between East and West. Bahr's response was not recorded, but it is clear that he did not seize upon this offer. None of this early maneuvering produced any real progress. Instead, on 17 February both Bahr and Gromyko agreed that a pause was needed to consider the positions advanced by both, thus ending the first of what would become three rounds of consultation. The only tangible success Bahr achieved came in the course of a conversation with Kosy-gin, not Gromyko, during which Bahr convinced Kosygin to let nearly 200 would-be émigrés of German background leave the Soviet Union.[24]

Bahr flew back to the FRG to talk with Brandt and take stock. He informed not only Brandt but also the three Western occupying authorities of the progress of his talks. An internal U.S. State Department report noted that Bahr's consultation—in which Bahr, a West German, explained cutting-edge developments in East-West relations to the Western allies, instead of the other way around—"forcefully demonstrated" both West German self-assurance and the interconnected nature of German Ostpolitik with global détente.[25]

Moreover, Brandt and Bahr realized that they were moving in advance not only of the Western superpower but of the Eastern one as well. According to his memoirs, Bahr reached the conclusion at this time that Bonn was in fact much more prepared for West German–Soviet talks than Moscow was. Bahr had gone to the USSR with the assumption that the Soviets had already established their negotiating goals with regard to the FRG; now he saw that this was not the case.[26] The uncertainty that Bahr sensed in Moscow may have been due not only to disagreements within the Soviet camp but also within the SED. Valentin Falin recalled that Gromyko had to defend his negotiations against criticism from Erich Honecker, criticism that some members of the Soviet leadership felt to be justified.[27]

The Second Round, 3–21 March 1970

By early March the two sides felt ready to try again. Bahr returned to Moscow and shortly afterward wrote Brandt a personal letter, which concluded with the sentence, "I would prefer that you destroy this." He informed Brandt that he had discovered a raw nerve: he mentioned China, and suddenly floodgates of insecurity opened. Moscow, he wrote, was "absolutely convinced that the Chinese want war," explaining that the Soviets believed the Chinese *needed* war because "they have too many people." A complete lack of any kind of intelligence operation in China, reported Bahr, exacerbated Moscow's fears. His Soviet counterparts were also telling him that "the Americans are probably much further along with the Chinese than either of us [the USSR and FRG] suspect." Bahr concluded that the Chinese situation clearly made the Russians interested in a rapprochement with the West.[28]

Perhaps because of this worry, the Soviets gave Bahr an important opening in this second round. They suggested that the FRG seek a treaty with the GDR that would have "the same legally binding nature as treaties with other socialist countries."[29] Although the phrase "same legally binding nature" was only one small linguistic step away from "legally binding nature," it was precisely the kind of step that could help Bahr to dance around constitutional concerns and enable talks to continue. Under the terms of the West German Basic Law, West Germany was bound to pursue the goal of unification. Hence, Bahr shied away from any kind of formulation that included such terms as "legally binding" with regard to the GDR, assuming that such language would, in the face of legal scrutiny, be found in opposition to this goal. Phrases weakened by modifiers such as "the same as," however, would stand more of a chance in West German courts—and in the court of public opinion.

Erfurt

The Secret Capital

The power of public opinion would be amply demonstrated at the Erfurt meeting between Brandt and Stoph. Brandt's overnight visit there on 19–20 March 1970 produced no formal agreements, accords, or even putative road maps for future relations. The German newsmagazine *Der Spiegel* concluded at the time that the two heads of governments had "nothing new to say."[30] Little scholarship has been produced about Erfurt since.

Nonetheless, a handful of scholars and contemporaries have appreciated that something intangible yet significant happened. Gordon Craig and Alexander George have compared the surprise of the Erfurt meeting to that which accompanied the unprecedented exchange of visits between King Edward VII of England and French president Loubet in 1903, which established the Entente Cordiale and redrew the map of European alliances at the time.[31] Dennis Bark and David Gress have argued that Erfurt became the secret capital of the united German nation for a day.[32] Valentin Falin, looking back, has asserted that Erfurt represented the beginning of the process of German reunification.[33] And no less a figure than Henry Kissinger himself found that "the classic Western position— that any European settlement presupposed the reunification of Germany . . . passed into history" with the meeting of the two postwar German leaders in Erfurt.[34]

An examination of SED sources shows that the shock of the events in Erfurt had a long-lasting impact on not only Soviet-GDR relations but also the entire network of relations between both Germanies and their respective allies. Given the enormous impact of the Erfurt meeting, the following questions merit detailed answers: How did the Erfurt meeting come about? Precisely what occurred? What did the aftermath reveal about SED expectations for it? What long-term impact did it have?

How Erfurt Came About: Hurried Requests for a Brandt-Stoph Meeting—in Berlin

The origins of the Erfurt meeting lay in the correspondence surrounding Ulbricht's draft German-German treaty of October 1969. President Heinemann had passed along Ulbricht's letter and draft treaty to Brandt, who chose to respond to his nominal equivalent in the state apparatus, Willi Stoph.[35] In his reply, Brandt ignored the draft treaty and instead suggested talks not only on mutual renunciation of the use of force but also on "all outstanding questions between our two states."[36] In a petulant tone, Stoph's reply of 11 February called attention to Brandt's silence about the draft treaty but nonetheless invited Brandt to meet with him—in Berlin in only eight days' time.[37] One day before, in a presumably not unrelated move, the Soviets had proclaimed to the three western allies their own interest in beginning quadripartite talks—in Berlin in only eight days' time.[38]

The reason for the timing of these sudden and hurried requests is not entirely clear, but once again it may have had its origins in the contemporaneous Soviet feeling that progress in talks with the Chinese on border issues was unsatisfactory. The previous autumn, a meeting between Chinese prime minister Zhou En-lai and Kosygin on 11 September 1969 had set the stage for the opening of Sino-Soviet negotiations in Peking. The goal in the short term was to prevent further armed conflict on the USSR-PRC border until some kind of agreement over the border disputes could be obtained.[39] However, by February 1970 the Soviets had come to believe that the Chinese were interested only in one-sided concessions and might use force to gain them.[40] "In an attempt to put the Soviet side under pressure," read a Soviet summary of the talks of February 1970, "the Chinese leadership has created both in and around the talks an atmosphere of extortion" and continually "tries to speak in the language of threats." The leader of the Chinese delegation had announced that, if the Soviets were not prepared to accept certain Chinese demands, then "the conflicts on the border would last quite a while, and it 'would be difficult to avoid new incidents on the border.' "[41] In light of this, the Soviets may have been more interested in preventing any possible incidents on their European borders and those of their allies.

Whatever their origins, these hurried requests for a meeting in eight days' time did not produce a welcoming response from the Western side. As Kissinger put it, the short deadline "was totally unrealistic, given the glacial procedures of interallied consultation."[42] Brandt also opposed the repeated attempts to establish preconditions for the talks (that is, those cited in Ulbricht's draft treaty, which had been made more stringent at Brezhnev's insistence).[43] However, Brandt was more eager than Kissinger that talks should begin; on 25 February he wrote to Nixon, as Kissinger recalls, "gently urging the early opening of Berlin negotiations" and told Stoph that lower-level delegations could meet in late February.[44]

Kissinger was not pleased by this West German eagerness. As he recounted in his memoirs:

The intricacies of the Berlin question, the need to develop a common Western position, and the sharply conflicting views built up over the years all ensured that Berlin [i.e., quadripartite] negotiations would be protracted. Brandt could set a much brisker pace in his bilateral initiatives; the style of Bahr, his chief negotiator, made it inescapable. All of this increased our leverage. To put it diplomatically, I did not consider the slow pace of the Berlin talks a tactical disadvantage.[45]

Kissinger held off the start of quadripartite talks until 26 March 1970.[46] In his memoirs, he reproduced a memo he wrote to Nixon a week after the hurried requests arrived. In it, Kissinger expressed worry that Brandt's initiatives could revive the old debate from the Adenauer era between those in the Federal Republic seeking Western integration and those who were "enthralled by the vision of Germany as a 'bridge' between East and West."[47]

The Switch from Berlin to Erfurt

Unexpectedly, the stalling on the part of the West in response to the Soviet and SED's hurried requests turned out to have a beneficial effect for the East German regime: it allowed time for a change of heart on the question of inviting the charismatic former Mayor Brandt of the Western half of Berlin to its Eastern half. At first, this SED change of opinion expressed itself outwardly in talks with the West Germans only as petty disagreements over the technicalities of Brandt's travel route to Berlin, not a retraction of the invitation. However, an internal Stasi report spoke far more plainly.[48] "There seem to be reflections [on the West German side] on how to make Brandt's ride through 'East Berlin' into a show," claimed the report. "There are also worries that he will be cut off via a cordon of policemen on motorcycles," which would prevent Brandt from coming in contact with ordinary citizens.[49] According to the Stasi, the Western side hoped that "a Brandt surrounded by the 'cheering East Berlin population' would confer so much prestige on his Administration that he would not have to listen to the CDU/CSU on questions of Ostpolitik any more."[50] Perhaps because of Politburo unwillingness to revoke its own invitation outright, Berlin nonetheless remained the putative meeting point well into March. What is not clear from the documents is why the SED had suggested Berlin in the first place. Presumably the imagery that Brandt would be visiting a "foreign capital" had appealed to the SED. Gromyko had made vague comments to this effect to Ulbricht in late February; Gromyko had suggested that, if Brandt were greeted enough like a visiting foreign head of state, his arrival could be made to seem like a de facto recognition of the GDR.[51]

The spectacle of the former long-serving mayor of West Berlin processing triumphantly through East Berlin would truly have been an international sensation in the middle of the Cold War. Indeed, the prospect might even have given the Western allies pause, had they been asked how they felt about Brandt visiting the eastern zone of their occupied city. However, they never had to decide on that issue. Citing the ongoing petty disagreements about the technicalities of the Berlin meeting, Brandt proposed a change of venue in a letter of 8 March.[52] Three days later, Gromyko had a similar message conveyed to the SED leadership. In it, he indicated that worries about using East Berlin as the meeting site should not prevent the meeting from taking place at all. The Soviets "suggested" a change of venue as well—indicating their desire that the meeting come about despite difficulties—saying that the conversation should take place in either Magdeburg or Erfurt instead.[53] The SED Politburo agreed to this "suggestion" on the same date, 11 March.[54] As a result, the lower-level FRG-GDR delegations meeting to prepare the Brandt-Stoph conversation—headed on the Western side by Ulrich Sahm, son of Berlin's mayor from 1931 to 1935—agreed on Erfurt.[55]

The reason for Moscow's pressure on the SED to keep the Brandt-Stoph meeting alive, according to Gromyko, was not so much its concern about German-German relations as its concern about public relations and world political opinion. This was neither the first nor the last time that this factor would weigh heavily on German-German contacts. As the Soviets saw it, if the talks fell through, the GDR's international reputation would suffer. They were afraid that Brandt could win leverage over the GDR by gaining the upper hand in the press and public opinion. Brandt could claim to the media that his offer to come to East Berlin had been refused and counter with the offer of a Bonn meeting. The Soviets felt that "the world should not be allowed to garner the impression that the GDR is turning down talks."[56] In other words, the value of Brandt's visit rested in its ability to increase the GDR's standing in the eyes of the world. Neither the dictators in Moscow nor those in East Berlin were impervious to the public opinion of the capitalist world.

Soviet pressure on the SED to meet with the FRG may also have been due to the beginning of secret talks between Kissinger and Le Duc Tho, although it is hard to guess when the Soviets might have learned of them. It cannot be assumed that Hanoi informed Moscow as soon as the talks began. Vietnamese-Soviet relations did not exhibit much cordiality. One of the disappointments of détente was that it did not result in greater Soviet pressure on North Vietnam to act in a more conciliatory manner. In what measure this was due to Moscow's *unwillingness* and in what measure to its *inability* has long remained an open question.[57] It now seems likely that it was due to the latter.[58] Historian Stephen Morris, a specialist on the topic of Soviet-Vietnamese relations, has found that the Moscow-Hanoi relationship was characterized by "recurring duplicity."[59] And Anatoly Dobrynin, long-time Soviet ambassador in Washington, has described relations between Moscow and Hanoi in the following way:

> The leadership in Hanoi, while our ideological allies, doggedly avoided informing us about their long-term plans in Southeast Asia or their policies toward the United States, notwithstanding our considerable military and economic aid. As a result, their actions often were a surprise to us and put us in difficult positions. Actually they did not pay much attention to how they affected our relations with Washington. On the contrary, they did not mind spoiling them. We learned much more from the Americans about their negotiations with Hanoi than we did from the Vietnamese.[60]

Welcoming Brandt to Erfurt

Whatever Soviet motives were, their "suggestion" that the meeting site be switched resulted in the location being changed on short notice from Berlin to Erfurt, which in turn necessitated a large amount of short-term tactical planning on the part of the SED hosts. East German files from the days immediately after the switch to Erfurt contain pages and pages of protocol for even the tiniest details of the visit. The arrival time of the train, exactly who would greet whom when, where carpets and flags would be placed, which room various delegation members would have at the hotel Erfurter Hof—no detail seemed too trivial to be fixed in advance.[61] The planning should have been a little less all-inclusive and a little more careful, however; giving Brandt a hotel room with a window on the large plaza outside, for example, proved to be an enormous mistake. Events soon showed that the security plans for the meeting had been inadequate, or as an internal Central Committee Secretariat discussion concluded afterwards, "*[T]he preparation for the Erfurt meeting was not fully recognized as a key component in the class conflict between socialism and imperialism. The dangerousness of the class enemy and his intent to prepare and conduct an organized provocative act was not recognized.*"[62]

In consultation with the Soviets, the GDR minister for state security, Erich Mielke, had ordered the Stasi, or MfS, to take responsibility for all measures necessary for the security of the talks.[63] The operation was given an unpromising code name: "Operation Confrontation." Before Brandt and his delegation even got to Erfurt, flaws in this operation became apparent.[64] After his train crossed into the GDR about 7:30 A.M. on the morning of 19 March, well-wishers waved from the tracks along the route to Erfurt.[65] Windows facing the train reportedly bore white signs with large "Y"s written on them, signifying the difference between the spelling of the names of the West and East German heads of government: Will*y* Brandt versus Will*i* Stoph.[66]

This secretly taken surveillance photo accompanied a report filed by Erich Mielke, the head of the Stasi, about the events in Erfurt. The picture shows a crowd waiting in Erfurt at 8:30 A.M., about one hour before Brandt's arrival. The report did not include a photo of the breakout, perhaps due to Mielke's obvious embarrassment at his failure to maintain order. (From File J IV 2/3A/1866 [Sekretariat], SAPMO)

In Erfurt itself, the local district leaders had suggested that a thousand party activists should line the streets. However, this plan never made it from conception to implementation, perhaps due to the last-minute change in venue.[67] Instead, members of the public crowded the streets hours before Brandt's arrival, to the consternation of the security forces.[68] Finally, at about 9:30 A.M., Brandt's train reached Erfurt station. In an effort to block the view of the crowds during Brandt's arrival, an on-site unit commander tried to position a street tram in front of them, by allowing it to enter a blocked-off area. But the positioning of the tram necessitated the raising of a barricade; this raising gave the crowds an opening in one of the lines of blockade.[69]

Erich Mielke's report to Erich Honecker described what happened next. As Brandt's delegation walked across the street from the train station to the hotel, "the agitated crowd broke through . . . the second blockade of reserve MfS forces [which] could not resist the force of the crowd and was torn asunder." Mielke estimated that a crowd of 1,500 flooded the plaza between the train station and Brandt's hotel, of which he claims 500 were journalists. While the crowd chanted, "Willy Brandt to the window," Mielke's men shouted "Willi Stoph to the window"; however, as the MfS men were "busy restoring order and clearing the plaza, their shouts . . . did not have the proper impact."[70] Brandt, who, after some hesitation, appeared at the hotel window overlooking the plaza, recounted in his memoirs that he made a quieting motion to the crowd with his hands, hoping to dampen symbolically expectations that he could not fulfill. When he turned away from the window, he recalled, his staff had tears in their eyes.[71]

Security forces succeeded in clearing the plaza shortly thereafter. Markus Wolf remembered that there was a panicky attempt to organize a counter-demonstration for Stoph: "Our colleagues [i.e., Stasi workers] were hauled in from far and wide," he said, in order to demonstrate in favor of the correct Willi.[72] Mielke's description of the Erfurt events ended with the sinister note, "[T]hose people who chanted or in other ways made themselves evident by their negative actions were documented and will be worked on."[73] There was little else he could say, after he and the MfS had failed so spectacularly to maintain a facade of order at the crucial first meeting between the Germanies.

If interviews of over twenty years later can be believed, not all responses within the SED to these events were negative. In a 1996 interview, a minor member of the GDR delegation, legal expert Günter Görner, discussed his reaction to the events that he had witnessed personally in Erfurt in 1970. He recollected that he personally felt moved by the sight of the demonstration in favor of Brandt. He found that the people gathered there were not concerned with abstract issues such as "full legal recognition" or codifying the status quo. Rather, they merely hoped that "Germans could speak normally with each other" and that Brandt could perhaps make progress on issues of human rights. Görner did not belong, however, to the group of SED decision-makers; rather, he wrote early versions of preparatory papers that were later edited by higher-ups. Hence, his personal opinion did not have a policy impact.[74]

The Conversation Itself

The overwhelming reception that Brandt received from the population of Erfurt overshadowed the formal conversation that followed. Indeed, Brandt even skillfully slipped in a reference to the greeting during the official session, using a cleverly ambivalent construction that could refer either to the official or the unofficial welcome he had received: "I would like to say thank you for the friendly reception that you have let be bestowed upon us here in Erfurt."[75] In contrast, Stoph's comments at the official session contained little heartiness and even less subtlety. "Is it your intention," he asked early on, "to repeat the politics of Stresemann? Politics that consist of strengthening the alliance with the Western powers and recognizing the borders in the West in order to keep the borders in the East open, just as happened in Locarno?"[76]

Stoph then complained about a series of what he viewed as aggressive acts on the part of the FRG against the GDR from the early Cold War, concluding that "the securing of our border in 1961 was an act of humanity."[77] He strove to emphasize the differences between the GDR and the FRG, calling it "fanciful" to say that the citizens of both "were just 'all Germans' . . . since the beginning of the last century, there have always been Germans who stood on the side of progress, of the working class and the working people, and others on the side of reaction and capitalism."[78] Stoph concluded by listing the goals of the SED: a clear official end to the Hallstein Doctrine; mutual renunciation of the use of force; membership for both Germanies in the UN; clear promises never to use atomic, biological, or chemical weapons; and discussion of questions on "remnants of the second World War" (which he did not identify more clearly) and of the debts and reparations that the FRG owed the GDR (also not specified). Significantly, at this point he called for "normal relations on the basis of equality . . . and the norms of international law," a slight semantic difference from the "full legal recognition" of the GDR, which Brezhnev had insisted be put into the draft treaty at the Moscow meeting.[79]

As he had done in written correspondence, Brandt chose in his oral communications to avoid replying directly to these demands. Indeed, he said plainly that he and his government had a very low opinion of the attempt to force a draft treaty upon them without any kind of discussion in advance.[80] He pointed out how unusual it was that the very first conversation between the two German heads of governments was a summit, not preceded by extensive lower-level talks. The fact that a summit was needed, he said, showed the extent of the division between the FRG and the GDR, a division which "had only been getting deeper until today."[81] He then listed the hopes of the West German side that both Germanies would declare their "duty to maintain the unity of the German nation" while still recognizing the rights of the four occupying powers. He further hoped they would renounce use of force against each other and attempt to establish cooperation in a variety of spheres.[82] Brandt stated specifically that such cooperation should go beyond "formal documents" and that "the people both on this side and on that side should get something out of it." Specifically, this should include the reuniting of engaged couples waiting to marry and of children "not yet reunited with their parents" (meaning, although he did not say so explicitly, those separated by the GDR's sealing of the border.)[83]

Unofficial conversations, whether during lunch or during a joint visit to Buchenwald, were hardly more cordial. During the lunch break, Stoph tried to draw Brandt out on the subject of American aggression in Vietnam, but Brandt proved evasive. According to the SED summary of the lunch conversation,

The official photo of the Brandt-Stoph meeting in Erfurt, 19 March 1970. Brandt and Stoph
(left and right, respectively) face each other across the center of the table. This is the meeting

Brandt blandly replied that "when I get asked a tricky question, I just say, I only
understand Europe."[84] Then, when Brandt commented on how useful the kind
of direct contact they were having that day could be, Stoph seized the opportunity to demand the maximum: that he and Brandt institutionalize this direct
contact on the spot by proclaiming that they would exchange ambassadors and
embassies.[85] Once again Brandt's evasive talents did not fail him. As with Vietnam, Brandt managed to get off the topic without a direct reply. Instead, the
conversation turned into a "small-talk" discussion of the works of Goethe.[86]

In the end, both sides avoided making any kind of firm commitments. Their
meeting did not advance much beyond mutual statements of demands and hopes
for German-German relations. Stoph, in a summary of his personal exchanges
with Brandt during Erfurt, concluded that Brandt was trying to set up minor
agreements or commissions to discuss specific issues but that he completely
avoided "the main issue," namely, the establishment of full legal recognition and
formal relations between the two Germanies.[87] For his part, Brandt stated explicitly his regret that the closing communiqué of the talks had nothing more
profound to say than that the meeting had occurred. He was at least gratified that
it had been possible, in a private conversation with Stoph after the visit to
Buchenwald, to agree that a return visit would take place on May 21 in Kassel.[88]

at which the East Germans gave the West Germans a copy of *Faust* as a gift.
(Signatur J 0319/01/6 N, Bundesarchiv, Koblenz)

Stoph closed the day with a television interview with Karl Eduard von Schnitzler, the broadcaster who later became infamous for his anti-FRG show "The Black Channel." Schnitzler asked Stoph what, from a Western journalist, would most likely have been considered a leading question: "How did Erfurters rise to the challenge of hosting this important meeting on such short notice?"[89] Bizarrely, Stoph went out of his way to thank the population of Erfurt for their hearty support: "We felt lifted by the support of the population, from their approval which expressed itself during the day in hearty rallies and numerous written tributes."[90] This attempt to suggest that the massive demonstration of support for "Y" had actually been for "I" was hardly convincing. It was nonetheless repeated in the next day's issue of the SED's party newspaper, *Neues Deutschland*. The paper did report that there had been a demonstration—of support for Willi Stoph.[91]

Optical Impressions: Lessons Learned by the Politburo and the Stasi in the Aftermath of Erfurt

In contrast to the outward attempts to breeze over the events of Erfurt, SED documents show that party leaders would spend many months involved in an extensive internal investigation of what had gone wrong. Papers from this investigation reveal further what the SED had hoped to achieve in Erfurt, and what a significant impact its failure made not only on the Politburo but also on the Stasi. In a meeting on 25 March, the Secretariat of the Central Committee conducted what was more or less an interrogation of various officials who had been present at the time of the fiasco. Simply the fact that it was the Secretariat doing the questioning, and not the Politburo, may hold significance for internal Politburo power struggles. Former party archivist Monika Kaiser has argued that Erich Honecker had begun to use the Secretariat as his own forum, taking advantage of the fact that Ulbricht rarely attended.[92] Hence, the fact that the Secretariat, and not the Politburo, carried out the questioning may be an early sign of Honecker's taking advantage of a position of authority to question the wisdom of an event conducted under Ulbricht's leadership.

Those called before the Secretariat made various excuses for themselves. One of those questioned, the district party secretary of Erfurt, defended himself by saying that he was only one of "thousands" of people had been involved in planning security. In his view, the main problem had been that the security design was "defensive," that is, there had been no uniformed officers aggressively patrolling. The goal as he understood it had been to convey an image of "normal life."[93] Another party official said that uniforms were avoided because "we had been told that a certain optical impression had to be secured."[94] These comments suggest that, like the Soviets, the SED had been primarily interested in the public relations dimension of the Erfurt talks. It avoided demonstrative security measures in an effort to offer a better "optical impression" to the visiting Western journalists. Hence, concern about public opinion had played a key role in planning for Erfurt. However, while this made sense from a public relations standpoint, it clearly did not have the intimidating effect on the locals that high-profile deployment of uniformed police or even army officers might have had. In other words, the GDR's security planning was undone by its concern for how its image would be conveyed to the world by visiting journalists. Perhaps out of a sense of betrayal that the journalists had not played their assigned role in conveying positive images of the GDR abroad, they were cited as *agents provocateurs*. One observer interviewed by the Secretariat reported seeing the Western journalists rush out of Brandt's train even before Brandt, in order to start distributing propaganda to locals—in cooperation with local youths.[95]

Despite all the contradictions and finger-pointing, however, there appears not to have been any kind of a purge, and certainly no top-level heads rolled, at least at that time. A final Politburo resolution did point out, ominously, that there had indeed been enough People's Police reserves stationed in the immediate area to handle the situation. However, the police leadership had failed to call on them. The fact that there had been reserves in the wings shows that, while the SED hoped to achieve a public relations success, it had also apparently prepared for the worst. One wonders what would have happened had these "reserves" in fact been activated; could there have been bloodshed in Erfurt? The final Politburo resolution did not explore this issue, however. Instead, it called for more centralized planning in the future and ordered that there should be a clear chain of leadership for "mobilization" in such cases.[96]

Although the topic does not specifically arise in the documents, the case of Erfurt shows some of the constraints on the leaders of a state defined by its ideology. A petty tyrant may not care if his citizens despise him, as long as they remain subservient. Ideological dictators either believe or try to believe—and, more importantly, hope to convince the world—that they share their ideology with their population. Hence, a visit from the head of an ideologically hostile foreign state poses huge difficulties. On the one hand, too obvious police suppression of public expressions of delight at the capitalist leader's presence reveals the bankruptcy of the notion that the public voluntarily subscribes to socialism. On the other hand, too little policing yields exactly the same result. In this way the SED Politburo was constrained by its need to keep up ideological appearances. Brandt's restrained reaction to his welcome in Erfurt was in some part an acknowledgment of this need. The events in Erfurt also weakened East Berlin's hand vis-à-vis Moscow. Ulbricht had, in a move of ideological daring, declared that socialism as it existed in the GDR might be a long-lasting formation in its own right; but the demonstration for Brandt spoke more of instability than longevity.

Furthermore, Erfurt showed that the SED Politburo could not ignore the wishes of the population of the GDR entirely. The greeting to Brandt was one of the few significant expressions of public opinion during the Ostpolitik era. It was fitting, because Ostpolitik had as its goal small improvements in the daily lives of both West and East Germans. But for the bulk of the détente era, the wishes of the GDR's average citizens are mostly notable for their absence. The SED state allowed no venue for their expression other than by mistake, as happened in March 1970.

"Absurd and Terrible Things"

Erfurt had both conceptual and practical impacts on the Stasi in particular. Markus Wolf recollected that Mielke took calls for more centralized planning of security during Western visits too much to heart. As a consequence, Wolf believed that "absurd and terrible things . . . developed." For example, Mielke came to insist that all passersby with whom a prominent Western visitor might come into contact while in the GDR should be Stasi operatives. In other words, if there were a museum or theater visit on the agenda, all the other visitors or theatergoers had to be Stasi agents. This kind of manpower-intensive operation became more and more difficult to maintain, Wolf remembered, as the numbers of visitors increased.[97] In general, Wolf found that the shock of Erfurt (on top of

Prague) had an "on-going effect" on security chief Erich Mielke, leading him to overburden the state security apparatus in this and numerous other ways in an attempt to prevent any possible repetition.[98]

In fact, after Prague, Erfurt, and the Ostpolitik accords, the numbers of Stasi employees began to rise dramatically. The need, for example, to guard the long transit ways between West Germany and East Berlin in addition to the border crossings meant that an increase in manpower was necessary. In other words, one of the unintended consequences of Ostpolitik was that, as it produced more and more institutionalized facilitators for German-German contacts, the ranks of the Stasi swelled.[99] In other words, Ostpolitik unintentionally sparked an increase in the size of the apparatus of repression within the GDR.

The SED saw, on the one hand, risks in increased German-German cooperation. Another document from the spring of 1970 shows that the party knew it could, on the other hand, achieve material gains as well. A letter in the private archive of former West German chancellor Helmut Schmidt summarizes a conversation on the fringes of the Hanover trade fair in April 1970 between the GDR's deputy minister for foreign trade, Heinz Behrendt, and a state secretary in the FRG economics ministry, Klaus Dieter Arndt. The East German, Behrendt, had sought an increase in the amount of interest-free swing credit that the GDR received from the FRG. The hard winter of 1969–70 had created this need, he explained. Arndt asked pointedly in reply, "Is your government fully aware of the extent to which the West German government has helped you this winter?"[100] Behrendt responded with unusual politeness and did not employ the standard SED rhetoric about how the FRG owed such help to the GDR because of past Western wrongdoing. "We are fully aware of the meaning of this help and we value it highly," Behrendt answered.[101] Arndt seized the opportunity to make a vague but nonetheless worrisome remark for the GDR: He pointed out that legal recognition of the GDR by the FRG, which the SED sought avidly, could invalidate some of the special aspects of German-German trade.[102] Although Arndt did not say so, it was clear that he was hinting at the withdrawal of the kind of swing credit that Behrendt was seeking to increase. The conversation ended without Arndt making any kind of a commitment. As will be discussed, the question of a swing credit increase remained an issue up to and during Basic Treaty negotiations in 1972–73.

Berlin

Soviet Worries and the Start of the Berlin Talks

Upon hearing of the events in Erfurt, U.S. president Richard Nixon reportedly commented, "This will scare hell out of the Soviets."[103] He was not far off the mark. The events of Erfurt made a lasting impression not only in East Berlin but also in Moscow. According to Markus Wolf, the events in Erfurt caused the Soviets a change of heart. Previously, they had encouraged East Berlin to go ahead with the meeting, despite squabbles over the meeting site. Now, Moscow began to worry about the SED's management of rapprochement with West Germany. The CPSU sent clear signals that the GDR should make no progress at the follow-up visit.[104] Wolf also remembered Erfurt as the beginning of open disagreement between Honecker and Ulbricht about how relations with the West should be managed. "The sudden shock of Erfurt, the euphoric greeting which Brandt received—it was terrible for Honecker," the former spymaster recollected.[105]

Party archive documents corroborate Wolf's account. Ulbricht, Stoph, Honecker, and Winzer held a consultation with Brezhnev and others on 15 May 1970 to plot strategy for Stoph's return visit to Brandt in Kassel.[106] What appears to be a summary of comments made at that meeting survives.[107] With regard to Erfurt, Brezhnev observed dryly that "there were moments, questions, which could have been avoided."[108] He also indicated his displeasure with comments made by Brandt at the recent SPD party congress, which indicated that the chancellor was not willing to follow Brezhnev's wishes and establish formal diplomatic relations with the East. Brezhnev's conclusion was, "We must approach the conversation in Kassel as a chance to . . . obtain a maximum profit in terms of propaganda for the GDR," once again stressing the public relations dimension. As for substantive German-German agreements, they should wait; as he put it, "We are in favor of a 'pause for reflection.' "[109] This term—"pause for reflection"—later was attributed to Brandt, who insisted that it came from Stoph. The original source, however, was Brezhnev.

Brezhnev's worries about the danger inherent in contacts with the FRG were clearly not so far-reaching that he saw the need to break off his government's own bilateral talks with Bonn. Indeed, on the very same days that Ulbricht and his colleagues were in Moscow, Egon Bahr was in Moscow as well, carrying out a third round of negotiations with Gromyko. The brief third round lasted only from 12 May until 22 May; shortly thereafter, in June 1970, a major fiasco temporarily stalled talks.

The fiasco was the unintended publication of confidential working papers from the negotiations. Via an unknown leak, the West German media gained access to materials from the Bahr-Gromyko talks. Excerpts appeared on 12 June 1970 in the popular newspaper *Bild*, and a longer version appeared on 1 July in both *Bild* and *Quick*.[110] This unauthorized publication—which came to be known by the shorthand term of the "Bahr Paper"—represented the first time the public really became aware of the stakes involved. Political scientist Richard Löwenthal has shown how hard it was for many West Germans, particularly older ones, to countenance the notion of an agreement with the Soviets that would confirm postwar borders.[111] The publication of the Bahr Paper subjected Bahr to criticism that he was moving too quickly. It also instantly turned what were offers under discussion into absolute minimum demands, because to retreat from them after publication would have meant to lose face; once again the importance of public opinion became apparent.[112]

But even this breach of confidentiality failed to derail the FRG-USSR talks, showing just how avidly interested Moscow was in their continuance. (The breach did cause Bahr to establish a "contact committee" to keep parliamentarians, including those of the opposition, informed of his negotiations, so that they could better assess press "revelations" for themselves. This group continued to meet throughout the course of the German-German negotiations.[113]) Although Brezhnev had told the SED to hold back after the difficulties of Erfurt, he saw no need to hold back USSR-FRG relations after the difficulty of the Bahr Paper publication. Once again it becomes apparent that Brezhnev was not so much opposed to contacts with the FRG as to contacts *that he himself was not managing*. In other words, his "double game" was still in operation. In fact, he may not have seen any contradiction in negotiating with the FRG while discouraging the GDR from doing so. As Raymond Garthoff has trenchantly observed, the Soviets viewed détente merely as a policy but saw the overarching class struggle as "an objective phenomenon in the historical process that could not be abolished by policy decision, even if the Soviet leaders wanted to do so." While this position was not without a self-serving dimension, says Garthoff, "it was not cynical artifice."[114] In other words, Marxist ideology showed that conflict with the West was unavoidable. If the GDR did not seem to have the wherewithal to manage it skillfully, then the Soviets would have to do so themselves.

U.S. Worries

The Soviets were not the only superpower to worry about the actions of a German ally; the United States had concerns as well. At times these concerns were lost amid the noise of Vietnam protests. As the Germanies were evaluating Erfurt and planning for Kassel, Americans were coming to grips with Nixon's speech of 30 April announcing the invasion of Cambodia, the killing of Kent State students on 4 May, and a 100,000-strong protest march in Washington on 8 May 1970.[115] On top of this, the U.S. Senate had decided on 9 April 1970, by a vote of 72-6, to ask that not only the United States but also the Soviet Union stop testing and deploying Multiple Independent Reentry Vehicles (MIRVs) during SALT negotiations, which had resumed in Vienna in April.[116] Nor were the protests confined to the United States; similar demonstrations in Europe introduced a popular element of anti-Americanism and indeed anti-capitalism to the relations between the United States and its West European allies.[117]

Nonetheless, if Ostpolitik did not receive much popular attention in the United States at the time, it inspired a good deal of worry among U.S. leadership elites.[118] Political scientist Wolfram Hanrieder has shown that a paradoxical situation arose with the beginnings of Ostpolitik. In the 1960s, U.S. leaders had accused the Germans of not keeping pace with détente developments and of "obstructing or retarding the solution of important East-West issues."[119] Hence when the new Brandt government evinced willingness to implement détente measures of its own, the West could hardly complain. On top of this, Brandt claimed to view the division of Germany not as a territorial but rather as a human rights issue, thereby offering "an unobjectionable political and moral rationale" for his Eastern policies.[120] However, Brandt's initiatives raised the fear that the FRG could (intentionally or unintentionally) go further than the United States thought wise. Indeed, Hanrieder even postulated a kind of double American containment—on the one hand, keeping tabs on the Soviets; on the other, on the West Germans. In other words, the FRG was in a difficult position: both too little and too much enthusiasm for détente were suspect.[121]

Doubts about the new West German course were aired by John McCloy, Lucius Clay, and Dean Acheson, all elder statesmen from the Truman administration. The three visited Nixon late in 1970 to complain about Brandt's initiatives.[122] To be sure, they had other concerns to discuss as well. But they particularly feared that West Germany was being run by experimenting West Berliners (rather than reliable Rhinelanders) who did not understand the importance of the "keep-the-powder-dry and don't-change-anything policy."[123] Dean Acheson in particular seems to have seen in Ostpolitik a "dangerous and alarming departure from Bonn's past diplomatic practice of conducting its Eastern policies under American tutelage."[124] For his part, Kissinger had his own worries. On the one hand, he feared that "Ostpolitik was more likely to lead to a permanent division of Germany than to healing its breach."[125] On the other, he worried that Ostpolitik could succeed too well in healing the breach. As he wrote in his memoirs, Brandt's policies "could, in less scrupulous hands, turn into a new form of classic German nationalism. From Bismarck to Rapallo it was the essence of Germany's nationalist foreign policy to maneuver freely between East and West."[126] In either case, it was clear to him that, since "the Brandt government was asking not for our advice but for our cooperation in a course to which its principal figures had long since been committed," it would be best to work "*with* Brandt rather than against him."[127]

Along with the United States, France was particularly concerned about Ostpolitik. Paris did want to maintain cooperative FRG-French relations, which would seem to include supporting Bonn's major foreign policy initiatives. However, the French saw hostility between the two Germanies as a kind of guarantee that German reunification would not occur, a guarantee that was not entirely unwelcome.[128] As a result, Ostpolitik led to much gnashing of teeth in Paris. Georges Pompidou's anxiety and jealousy were plainly on display when he met privately with Nixon in late 1971, just after Willy Brandt won the Nobel Peace Prize. According to the U.S. summary of their conversation, Pompidou dismissively remarked to the U.S. leader that "Ostpolitik is a nice concept and can win a Nobel Prize," adding that either Pompidou or Nixon could easily have done the same themselves, but for the fact that *they* were wise enough not to "risk old friends for those who would never be friends."[129] An expert on French Cold War foreign policy, Georges-Henri Soutou, has argued that Pompidou viewed Ostpolitik as acceptable enough in the short term but potentially quite dangerous in the long term.[130] Cold War politics expert John Young argues that "it was probably in order to control German ambitions that Pompidou allowed Britain into the European Community."[131]

The irony is that becoming a more neutral factor in European politics and pulling away from the Western Alliance did not seem to be one of Brandt and Bahr's many goals. SED documents contain no FRG appeals to the GDR to join in establishing some kind of a neutral Germany that would be independent, or more independent, of West or East. Neither SED documents nor interviews with persons involved have contained any clear indications that West Germany was, by taking up negotiations with the East, intentionally trying to weaken its NATO ties. Indeed, as described above, Bahr had made clear at the Moscow talks that West Germany's NATO obligations came first. Hence the worry of the Western allies, while a significant factor in their decision-making, does not seem to be justified by the documents available so far.

Bahr speculated in 1997 that Washington's expressions of fear about German neutralism may in fact have been exaggerated in order to put pressure on the West Germans to be apologetic about their actions. Bahr personally believed that Kissinger was far too aware of the realities of the Cold War balance of power to suspect that the West Germans would strike out on their own. What may in fact have been a real worry, Bahr suggested instead, was fear that Brandt might unintentionally set in motion events whose consequences he could neither foresee nor control.[132] In other words, Brandt might repeat on a large scale what he had unintentionally done in Erfurt on a small scale. Or the Soviet Union might offer some kind of unexpected bargain on German unity—as Stalin had done in 1952.[133] In short, the United States feared unpredictability. As Hanrieder has put it, "Ostpolitik contained at least the seeds of future German neutralism, irrespective of the intentions of the current German government."[134] Kissinger similarly stated in his memoirs that "resurgent nationalism was a danger whichever course the Federal Republic pursued" and later complimented Brandt retroactively for having assumed "the burdens and the anguish imposed by necessity."[135]

In short, there seems to have been ironic similarity between Soviet and U.S. worries about the conduct of each of their respective German allies in opening talks with the enemy. Both superpowers worried about Germans showing too much initiative. Given these worries, it is unsurprising that the talks between the Soviets and the three Western allies about Berlin got off to a slow and unpromising start. The first round of quadripartite negotiations, which Kissinger called the "Berlin talks," achieved little. The U.S. ambassador, Kenneth Rush, insisted on speaking about "Berlin as a whole" and the practical goals that the Western Allies hoped to obtain during the talks, while the Soviets preferred vague statements such as "the Soviet people will never forget that in the battle for Berlin 300,000 of our soldiers and officers were killed or wounded."[136] The next two meetings, on 28 April and 14 May, similarly made little progress.[137] It was probably, then, to the superpowers' mutual relief that the follow-up Brandt-Stoph conversation in Kassel ended without any kind of concrete result. Indeed, if the papers of Markus Wolf and Erich Honecker are to be believed, this was the intent of the Soviets.

Kassel

Preparing for Confrontation

Stoph, following the Soviet lead, intentionally took a demanding stance and prevented progress when he paid a return visit to Brandt in the West German city of Kassel. The final preparatory papers for the 20 May meeting, approved by the Politburo the day before, made clear that Stoph should demand the establishment of diplomatic relations as a prior condition to any detailed discussions.[138] Given that the FRG had already refused such snap recognition at Erfurt, this was hardly a prescription for making progress. The preparatory papers also indicated precisely how Stoph was to respond to any attempts to schedule a third meeting, which a Stasi advance report on Brandt's intentions for Kassel had suggested would be forthcoming.[139] The pre-scripted reply to such a suggestion was, "The course of this meeting has not produced the needed conditions for a further one." The fact that this reply was written *before* the meeting suggests that what would actually happen there would be irrelevant.[140]

Even the preparations for the more mundane aspects of the meeting bespoke rigidity. Every comrade traveling in Stoph's delegation had to follow a strict code of behavior. He was to remain at whatever place he was instructed to stay in the interest of his own safety. Alcohol intake was to be avoided.[141] The gastronomic needs of the delegation would be tended to solely by Stasi officers, insuring perhaps the safety if not the tastiness of the offerings.[142] In short, the immediate advance planning for Kassel did not suggest that a fruitful meeting would follow.[143]

This hard-line stance in advance of the meeting is more notable for the fact that it followed shortly after Behrendt's request for an increase in swing credit in mid-April and the postal agreement of late April 1970 between the two Germanies. For processing West German mail sent to East German citizens, the GDR would receive 30 million DM a year, and that retroactively to 1967 and until 1973.[144] Given the desire of the FRG to reach agreements on a host of other practical issues, it could be assumed that other similarly lucrative accords could be reached in the future, if the GDR would cooperate. Nonetheless, the SED attitude going into Kassel was clearly not one of cooperation, which suggests that material gain from the FRG was not always the SED's top priority. Indeed, the GDR's provocative raising of tolls on truck and barge traffic by 20–30 percent on 28 April did little to improve the likelihood that an accord would be reached.[145]

The Meeting Itself, 21 May 1970

The SED delegation's legal expert, Günter Görner, remembered that there was, at least for him, a brief moment of hopefulness during the GDR delegation's train ride to Kassel. He recalled in a 1996 interview that he was surprised and heartened by the sight of some friendly well-wishers waving from the side of the train tracks in the FRG and felt that it was an appropriate counterpoint to the welcome Brandt had received in Erfurt. The heartening moment did not last long, however. Görner immediately felt saddened by the knowledge that, in his words, "We weren't exactly the great bringers of peace." He knew that Stoph's preparatory papers, the initial drafts of which he had written, had become more hard-line in subsequent versions.[146]

Another member of the GDR delegation, the West German expert from the GDR Foreign Ministry, Karl Seidel, remembered that the Kassel meeting itself was characterized by an atmosphere of "on-going confrontation."[147] He also recalled that private conversations with Stoph outside of the official rounds were conducted with both loud radio music playing and the television on. The goal of this was to confound potential West German eavesdroppers, but it also exacerbated the tension that the SED delegation was feeling. "Stoph," recollected Seidel, "was understandably very nervous."[148]

A large anti-Stoph protest was waiting for the GDR delegation in Kassel and intensified the sense of confrontation. Protesters tore down the GDR's flag even as Stoph and Brandt greeted each other at the opening of the official meeting. On being handed a note with this information, Stoph interrupted Brandt to issue "the sharpest of protests."[149] The next day, the SED newspaper *Neues Deutschland* referred to the demonstration as nothing short of "Nazi-style terror."[150] Brandt expressed his regret and tried to turn to substantive issues. Stoph, however, repeatedly complained about the incident, wondering aloud

An official East German photo of Willi Stoph and Willy Brandt in Kassel. (From File DC20-4677, Bundesarchiv, Potsdam)

"why it was permitted" that official guests of the federal government should be subjected to such "murderous propaganda."[151] Brandt tried to explain that the insult was not intentional and that the legal structure of the Federal Republic permitted demonstrations to occur, but Stoph persisted in seeing the occurrence of a protest as the personal fault and perhaps even intent of Brandt. In short, the tone of the Kassel meeting was hostile from the outset and changed little during the rest of the official and unofficial meetings.

When the talks finally turned to substantive issues, Stoph began by demanding full legal recognition and complaining about the fact that the FRG still had not responded to the draft treaty.[152] Brandt tried to switch the discussion to more specific aspects of German-German relations by listing what later became known as the "Twenty Points," or twenty areas in which the FRG was seeking accord. These would later serve as the basis for Bahr's negotiations with Michael Kohl. Among them were general appeals, such as calls to base German-German relations on the principle of human rights, to avoid the use of violence, to respect each other's "independence and self-sufficiency," to allow each side to represent itself diplomatically, to acknowledge that both Germanies belong to one nation, and to recognize the authority of the four occupying powers. The

West German police attempt to control protesters (both for and against the GDR) during the Kassel meeting. The banner at top reads "Down with the traitors in the German East"; the other, "Full Legal Recognition for the GDR." (From File DC20-4677, Bundesarchiv, Potsdam)

points also included more specific goals, such as the desire to solve the problems of families torn apart by the German division or to address the issues of people living in border towns.[153] Brandt did not succeed, however, in getting Stoph to discuss these issues in more than a superficial way. Nor did a private conversation with Brandt mitigate the sense of confrontation; Stoph complained once again about the protests.[154] According to a summary of the Brandt-Stoph conversation in Helmut Schmidt's private papers, Stoph pressed for UN membership, but Brandt felt that the time was not yet ripe. Stoph then reportedly indicated his concern that there be no "damage" done to trade between the two Germanies, possibly in reference to the idea voiced by Arndt that the GDR could lose certain advantages were it to seek full recognition. The two ended by agreeing on a "pause for reflection."[155]

SED Assessment of Kassel

The sensational protest against Stoph received much attention in the West German press. *Der Spiegel,* for example, entitled its cover story "The Confrontation in Kassel," thereby unwittingly using the same name as the Stasi security plan for the meeting.[156] As for East Berlin, the SED reaction suggested that it was pleased with itself. A GDR Ministry for Foreign Affairs summary of Kassel, produced the day after the meeting, evinced a self-congratulatory tone. The report noted that the GDR delegation had succeeded in following the plan for the meeting laid down by the Politbuero.[157] Moreover, it had been "absolutely correct" to demand the establishment of full legal recognition.[158] In other words, there was no sense of regret about a missed opportunity. The report also complained that Brandt had "covered for neo-Nazism" in comments made at the meeting. ("Neo-Nazism" was a reference to the protest against Stoph.)[159] Another summary report, produced by a Stasi agent, noted Brandt's insistence on close cooperation with the United States. "He is not even willing, in the face of US resistance, to agree that the FRG and the GDR should apply for UN membership."[160] In short, after Kassel there emerged a tense, confrontational, and altogether unproductive atmosphere and a temporary halt to high-level German-German conversations.

In existing historiography, Ulbricht usually receives the blame for being the "hard-liner" behind this outcome.[161] However, SED documents suggest the opposite, namely that Ulbricht may have been in favor of a third meeting. What appears to be a partial text of Ulbricht's speech for the thirteenth plenary session of the Central Committee, held on 9 June 1970, contains the following remark, underlined for emphasis: "*We hope that a third round of talks between the GDR and the FRG will lead to negotiations on taking up diplomatic relations.*"[162] In his memoirs, Hermann Axen stated that he remembered Ulbricht making just such a proposal, and not for the first time.[163] The desire to hold a third round stood in clear contradiction to the advice of the Soviets and the decision of the Politburo, made on 19 May 1970 (when Ulbricht was not present), not to seek a third meeting.

In summary, Ulbricht was in favor of further high-level contacts, and the Soviets were opposed.[164] It is also apparent that the varying contacts and conversations—Moscow, Erfurt, Berlin, and Kassel—mutually influenced each other, despite their disparate locales and differing participants. As will be discussed in the next chapter, these mutual interactions so worried Brezhnev that he deemed it necessary to put tricky German-German talks on ice while the USSR reached some kind of conclusion in its own talks with West Germany.

It would become obvious in 1970 that Moscow was intensely interested in concluding an accord with Bonn and would not tolerate any dangers to the accord—even if they came from within the Soviet Bloc. The CPSU under Brezhnev had come to see a treaty with Bonn as a way to solve many problems at once. It could confirm post–World War II borders, thereby affirming Soviet territory gains; reduce the chances of conflict in Europe at a time when tensions with China were rising; and create the kind of closer relationship with West Germany that, in a best case scenario, would harm Bonn's relations with Washington. These were the gains Moscow sought from the Faustian pact; but their price was still unclear.

Discovering the Perils of Bargaining in the Second Half of 1970: The Moscow Treaty, the Quadripartite Talks, and the Beginning of the End for Ulbricht

three

The commencement of face-to-face conversations revealed to all sides that there would be costs to pay for détente. Those who found themselves in the role of helpless spectators to the events of Erfurt—namely, the Soviets and the members of the SED Politburo who doubted the wisdom of Ulbricht's course—were especially worried about the risks involved and felt the need to limit potential damage. In the second half of 1970, Moscow and a growing anti-Ulbricht faction joined in a desire to manage the risks of German-German rapprochement. Their efforts constrained negotiations both from without and from within.

From without, the Soviets applied pressure on their German ally to cooperate less with the FRG and more with the USSR. Moscow was particularly interested in keeping the SED sidelined while it finished its own negotiations with West Germany. In a striking parallel, available documentation suggests that the United States similarly disagreed with its own German ally about how quickly negotiations should proceed. The fact that both the USSR and the United States worried more about the pace and control of negotiations than about whether or not they should occur—the superpowers were, after all, pursuing their own rapprochement at the same time—did not mitigate the seriousness of their disagreements with their respective allies.

From within, Ulbricht faced political opposition at home, much as Brandt did. But whereas the most severe domestic criticism of Brandt came from the opposition—namely, the CDU/CSU and the media sympathetic to those parties—in East Germany no parties or media played the role of opposition. Hence, the strongest criticism of Ulbricht came from within the Politburo, in the form of a faction headed by Ulbricht's erstwhile protégé, Erich Honecker. Honecker shared, or at least convincingly acted as if he shared, Soviet concern about Ulbricht's eagerness to secure economic gains through cooperation with West Germany. In late 1970 and early 1971, Honecker seized upon not only Soviet but also SED discontent with both Ulbricht's policies and person as a means of assembling a coterie of supporters for himself within the Politburo. This coterie included Willi Stoph, foreign affairs specialist Hermann Axen, and economic affairs specialist Günter Mittag. To garner support for himself, Honecker capitalized on worries over FRG-GDR relations, the course of East German economic development, and the proper conduct of GDR relations with the Soviets. The assembly of an opposition faction within the party, or "factionalism," was usually considered one of the most grievous party crimes. However, Honecker mustered enough support to convince his fellow Politburo members that his increasingly less subtle campaign against Ulbricht was more compelling than criminal.[1]

Hence, throughout 1970 the German-German rapprochement was subject to external and internal restraints. What do these restraints reveal about the motives of the individuals who were applying them—namely, the Soviets and the Honecker faction members? To answer this question, it is necessary to examine three parallel and partly contemporaneous issues in the second half of 1970: (1) the conclusion of the Moscow talks, (2) the desultory continuance of quadripartite negotiations, and (3) the development of increasingly vocal opposition to Ulbricht within the Politburo. While the first two sets of talks may at first glance appear to be a detour away from topic of SED politics, since they nominally did not involve the East Germans, they in fact had enormous significance for the SED's conduct of its own relations with West Germany. During most of 1970, the Soviets under Brezhnev's leadership kept the SED's German-German contacts on ice. Moscow repeatedly expressed worry to the SED about the wisdom of GDR-FRG rapprochement while Soviet efforts to conclude the Moscow and Berlin talks were still ongoing. In October 1970, however, Moscow shifted its attitude. The CPSU stopped trying to keep the increasingly factious SED Politburo on the sidelines and allowed East Berlin to reopen contacts with the West Germans. In other words, it was the shift of opinion in *Moscow* that permitted East Berlin to resume conversation with Bonn. To understand why

Moscow's shift occurred, it is necessary to first explore the history of the Moscow Treaty between the Soviet Union and West Germany and that of the four-power talks.

The Moscow Treaty

Historian and journalist Peter Bender has argued that Brezhnev found détente too serious a matter to be left to the Germans.[2] This is a particularly apt description for Soviet attitudes in the wake of Erfurt. As described in Chapter 2, Moscow blocked any kind of progress at the follow-up meeting in Kassel, instead calling for a "pause for reflection." Subsequent events show that the Soviets used this pause to forge ahead in their own talks with Bonn.

They also used it to keep the SED in the dark. In general, the Soviets kept East Berlin surprisingly well informed about their foreign relations, but the close of bilateral negotiations with the West Germans represents a significant exception. As late as 8 August 1970, four days before the official signing, the SED foreign ministry officials faced with the task of summarizing Soviet–West German talks complained about the paucity of sources from which they could work. The cover note to their summary explained apologetically,

> As a basis for this analysis we could naturally use only that which was known to us; and that was the text of the West German paper about the Bahr-Gromyko conversations [possibly a reference to the Bahr Paper], some further materials . . . [taken] from individual MfS reports, and the published statements of the Bonn government.[3]

In other words, the officials were admitting that, mere days before the Moscow Treaty signing, SED information on it was limited to a few Stasi materials and published West German sources.[4] Sovietologist Michael Sodaro has suggested one compelling reason why Moscow kept East Berlin in the dark: the distress of the SED leadership "at the prospect of a political deal behind East Germany's back (particularly one that fell short of full-scale de jure recognition of the GDR)."[5]

Eagerness on Both Sides for an Agreement

Moscow may have felt that it was impossible to fulfill the wishes of both Germanies and that, given the importance the agreement, a free hand was needed in negotiating with Bonn. The Soviets also felt they could, in turn, use West German interest in bilateral negotiations to help check the potential excesses of German-German rapprochement. For example, Bahr wrote in his memoirs that Brandt's behavior toward the cheering crowds in Erfurt actually reinforced Bahr's negotiating position in Moscow. Brandt had signaled with his hands that the Erfurt crowd should quiet down. Bahr remembered that Brandt's "calming hand movement . . . functioned as a confirmation of the statement I had made to Gromyko in Moscow that it would be in our common interest to keep the course of events which we had set in motion under control."[6] Furthermore, the Soviet back-channel courier between Brezhnev and Brandt, Kevorkov, reported on Bahr's eagerness for progress. It was clear "that he wanted to reach an accord between our countries at any price, and preferably in the course of one day."[7] In short, West German willingness to negotiate, combined with Brandt's restrained behavior in Erfurt, appealed to the Soviets and matched their own desire to reach an accord.

Despite the eagerness on both sides, there remained many difficulties, and the course of West German–Soviet negotiations was hardly smooth. Moscow insisted on full legal recognition of East Germany, a demand that it dropped only toward the end of the talks, and refused to accept the FRG's insistence on some kind of mention of German unification or national unity.[8] The West Germans, in particular Minister of the Interior Hans-Dietrich Genscher, made it clear that such a mention was absolutely necessary to insure the constitutionality of the treaty. Genscher—who was known colloquially as "the brake" on Brandt's enthusiasm for Ostpolitik—claimed in his memoirs that he had told Brandt he would resign if such a mention were not included.[9]

Nonetheless, the Soviets and the West Germans were able to reach an accord by the summer of 1970. The key breakthrough was the idea that the mention of German unity should be contained in a separate letter, not in the actual treaty.[10] A note from Walter Scheel, indicating that the FRG intended to pursue the cause of German unity, was to be handed over on the day of the signing. This face-saving move gave the Soviets an element of deniability. As Soviet diplomat Yuli Kvizinski recalled, Gromyko accepted the idea of the letter because he found that it would have no legal connection to the treaty or binding force. Indeed, Kvizinski remembered Gromyko saying that he considered the German letter to be merely one of "dozens, even hundreds" of such notes received by the foreign ministry, none of which required the least Soviet response or action.[11]

The Terms and the Signing of the Treaty

The Moscow Treaty itself was more significant for its symbolic gestures than for its practical achievements.[12] Both sides agreed to work for a relaxation of tensions and renounced the use of violence in their dealings with each other. They proclaimed their mutual interest in maintaining peace. Both affirmed that they had no territorial claims outstanding and would not press any such claims in the future.[13] Both parties defined the borders in Europe as they existed on the day of the signing, including the German-German border, to be inviolable.[14]

The West Germans received a sought-after mention that the treaty did not affect other agreements, meaning particularly the four-power authority in Germany. West Germany also declared a series of intentions, not least of which was to conclude agreements with the GDR.[15] The mention of the GDR by name constituted the first official acknowledgment of East Germany by the FRG. Diminishing this gain for the GDR, however, was the fact that the West Germans also formally recognized the "Oder-Neiße line." Theoretically, since the Oder-Neiße was the border between the GDR and Poland, and the treaty at hand was between West Germany and the Soviets, the Moscow Treaty should have had nothing at all to say about it. The fact that the Soviets sought, and received, an explicit *West* German guarantee showed whose German guarantee they truly valued. The guarantee would be strengthened in an FRG-Poland treaty later in 1970.

Bonn's recognition of existing postwar borders, particularly the Oder-Neiße line, carried with it an unintended consequence. One of the legitimating strategies of Warsaw Pact communist regimes was to claim that they were there to guard against German revenge for the loss of World War II. Poland in particular had taken huge swaths of Germanic territory and expelled millions of Germans. Hence, the Soviet bloc regimes could justify themselves by claiming that only communism and Soviet troops could possibly hold back German revanchism. By 1970, this was in fact one of the very few legitimating strategies the Polish regime had left. West German recognition of Cold War borders undermined this strategy.[16]

This unintended consequence did not worry the Soviet Union enough at the time to prevent agreement with the West. Instead, Moscow played up the signing of the treaty. The details of the actual signing ceremony in the Soviet capital on 12 August 1970 merit attention because they would later play a role in internecine SED Politburo struggles. Although Bahr and Gromyko had negotiated the treaty, protocol demanded that Foreign Minister Scheel take part in the closing rounds and that either he or Brandt actually sign the accord. Brandt decided to fly in and sign it himself, which in turn caused a protocol problem for Brezhnev. Brandt's official equal was Kosygin, but Brezhnev clearly did not want to be left out of the signing festivities. He reportedly decided that Brandt and Kosygin should be photographed while seated to sign the treaty, so that Brezhnev could stand regally above them, looking over their shoulders.[17] *Pravda* reproduced this photo on its front page the next morning, which—as will be described later—caused consternation among the Honecker faction.[18]

The Significance of the Treaty to Moscow and East Berlin

Why did Moscow desire this accord? The documents and later analysts have suggested three major reasons. First, the Soviets wanted to formalize relations

The signing of the Moscow Treaty on 12 August 1970, as staged by Brezhnev so that he could look down on the signatories. (Bundesrepublik Deutschland, Fotodienst 1/2-79/Nr. 788, Bild 146/99/0/1, Bundesarchiv, Koblenz)

in Cold War Europe and thereby quiet tensions on the European "front," in order to deal better with the rise in tensions on a more important "front"—the Chinese.[19] Second, the USSR hoped to profit from increased economic contacts with the West Germans, having already received benefits in the form of pipeline purchases on favorable financing terms. Third, there were hopes that, as Bahr's aide Antonius Eitel remembered, "via a policy of embrace, the FRG could be swayed from its pro-Western course" and perhaps encouraged to lean toward neutrality.[20] Political scientist Richard Löwenthal developed this point further, arguing that Moscow in this time period as a whole had a double goal: it sought not only to consolidate and legitimate its holdings in Eastern Europe but also "to explode the Western alliance and in particular the [FRG's] ties to the United States."[21] In a best-case scenario, the FRG could perhaps be persuaded to leave NATO.[22] It is probably with this scenario in mind that Brezhnev, in a conversation with Brandt at the time of the treaty signing, warmly commended the example of De Gaulle to the West German chancellor. As Brezhnev put it, "the more independent a state is in its foreign policy . . . the greater the chances are for an expansion of the cooperation between our states."[23]

Political scientist Wolfram Hanrieder found that "from Moscow's perspective, the developments of the early 1970s were of a magnitude perhaps un-paralleled in postwar Soviet diplomacy." Indeed, he has argued, the USSR "had all along aspired to be a superpower equal to the United States, an aspira-tion that lacked plausibility except in two important areas: the Soviet Union had achieved nuclear parity, and it headed (like the United States) a powerful military-political alliance." Now Brezhnev had signed a treaty with the West Germans, which implied legitimization of Soviet influence in Eastern Europe. Along with SALT, the agreement "must have appeared to Leonid Brezhnev not only as the crowning point of his career but of Soviet postwar diplomacy."[24] As will be discussed in subsequent chapters, the USSR did indeed prize this accord quite highly. By mid-1971, it would declare ratification of just this treaty to be its *top* foreign policy priority, a surprising claim given the many other concerns facing the USSR in that year.

The East German response to the treaty was muted. The files from a Polit-buro meeting in July 1970 contain only the notice that the Moscow talks were discussed but not what was said.[25] Notes from a meeting on the day before the signing indicate only approval of the publication of an article in the party newspaper, *Neues Deutschland* (on the theme of "A Success for Everyone Who Supports Détente and Peace").[26] Less official sources indicate worry on the part of Honecker. Valentin Falin recollected that Honecker, during a visit to Moscow in August 1970, complained bitterly about the treaty.[27] Indeed, there exists a document in Honecker's handwriting about a conversation of this nature with Brezhnev on 20 August 1970. According to this account, it seems that Brezhnev conceded that the Moscow Treaty had "not only a positive but also a negative side—especially for the GDR." Brezhnev also agreed with Honecker that "the politics of the Brandt administration are intended to rattle the GDR."[28] In other words, Brezhnev seemed to acknowledge Honecker's worries that Moscow had let Bonn get away without full legal recognition of the GDR.

The Desultory Quadripartite Talks

With the signing of the Moscow Treaty, the next open question was the status of Berlin, long a source of Cold War crises. The need for normalization of its status was apparent to all, but not the way to achieve it. Like the SALT talks, which had opened in November 1969 but made little progress during the first year and a half, so too did the quadripartite talks proceed desultorily.[29] The slow pace suited both sides. Kissinger found that stalling worked to the advantage of the United States while it sorted out its contacts with China. Likewise, Brezh-nev wanted to hold the Berlin agreement hostage to a higher goal—getting the new Moscow Treaty ratified by the West German parliament. Hence, both the

Westerners and the Soviets proceeded only with the greatest caution and reserve in the four-power Berlin talks. As Bahr's aide Antonius Eitel described the early rounds, both sides presented their positions "without even a hint of willingness to compromise."[30] Kissinger remembered that the Soviet ambassador, Pjotr Abrasimov, was especially obstructionist. Kissinger found him to be "peremptory and abrasive even by Soviet standards," noting, "He found it hard to accept that he could not simply issue directives to the Western negotiators."[31]

In consequence, the negotiations made scant progress on the task at hand, namely, codifying the status of Berlin and its transit routes in order to ease tensions and improve the daily life of West Berliners.[32] Instead, the talks in the second half of 1970 seemed more like a historical debating forum than negotiating rounds. For example, at a meeting on 9 June 1970, U.S. ambassador Kenneth Rush challenged the Soviets' insistence that their wishes should have priority in Berlin because the Western allies had come there only after the Soviets had conquered the city in World War II. In a speech that incensed the Soviet ambassador, Rush implied that the Western allies could have taken Berlin but held back out of respect for their Soviet allies.[33] Rush then went on to point out that at the end of the war the Western allies had conquered a significant amount of German territory which they then relinquished and allowed to become part of the Soviet zone of occupation.[34] Abrasimov responded that, while the Soviet Union did respect the contributions of its former allies, "it was above all necessary to point out that the outcome of the war was determined by the Soviet army, by the grandiose battle for Berlin," and he rejected the notion that the Western allies could have just marched into Berlin.[35]

After a couple rounds of such time-consuming and ultimately pointless debating, the American delegation indicated on 21 July that it wanted to move beyond historical generalities and address specific issues. It indicated that it had four main areas of interest: improving access to Berlin, improving travel conditions for Berliners both to and around Berlin, codifying the city's relations "with the countries of Eastern Europe," and doing the same with its relations with the FRG.[36] Rush specifically spoke about "Berlin" and not "West Berlin." Any agreement that did not cover these four bases, he said, would be considered provisional. Furthermore, the Western allies declared themselves unwilling to discuss the presence of Bundeswehr reservists in the Western sectors as long as a discussion of East German military deployment in the Eastern sector was taboo.[37] This Western attempt to move the talks on to practical issues was effectively put on hold for months, however, because after the close of this July meeting the talks went into summer recess for over two months. Clearly neither side was in a rush to make progress.

When meetings resumed in late September, the Soviet ambassador complained that what they viewed as the most important element had been left out.

This was a promise that the exploitation of West Berlin to the disadvantage of the USSR and its allies would cease.[38] By this, the Soviets seemed to mean any kind of official presence of the FRG in West Berlin, such as the holding of the federal presidential election there in March 1969. The Soviets made these wishes more specific in the meetings that followed. On 4 November, they made clear that there should be no kind of official FRG political activity in West Berlin, meaning no sessions of the parliament or any other organ of government. No party congresses of any of the established West German parties should take place in Berlin. FRG officials could visit West Berlin only as guests. Furthermore, in a challenge to the Western insistence that there could be no talk of troop removals in West Berlin without a concomitant discussion about troop removals from East Berlin, the Soviets insisted that "in West Berlin, the quadripartite agreements and decisions on demilitarization should be strictly observed." Exactly which agreements these were remained unspecified.[39] Two very public events at this time did little to improve the Soviet mood. In late October 1970, the Soviet dissident writer Aleksandr Solzhenitsyn won the Nobel Prize for literature. On 7 November 1970, the fifty-third anniversary of the October Revolution, a West Berliner shot a Soviet sentry at the Russian war memorial in the British sector.[40]

An even more effective stalling maneuver was the disingenuous respect that the Soviet ambassador began showing for GDR sovereignty with regard to its authority over transit to Berlin. One of the key Western goals was securing an accord on transit to West Berlin; but the Soviets insisted at the 16 November meeting that, since the transit routes obviously ran through GDR territory, "there were no such things as four-power agreements about it [transit] and that an agreement with the GDR would be unavoidable."[41] Since the Western allies did not recognize the GDR at all, and therefore could not negotiate a treaty with it, this clearly put them in a problematic position. Just to drive the point home, Abrasimov once again insisted at the 10 December meeting that specific accords could be reached only if "it was understood, that there could be no infringement . . . on the sovereign competencies of the German Democratic Republic."[42]

Reasons Both Sides Were Interested in Stalling

The Soviets had various reasons for stalling. They used the time to seek ways in which they could gain increased leverage over the West. For example, the two geographically disparate locales of Berlin and Cuba once again became linked.[43] Moscow repeated an earlier gamble: it attempted again to fortify Cuba militarily. In late August 1970, a U-2 flight over Cuba had detected construction of naval facilities in Cienfuegos Bay. Of particular worry to Washington was the fact that the new construction included a soccer field for the troops stationed there. Cubans played baseball; Russians played soccer. U.S. intelligence reports also indicated a flotilla of Soviet ships moving toward Cuba, including tenders and barges of the type that usually serviced nuclear submarines. As described in Kissinger's memoirs, U.S.-USSR back-channel talks resulted in a Soviet promise on 6 October that the base would not in fact be completed, although cat-and-mouse games continued throughout the fall while a Soviet sub tender came and went.[44] This sequence of events averted a crisis but showed that the Soviet commitment to détente had its limits.

Moreover, the Soviets also explored the option of undermining the Western alliance via bilateral contacts with the French. In his account of the quadripartite talks, Kissinger acknowledged that he was describing "a complex multilateral negotiation from the perhaps inadequate perspective of a single participant" and speculated it was quite possible "that there were other bilateral contacts with the Soviets."[45] SED files reveal that such contacts did in fact take place. East German archives contain at least four summaries of bilateral conversations between the Soviet and French ambassadors.[46] Such contacts may have induced the Soviets to believe that they could perhaps split the allies if they held on to a hard-line stance. For example, a relatively cordial French-Soviet meeting took place on 1 October. According to the Soviet summary passed on to the SED, the French ambassador to the FRG, Jean Sauvagnargues, told Abrasimov that, although France appeared together at the four-power meetings with the United States and Great Britain, one should not think that this meant France stood with the other two against the USSR.[47] For his part, Abrasimov spoke of common French-Soviet interests. He said bluntly that "France and the Soviet Union share common positions on the necessity of ending U.S. intervention in Vietnam; our countries have similar points of view with regard to the crisis in the Near East."[48] The SED Politburo, presumably with Soviet blessing, had also sent foreign policy specialist Hermann Axen to Paris over the summer to try (unsuccessfully) to flatter French foreign minister Maurice Schumann into agreeing to a French recognition of the GDR in advance of official West German recognition.[49]

For its part, the United States also hesitated to make progress in the Berlin talks. As mentioned earlier, Nixon and Kissinger decided to give overtures toward China the highest priority. The relatively moderate faction of Zhou En-lai had triumphed at the Central Committee plenum in September 1970. In a harbinger of things to come, an American journalist had been invited to appear on the reviewing stand at the Chinese National Day Celebration on 1 October, the first time an American had ever been so honored.[50] Kissinger and Nixon decided to enlist President Yahya Khan of Pakistan as an emissary. Nixon convinced Khan to carry a secret offer to the Chinese, stating U.S. willingness to send an emissary to China for confidential talks on Sino-American relations.[51] Given that Kissinger hoped to use rapprochement with the Chinese to force the

Soviets to be more conciliatory, he needed to find out just how accommodating the Chinese were before he could apply pressure to the Soviets. Moscow was not being as cooperative as Kissinger had hoped in planning a U.S.-USSR summit, despite the fact that Dobrynin issued "periodic feelers" on the topic.[52]

As Soviet ambassador Dobrynin recollected in his memoirs, Gromyko felt that the USSR should demand a resolution to the Berlin talks before it agreed on a summit date and that most of the Politburo agreed with Gromyko that "a meeting with Nixon can wait."[53] In essence, Moscow wanted to "sell" a summit, and the price was progress over Berlin. Dobrynin realized only later that the Soviet delay had caused the Americans to put their primary efforts into organizing a Chinese rather than a Soviet summit.[54] In fact, when Kissinger called Dobrynin on the morning of 15 July 1971 to inform him in advance of the China announcement he was about to make, Dobrynin recollected that Kissinger "sounded noticeably pleased, clearly implying that our delays in responding to the president's requests about a Soviet-American summit played into the hands of the Chinese. In my heart of hearts, I could only agree with him."[55]

Hence, in this time of transition in U.S. relations with the USSR and China, Nixon and Kissinger chose to proceed very slowly in the Berlin talks. Nixon's office produced National Security Decision Memorandum (NSDM) 91 in early November 1970, a document presumably drafted by the national security adviser, Henry Kissinger. According to the secret internal state department history, NSDM 91 made it clear that, while the president did hope for improvements in Berlin, "he considered the current arrangement to be an adequate basis for fulfilling American obligations," concluding, "Therefore, a new quadripartite agreement was not an essential requirement 'in terms of our interests or our policy.'"[56]

The sense that the United States did not in fact want progress in the Berlin talks strained U.S.-West German relations. Political scientist Honoré Catudal has argued that another long recess in the quadripartite talks (this time around Christmas 1970) touched off a crisis between Bonn and Washington. Brandt was deeply dismayed by the slow progress and wrote to Nixon in early December to encourage an acceleration of the talks. Brandt's letter was, as Kissinger remembered "not without implied criticism." The West German chancellor recommended that negotiations "go into 'continuous conference.'"[57] According to Catudal, he also sent numerous emissaries to Washington and wrote personal letters to Pompidou and Heath as well.[58]

New Levels of Negotiations

It seems that the introduction of two new negotiating levels in late 1970 and early 1971 helped make possible the quadripartite agreement that would eventually result from the talks in mid-1971. At the suggestion of the British, one new level of negotiations was established in November 1970 when a series of "expert meetings" began. These allowed chief aides to the ambassadors (Yuli Kvizinski for the Soviets, Jonathan Dean for the Americans, Christopher Audland for the British, and René Lustig for the French) to thrash out details of draft agreements in advance of ambassadorial meetings. This proved to be a more expeditious method of negotiating.[59] A second, more important level opened when Kissinger decided to get personally involved in the Berlin talks in January 1971, after conversations with Dobrynin on the topic. Kissinger recalled that he decided to conduct the SALT and Berlin talks in tandem, even though this put him "on thin ice with the rest of the government" for assuming so much authority and even though his staff "was too small to backstop two complex simultaneous negotiations."[60] At the end of January, Kissinger had both Rush and Bahr visit him to discuss ways to speed up negotiations.[61]

Bahr eventually made the suggestion that he and Rush should conduct what were in effect the real negotiations with the Soviet ambassador in Bonn, Valentin Falin.[62] The agreements reached by this so-called "Group of Three" could then be introduced into official levels by Rush.[63] The trio's talks were conducted completely off the record and without translators; the language used was English, although this was not an easy language for Falin or Bahr. Bahr later called the group an ideal set-up, because each of the three reported directly to the key decision-maker—that is, Falin to Brezhnev, Bahr to Brandt, and Rush to Kissinger and Nixon.[64]

The Soviet diplomat in the "expert group" in Berlin, Kvizinski, remembered the work of the Bonn "Group of Three" less fondly. In his memoirs, he wrote of the difficulty of working in Berlin while knowing that a more high-powered group in Bonn was making the important decisions. As he recalled,

> After a while it seemed to me that this construction was an especially well-refined method of pulling the wool over our eyes. First, Bahr and Rush would, after much struggle, reach a compromise agreement with Falin on a certain question. We would concede the maximum in Bonn. Then we would find out in Berlin that this was not enough, because the British and the French would not accept the agreed-upon formulations. But we could hardly say at that point that we had made an agreement with the Americans [in Bonn]. That would have resulted in an international scandal. We could only appeal to the conscience of the Americans, and when that did not help, make further concessions.[65]

Despite Kvizinski's complaints, the Bonn "Group of Three" did eventually produce results. These two new levels contributed to the ability of the quadripartite talks to make substantive progress in 1971, especially after the dramatic alteration in the strategic landscape with the announcement of Kissinger's visit to China. As will be discussed later, this announcement "seemed to concentrate Soviet minds" and produced movement in both the four-power and the SALT talks.[66]

In summary, the quadripartite talks proceeded slowly in 1970 because this was what the superpowers wanted. The transcripts of their sessions show little willingness to compromise. Furthermore, both sides wanted to explore other options. On the Soviet side, these included the Cienfuegos Bay naval base construction and their bilateral contacts with the French. On the U.S. side, these were primarily the preparations for what would become the surprise announcement about the visit to China in 1971. Raymond Garthoff has found that one of the reasons the SALT talks made such slow progress for a long time was "Kissinger and Nixon's lack of interest in SALT as arms control," since they chose to see it rather as "simply one key piece on the political chessboard."[67] The same could be said for the quadripartite talks as well.

The Beginning of the End for Ulbricht

The coolness the Soviets displayed in the quadripartite talks mirrors the coolness that they showed in this period to German-German rapprochement.[68] Earlier scholarship tended to assume that East Berlin was the brake on rapprochement; new documents suggest that in fact Moscow was to blame. What also needs reassessing are SED interests and motives, specifically the degree of enthusiasm that Walter Ulbricht showed toward Ostpolitik. As suggested in the last chapter, he seems actually to have been in favor of a third Brandt-Stoph meeting, to the dismay of the Soviets. Throughout the second half of 1970, there were further hints that Ulbricht was in fact too interested in contacts with the West for Soviet tastes. As political scientist James McAdams has pointed out, Moscow was finding Ulbricht's independent initiative highly suspect.[69]

Markus Wolf has speculated plausibly that Ulbricht recognized Brezhnev's "double game" early on. Despite words from Brezhnev to the effect that dealings with the FRG were dangerous, Ulbricht saw that Moscow itself was proceeding eagerly in that very direction. Wolf recollected that Ulbricht "didn't want to sit on the back of the train, he wanted to be up front on the locomotive" and show initiative of his own in relations with the FRG.[70] In fact, Wolf found that Ulbricht's real hope was that the GDR could benefit from what in SED parlance was referred to as the "scientific-technical" revolution, or technology-intensive means of production, in order to improve its economic indicators. Wolf also recollected that Ulbricht at this time voiced the idea of an economic confederation with West Germany, a recollection shared by Politburo member Hermann Axen and Ulbricht's economic adviser Wolfgang Berger.[71] Berger stated explicitly in a 1991 interview that Ulbricht had hoped for some kind of confederation between the two German states in order to produce economic and "scientific-technical" benefits for both.[72]

Neither documentary hints nor Wolf's nor Berger's comments, however, suggest that scholars have misunderstood Ulbricht all along and that he was in fact a closet liberal and a reformer during the whole of the 1960s, as Monika Kaiser has argued. Rather, documents suggest something more limited: that his attitude toward Ostpolitik was more welcoming but also more complex than has been understood.[73] The files also show that nascent opposition to Ulbricht—arising in reaction to his economic ambitions, his attitude toward the FRG, and, last but not least, his personal arrogance—coalesced around Erich Honecker starting in the summer of 1970 and became increasingly vocal.[74]

The "Argumentation" of 2 June

It seems that Honecker took advantage of Ulbricht's routine absence from meetings of the Central Committee Secretariat, as well as his frequent absences from Politburo meetings, to undermine Ulbricht's plans.[75] SED documents show that, in the second half of 1970, Honecker presided over a large number of Politburo meetings that an ailing Ulbricht did not attend. At many of these meetings, the Politburo under Honecker's chairmanship approved documents endorsing a hard-line, demanding stance in relations with the West. Such a stance in some cases directly contradicted Ulbricht's preferences.

For example, at a Politburo meeting without Ulbricht on 2 June 1970, Honecker secured approval of an "argumentation," or an extensive set of documents and appendices, on "questions of foreign trade with Western Germany."[76] This included a treatise "on the duty of the FRG to compensate the GDR for debts and damages."[77] It argued that compensation was necessary because West Germany was conducting "economic warfare" in its relations with East Germany and hence the GDR deserved reparations. What exactly the warfare comprised was discussed only vaguely; it was said to include manipulation of currencies and exchange rates.[78] Moreover, the FRG was held to be indebted to the GDR for, among other things, its use of East German postal services. An appendix contained an overall sum that West Germany owed the East: "over 100 billion DM-West."[79] The argumentation noted proudly that, despite such extensive damages and debts, the GDR had achieved "a respectable place among the leading industrial states of the world."[80] It pointed out, however, that Bonn had to realize that "it would not be able to escape the demands of the GDR for compensation for all debts and damages."[81] Further contacts with West Germany, noted an addendum, should "offensively" try to secure payments.[82]

A similar hard-line document resulted from the 23 June Politburo meeting, which Ulbricht also did not attend because he had undergone surgery the previous day.[83] Under Honecker's chairmanship, the Politburo approved an awkwardly named set of "instructions for achieving the political and economic interests of the GDR in the foreign economic relations of the GDR with the FRG and the independent political entity of West Berlin."[84] These "instructions" amounted to a long summary of Bonn's sinister motives for instituting Ostpolitik. It found that the policy was a covert attempt to damage the GDR economically. It maintained that the "leading circles" in West Germany were trying to "put the socialist economy of the GDR into a relationship of dependency to the state-monopoly economic system of the FRG"—ironic claims, since Honecker in the later years of his own rule would show no understanding of how debt created dependency.[85] The instructions charged that both political and trade activities were being coordinated in an attempt to "support so-called inner-German special relations," which the report viewed as a sort of Trojan-Horse threat to the GDR.[86] In its conclusions, the report found that "only such treaty agreements should be made which bring the GDR maximum economic benefit and avoid dependencies."[87] In addition, the personnel involved in economic cooperation should be limited; the number of business and official trips taken by citizens of the GDR into West Germany should be kept to an absolute minimum. In essence, the Politburo in Ulbricht's absence made a clear statement of its concern over the risks of contacts with the FRG and the need to manage those risks.[88]

Ulbricht's View: Seek Dependency

Notes from a conversation two days later between Walter Ulbricht and Kosygin's deputy Nikolai Tikhonov indicate that Ulbricht had not heeded his own Politburo's call for restraint.[89] Rather than submit to the Politburo's desire to reduce dependency to a minimum, Ulbricht held the opposite to be necessary. "In the time of the open border we suffered gigantic losses," he remarked to Tikhonov and Abrasimov, who was also present.[90] "Why am I explaining all this to you, Comrade Tikhonov? Because Moscow asks us now and then the question, 'What are all these contracts with the French, with the West Germans, with the Japanese[?]'" The justification was in Ulbricht's eyes "very simple": "We are going to go as far as possible into debt with the capitalists, so that somehow we can make it through." After all, he argued, "a portion of the products from new factories will have to be exported to those places from which we got the machines and the debts." This was a clear statement of Ulbricht's notion that Western machinery could be used by GDR labor to produce goods that could be exported back to the West in exchange for hard currency. The unspoken corollary was that raw goods for production would come from the home of Ulbricht's conversation partners. Ulbricht concluded his conversation with Tikhonov in a didactic tone (for which he would be criticized during his ouster): "I have to explain this to you as a Soviet leader so that you realize what we can do and what we cannot do."[91] Then at the Politburo meeting of 29 June, the first he attended after his operation a week earlier, Ulbricht suspended the very same "instructions" that the Politburo had approved in his absence.[92] In other words, he negated the statement of worry made by the Politburo in his absence.

Showdown

Ulbricht's actions prompted a highly unusual Politburo meeting on 1 July 1970. One sign that something unusual occurred is the particularly uninformative nature of the summary for that day. It records only that "questions of the method of work of the Politburo and the Secretariat of the Central Committee" were discussed—that is, the bodies where, according to the former SED party archivist Monika Kaiser, Ulbricht and Honecker respectively dominated.[93] Kaiser has argued that, at this meeting, Ulbricht had in fact dismissed Honecker but had been forced to reinstate him at Soviet insistence.[94]

Whether or not Ulbricht actually went so far as to dismiss Honecker, one larger point remains clear: by July there were serious tensions within the SED Politburo.[95] These disagreements had reached the level where they merited Soviet intervention. The notes for the subsequent SED Politburo meeting, on 7 July, related that, at the suggestion of the Central Committee of the CPSU, discussion of "questions of the method of work" would be postponed until a later joint session with the Soviet Politburo.[96] Unusually, there exists a file from another SED Politburo meeting on the same day, although it is not clear why two took place.

Shortly thereafter, Ulbricht gave a speech in Rostock during the "East Sea Week" celebration, referring to a "new situation in the FRG" and suggesting that the new Brandt government had made "some progress in recognizing reality," a phrase that was usually a complimentary one in the socialist vocabulary. This conciliatory speech, which was published in *Neues Deutschland* on 17 July, seemed to imply that Ulbricht saw potential for productive cooperation with the Brandt cabinet.[97] Yet at the Politburo meeting on 28 July, the "instructions" that Ulbricht had voided were once again reinstated, thereby overturning Ulbricht's decision to overturn them. The protocol noted that Willi Stoph would be in charge of the distribution of the "instructions," clearly identifying him as a sponsor of the document.[98]

Furthermore, there also exist notes from what seems to have been an extremely significant conversation between Erich Honecker and Leonid Brezhnev on 28 July. According to the notes, Brezhnev told Honecker, "The way the situation there [in East Berlin] has so unexpectedly developed has deeply disturbed me."[99] Brezhnev further complained, "[U]ntil recently, the GDR was something that we could rely on. Now, however, a danger is appearing." In a statement that contrasted strangely with the fact that Brezhnev was at that time in the process of signing an amicable accord with the Brandt administration, Brezhnev warned against letting "the danger" (of disharmony in the Politburo) become known to Bonn. "It won't be long before the enemy, Brandt, will recognize this and use it for himself."[100] Brezhnev then compared the GDR of 1970 to Czechoslovakia in 1968: "Just so you see clearly. We are keeping the CSSR [Czechoslovak Socialist Republic]. There were many promises to us. Everything turned out differently."[101] He also made veiled threats: "We cannot just stand aside and watch such a development. We must and will react."[102] These comments suggest that Brezhnev did indeed sense that a satellite was showing too much initiative and in need of correction. Indeed, he complained specifically about Ulbricht's interest in cooperation with the FRG. "There is no, and it should not come to, any process of rapprochement between the FRG and the GDR."[103] Brezhnev then got more specific: "To any steps of Walter's that affect the unity of the Politburo, of the SED, we will respond accordingly."[104] In extremely blunt language, reminiscent of that which he had reportedly used with the beleaguered Czechoslovakian leadership in 1968, Brezhnev told Honecker: "I tell you in all openness, it will not be possible for him to rule without us. . . . We have troops in the GDR." He put it quite starkly: "Without us, there is not GDR."[105] Brezhnev did urge caution about simply ousting Ulbricht immediately and entirely, again citing the threat of the enemy. He made it clear, though, that he was tired of what he regarded as uppity behavior on the part of Ulbricht. Brezhnev did not like references to the GDR as the "best model of socialism" or comments to the effect that "one does everything better in the GDR."[106] He complained about a past conversation in which Ulbricht would not cease talking to Brezhnev even though Brezhnev had been hot and uncomfortable. Brezhnev revealed his own personal chagrin with Ulbricht by saying, "One just cannot treat someone like that."[107] In short, there is a great amount of circumstantial evidence not only that Ulbricht's position was in danger as early as July 1970 but also that the danger arose in large part from his willingness to pursue rapprochement with the West.

In other words, Ulbricht was in danger from doing exactly what Brezhnev was doing himself. Even as Brezhnev voiced worry about FRG-GDR relations to Honecker, the Soviet leader played up his own relations with Bonn. Markus Wolf vividly recalled a lesson that Honecker and his supporters learned about Soviet ambivalence during a vacation in Bulgaria in August 1970. Wolf recollected that he and "half the Politburo, the Honecker wing" were spending a holiday there as Brandt traveled to Moscow to sign the Moscow treaty with Kosygin. The Honecker faction felt absolutely certain that the coverage in *Pravda*—a sure indicator of CPSU Politburo attitudes—would be minimal. Instead, the day after the signing, the unusually large photo with Brezhnev looming over the seated Brandt and Kosygin dominated the front page. Wolf remembered getting up early to look at *Pravda* when the pack of the day's copies for the SED Politburo vacationers arrived. He said he laid out copies on the breakfast tables so that no one would miss the point.[108]

The SED Delegation to Moscow in August 1970

Shortly after the signing of the Moscow Treaty in mid-August, a tense SED delegation that included Ulbricht, Honecker, Stoph, Axen, and Mittag traveled to Moscow to meet with Brezhnev and others. Honecker seems to have managed to have a private talk with Brezhnev during this visit.[109] In the private conversation, Brezhnev dismissed the notion that the GDR could surpass West Germany without any risk of becoming more like it, a notion that seems to have been Ulbricht's.[110] Moreover, Brezhnev repeated a long-standing complaint about Ulbricht's idea that the GDR was some kind of model. Brezhnev grumbled, "One should not extol one's own model of socialism. One should not give other countries the idea that one does everything better."[111]

The official meeting took place the next day, and what seem to be notes from this discussion have survived.[112] According to the notes, Ulbricht once again made arrogant remarks. Referring at one point to cooperative economic endeavors with the USSR, Ulbricht remarked disparagingly, "We're not Byelo-Russia, we're not a Soviet state. So this will be real cooperation."[113] Brezhnev in return expressed a clear preference for a delay in German-German rapprochement. "We have decided that the negotiations with the FRG don't need to be pushed along. We want to see first . . . how the ratification [of the Moscow Treaty] proceeds, how the negotiations with the People's Republic of Poland proceed [on what would become the Warsaw Treaty]."[114] Brezhnev did not challenge Ulbricht personally at the official meeting but did note, "We have received in recent times some signals and rumors that there are, shall we say, differences and quarrels in the SED Politburo," and stressed that the maintenance of unity was crucial.[115]

If Honecker was hoping that this would be the meeting where his promotion to the number-one spot would occur, however, he was to be disappointed. Brezhnev praised Ulbricht's long years of work and made it clear that a change was not immediately in the cards, perhaps as part of Brezhnev's wait-until-ratification policy. In essence, Brezhnev cautioned both Ulbricht and Honecker. He served Ulbricht notice that he was not happy with his leadership, but he also cautioned the Politburo generally (and it seems Honecker particularly) against sudden dramatic changes while the Moscow Treaty was not yet ratified.

Honecker Continues Pressure on Ulbricht in September 1970

Honecker does not seem to have been satisfied with the results of the August meeting, however, because he continued to apply pressure to Ulbricht throughout September 1970. At yet another Politburo meeting without Ulbricht—indeed, one without most members of the Politburo attending (perhaps because it was at the end of vacation season)—the Politburo passed a resolution that would often be cited afterwards. On 8 September, it approved an "analysis" of the five-year plan and charged Stoph with its implementation.[116] While this sounds rather innocuous, and indeed the documents are rather unrevealing, subsequent references to this date suggest that those who voted for it considered it to be a serious challenge to Ulbricht. It served as a de facto end to Ulbricht's cherished "New Economic System."

The analysis was produced by Willi Stoph and Günter Mittag and contained general suggestions for altering the implementation of the existing—that is, Ulbricht's—five-year plan. All ministries were directed to concentrate on executing the plan "on the basis of already existing long-term agreements with the Soviet Union and other socialist countries."[117] By endorsing a return to a stronger Soviet and Warsaw Pact orientation, the analysis seems to have been an attempt to address Brezhnev's complaint that the GDR arrogantly saw itself as a model of innovation.

Yet again, however, Ulbricht willfully ignored the message coming both from without (that is, from Moscow) and from within (that is, from the Honecker faction), saying that his economic direction needed revision. On 21 September, Ulbricht gave a speech to the first secretaries of the GDR's districts on the exact same topic the Politburo had addressed, namely, the execution of the current five-year plan. In it, he emphasized the need for "a breakthrough" in high technology, an aspiration that implied cooperation with the West. He argued that the GDR was "faced with the necessity to master the scientific-technical progress as quickly as possible," saying this was necessary "because the political fight with the West German imperialism makes it so."[118] In other words, he argued that keeping up with the West German standard required an all-out effort in the realm of "scientific-technical progress," which was the main euphemism for technology-intensive production.

In a surprisingly blunt statement, Ulbricht implied that this task would involve taking advantage of the ability to get cheap raw goods from the USSR: "We are a country that is relatively small and has little in the way of raw materials, so only in cooperation with the Soviet Union and the other socialist states could the problem of the scientific-technical revolution be successfully mastered."[119] Mentioning such a venal motive for working together with the Soviet Union—as opposed to explaining that one did so out of voluntary, respectful, ideological agreement—verged on the heretical.

Next, Ulbricht indirectly acknowledged Politburo criticism of his goals, but implied that such complaints were pointless. He admitted that in the pursuit of his economic aims, there had been "injuries done to the principle of democratic centralization." He brusquely observed, however, "There is no point in remarking on the injuries to democratic centralization; that doesn't help us move forward. Our point of departure must be the thoughtful application and use of the economic laws."[120] It is perhaps not surprising that typed on the top of the text of the speech are these words: "Strictly confidential, was not published!"[121]

Erich Honecker did not relent. In speeches of his own at the same time, he contradicted Ulbricht's claims that there was "a new situation" in Bonn and that cooperation with it would give the GDR a high-technology boost. In two similar talks given on 14 and 25 September 1970 in Dresden and Erfurt respectively, Honecker described the Bonn government in terms very different from those Ulbricht had used. In Dresden, he cautioned that no one should be deceived by the West German initiatives, asserting, "They have not changed their goal at all." The Brandt government was not slackening the long-standing FRG hostility to the East, he charged; it was in fact intensifying it in a new fashion.[122] In Erfurt he was more blunt; saying that between socialism and social democracy "there could be no cooperation."[123] Honecker's divergence from Ulbricht, as expressed in these speeches, seems to have received Soviet support.[124]

Markus Wolf recollected in 1996 that this divergence between Ulbricht's and Honecker's speeches caused much confusion in the top ranks. He remembered that he and others found themselves asking, "What is the party line now—is it what Ulbricht says or what Honecker says?"[125] An all-out confrontation between Ulbricht and his crown prince was clearly on the way.

A Significant Shift in Soviet Attitude

Attitudes were changing not only in East Berlin. Soviet guidance to the SED on the question of relations with West Germany abruptly changed direction in late October 1970. Valentin Falin, who was at the time head of the Third European Department of the Soviet Foreign Ministry and already recognized as the leading point-man on German issues in Moscow, appeared in East Berlin for consultations with the SED on 27 October. East German files contain a summary of Falin's conversation with an unspecified high-ranking SED functionary. In it,

Falin and the functionary agreed that high-level contacts with the Brandt government should resume. The general tone was still confrontational toward the FRG; both Falin and the East German agreed that the "internal order" of the GDR would not be a subject of discussion and that there would be "not even a hint" of a mention about "inner-German" relations, a phrase that the SED regime thought implied that it was something less than a separate, sovereign state.[126]

It came out in the conversation that both Moscow and East Berlin were aware of the Brandt government's intent to press publicly for some kind of resumption of German-German contact. Falin ordered a kind of preemptive strike. He told the SED leaders to pass on a message to Bonn offering a resumption of talks and for good measure gave the SED a draft of exactly what Moscow wanted the message to say.[127] Falin mentioned specifically that the message should not to go to the mayor of West Berlin but rather to Brandt, because it would take the Americans longer to hear about it from Brandt.

Why should the mayor of West Berlin have come into question at all? It seems that Falin, and by inference Moscow, had decided to link several issues. Falin's draft of the message that the GDR was to pass on to the FRG stated that German-German talks should resume in order to help the Berlin talks come to a "positive result."[128] In this way Moscow could simultaneously press for progress over Berlin and assert the sovereignty and indispensability of the GDR. Indeed, Falin's draft message explicitly stated this goal: German-German talks would be possible only "with the recognition of the sovereign rights of the GDR."[129]

Apparently, Moscow had decided to try a new tack by getting the factious SED Politburo more involved, rather than keeping it on the sidelines. In other words, a significant shift in attitude had taken place. Moscow's primary interest was in getting the Moscow Treaty ratified; by late 1970 it had decided that making progress in both the Berlin talks and the German-German rapprochement would be the best way of promoting ratification. Markus Wolf recollected that this October 1970 shift took place rather quickly and caught even some SED Politburo members off guard. As Wolf recounted in his memoirs, two Politburo members were conducting talks with the French in Paris at the time. "Workers in my service received the alarm that they had to get new directives to them" so that they would cease using old phrases in conversations with the French, Wolf recalled.[130]

The Bertsch Delegation

Following orders, the SED delivered Falin's message almost verbatim to Brandt immediately.[131] A delegation traveled to Bonn the next day, 28 October 1970, and gained an audience with Brandt personally the following morning. According to the report of the head of the delegation, Herbert Bertsch, the deputy head of the Press Office of the GDR's Council of Ministers, the chancellor was extremely receptive. Bertsch reported that Brandt endorsed the goal of helping the four powers to reach an agreement.[132] Indeed, Bertsch quoted Brandt as saying that the "exchange of opinion" should begin "as quickly as possible," and that as soon as the GDR named its representative, talks could begin "immediately" with Egon Bahr representing the Western side. The GDR could choose the meeting site "at any time." Brandt repeated that Bahr was ready "to come to you immediately."[133] Bertsch speculated that the cause for the rush was a series of upcoming state elections. He recorded Horst Ehmke, Brandt's *chef de cabinet*, as saying, "We have to make sure that there are some practical results, so that the whole thing does not just look like a cheap election maneuver."[134] The only FRG reservations noted by the report were Brandt's worries that any kind of German-German conversation not compete with the four-power talks, and that there be no preconditions.[135] Even at the time, the West Germans sensed the guiding hand of the Soviet Union. As Bahr wrote to Kissinger, "The Soviets caused this step to happen."[136]

A Month's Delay

Despite the readiness of both sides, it took a month of telegrams and letters to agree on a meeting time and place.[137] The reason for the delay is not clear; it might have been the result of lingering tension between Brezhnev and Ulbricht over the nature of relations with the FRG. The two leaders exchanged tense letters about various details of FRG-GDR cooperation.[138] At its heart, however, the basic tension between Brezhnev and Ulbricht was not about details. As Wolf observed in his memoirs, "Brezhnev wanted to control the opening to the West himself. Nothing could be more inconvenient for him than independent, hard-to-oversee contacts between the GDR and the FRG."[139]

Bonn and East Berlin finally agreed on a time and a place. The "pause for reflection," the beginning and ending of which had both come at Soviet suggestion, ceased on 27 November 1970. On that date, Egon Bahr traveled to East Berlin to begin what would become more than three years of nearly continuous negotiations with Michael Kohl, a GDR foreign ministry official who had been involved in the "Pass Agreement" negotiations previously. Both men would be the wiser for the lessons learned from bargaining in late 1970. They knew that the various unfinished processes—the unratified Moscow Treaty, the unfinished Quadripartite Accord, the unresolved tension in the Politburo—were all intimately linked to each other. An awareness of these links would inform their negotiations. Both men would have to walk a tightrope between the mandates of their immediate political masters, who seemed inclined to take risks, and the concerns of the allied superpower looking over their shoulders, who were eager to manage risk and direct matters themselves. It would not be an easy balancing act.

Expediting Negotiations in 1971:
Superpower Maneuvering and
the Importance of China

four

The Soviet shift of October 1970—toward encouraging German-German contacts rather than blocking them—became more pronounced throughout 1971. The reason was Soviet desire for ratification of the Moscow Treaty by the West German parliament as soon as possible. However, as will be described below, by 1971 the Soviet leadership realized that the Western powers had decided to make ratification contingent on progress in the four-power Berlin negotiations. Hence, Moscow had no choice but to expedite the Berlin talks in hopes of achieving ratification.

In fact, *both* superpowers showed new interest in making progress on the German question in 1971, but both were dependent on their German ally to do so. To understand why, it is necessary to examine the linkages between four events: (1) the talks between East and West Germany, (2) superpower relations in 1971, (3) increased superpower involvement in German-German affairs in 1971, and (4) the ouster of Ulbricht. The story of 1971 is the story of the links between these events.

Enter Bahr and Kohl

As described in Chapter 3, Willy Brandt responded to the invitation of the Bertsch delegation to begin talks by indicating that his emissary, Egon Bahr, would be willing to travel to the GDR as soon as possible. The GDR accepted this offer. As a result, both the first and second meetings took place in East Berlin. As the site of the meetings, the SED chose the Council of Ministers building—a *government*, not a *party*, building, chosen to imply that one legitimate government was negotiating with another.

Michael Kohl

Awaiting Bahr's arrival in November 1970 was the man chosen by the SED to represent the GDR in the talks, Dr. Michael Kohl.[1] His résumé exuded party loyalty. Born in 1929, Kohl chose to study law and went on to teach international jurisprudence at the University of Jena.[2] In 1963, he moved to Berlin to head the legal department of the East German Foreign Ministry. From 1965 on, he worked as a state secretary in the Council of Ministers but maintained a close affiliation with the foreign ministry. In particular, he was responsible for the issue of West Berlin. Kohl, who does not appear to be related to his namesake Helmut, participated in some of the negotiations that resulted in the "Pass-Agreements" of the mid-1960s. When he began conversations with Bahr in 1970, he was on the staff of the Council of Ministers and hence was Bahr's protocol equal.

What characterized Michael Kohl as a negotiator?[3] In a 1996 interview, Bahr recollected that Kohl's negotiating style underwent a profound transformation over the course of the nearly three years during which they dealt with each other. At first, Bahr found Kohl to be extremely remote, distant, and inflexible.[4] On top of that, he found that Kohl suffered personally from the kind of "inferiority complex" that afflicted the GDR as a whole. Bahr thought that this was to be expected—as he put it, "That was what the top product of a GDR education was like."[5] Moreover, having to deal with someone who had just successfully negotiated a treaty with the impenetrable Gromyko (namely Bahr) made Kohl uneasy. He also seemed unsettled by both the prospect of, at times, doing so on Western soil and having to face Western reporters. Bahr remembered in particular their first joint press conference in Bonn, when he saw "the sweat beading up on [Kohl's] forehead."[6]

Two years later, however, relations between Bahr and Kohl had improved to the point where they could make jokes with each other. Eventually, Bahr came to respect Kohl as an intelligent negotiating partner. They even reached a point where Bahr could, in Kohl's presence, make calls to leaders of the West Berlin Senate to discuss Berlin-specific details of their negotiations. Officially this was

Egon Bahr (center) and Michael Kohl (far right) speak to journalists outside the GDR's Council of Ministers' Building in East Berlin in 1972. (Signatur L 0928/26 N, Bundesarchiv, Koblenz)

taboo, since the GDR maintained a strict separation between negotiations with the FRG and with West Berlin.[7] Moreover, delegation members from both the Eastern and Western sides praised Kohl for developing a sense of teamwork on the Eastern side, which had no parallel in the Western group.

The Composition of Kohl's Delegation and Stasi Involvement

To understand the composition of Kohl's delegation, it is essential to consider the role of the Stasi—or the MfS, as it called itself. First, it is clear that MfS involvement was extensive. Second, the nature of the involvement suggests that the ministry functioned in many ways as an "ersatz" foreign service. Finally, and most importantly, involvement was not synonymous with being in charge.

The involvement began at the top. Documents from the Stasi archive suggest that Kohl may have been more multifaceted at the beginning of negotiations than Bahr's picture of him as an insecure, inexperienced negotiator would suggest. While not providing absolute certainty, they suggest strongly that Michael Kohl had a secret title to put next to his public one: "IM Koran."[8] In Stasi usage, the abbreviation "IM" stood for "inoffizieller Mitarbeiter," or "unofficial co-worker." This was the designation for the largest and most diffuse category of Stasi agents; a recent study estimates that during the lifetime of the GDR, approximately 600,000 people worked as IMs at some time or another.[9] Exactly what such activity entailed varied widely. IMs were subdivided into several different gradations; one could be anything from an "IMK," an IM who merely made his or her home available for a conspiratorial meeting in which he or she did not take part, to an "IME," an IM assigned to carry out a particularly delicate task requiring specific skills.[10] It is not clear from existing documents into which category "Koran" fell, nor when he officially began working for the Stasi. Documents make it clear, though, that he was actively reporting during the German-German negotiations.

In fact, it seems that Kohl's link to the MfS was one of the reasons he was chosen to head the delegation. When asked directly if Kohl was "Koran," MfS espionage chief Markus Wolf refused to answer the question. He did say, however, that his office had been consulted on whom to pick as the head of the GDR delegation. Wolf remembered that someone with legal training was called for, because the negotiations would concern issues of legal recognition. As a result, Wolf said, his office nominated Michael Kohl.[11] When asked why the MfS had proposed Kohl in particular, Wolf responded, "We tried but could not find anyone else. Moreover we had a relationship of trust with him," a euphemism that sometimes implied an established working relationship.[12]

The active involvement of the MfS in the German-German negotiations, while sounding sensational at first, is on second glance less surprising, considering the role that the MfS played in the GDR's relations with other states. Given that the GDR did not have formal diplomatic relations with most Western countries, contact with them often had to be established clandestinely. Such contacts were by and large the responsibility of Markus Wolf's intelligence apparatus.[13] Also especially important in dealings with the West was the lawyer Wolfgang Vogel, who served as a go-between to the MfS, the Politburo, and the West German federal government in bargaining to allow would-be émigrés to leave the GDR.[14] The MfS at times fulfilled the functions that usually belonged to a foreign ministry or trade ministry.[15]

As a result, it was to be expected that the Stasi would be actively involved in the German-German talks, and not just to pursue espionage. As delegation member and GDR foreign ministry representative Karl Seidel recollected, the GDR delegation needed staff with technical expertise in areas such as customs and transit, and that sort of expertise was to be found most readily in the MfS.[16] Hence, one would expect that Kohl would not be the only Stasi representative on the GDR delegation; and indeed MfS documents reveal that he was not. Two of the visa and customs experts, Alwin Brandt and Helmut Nacke, were "HMs," "hauptamtliche Mitarbeiter," that is, "official" or "senior co-workers" of the

MfS.[17] As official Stasi staff, they did not use cover names, although they were not identified to the West Germans as MfS operatives. Furthermore, in the past Seidel himself had worked as an IMK (the least demanding category) under the code name "Ingrid." Finally, the traffic expert, Heinz Gerber, reported on the German-German talks as IM "Walter Mehlhorn." In an interview in 1996, delegation member Görner (for whom there is no evidence of Stasi activity) conceded quite openly that the MfS was involved in every phase of the negotiations, and that seemed to be nothing out of the ordinary.[18]

It is clear that Mielke, Wolf, and the MfS were quite well informed about the progress of German-German talks throughout.[19] Indeed, there even exist protocols typed up from bugging private conversations between Egon Bahr and Michael Kohl. In one case the protocol was accompanied by a report comparing Kohl's spoken comments with the written report he himself had submitted afterwards.[20] In other words, the MfS was spying not only on strangers but also on its own. In an interview, Seidel recounted that at the time he had gotten the impression that Kohl sensed he was under surveillance. Seidel emphasized that this was only his personal impression and that he and Kohl never discussed it directly. However, he remembered that Kohl's comments or actions would suggest an awareness of eavesdropping, such as when Kohl would request Seidel to turn up the radio when the two of them were talking.[21] Moreover, it must be remembered that the MfS was not the only large intelligence organization in the GDR; as intelligence historian Christopher Andrew has pointed out, "the KGB base at Karlshorst in the Berlin suburb was the biggest outside the Soviet Union."[22]

The key question is, did the MfS involvement enable it to control the direction of the talks? The answer—in contrast to the oft-voiced notion that the Stasi was some kind of a rogue state within the East German state—is no. Despite the copious information they were receiving from these various sources, documents do not suggest that Mielke and Wolf were directing negotiations themselves. Rather, direction came from the SED Politburo in the form of directives to Michael Kohl that were approved in advance by the Soviets. It seems logical to assume that Mielke's opinions as head of the Stasi received consideration when these directives were formulated. Moreover, surviving correspondence shows that Mielke had a close working relationship with both Ulbricht and Honecker.[23] Starting in 1971 (after Honecker came to power), Mielke was a candidate member and then a full member of the Politburo as well. Hence, he certainly had many ways of making his opinion known. And the MfS had an ongoing means of voicing its concerns in the form of the delegation members in its service. In other words, the MfS reports most likely helped shape the directives to Kohl and occasionally caused specific changes (such as when Stasi reports deterred the Politburo from inviting Willy Brandt to travel to East Berlin), but the Stasi did not have ultimate control over the East German delegation; the Politburo did.[24] Furthermore, none of the available evidence suggests that the Stasi as an institution had interests distinct from those of the Politburo concerning German-German rapprochement. There was certainly worry within the MfS about the security implications of closer cooperation with the West, but that worry was equally strong within the Honecker faction of the Politburo. In summary, the Stasi in the Ostpolitik era functioned as it was designed to—providing intelligence to the Politburo, which then acted upon that information.

The Composition of the West German Delegation

SED papers make clear that the official composition of the FRG group looked similar to that of the GDR. As with the GDR delegation, the FRG group comprised numerous experts and specialists who took part in only a subset of meetings, so only the most significant and regularly attending delegation members merit description.[25]

The FRG had a foreign ministry representative in its delegation too, in the person of Hans-Otto Bräutigam. When asked in 1996 why he was chosen for the delegation, Bräutigam responded that the West German Foreign Ministry had wanted to send as young a representative as possible so that his actions could be disavowed as easily as possible. Bräutigam recollected that the German-German negotiations caused his employer, the West German Foreign Office, an "approach-avoidance" conflict. On the one hand, it did not want to conduct the negotiations itself, because that would have implied that they were foreign relations; on the other hand, it wanted to be as well informed as possible and to have as much influence as possible. Just as the U.S. State Department felt shut out by Henry Kissinger, so too did the FRG Foreign Ministry worry that Bahr would cut it off from information about the talks. Hence, Bräutigam's task was in essence twofold: he had both to keep his employer informed about the talks and to represent its interests therein. Among others, these interests included guarantees of respect for the agreements reached with the Western allies in the first two decades of the Cold War, as well as some kind of acknowledgment that "the German question" remained open.[26]

Bräutigam succeeded in developing a good working relationship *with* Bahr, he says, despite the fact that he essentially had to report *about* Bahr to the Foreign Ministry. Moreover, he found that Bahr was motivated by a sense of maintaining "the national integrity" of Germany as a whole as much as possible. Bahr's personal aide, Antonius Eitel, who also took part in the negotiations, shared this assessment of Bahr's motives.[27] Both praised Bahr's negotiating talents; Bräutigam characterized them as brilliant.

The Foreign Ministry had further representation on the West German side in Ulrich Sahm, who was (as previously mentioned) the son of a Weimar-era mayor of Berlin. Sahm already had experience in dealing with the East, having headed the talks with the GDR on the practical details of the Brandt-Stoph meeting. He was officially "on loan" to the Federal Chancellery during the talks; Willy Brandt had invited him to head its foreign policy department.[28] Among other tasks, Sahm headed the working group that prepared speaking points and other papers for Bahr during the negotiating rounds. Fellow delegation member Antonius Eitel remembered these preparations as enormously complex affairs, made complicated by the efforts of various West German ministries and agencies to ensure that their views were represented therein. As Eitel recalled, the Ministry for Inner-German Relations in particular had more or less spent its entire existence preparing for such talks; as he put it, "much official sweat" had been shed already.[29] This ministry also had its own representative on Bahr's delegation, in the person of Jürgen Weichert.

Just as with Kohl and Bahr, the two delegations came to know each other quite well over the course of the three years they spent together. During the day, while Bahr and Kohl held increasingly lengthy one-on-one conversations, the two delegations would be forced in their absence to make small talk with one another, since they did not have the authority to discuss more substantive matters. Bräutigam recollected that long hours spent in this manner allowed a certain measure of camaraderie to develop.[30] As his GDR counterpart, Seidel, recalled, "It wasn't as if we were sitting there with knives in our hands."[31] However, there was always a certain reserve; as Bräutigam remembered, "We were a class enemy, and they never forgot that."[32] Usually Kohl and Bahr would reappear after a long consultation with each other and issue directives about what was needed for the following day. Hence, a day spent in idle small talk would often be followed by an intensive, sleepless night of work for both sides, to be followed in turn by another day of small talk.

Initial Motives of the GDR Delegation

What motivated the SED delegation at the beginning of talks? At Ulbricht's request, GDR foreign minister Otto Winzer produced a summary of the SED's goals before the first Bahr-Kohl meeting. His summary stated that, first and foremost, the GDR should seek an agreement on transit, meaning transit through East German territory to West Berlin. This was the prime task assigned to the SED by Moscow. If Bonn were unwilling to talk about transit, however, then Kohl should try to proceed to questions of "a basic regulation of the relations between the GDR and the FRG." It is notable that the second option did not actually call for Kohl to seek "full legal recognition."[33]

In a 1996 interview, the East German legal expert Günter Görner offered another perspective on the motivations of the SED delegation. He maintained that the SED delegation was sincerely interested in the maintenance of peace and the status quo in Europe. All of the GDR delegation members shared a memory of World War II, even if it was, as with Görner, from the perspective of a young child. "In each of us hovered somewhere the fear of war," he recalled. "Our real goal was to prevent war ever proceeding forth again from German soil."[34] Görner belonged in the ranks of those who prepared technical papers, however; he was not one of those who made the decisions.

Yet another SED priority—one not discussed openly—was to increase the amount of financial transfers, in various forms, that the GDR received from the West Germans. This priority is difficult to describe using documentation, because it was usually discussed in highly coded language, if at all. Too much desire for the currency of the enemy state was unseemly. Nonetheless, the documents show that the SED badly desired hard-currency payments. The party believed it deserved these payments, either for restitution of the "damages" inflicted by the FRG's "economic warfare" against the GDR or in exchange for services rendered, such as delivering mail. To what use the SED intended to put these payments was not clearly spelled out. Post-1989 revelations about the lifestyle of Politburo members and senior Stasi officials—who enjoyed Western cars, appliances, and bank accounts—show that some of the income found its way into personal use. However, the most basic cause of the need for cash, which became more pronounced through the 1970s, was the simple fact that the economic productivity of the GDR was not sufficient to finance Politburo plans to improve both East German economic indicators and the populace's standard of living.[35] Ulbricht hoped to use hard currency to improve the GDR's economic performance by purchasing modern industrial equipment from the West, as discussed previously.

These were the overall goals. Specific goals for each negotiation round were set by the SED Politburo in consultation with the CPSU and then forwarded in a directive to Kohl. In shaping these directives, the SED had to bear in mind what the USSR had already agreed to, whether it be with the West Germans in Moscow or the Western allies in Berlin.[36] After the Politburo issued a directive and received the go-ahead from Moscow, Görner and others prepared detailed papers for the individual negotiating round. This preparation seems to have been less complex on the East German side than on the West German. Görner remembered that, essentially, the papers were written by Kohl, Seidel, and himself.[37] In contrast to Bahr, Kohl also seems to have shared with the rest of his delegation the details of their one-on-one conversations.[38]

The First Bahr-Kohl Meeting, 27 November 1970 in East Berlin

As with Erfurt and Kassel, the SED's preparations for the initial Bahr-Kohl meeting on 27 November 1970 reveal concern not only with large goals but also with the tiniest protocol details. For example, Seidel recalled the decision to not greet Bahr outside, in front of the Council of Ministers building (presumably to minimize the risk of any kind of public scene, such as that in Erfurt). This created a simple problem: how would Bahr get inside the building if no one were allowed to greet him? Seidel was given the task of opening the door "as if by an invisible hand" when Bahr walked up the steps so that the welcome could take place inside.[39]

Only Kohl and Seidel attended the first meeting; they met Bahr, Eitel, and Weichert from the FRG.[40] The tone could hardly be described as friendly; the discussion began with petty squabbling.[41] However, the tone was not so hostile as to prevent substantive discussion. Both sides aired some of their general goals. For the GDR, these were to promote détente "in the heart of Europe," an important part of which would be reaching an agreement over transit to West Berlin.[42] Moreover, the GDR wanted to encourage those on the Western side who held "realistic positions"—which seemed to be an indirect, complimentary reference to Brandt. Kohl specifically mentioned that the GDR wanted to help "as much as possible to make the conflict with the forces of a rightist-extremist nature and with the CDU/CSU easier for you [meaning, presumably, Brandt and Bahr]."[43]

For his part, Bahr emphasized the statement Brandt had made in his inaugural speech and elsewhere that the FRG was willing to regard the GDR as a separate state, one with which it needed to regularize relations.[44] He also repeated the West German position that neither state could speak for the other. This represented a significant deviation from the view prevalent in Bonn for the first two decades of the Cold War, that the FRG alone legitimately represented the interests of a notional greater Germany.[45] The FRG further indicated that it would use as the basis of its negotiations the twenty points laid out by Willy Brandt in Kassel.[46] In this way the GDR would be forced to deal with the issues Brandt had raised there, which had received no substantive discussion at the time.

Bahr made it clear, though, that there were limits to how far the FRG was willing to proceed in relations with the GDR, remarking, "We could not, for example, agree, without the approval of the four powers, to some kind of a confederation such as has been proposed in earlier years by the chair of the council of state [Ulbricht]."[47] Bahr also pointed out that there were unquestionably unique aspects to German-German relations. This was a sore point for the GDR, which maintained that relations between the two Germanies were no different from those between any two foreign states. However, Kohl could not challenge Bahr's remark that "even Stoph and Brandt could agree on one thing: they didn't need a translator, and we don't either."[48]

At the end of this initial meeting, Bahr asked if he had understood properly that the GDR was primarily interested in talking about transit to West Berlin but only in exchange for a reduction of the activities of the West German federal government in that city. Kohl confirmed this.[49] For his part, Kohl asked Bahr about the FRG's choice of phrases. He asked why Bahr was avoiding using the adjective "völkerrechtlich," meaning roughly "legal" or "according to international legal norms." Kohl asked if Bahr avoided it "out of cosmetic reasons." Bahr answered in the affirmative and added, "When I say, we want that which is usual between states. . . ." Kohl cut him off and finished his sentence: ". . . then you mean full legal relations but are only formulating it differently for cosmetic reasons?" "Exactly," replied Bahr.[50]

An unofficial, one-on-one conversation between Kohl and Bahr followed the official session, thus setting a model for all future meetings.[51] According to Kohl's summary from this private conversation, Bahr complained about the rivalry between his office and the foreign ministry, where he found that "twenty years of CDU personnel politics was having an effect."[52] The two discussed minor controversial issues, such as the fact that Bahr had entered the GDR using only his Berlin personal ID card (using his passport would have had the undesirable connotation that he was traveling abroad) and that he had an FRG flag on his car.[53] Bahr emphasized that Kohl and his delegation would be allowed to enter the FRG without any kind of emigration control and that they were free to place an East German flag on their vehicle too. This privilege had an unintentionally comic consequence on the first GDR trip to the West; the GDR delegation hoped to drive across the entirety of West Germany with a flag on the car, but the flag flew off almost as soon as they crossed the border.[54] The delegation did have a spare, though, which it could at least display on its arrival in Bonn. On more substantive matters, Bahr emphasized that negotiating the issue of transit would be difficult for the FRG and the West Berlin Senate because they were more or less dependent on the consent of the three Western allies.[55] Bahr also noticed that East Berlin had avoided making any clear statement about the intentions of its ally, the Soviet Union, and interpreted this as a sign of insecurity on the part of the GDR.[56] Kohl's unwillingness to choose a date for a follow-up meeting only increased Bahr's sense that the SED was unsure how to proceed.[57]

In short, the first meeting showed that there would be no speedy resolution to the issues dividing the two German states. When facing the West German press afterwards, Bahr strove to counter any expectations of speedy progress. As he told *Der Spiegel*, the FRG had to take a "deep breath" and give the talks as much time as needed.[58] At the initial meeting, Kohl had expressed concern about the amount of press attention the talks were receiving in the West.[59] However, as the talks stretched on and became more routine, the press attention became less intense, and Kohl did not make this issue a priority in later meetings. Bahr does not seem to have tried to manipulate the GDR through hostile leaks or similar actions; rather, he was more concerned simply to fend off the attacks of the right-leaning press, particularly the papers owned by Axel Springer. He had received a good deal of criticism for the publication of the so-called "Bahr Paper" during the Moscow Talks and was determined not to repeat the experience.[60]

Superpower Maneuvering Creates a Complicated Chain of Dependencies

Before Kohl and Bahr could meet again, however, three developments would alter the context of their negotiations. Brezhnev came to suspect that the West had linked ratification of the Moscow Treaty to the Berlin talks. The FRG would achieve a degree of reconciliation with Poland via the Warsaw Treaty of 7 December 1970. Finally, Honecker's campaign against Ulbricht would reach a new height with the fourteenth plenary meeting of the SED Central Committee on 9–10 December.

Brezhnev's Suspicions

Brezhnev announced his suspicions at a meeting in Moscow of the Political Advisory Committee of the Warsaw Pact on 2 December 1970, with Ulbricht and other SED Politburo members in attendance.[61] There they heard Brezhnev complain that the Brandt government was not moving forward as aggressively as it should on the question of ratifying the Moscow Treaty. The Soviet leader found that the Americans and their allies were to blame and accused them of playing both sides. On the one hand, they seemed to be openly supportive of Brandt and Ostpolitik. On the other hand, Brezhnev suspected that they had forced a "Junktim," or "linkage," on Brandt, that they were insisting that Brandt make ratification of the Moscow Treaty dependent on progress in the Berlin talks.[62] Brezhnev fumed, "They are playing games with it [ratification] and want to use the problem of putting the USSR-FRG Treaty into force to get one-sided advantages for themselves."[63] These were not groundless suspicions. In January 1971, Brandt confirmed the Soviet leader's fears by pledging publicly not to submit the Moscow Treaty for ratification by the Bundestag until there was a Berlin settlement that the FRG and its allies found acceptable.[64]

Originally it had been the Soviets who had established linkage between the Berlin talks and the German-German talks. As discussed previously, Falin's visit and draft message of October 1970 showed that the Soviets had decided to tie progress in the former to progress in the latter. The USSR decision to do so was consistent with its claims in the quadripartite negotiations that the issue of transit fell under the sovereign authority of the GDR. Since the Western allies had not recognized the GDR, they could not deal with East Berlin. Hence, it was up to the FRG to reach a transit agreement with the East Germans. Brezhnev's comments of December 1970 show that the Soviets realized that the Western allies had decided to turn the tables and construct a link as well. Their link was to Bonn's ratification of the Moscow Treaty, which Brezhnev greatly desired.

In other words, the two superpowers had established a complicated chain of dependencies. The Soviets had declared that progress in the German-German talks was a necessary precondition for progress in the quadripartite talks. The Western allies had in effect trumped this by declaring that progress in the quadripartite talks was a necessary precondition for ratification of the Moscow Treaty, thereby taking advantage of one of the Soviet's main motives for dealing with the West. Hence, if the Soviets were to stick to their original link, then progress in the German-German talks would become a necessary precondition not only for the success of the Berlin talks but also for the more important process of ratification of the Moscow Treaty. The German-German talks thereby became a bottleneck on the flow of events.

Brezhnev considered this an unfortunate development. He was already worried about Ulbricht showing too much initiative. Now Brezhnev had even greater need for a compliant SED Politburo, because he needed smooth-running German-German talks to achieve the desired ratification of the Moscow Treaty. Perhaps this motivated him to emphasize the necessity for coordinated action in his speech to the assembled Warsaw Pact representatives: "I think that we are all agreed that the steps we will be undertaking next must be coordinated and that their execution should be determined by progress on many fronts."[65]

The Warsaw Treaty of 7 December 1970

Brezhnev did find at least one cause for optimism: the fact that negotiations between the West Germans and Poland, which had begun in February 1970, had resulted in a treaty.[66] Five issues had divided Poland and the FRG: the inviolability of the Oder-Neiße line, the expulsions of Germans from Poland after the war, the status of those of German origin still in Poland, the status of economic links, and diplomatic relations between the two states. The Warsaw Treaty of December 1970 confirmed the first, remained vague on the second and third (although it did call for more emigration), and voiced encouragement for expanding the fourth and fifth.[67] As mentioned earlier, neither the Communist regime in Poland nor the Soviets could view this treaty as an unmitigated success. It posed an implicit challenge to the Soviet claim that the USSR was defending Poland's post-1945 frontier against German revanchism.[68] Taken together, the Moscow and Warsaw Treaties were the beginning of the end for that legitimating strategy. Moreover, while the treaty language was unambiguous in its affirmation of the existing borders, the future was less clear.[69]

Would this treaty remain in force if the two Germanies were to form some kind of a union, or if a peace treaty to World War II were ever to be written?

For the time being, however, the treaty was taken as an earnest of West German willingness to normalize relations with the Warsaw Pact. Brandt further strengthened this impression with his behavior in Warsaw following the signing ceremony. While in Poland, he paid a visit to a memorial for the victims of the Warsaw ghetto uprising. In a surprising and moving gesture of atonement, he fell to his knees on its steps. As his biographer Barbara Marshall aptly put it, "[T]his gesture captured the imagination of the world and did a great deal to restore respect for Germany. It singled Brandt out as a politician with a moral dimension which had been lacking in his predecessors." The graciousness of his gesture failed to impress the FRG domestic audience at the time. Contemporaneous opinion polls in the West German press showed that a majority disapproved of the gesture, providing a sobering measure of the uphill public relations battle facing the West German leader.[70]

Henry Kissinger believed that Brandt's visit to Warsaw, like that to Erfurt, had unintended but serious consequences. Kissinger argued in his memoirs that the Polish leader at the time, Władisław Gomułka, hoped to use the public relations boost that Brandt's visit had provided to take unpopular measures to cure economic woes. Only a week after Brandt departed, Gomułka raised the price of meat on 13 December (shortly before Christmas in a country with a strong Catholic tradition) and carried out other similarly ill-advised moves. These moves provoked rioting and eventually led to the replacement of Gomułka by Edward Gierek on 20 December.[71] Kissinger's view is controversial.[72] However, the accuracy of Kissinger's reconstruction is less important than the fact that he believed in it. In other words, he felt confirmed in his view that Brandt's presence could produce a chain reaction leading to risky outbursts of public sentiment. This view meant that he had little enthusiasm for allowing Brandt to fly solo as he reshaped relations with the East. Kissinger felt that he was not alone in this worry; as he recalled, even Zhou En-lai "shared the view of several of West Germany's allies that Chancellor Willy Brandt's Ostpolitik . . . contained the risk that what started as gestures of reconciliation would turn into a freewheeling German nationalism that might demoralize Europe."[73]

The Campaign against Ulbricht Gathers Momentum

Brandt's initiatives were not the only ones causing concern. Although the two superpowers did not have similar relations with their German allies, they did have similar fears about them. Kissinger worried about the risks inherent in Brandt's initiatives. Brezhnev worried similarly about Ulbricht. The ever-eager Erich Honecker was wise enough to take advantage of Brezhnev's uneasiness. The Honecker faction intensified its campaign against Ulbricht in 1971 by playing up the perceived perils of Ulbricht's course of action. In particular, a unified show of defiance occurred in the wake of the fourteenth meeting of the Central Committee of the SED in early December 1970.

The controversy centered on Ulbricht's closing remarks at the fourteenth meeting.[74] Ulbricht had once again made impolite references to base motives for cooperating with the Soviets (such as to gain raw materials). He had also asked whether, in the wake of the Moscow and Warsaw Treaties, it was not "time to sign a treaty to secure the peace in Europe."[75] References to a "peace treaty" were by this time taboo in socialist parlance. They drew attention to the ongoing lack of a peace treaty to World War II, the negotiation of which would reopen precisely those old controversies over borders that the Moscow and Warsaw Treaties were designed to resolve.

In response to his closing remarks, Ulbricht received a surprising series of letters and notes from members of the Politburo. These missives, the first unmistakable written expressions of opposition to Ulbricht, represent a kind of write-in campaign, which had as its goal the prevention of publication of Ulbricht's closing remarks. The fact that all of the letters that bear dates share the same one—17 December 1970—and that the undated ones appear to have been sent on that day as well show that they were part of a coordinated action. Some of the letters, such as Paul Verner's, were quite lengthy. Verner complained that Ulbricht did not take account of the Politburo's report of 8 September 1970, which had pointed out flaws in Ulbricht's management of the GDR's economy.[76] Hermann Axen, Kurt Hager, Walter Halbritter, Werner Lamberz, Horst Sindermann, Günter Mittag, and Albert Norden all repeated this criticism.[77] The fact that so many of the letters shared the same complaint shows that one of the prime motives of the Politburo in toppling Ulbricht was to seek an improvement in the GDR's economic performance, which, ironically, is what Ulbricht was seeking as well.

Axen's letter also complained that Ulbricht had not acknowledged remarks made by Stoph to the effect that the goals of the economic plan for 1970 were unrealistic.[78] Such a lack of acknowledgment on Ulbricht's part was hardly surprising, given that the goals were set under his leadership. Axen's letter also showed that there existed displeasure within the party about Ulbricht's penchant for bypassing the Politburo and seeking economic and technical advice from a hand-picked group of his own experts.[79] Ulbricht was reportedly fascinated by the idea that "scientific foresight" provided by scholars could allow the GDR to overcome its shortfalls.[80] In consulting with outside experts, Ulbricht excluded the Politburo; Axen's comments reflected bitterness at such bypassing.[81]

In response to this write-in campaign, Ulbricht capitulated. He decided that his closing remarks would not be published.[82] Still Honecker did not let the matter drop. He would later produce a condemnatory study called "On the

Correction to the Economic Policies of Walter Ulbricht at the 14th Meeting of the Central Committee of the SED." This 26-page, single-spaced document offered a retroactive vilification of Ulbricht's policies, charging him personally with "arrogance in relation to the Soviet Union."[83] It specifically listed as a grievous error his habit of "referring to the GDR and its experiences as a model at every opportunity."[84] Ulbricht's drive to increase the technological modernity of GDR industry received the blame both for the shortage of consumer items in East Germany and for the GDR's indebtedness to the FRG. In short, Honecker skillfully cast Ulbricht in the role of scapegoat and deftly excluded the party from the circle of those deserving blame for the economic mismanagement of the GDR.

The Second Bahr-Kohl Meeting, 23 December 1970

Given all of these major developments, it is perhaps unsurprising that the second meeting between Bahr and Kohl, on 23 December 1970, achieved nothing of substance. A contentious one-on-one meeting between the two preceded the official round. In it, Bahr complained that it was completely incomprehensible to him why Kohl refused to give him some kind of telephone contact number. Kohl justified this by saying that telephone lines were not secure enough for their conversations. Bahr seized upon this remark to voice a threat that revealed FRG awareness of SED motives. First, he used Kohl's comment about telephone lines to segue into a complaint that the installation of various German-German telephone connections, which had been agreed upon in April 1970, had not been realized.[85] Particularly painful was the situation in Berlin; by 1971, all telephone connections between the two halves of the city had been cut off for eighteen years.[86] According to Kohl's summary of the conversation, Bahr said that this breach of trust was causing the FRG to wonder if the GDR lived up to the treaties it signed. If it did not, then "the payment of the promised DM 30 million would not occur."[87] This was a rare instance of the FRG openly saying it would withhold one of the GDR's main desiderata, namely, Western currency. The threat suggests that Bahr valued hard currency as a weapon that could force SED minds to concentrate. Kohl avoided replying by saying that although he bore no responsibility for telecommunications issues, there could be no doubt that the GDR lived up to its contractual obligations.

In the official meeting, the two basically repeated positions established at their previous encounter. Kohl made it clear that the aim of the GDR was to discuss a transit accord with West Germany in exchange for a decrease in the representation of the FRG in West Berlin.[88] Now it was Bahr's turn to be evasive; he responded that he could not discuss transit until the four-power talks concluded.[89] Exasperated, Kohl argued that a decrease in the "federal presence" of West Germany in West Berlin would help to build a bridge between the two Germanies. Hence, he did not understand "why you do not want to walk this bridge."[90] As 1970 came to a close, the German-German conversation seemed to be stalling almost as soon as it had started.

"The Atomic Bomb Is Hanging Over the Negotiating Table": The Superpowers Increase Their Role in German-German Talks

Recognizing a logjam in the making, both superpowers took steps in early 1971 to expedite German-German talks. Falin and the Soviet deputy foreign minister Vladimir Semenov pressured the GDR deputy foreign minister, Ewald Moldt, when he visited Moscow on 6–7 January 1971. The two Soviet officials made clear to the SED that it should not block progress by demanding concessions from the Brandt government.[91] Four days later, Gromyko reemphasized the need for progress in his own conversation with GDR foreign minister Otto Winzer, who was also in Moscow. Falin attended this Gromyko-Winzer meeting as well and told both men about a recent conversation with Bahr. According to Falin, Bahr had complained that the Americans showed little interest in making progress in the four-power talks on Berlin.[92] However, Bahr reportedly found the most important problem facing him was not the lack of American interest but rather the lack of East German interest in progress.[93] Bahr even hinted that, were German-German talks to fail, the Brandt government could be forced to leave office. Such a prospect worried the Soviets because it would endanger the ratification prospects of the Moscow and Warsaw Treaties. In order to make progress, the FRG was in fact willing to give up some aspects of "federal presence" in West Berlin, precisely what Kohl had been seeking. These aspects included meetings of the Bundestag and Bundesrat as well as official appearances in the former capital of the federal president and chancellor.

In response to this sustained Soviet pressure to make progress, Winzer tried to make clear the concerns of the SED about its talks with Bonn. He specifically stated that the party's goal was to avoid the spectacle of having a German-German accord on transit become a mere appendage to a four-power agreement—which would in fact happen later in the year. Such an outcome, he felt, would damage the authority of the GDR, by which he seemed to mean that it would carry the unfortunate (and regrettably correct) implication that the GDR's foreign policy was merely a corollary to that of the Soviet Union instead of that of a sovereign state. The SED hoped instead that the German-German accord would stand on its own and that the Soviet Union, in its dealings with the three Western powers, would merely take official note of it.[94] In reply, Gromyko did not respond directly to Winzer's concerns but instead emphasized that ratification of the Moscow and Warsaw treaties was currently the Soviets' most important goal and that all efforts were needed to make sure that this happened as soon as possible.[95]

That ratification of the treaty with the FRG should be the Soviet's top foreign policy goal, a statement that Gromyko and others would repeat often, remained puzzling to the West. As Kissinger remarked in 1994, "That the Soviets should place such emphasis on West Germany's recognition of the borders established by Stalin in fact indicated weakness and insecurity. The Federal Republic, a rump state, was on the face of it in no position to challenge a nuclear super-power."[96] Nonetheless, documents make clear that the Soviets did indeed place great emphasis on West Germany's recognition of existing borders. Also on the minds of the Soviets at this time, although Gromyko did not mention them directly during this visit, were relations with China. Moscow had offered to sign a nonaggression pact with the Chinese in January 1971. Peking had rejected this proposal.[97] Then, in February, the Soviets tried again, by inviting the Chinese to begin consultations over possible joint action to support the people of Indochina against American aggression; but again they were rebuffed.[98]

Falin took advantage of an informal conversation with the departing East German guests on the way to the Moscow airport after the meeting to make the Soviet point once again. Falin told Kohl that he and Gromyko believed that the SED was interpreting the notion of "full legal recognition" too narrowly. Falin suggested that some aspects of the Moscow Treaty actually *implied* recognition of the GDR (presumably a reason for the SED to be interested in creating conditions conducive to its ratification).[99] Falin suggested that rather than seeking a complete FRG withdrawal from West Berlin, East Berlin should specifically seek a reduction of the FRG's *political* presence. This meant that the SED should be more tolerant of nonpolitical forms of representation, such as economic and cultural institutions. The Soviets were also of the opinion that meetings between Bahr and Kohl should occur with greater frequency and last longer. The implication seemed to be that the SED should see its way clear to making progress in the German-German talks out of Soviet concern for the future of the two treaties.

The conduct of the next Bahr-Kohl meeting indicated that Kohl had taken Falin's and Gromyko's suggestions to heart. At a relatively short meeting on 15 January 1971, the first to take place in Bonn, Kohl called for a reduction of the *political* presence of the FRG in West Berlin, as opposed to his previous calls for reduction of the *federal* presence, a more inclusive term. He hinted that the GDR would be willing to make progress on a transit agreement in exchange.[100] According to Kohl, Bahr responded that he now realized that the GDR was indeed willing to make progress on a transit agreement.[101] Bahr and Kohl also seem to have reached some agreement over their earlier dispute as to whether the GDR was living up to the terms of the postal treaty, because Bahr thanked Kohl and indicated that he would have the "remaining DM 30 million" paid to East Berlin.[102] According to Kohl, the lunch that ended the meeting was characterized by a "relaxed" mood.[103] In short, following the suggestions of the Soviets, Kohl's remarks interjected a note of hopefulness into the German-German talks. Bahr's personal summary for Willy Brandt noted that SED willingness to talk not only about transit but about other issues represented a significant change, one that the FRG should not let pass.[104]

Kissinger Decides to Involve Himself Personally

This pressure on the East Germans shows just how much the Soviet attitude had shifted between 1970 and 1971. Before, the Soviets had insisted that the two Germanies take a "pause for reflection"; now, Moscow was eager for the two to make progress. In his memoirs, Kissinger recollected that he took particular note of this shift at the time it was happening. He found that Moscow "was hinting at a readiness to move on Soviet guarantees of access and improvement in life in Berlin" and thought that "on this basis a serious negotiation was possible."[105] Because of this, Kissinger decided to get personally involved in the Berlin talks.[106] Although he remained geographically removed, he became intellectually involved, conducting his secret diplomacy via conversations with Dobrynin in Washington and Rush in Bonn. Hence, at exactly the same time the Soviets were promoting progress in the German-German and Berlin talks, the United States began actively trying to spur progress as well. In particular, Kissinger told Dobrynin on 9 January that his main interest was twofold. He wanted improved access to West Berlin, but equally important were Soviet guarantees of the improvements, so that the United States did not have to "depend on the goodwill of the East German regime," against which it had little leverage.[107] Kissinger also decided that he should conduct the Berlin and SALT talks in tandem, playing one off the other as much as possible to achieve concessions. This view found expression in comments that Rush, Kissinger's voice in Bonn, made to Abrasimov in their conversation of 18 January. On that occasion, Rush made it unmistakably clear that it was "not possible to separate the Berlin question from other issues that influenced the relations between our states," such as the SALT talks and the efforts to establish a European-wide conference on security.[108]

Politburo Infighting

Just as both superpowers began hoping for more progress in the German-German talks, however, the SED Politburo became less and less capable of achieving such progress. Instead, its internal divisions grew worse. Opposition to Ulbricht reached a new height in January 1971. The "write-in campaign"

Honecker out in front: Erich Honecker congratulates the Soviet ambassador to the GDR, Pjotr Abrasimov, on the occasion of Abrasimov's return to Moscow in September 1971. Honecker, with the help of Abrasimov and Willi Stoph (left) had succeeded by this point in pushing Walter Ulbricht (rear center) completely to the background. (Signatur K 0913/30 N, Bundesarchiv, Koblenz)

against him had been an internal affair; now, however, Honecker took a calculated risk and decided to begin waging a battle external to the Politburo as well. He appealed openly to the Soviets to get involved in the internecine SED power struggle. Hence, the increased involvement of the Soviets occurred by invitation as well as by their own inclination.

In an interview in 1990, Honecker innocently claimed that "it was not as if there was an inner-party putsch . . . or as if someone put together a faction . . . and then surprisingly forced a resignation."[109] Yet SED documents show that this is exactly what happened. Honecker and twelve other Politburo members—in other words, a faction—sent an unprecedented letter to Brezhnev on 21 January 1971.[110] Axen recollected in his memoirs that Honecker organized the letter with the support of at least one prominent Soviet representative, namely, Ambassador Abrasimov.[111]

The letter detailed a series of grievances about Ulbricht. It accused him of opposing Politburo decisions and complained that he had an unfortunate tendency to propose "pseudo-scientific" theories, which was a reference to his inclination to take advice from nonparty experts.[112] It pointed out that his closing remarks to the fourteenth plenary session had contradicted party decisions. In his conduct of relations with the FRG, it accused Ulbricht of following "a personal line"—a condemnatory term implying that one was not following the party line—and that this stubbornness was endangering the conduct of negotiations with the West Germans as agreed upon with Moscow.[113] Moreover, it had become more and more difficult to deal with him personally; in recent months, the letter alleged, his "already quite difficult character" had expressed itself in a new level of rudeness toward his colleagues.[114] Indeed, it charged, Ulbricht seemed to believe in his own infallibility and saw himself "on a level with Marx, Engels, and Lenin."[115] The Honecker faction's letter ended with a dramatically direct plea. It requested that Brezhnev try to convince Ulbricht to resign of his own accord.[116]

A Lull in Both Sets of Talks in Germany

Given the extent of inner turmoil, it is not surprising that the next Kohl-Bahr meeting, five days after the letter to Brezhnev was mailed, once again made little progress. The Politburo was preoccupied with its own internal bloodletting. Kohl did once again emphasize that the GDR was offering a "golden bridge" to the West through its willingness to talk and wished the FRG would show more appreciation of this.[117] Bahr responded that Kohl needed to understand that even if the GDR were to offer Bahr a dream treaty with every single clause the FRG wanted, he could not accept it without the agreement of the Western occupying powers.[118] In his one-on-one conversation with Kohl at the same meeting, Bahr further emphasized that the West German rate of progress was limited above all by the Americans. In fact, according to Kohl, Bahr foresaw a lull in both the German-German and the Berlin talks, because Kissinger needed time to get himself up to speed on both, now that he was personally involved. Until he did so, Bahr expected little progress in the quadripartite negotiations, at least during the next month.[119] Bahr's expectations were fulfilled; both the Bahr-Kohl and the Berlin talks went into a kind of holding pattern.

Kissinger, in a conversation with Rush, expressed worry that too little progress in German-German rapprochement could perhaps be as dangerous as too much. "If the stalemate proved too protracted, Brandt might seek to break out on his own, blaming us for Germany's unfulfilled national aspirations and perhaps charting a new and far more independent national course," Kissinger remarked. Rush revealed the extent of U.S. worries at this time, when he asked Kissinger whether the country "could handle a Berlin crisis and its accompanying German domestic uproar while the war in Vietnam was going on."[120]

However, there is no evidence available in the East German documentation that the West Germans were in fact hatching the kind of nationalist plot of which Rush suspected them. Rather, Bahr at this time was continually remarking to the East Germans that his hands were tied by the cautious nature of the Western powers. There are no signs of Bahr suggesting to Kohl that, since the West was hesitating, the two Germanies might as well strike out on their own.

Even had Bahr made such a proposal, in the spring of 1971 it would not have been clear who on the East German side would have responded. Ulbricht was still nominally in charge, despite the difficulties that the Honecker faction was causing. The relatively uneventful fifteenth plenary session of the SED Central Committee on 28 January, which coincided with Brandt's equivalent of a "State of the Union" address, produced no changes in the SED top leadership.[121] Shortly thereafter, Ulbricht left for the Soviet Union, where he spent most of February and half of March.[122]

In the midst of the uncertainty in the SED Politburo, the Soviets seem to have undermined the GDR with regard to Berlin. In his talks with Gromyko at the beginning of January, East German foreign minister Winzer had made clear that the GDR hoped for a free-standing German-German accord on transit as a means of asserting East German sovereignty. This was hardly an arrogant request, considering that the Soviets had told the three Western powers that just such an accord was necessary. In other words, the USSR maintained in the quadripartite talks that it would not address an issue—that is, transit—that fell into the competency of another sovereign state—that is, the GDR. According to Kissinger's memoirs, however, Dobrynin overturned this stance in early 1971. The United States wanted not only improved transit rights but, crucially, *Soviet* instead of *GDR* guarantees of those improvements. On 10 February, Dobrynin essentially acceded. He indicated to Kissinger that the Soviets would be willing to adopt a face-saving construction: they would, as part of the quadripartite accord, include a Soviet statement of the East German view. In other words, they were offering to include discussion of transit provisions in the four-power agreement, something that they had hitherto refused. By inserting such a statement in the form of a summary of East German interests, the Soviets presumably hoped to massage SED egos. Kissinger found that this suggestion had promise but needed to be investigated further.[123] Perhaps the Soviets offered this concern at this time because receipt of the Honecker faction letter had increased their worry about the ability of the GDR to manage the delicate matter of transit rights.

With Ulbricht on an extended stay in the USSR and a strong faction within the Politburo at home seeking his dismissal, the SED leadership was clearly in a fragile state. Yet it seems that Brezhnev did not act immediately on the Honecker clique's request of 21 January to exert pressure on Ulbricht to resign. In a letter Ulbricht wrote to Brezhnev at the end of his visit, on 12 March 1971, he thanked the Soviet leader for granting him and his wife their time at a spa and asked whether it would not be advisable to publish word "of our friendly conversation."[124] A brief article noting that Ulbricht and Brezhnev had spoken subsequently appeared on the first page of the 15 March issue of *Pravda*, indicating that Ulbricht was still in favor.[125] In short, the letter and article hardly suggest that Ulbricht had received the kind of stern talking-to that the Honecker faction had hoped for.[126]

The Twenty-fourth Party Congress of the CPSU, March–April 1971

Brezhnev may not have acted on the Honecker faction's request immediately because he was involved in planning the twenty-fourth party congress of the Communist Party of the Soviet Union, held from 30 March to 9 April 1971. This congress was overshadowed by Soviet economic difficulties. As the Soviet ambassador to the United States at the time recalled, "[Moscow] knew that the country was in a difficult situation. The Soviet economy and living standards were stagnant."[127] Brezhnev made clear at the congress that he thought American capital and technology could be the answers to the economic problems plaguing the USSR.[128] This is an argument strikingly similar to that which Ulbricht had made vis-à-vis the FRG.

Kissinger, in his memoirs, particularly remembered this Soviet party congress for another reason, namely, the astonishingly hostile Chinese press campaign against the USSR that directly preceded it. As he recalled, "The Chinese showed what pinnacles of invective they were capable of when they meant business: They launched a fire-breathing verbal assault *on the Soviet Union* . . . Brezhnev was denounced as a 'renegade.'" Kissinger argued that the significance of this press campaign was its startling implication that the USSR "had replaced [the United States] as the principal enemy of Peking."[129] Soon, on his own visit to China few months later, he would discover that the Chinese leadership had built underground shelters in Peking because of their anxiety about the Soviet troops along the Chinese border.[130] Kissinger saw Chinese receptiveness toward improved U.S.-Chinese relations as the result of growing concern about the USSR. The Chinese reinforced this implication with a small but significant gesture on 6 April when they invited a U.S. Ping-Pong team to visit and compete in China; the team arrived eight days later.

In his remarks at this party congress, Brezhnev expressed regret over the sorry state of Sino-Soviet affairs but maintained a hostile stance toward the Chinese leadership.[131] A Soviet assessment of the Chinese press attack, provided to the SED, found that the attack demonstrated "irreconcilable hostility" and served as an "encouragement of American aggression."[132] The informational material for the party congress, distributed to the heads of Warsaw Pact delegations in attendance in Moscow, painted an even grimmer picture. It reported a threatening comment made by the Chinese: that " 'the atomic bomb' is hanging over the Chinese-Soviet negotiating table."[133]

Exit Ulbricht

Leaders of the SED attended this party congress in Moscow personally. Exactly who would travel with the delegation had been a matter of controversy. The East Berlin Politburo under Honecker's chairmanship had tried to prevent Ulbricht from joining the delegation. It had decided that Ulbricht's health would not permit him to travel and instructed him to revoke his decision to be part of this delegation.[134] Ulbricht ignored this pronouncement, however, and journeyed to Moscow nonetheless, where his arrival (as well as that of other delegation members) received a first-page mention in *Pravda*.[135] He even delivered a speech.[136] His personal papers contain his handwritten notes from the congress, including one emphasizing "the danger of a new world war," perhaps a reference to the kind of Sino-Soviet tension described above.[137] His attendance at this conference turned out to be his last visit to Moscow as head of the SED, because he "resigned" a month later, on 3 May 1971.

Why did Ulbricht abandon office? Unfortunately, the East German documentary record yields little information about precisely what happened between Ulbricht's attendance at the Moscow congress in late March and early April and his appearance at the sixteenth plenary session of the SED Central Committee on 3 May, at which he formally requested to be relieved of his duties.[138] There does exist a letter from the entire Politburo to Brezhnev, thanking him for his recent consultation with Ulbricht (but not revealing its result).[139] The letter is dated 27 April. There also exists a note in a Politburo file from the same date that mentions an Ulbricht-Brezhnev conversation and thanks Brezhnev as well.[140] Hence a decisive Brezhnev-Ulbricht conversation must have taken place sometime before the end of April.[141] The 13 April issue of *Pravda* noted that Brezhnev and Ulbricht had met the day before; perhaps that was the fateful conversation.[142]

Ulbricht's contemporaries have shed some light on what may have transpired. Herman Axen recollected that Brezhnev talked to Ulbricht for over five hours about the latter's leaving office. Former SED archivist Monika Kaiser has argued that the desire to resign was Ulbricht's; however, given the unhappy state of relations between Brezhnev and Ulbricht by the spring of 1971, it is hard to imagine that Brezhnev would spend so many hours convincing Ulbricht not to go.[143] In addition to these hints of some kind of decisive Brezhnev-Ulbricht conversation, Markus Wolf has recounted that a dramatic showdown between Honecker and Ulbricht also occurred back on East German soil. Wolf did not say when, but he recalled that Honecker drove out to Ulbricht's summer house in on Lake Dölln and took along armed bodyguards. Honecker ordered guards posted at all doors and gates and gave instructions that all connections to the outside world should be cut off. According to Wolf, Honecker managed by these and other means to convince Ulbricht of the need to resign.[144]

Kaiser hypothesized that Ulbricht was "without a doubt" intending to resign.[145] However, the SED documents and sequence of events described above suggest that doubt is warranted. The continuing efforts of the Honecker faction in 1970 and 1971 to remove Ulbricht suggest an unwillingness on his part to relinquish power. The need for lengthy conversations with both Brezhnev and Honecker in the spring of 1971 further implies reluctance on the part of the long-term SED leader. Even after his dismissal, Ulbricht tried to play as active a role as possible in East German politics, despite the opposition of Honecker.[146]

As a consequence, the conclusions reached in previous historiography about the ouster of Ulbricht require reassessment. Pre-1989 works usually cited Ulbricht's opposition to Ostpolitik as a prime factor in his fall from power.[147] (A notable exception is James McAdams, who offered a more differentiated picture of Ulbricht.) Post-1989 works have either maintained this view or, in the case of Kaiser and Jochen Stelkens, claimed the exact opposite—namely, that it was Ulbricht's fervor for Ostpolitik that worried the Soviets.[148]

Yet these questions are not the most informative way to examine the transition from Ulbricht to Honecker, nor are they the best route to understanding the period that followed. Instead of asking which of the two men was more pro- or anti-Ostpolitik, it is more informative to look at the extent to which they were willing to follow Moscow's lead at all times, including sudden changes of course. As preceding chapters have shown, Moscow was at times less and at times more interested in having the GDR deal with the West; the problem with Ulbricht was his unwillingness to subjugate himself immediately to all changes of Soviet opinion. He had his own goals. There are even hints that he was motivated by the notion of some kind of an economic confederation, which seemed to be a more mild version of the kind of political confederation that the GDR had sought in the first half of the Cold War.[149] Honecker, in contrast, seems mainly to have gained power by successfully convincing Moscow of his willingness to allow the CPSU to set the goals.[150] Egon Bahr sensed this at the time. After Ulbricht's ouster, he wrote to Kissinger that Honecker would prove to be "an easier partner" for Moscow.[151]

Perhaps the most convincing evidence that the "pro- or anti-Ostpolitik" question is irrelevant is that fact that, after assuming office, Honecker allowed the German-German talks simply to continue as before. In fact, it is impossible to tell from the negotiation files alone at what point Honecker took over. The transition caused neither practical nor ideological disruption to the talks that

Ulbricht had begun. To understand why, it is necessary to understand that the crucial criterion that had brought Honecker into power had not been his anti-Ostpolitik stance but rather his willingness to conform to Soviet desires. Viewed in this way, Honecker's willingness to continue negotiations that he had criticized no longer seems surprising. The Soviets were interested in having him do so, and that was the deciding factor.

In summary, by mid-1971 a complicated series of dependencies had been erected. The Soviets had themselves made the Berlin talks dependent upon German-German rapprochement. They had created this linkage by insisting that the crucial issue of transit from West Germany to West Berlin fell under the jurisdiction of the GDR. Obviously, any treaty bearing on the status of the island-city of West Berlin needed to address the issue of transit to that island; but, given that the Western powers had no diplomatic relations with the GDR, they could not negotiate with it on this key component of the would-be quadripartite accord—the West Germans had to do so in their stead. Thus, in order for the Berlin talks to move forward (and make ratification a possibility), the two Germanies had to resolve transit questions between themselves. The necessity for West German involvement dovetailed neatly with Brandt and Bahr's own interest in negotiating with the East on a broad range of issues in the hope of normalizing relations. Meanwhile, to inspire the Soviets into making progress over Berlin, the West in turn linked the ratification of the Moscow and Warsaw Treaties to the Berlin talks. So, it was with a new complexity but also with both superpowers in favor of progress and a new head of the SED in place that negotiation proceeded, in the second half of 1971, to produce results at last.

Achieving Initial Aims in 1971–1972:
The Quadripartite Agreement, the
Transit Accord, and the Traffic Treaty

five

Erich Honecker received official confirmation of his tenure as top man at the SED's eighth party congress in June 1971. His ouster of Ulbricht could have been an extremely disruptive event, because it represented the first change ever in East German leadership. To minimize the sense of upheaval, Honecker tried to portray an image of a friendly handover. Rather than one large picture of the new leader, the party newspaper *Neues Deutschland* had carried equal-size photos of Ulbricht and Honecker when Ulbricht announced his "resignation."[1] Ulbricht was also spared the fate of becoming an unperson. Instead, he received the honorific title of "Chairman of the SED." The party under Honecker's new leadership took pains to project the image of a smooth transition and conceal the contentious events that had transpired to oust Ulbricht. As it turned out, the images of continuity were borne out by the reality of Honecker's rule. Internally, he ran the party in much the same fashion as his dictatorial predecessor.[2] Externally, he continued the contacts with the West that Ulbricht had begun.

Honecker did make some changes, however—including a deadly decision kept secret from the FRG at the time. The SED under his leadership decided to install lethal shrapnel mines along its Western border.[3] These were far more brutal than simple mines because they expelled hundreds of steel projectiles when triggered.[4] Their covert installation contrasted sadly with the hope for a more humane future in German-German relations that negotiations seemed to promise.

On top of the transition in East Germany, the international political context changed significantly in the summer of 1971 as well. The most dramatic alteration came as a result of American president Richard Nixon's surprise announcement on 15 July 1971 of Kissinger's visit to China. This U.S. initiative altered the Cold War geopolitical landscape in a single stroke.[5] Then, just one month later, Nixon showed again that he had no hesitation about taking risky steps without consulting U.S. allies by announcing that he would suspend the convertibility of the dollar to gold. This so-called "Nixon Shock" unnerved world markets in general and Western allies in particular.[6]

In part despite and in part because of these changes, the ongoing negotiations—the German-German talks and the quadripartite or Berlin talks—finally yielded results in late 1971 and 1972. As before, the two sets of negotiations mutually influenced each other and interacted increasingly with ongoing superpower talks on arms control as well. Hence, an understanding of the results of German-German negotiations, namely the Transit Agreement and the Traffic Treaty, requires a grasp not only of the result of the Berlin talks—that is, the Quadripartite Agreement—but also the progress made in the Strategic Arms Limitation Talks (SALT).

The Quadripartite Agreement:
Capitalizing on Soviet Eagerness

In mid-1971, the quadripartite negotiations managed to escape from the doldrums in which they had languished throughout 1970.[7] This was due not least to the development, as detailed in Chapter 4, of new Soviet and U.S. interest in expediting the talks. By mid-1971, Kissinger sensed willingness on the part of the Soviets to retreat from their insistence that only East Germany could discuss issues of transit to West Berlin.[8] Seeking to capitalize on it, the Western powers submitted a draft agreement to the Soviets on 5 February. The Western draft directly addressed issues of transit, which the Soviets had previously insisted were the exclusive domain of the GDR. The draft proposed a face-saving formulation: the Soviets would enter into agreements on transit only "after consultation thereon with the Government of the German Democratic Republic," implying that GDR approval was necessary in advance.[9] This served essentially as a sop to East Berlin's sensitivity about recognition of their jurisdiction over transit routes. The Western draft further accommodated the GDR by stating that East Germany should "expect to receive from the Federal Republic of Germany an appropriate compensation for the costs related to surface traffic between the Western sectors and the Federal Republic of Germany in the form of an annual lump sum to be agreed upon between their authorities."[10] In the first meeting following the handover of this draft, the Soviet ambassador remarked upon it favorably.[11]

The extent of Soviet optimism was limited, however. In the next official meeting, Abrasimov reemphasized the sovereignty of the GDR. He complained that some components of the Western draft, particularly the rather unsettling provisions that would allow sealed cargo containers to cross GDR territory without inspection, "belittled the legitimate interests and sovereign rights of the GDR."[12] For their part, the Western allies, headed by the British, called upon the Soviets to give a name to the area under discussion rather than merely using the term "Central Europe," a concept that they considered to be too vague.[13] In short, it seemed in early 1971 as if there might be the potential for progress in the Berlin talks, but the terrain ahead clearly would be difficult to maneuver. In light of this, the Western allies decided to try to simplify their negotiating stance somewhat, by circumscribing their German ally's room to maneuver.

Bahr Gets "Muzzled" in March 1971

The allies did so just as that ally was in fact trying to broaden its authority. In February 1971, Bahr had tried to widen the topics he could negotiate with the GDR. He told Kohl that the FRG wanted to discuss both a transit treaty and fundamental issues of German-German relations with the GDR simultaneously.[14] This fit awkwardly with the GDR interests as laid out in Kohl's directive from the SED Politburo; following the guidance given by Gromyko, the SED directive instructed Kohl to pursue a transit accord as his highest priority. The Soviets wanted this accord as quickly as possible to improve the chances that the Moscow and Warsaw Treaties would be ratified. Kohl was told to hinder the FRG's distracting attempts to discuss broader issues of German-German relations.[15] Hence, when Bahr reiterated many of the original "Twenty Points" presented by Willy Brandt to Willi Stoph at Kassel as a basis for some kind of basic treaty between the two Germanies, Kohl tried to shift the discussion back to transit.[16] The three Western powers unintentionally came to Kohl's aid at this point by sharply circumscribing Bahr's room to maneuver.

Kohl found out about this turn of events in a private conversation with Bahr in March 1971 which was bugged by the Stasi.[17] Bahr told Kohl that he found himself in "a difficult position" and that he had decided to be "totally open about it." Bahr explained that he had been summoned to an audience at midnight the night before with representatives of the Western powers. "They showed up in force, all three ambassadors personally, with all three deputies," he recollected.[18] The purpose of the summons was to veto any attempts by Bahr to negotiate a transit agreement with the East Germans. In their opinion, the issue of transit was now "at the heart of the four-power negotiations" and hence they wanted Bahr to distance himself from any independent initiatives while they dealt with the Soviets.[19] In other words, the Western powers had realized that the transit agreement was their point of greatest leverage against the Soviet Union. Bahr added that the three allies seemed unsettled by Kohl and Bahr's one-on-one conversations, which inspired in them a feeling of "mistrust." Despite this, Bahr emphasized that he personally valued his one-on-one conversations with Kohl, "even if they are not really private conversations"—perhaps a reference to the fact that he suspected he was under Stasi surveillance.[20]

In an interview in 1996, Bahr recollected that this midnight summons was the only time the three Western powers had directly intervened in the German-German talks.[21] He admitted, "I had wanted to speed things up." According to Bahr, the three powers sensed this and thought, "Good God, he will destroy our negotiating position with regard to the Russians, if he's already talking about transit!"[22] Kissinger in particular praised Kenneth Rush for having "curbed Bahr's impatience."[23]

The Soviets became aware of the American worries about West German overeagerness. At the end of May, almost two months after the Allies had "muzzled" Bahr and forced the German-German talks into a holding pattern, Moscow informed East Berlin, "The Western Powers react again and again to the talks between the delegations of the FRG and GDR with great nervousness. They are unsure about what is really going on." The talks with Bahr therefore offered an advantage, the Soviets thought, in that they provided incentive for the Western allies to keep moving in their own talks. While it was clear that Brandt and Bahr were working in cooperation with the United States, it was also obvious to the USSR that the Americans feared the two Germans could "step out of line."[24] In short, both superpowers realized they could use their opponent's worry about their respective German partner to gain leverage in the four-power talks.

The United States attempted to limit Moscow's ability to gain leverage in this manner by issuing a kind of ultimatum. On 9 March 1971, the day after the three Western powers had summoned Bahr at midnight, another four-power meeting took place.[25] Rush described the "muzzling" of Bahr to the Soviets by announcing that the Western powers had reached an "arrangement" with the West Germans. Bahr could not negotiate on issues of transit to Berlin as long as there was no agreement between the four powers on the topic. Rush concluded by saying that the future of the talks depended on the Russian reaction.[26] Put bluntly, Rush had given Abrasimov an ultimatum: you have to deal with us on the subject of transit to Berlin; you cannot do so by proxy via the Germanies.

According to his memoirs, Kissinger seconded Rush in a conversation of his own with Dobrynin on 22 March. Kissinger made clear to Dobrynin what he thought were the key issues in the Berlin talks: the West sought Soviet acknowledgment of West Berlin's ties to the FRG and the latter's right to represent the former abroad; a guarantee that surface transit, whether civilian or military, could pass unhindered; a commitment to improve access between the two halves of the city; and willingness to establish a Soviet consulate in West Berlin in a separate accord (so that the Soviets could not claim that problems with the consulate were cause for negating the rest of the quadripartite accord).[27]

The Response of the SED and the Soviets

The SED directive for the first Kohl-Bahr meeting after the Allies had placed restrictions on Bahr, written on 15 March, lamented the FRG's lack of backbone and its willingness to submit to the pressure of the Western powers. This lament was ironic, given that nearly all of Kohl's directives began with the instruction that he was to follow the "line" agreed upon with Gromyko or some other Soviet representative. Kohl's most recent directive suggested that he should continue to pursue the goal of a transit accord despite the restrictions on Bahr. He should try to do so covertly, under the guise of seeking a "traffic treaty," a euphemism for an accord on the small amount of German-German traffic other than that traveling to Berlin.[28]

For their part, the Soviets produced a draft four-power treaty of their own and handed it to the three Western powers on 26 March. This draft employed a face-saving formulation with regard to the GDR. It stated unequivocally that the GDR expected a lump-sum payment for giving away transit rights and specified that this sum should be enough "to cover in full the costs incurred to the GDR because of transit, including the upkeep of the roadways."[29] The Soviet draft also avoided using the name "Berlin" and instead referred to "the area whose situation is under negotiation by its representatives."[30] In handing over the Soviet version, Ambassador Abrasimov heaped praise upon it. He remarked that it contained "all of the main components that the final agreement would contain" and left no important issue untouched.[31] Unsurprisingly, the Western allies were less enthusiastic and indicated that they needed time to look over the draft.

In the meantime, the German-German talks had to avoid any issues of substance until the quadripartite talks reached a conclusion; the conversation between the Germanies temporarily became an exercise in point-scoring. For example, on 31 March, Bahr quoted from a study written years ago by a young

Michael Kohl. Kohl had referred to the Koreas and the Germanies as two states in a common nation.[32] Unfortunately for Kohl, this was a very unfashionable notion in 1971; now the SED claimed that East Germany was not merely a separate state but rather a separate nation. Kohl had to distance himself as best he could from his own earlier writing.

Bahr also challenged Kohl on the subject of "border incidents" in early April. Although Bahr did not use names, it seems he was referring to the case of eighteen-year-old Klaus Seifert, who had fled the GDR on the evening of 8 April. Seifert had stepped on a mine, which obliterated his left foot. He still made his way to the border, where he collapsed and was found by a passing hunter. He died in a West German hospital a couple of weeks later.[33] Bahr, citing both bloody scenes and fires caused by GDR artillery on the border, lodged a protest and sought some kind of apology.[34] Kohl implied that the incidents had been provoked by the West and said that the only regret the GDR had was that the FRG refused to establish formal legal relations with the GDR.[35]

In short, the German-German conversations essentially became a forum for rhetorical dueling but made little progress for several months. At a meeting on 21 May, Bahr came close to saying outright that this was the case. Kohl reported that, in a private conversation with Bahr, the latter remarked that "the four-power negotiations must reach a conclusion first, before the GDR and the FRG can really get going."[36] What Bahr did not add was that he himself had become heavily involved in the quadripartite talks by the end of May, and that this change forced him to focus his energies primarily on that forum instead of on the German-German talks.

Kissinger Links Berlin to SALT

The months of April and May 1971 saw several important changes take place both inside and outside of negotiating rooms, all of which would affect progress inside. According to Kissinger's memoirs, the United States scored various breakthroughs in secret diplomacy in April. On 21 April, a message from the Chinese arrived, inviting President Nixon or a representative of his choosing to visit China. On 23 April, there was a minor but significant breakthrough in the SALT talks, as the Soviets agreed to talk about a limitation on offensive weapons at the same time as an ABM—that is, a defensive—agreement.[37] This was followed by Brezhnev's public announcement in early May that the Soviets would be interested in discussing a treaty on reducing conventional forces deployed in Europe.[38] The introduction of an "expert level" in the Berlin talks, in which specialists thrashed out details that then only needed approval at the ambassadorial level, helped to expedite matters as well. Finally, in May, Bahr became part of the Bonn "Group of Three" (as mentioned previously), which began to tackle the outstanding issues of the Berlin talks in an expeditious fashion.[39]

The Group of Three, which remained a secret from not only Great Britain and France but even the U.S. State Department at the time, produced little in the way of formal documentation.[40] Kissinger repeatedly reminded his German ally to keep it that way.[41] Indeed, Bahr recalled that the agreements that the Group of Three reached would be presented by either the Soviet or the American side at the official level, often to the surprise of the British and French, to whom the formulations suddenly appeared "as if from a miracle of immaculate conception."[42]

By June 1971, the Soviets commented to the SED that the official level seemed to have become just for show. The Western powers were keeping the ambassadors " 'running in neutral' and limiting them to making general statements and eating lunch."[43] In contrast, talks at the secret level were quite productive.[44] Kissinger recounted in his memoirs that the Group of Three managed in the course of June to produce a more-or-less complete draft of what became the Quadripartite Agreement. Falin remembered in 1996 that the working cooperation was "very intensive . . . just the three of us, without translators or aides."[45] However, despite the substantial progress made in June, the formal signing did not take place until September. This delay was much to Brandt's dismay, who wanted a speedy resolution.[46] The wait was due to Kissinger. In his view, the Group of Three had succeeded a little too well. He felt that a Berlin agreement should not be announced too soon, because then it could no longer be used to put pressure on the Soviets to behave well in the wake of the China surprise that he would soon be springing. As a result, Kissinger slowed progress, because he wanted to capitalize on Soviet eagerness for a Berlin agreement to prevent protests in response to the upcoming announcement about his visit to China.[47]

Kissinger also wanted to force progress in the SALT negotiations.[48] The USSR had finally succumbed to U.S. pressure to agree to "simultaneity," that is, to discuss limitations on offensive weapons before, or along with, a defensive accord on ABMs.[49] In a May 1971 note to Erich Honecker, the Soviets informed him of this decision but also complained bitterly about the lack of American willingness to include all U.S. offensive weaponry in SALT, "regardless of whether these arms are on the national territory . . . [or] the oceans and seas or on the territory of third parties."[50] In other words, the United States was not willing to include forward-based systems (FBS) in their talks. As historian Jonathan Haslam has pointed out, the inclusion of such systems was anathema not only to the Pentagon but also to the European allies of the United States, and hence was politically untenable.[51]

Nixon and Kissinger were especially concerned that they, and not the official SALT negotiators under the lead of Gerard Smith, get credit for the "simultaneity" breakthrough. Kissinger, in a move recorded in his memoirs and masterfully criticized by Raymond Garthoff, delayed progress in the quadripartite talks out of pique, when the Soviets at one point bypassed Kissinger's back channel and dealt with the official SALT negotiators under Smith in Vienna. Kissinger feared greatly that the U.S. official negotiators would find out about his secret dealings.[52] To insure that the White House and not the official negotiators would receive credit for "simultaneity," Nixon himself announced the breakthrough at a 20 May press conference, the first of many 1971 surprises (followed by the China announcement in July and the "Nixon Shock" in August).[53] Kissinger considered the 20 May announcement one of three happy signs that the White House was in control of U.S. foreign policy. As he recollected, "three major initiatives were being negotiated of which the regular bureaucracy was ignorant: The May 20 SALT agreement, the Berlin negotiations, and the opening to China." He considered this ignorance highly desirable, even if it was "demeaning" to some of the bypassed bureaucrats.[54]

The Soviets tried to retreat on simultaneity somewhat following the 20 May public announcement, but Kissinger insisted on it. He had the Berlin agreement as his ace in the hole. As he put it, "The Soviets could not risk a crisis with us if they wanted the Berlin agreement concluded or the German treaties ratified. This linkage was never made explicit, but it was clearly reflected in the pace of our negotiations."[55] To make sure that the ace was not played too soon, Kissinger told Rush to slow progress in the Berlin talks until after 15 July (without telling Rush that that was to be the day on which the China visit would be announced).[56] One of the ways in which the delay was effected was by "recalling" Rush to Washington temporarily. Not only the Soviet but also the French ambassador expressed complete "astonishment" that Rush would absent himself from the Berlin talks for three weeks at a stretch "for no reason" just when they had reached such a productive phase.[57] Soviet willingness to put up with this behavior and accept concessions left no doubt in Kissinger's mind of how badly the Soviets wanted a Berlin accord. In July, Nixon announced the China visit. Bahr wrote to Kissinger via their secret channel that the Russians had reacted "emotionally" to the news.[58] Afterwards, the Berlin talks drew to a rapid close.

The Quadripartite Agreement of September 1971

The four ambassadors signed the Quadripartite Agreement on 3 September 1971.[59] Even though the treaty was about Berlin, it did not mention the city as a whole; rather, it used the vague geographical reference favored by the Soviets, referring to the city as "the relevant area." The treaty did mention the occupied sectors of the city, though, and specifically addressed the relationship of the Western sectors to the FRG. The Group of Three held the sectors "not to be a constituent part" of the FRG and not governed by it.[60] In addition, the treaty provided a legal basis for civilian transit from the Western sectors to West

The four ambassadors pose for photos after the signing of the Quadripartite Agreement on 3 September 1971. The signing took place in the American sector in West Berlin, in the building that had previously been used by the Allied Control Council. From left: British ambassador R. W. Jackling, Soviet ambassador Pjotr Abrasimov, U.S. ambassador Kenneth Rush, and French ambassador Jean Sauvagnargues. (Signatur ᴋ 0903/102 ɴ, Bundesarchiv, Koblenz)

Germany and vice versa; it was left up to the two Germanies to negotiate the details, and the treaty would not go into force until a transit agreement existed.[61] The Soviets, in return for the right to open a consulate in West Berlin and a decrease in activities of the FRG government in West Berlin, agreed that the FRG could represent West Berlin abroad. West Berliners could hold West German passports for foreign travel.[62] For their part, the Western powers recognized the GDR's de facto control of East Berlin and precluded any attempt to make West Berlin a more integral part of West Germany.

A bizarre coda to the close of treaty negotiations occurred when the SED produced its own German translation, which varied extensively from Bonn's version. Formulations in the East German version were much sharper than those in the Western draft. For example, where the Western translation referred to the laws of the FRG as "suspended" with regard to West Berlin, the East German document said that they were "no longer in force."[63] Discrepancies forced a postponement to the signing. According to Kissinger, French stubbornness provided a way out. The French ambassador did not join his allies in pressing for one single official German version, since he did not agree that German should be one of the official languages for a treaty about the divided Germany, negotiated in the former German capital, concerning German territory, whose execution would be largely left to Germans. As a result, a face-saving formulation was reached in which the Allies agreed that only the English, French, and Russian versions of the treaty were official.[64]

The Quadripartite Agreement must be judged a success. After its signing, it had the desired effect of making Berlin much less of a flashpoint than it had previously been.[65] Writing in 1974, historian Adam Ulam concluded that "the emotions the city had aroused in 1948, 1953, and 1961, when it stood as the symbol of the clash between the free and the Communist worlds, have now largely receded."[66] The agreement also created a positive climate for future European security measures such as Conference on Security and Cooperation in Europe (CSCE) and Mutual Balanced Force Reductions (MBFR).[67] Even such a staunch critic of Nixon and Kissinger as Seymour Hersh found the accord "remarkable." As he put it, "It provided a Soviet guarantee for unimpeded access from West Germany to West Berlin, and it gave West Berliners the right to visit East Germany and East Berlin. It also permitted West Berlin to retain its ties to the Federal Republic of Germany, including the right to travel on West German passports," while assuring the Soviets that Bonn would reduce its presence there.[68] Historian Peter Pulzer found that this accord showed that détente "could operate in a number of arenas—in South East Asia, in the Middle East, or in arms limitations. But unless it also operated in Germany . . . the remainder would be no more than a series of partial and peripheral deals."[69] Memory of the success of the Quadripartite Agreement lingered in the minds of specialists even until 1995, when negotiators in the Bosnian conflict used it as a template for the Dayton Accord.[70]

What were the motives of the Soviets in signing this agreement? As historian Keith Nelson has rightly observed, "Brezhnev wanted a Berlin agreement primarily because he wanted the Soviet–West German treaty of August 1970 ratified." Nelson erred, however, by saying that Kissinger's contact with Dobrynin on Berlin did not matter and that "China was not an appreciable factor in the bargaining."[71] Documents clearly show that once Kissinger decided to get personally involved, talks finally began to make substantial progress. He took advantage of constant Soviet concern about the threat of Sino-Soviet conflict. Another source of Soviet interest was the international political recognition of the Cold War status quo implied in the Four-Power Accord, which was precisely what the Soviets cherished about the Moscow Treaty. As Philip Zelikow and Condoleezza Rice have pointed out, the Quadripartite Agreement "served principally to help cement the partition of Germany."[72] A friendly visit by Brandt to

Brezhnev's summer house at Oreanda two weeks after the signing seemed to indicate West German acceptance of the newly enshrined reality.[73]

Diverging East German and Soviet Interests and the Transit Accord

Political scientist Peter Merkl has argued that the GDR's position was "intolerably worsened by the conclusion of the four-power agreements on Berlin."[74] Yet, upon closer examination, the story is not so one-sided. It bears remembering that the signing of the Four-Power Agreement did not put its terms into force. Before it could take effect, the two Germanies first had to reach a practical agreement over the details of transit. In other words, the two German states now held sway over the treaty. They began to talk in earnest in the second half of 1971.

The SED was quite keen to sign a transit treaty.[75] One of the reasons for this eagerness was financial. It hoped that such a treaty would allow it to "levy such fees and charges necessary to cover the costs of traffic of goods and people . . . through its sovereign territory."[76] Given that the citizens of East Germany would hardly be transiting across West Germany en masse, this provision would clearly be more profitable for the East than the West. The GDR estimated that, for the years 1972–75, the costs of providing transit ways would amount to around DM 160 to 200 million per annum.[77] The SED hoped to commit Bonn to paying this amount for each of those years in advance.[78] The party instructed Kohl to request payment in the form of a lump sum. Were this request to fail, then, as a negotiating tactic, he should say that the SED would take payment in a lump sum for 1972 only and then assess the actual charges for subsequent years on a year-by-year basis. To dissuade Bonn from pursuing this option, however, he should claim that the SED might decide to charge more retroactively for 1972 and on top of that it might additionally bill the FRG for the costs of assessing its costs.[79] For good measure, Kohl was also to make the daunting observation that the immense bureaucratic effort needed to assess costs would mean that the "improvements in travel and transit, as desired by the four powers, would probably not be achieved."[80]

The Western side was hesitant and foresaw several major hindrances. First and foremost was the question of the range of jurisdiction of an FRG-GDR treaty. Could it include West Berlin? Bahr hoped to provide regulation for both West Germany and West Berlin via two separate agreements. One would address traffic (that is, that between the two Germanies generally) and the other, which would serve as the needed corollary to the Quadripartite Agreement, would address transit (that is, to West Berlin).[81] The SED, insisting that West Berlin was not part of West Germany, argued that the latter agreement was a matter for direct talks between itself and the Senate of West Berlin (and talks had in fact already begun, addressing other, less controversial issues).[82] Yet another problem was the quarrel over the differing German translations of the Four-Power Agreement. Since the transit treaty was to serve as an extension thereof, it was essential that the two delegations agree on what they were extending. Bahr told Kohl on 9 September that the Western allies would not allow him to begin serious talks with the East until a common German translation existed.[83] The wait for such a translation held up talks until the beginning of October 1971.

The Significance of the German-German Talks

How quickly the two Germanies could overcome these obstacles and reach an agreement between themselves was not merely a matter of local concern. The German-German Transit Treaty represented interlocking global and local concerns. On the one hand, the quadripartite agreement waited on its conclusion, which meant that the much-hoped-for ratification of the Moscow and Warsaw Treaties depended on it as well. Indeed, the Stasi recorded a comment by Bahr that the three Western powers were even letting German-German talks influence the timing of a pan-European security conference and SALT.[84] In other words, the wrangling of the two Germanies over what were often municipal issues of access from one half of Berlin to another affected policy-making on the European and even superpower level; the local was affecting the global. The global also affected the local; the international context—particularly the Sino-Soviet rivalry—put pressure on the two Germanies to reach an accord. A briefing on Sino-Soviet relations given by Moscow to East Berlin at this time lamented yet again the sorry state of Sino-Soviet relations. The Soviets expressed regret that the Chinese had rebuffed offers both to take joint action against U.S. aggression in Indochina and to renounce use of conventional or nuclear weapons.[85] Indeed, Moscow found that "now as ever, anti-Sovietism stands at the core of both the domestic and foreign policy of the Chinese leadership."[86] The briefing noted that Chinese civilians and soldiers were continually provoking border incidents.[87] It also argued that China was essentially complicit in U.S. aggression against Vietnam, since various Chinese signs of friendliness towards the United States had emboldened the Americans to take a harder line in Vietnam.[88] They made the decision in October 1971, as China gained admission to the UN and Kissinger went back for another visit, to invite Nixon to Moscow.[89] (Kissinger saw a clear cause-and-effect relationship; as he viewed it, the "suddenly blooming" U.S.-Soviet relations, as shown by the signing of the Quadripartite Agreement and the Soviet invitation, arose from his overtures to

China.)[90] In short, domestic, even municipal, concerns were closely intertwined with international politics.

The SED's Deadly Fortress Mentality

Even as the SED under Honecker obediently followed Soviet instructions to seek a transit accord, it simultaneously fortified itself against the consequences of such an accord. A kind of fortress mentality became evident as the SED Politburo took four major steps. First, formalizing a decision made by the Politburo in July, the Council of Ministers on 8 September called for an increase in the "security and order on the state border of the GDR to the FRG and to West Berlin."[91] In other words, the deadly zone behind the wall should be made both larger and better fortified militarily. This included the installation of particularly lethal shrapnel mines. The fact that these fortifications would require those unfortunate East Germans who lived in the proposed area of enlargement to move out did not bother the Politburo; "temporary solutions" could be found.[92] Second, the Politburo called for an assessment of whether current GDR laws provided sufficient legal justification to force the border dwellers to move. It was considered important to be able to force "unsteady and asocial elements"—that is, those who had not been indicted for any reason but who were nonetheless undesirable—to move away from the border. If existing laws were not sufficient, then new ones should be written.[93] Third, the Politburo established the "West Commission." This commission was to provide the party with advice on political, economic, and cultural developments in the West and to counter Western propaganda with its own. Such measures were deemed necessary for the all-important "fight for ratification of the treaties."[94] Finally, at its meeting on 21 September 1971, the Politburo began considering "measures to secure the rights of the GDR with regard to possible claims from other states" on property in East Germany.[95] This move was a kind of preemptive strike against those Westerners who might use their new visiting rights to reclaim old property.

The SED implemented these measures in secret; in public, it continued to negotiate productively. Bahr and Kohl had a substantive conversation on 6 October about the possible terms of a transit accord.[96] The SED also took a step that may have made it feel more secure about negotiating: it added three "scientific experts" to the GDR delegation—in other words, Stasi.[97] This addition actually seems to have come about in response to a suggestion by Bahr. In a parallel to the four-power talks, Bahr had suggested to Kohl that they should employ "experts" to discuss technical matters. The details of customs procedures and transit arrangements with which they would be faced called for the skills of customs and traffic experts. As Bahr pointed out to Kohl with characteristic directness, it would be much better to let experts handle the details, since, as

Bahr said, "I have (a) no interest in and (b) don't understand the first thing about them."[98] Since in the GDR these were issues regulated by the MfS, it is not surprising that the SED would reach into that ministry to find experts on these issues. They were not identified as such, however.[99]

With experts now handling the technical details, the two delegation heads focused on topics that had become highly controversial.[100] Two questions soon emerged as decisive. Who would receive permission to transit through the GDR? And how much payment, and in what form, would the SED receive in return for granting permission for transit?

The sordidness of both topics was partially hidden by short-hand euphemisms. The issue of who could receive permission for transit was often referred to under the term "misuse." This, Kohl and Bahr agreed, meant misuse of transit pathways by persons with criminal intent. Where the two Germanies differed was in their definitions of criminal intent. The FRG, hoping to avoid the SED arbitrarily labeling would-be travelers as having "criminal intent," sought to nail down exact descriptions of who would be granted permission and what would constitute an actionable violation of transit rights.[101] As Bahr quite bluntly put it, "The fact that a man has long hair is not a reason to deny him transit"—a point of some importance in the hair-loving year of 1971.[102] The Politburo, in contrast, wanted as much flexibility as possible to refuse right of transit, especially to former refugees from the GDR. The SED even wanted the right to take action against those who planned "misuse" behind the scenes but did not transit personally, presumably meaning those who helped organize escapes from East Germany.[103] At its meeting on 12 October, the Politburo softened its stance in this regard slightly. It gave Kohl permission to indicate to Bahr that the GDR might be willing to provide full right of passage to émigrés who had left the GDR before some yet-to-be-specified date.[104]

On top of these issues, the question of "misuse" involved yet more complicated subcomponents. There was the question of whether transit could occur on an individual basis, that is, whether someone could drive in his or her own car or whether it had to take place in a group form of transportation, such as by bus. The former would both allow GDR citizens to see the superiority of Western automobiles and perhaps to bargain for illegal transit on an individual basis. There was also the very basic question of whether vehicles would be allowed to stop while in transit for a minor reason—such as to answer the call of nature— or only for a major reason—such as in case of a natural disaster.[105] The Soviets and the Politburo preferred the latter, because that would reduce chances for its citizens to gain access to vehicles transiting to the West. In general, the SED felt that Bonn did not pay sufficient attention to what it viewed as its need to secure the transit ways. Kohl complained to a sympathetic Politburo that Bahr, although saying that he wanted to avoid turning the transit ways "into an El Dorado for criminals," in fact kept "trying to reduce the GDR's control measures to a minimum."[106] Yet another subcomponent of the issue of "misuse" arose under the heading "range of validity," that is, the question of to whom transit rights would be granted.[107] The FRG felt that it was negotiating for all who wished to travel to West Berlin, while the GDR argued that the accord would apply only to West Germans. Since many employees of West German firms were technically "foreigners," often Turkish citizens who were not eligible for West German citizenship, the issue of the range of validity was of great importance to the FRG. The SED eventually conceded on this issue.[108]

The second major issue in the transit accord negotiations was the question of how the SED would receive payment. It was discussed under the shorthand of "visas" and "taxes." At issue was whether each individual would pay for a visa as he or she crossed or whether Bonn would pay a lump sum (which the GDR preferred, as mentioned above). Kohl also explained to Bahr at their meeting on 13–14 October that East Berlin planned to levy not only a visa fee but also additional fees for the use of GDR streets and a tax on the "profit which FRG companies earned using the streets of the GDR."[109] Kohl reported that Bahr was "outraged" upon hearing the latter.[110]

On top of these two concerns—who could transit and what the GDR would be paid—the SED delegation continued to emphasize its concern for its international standing by expressing interest in receiving UN membership as quickly as possible.[111] On 14 October, Bahr's delegation provided its own reminder of the international context of the negotiations. Over Kohl's protests that the German-German conversation was not an appropriate forum for such a communication, Bahr gave Kohl a message from the secretary general of NATO. The message, produced at the Lisbon meeting in early October, said that NATO hoped to begin talks with the USSR and "other interested governments" over troop reductions in Europe.[112] While vague, invoking the name of NATO served as a reminder of Bonn's backers.

The GDR Seeks Soviet Advice

In light of the difficulties these many issues were causing, the SED Politburo requested a consultation with the Soviets. Gromyko arrived for a visit in late October (and Brezhnev personally stopped by East Berlin as part of a trip to France at the end of the same month). The Politburo complained about the fact that West Germany was trying to make the transit agreement merely a corollary to the Quadripartite Agreement (which it in fact was) rather than a formal treaty between two sovereign states.[113] The SED also worried about Chancellor Brandt's recent statement to the effect that it was not necessary to recognize the division of Germany in order to regulate it.[114] The party did not like the notion that the division might be temporary and not worth acknowledging. The award of the Nobel Peace Prize to Brandt on the same day as Gromyko's visit to East Berlin, 20 October 1971, added extra weight to Brandt's policy ideas and pronouncements.[115]

Gromyko's words soothed East Berlin's ego (he agreed that the transit treaty was not merely a corollary but a significant treaty), but his actions undercut the SED's position. First, he informed his Germany ally that it should be open to the (for the SED heretical) notion that the FRG could in fact negotiate transit for West Berlin. Second, he gave the SED further unhappy news about the payment it was to receive from the FRG. The SED had realized that the method of lump-sum payment from Bonn, which Moscow preferred, carried the unfortunate connotation that Bonn was paying for West Berlin's travelers—nominally not West German citizens—as part of the lump. Should the lump sum be abandoned for this reason in favor of separate payments from the FRG and West Berlin? Gromyko replied no, thus showing that for Moscow, securing a hard-currency income flow had priority over the SED's sensitivity about West Berlin.[116] Finally, Gromyko made light of yet another of the SED's concerns when he said that East Berlin's hope for an invitation to attend a plenary session of the UN was unrealistic.[117] Where Moscow and East Berlin's interests diverged, Moscow prevailed. The Politburo, noting that "the basic orientation for negotiations is the line agreed upon in consultation with the Soviets," obediently transformed Gromyko's suggestions into instructions for Kohl's next meeting with Bahr.[118] Clearly, replacing Ulbricht with the more compliant Honecker had paid off for Brezhnev.

Thrashing Out a Transit Agreement

Negotiations on the transit accord remained quite contentious throughout the fall of 1971. Bonn stayed vehemently opposed to the SED's "tax" on the profits of FRG firms.[119] According to Bahr, FRG financial experts also considered the SED's estimates of the costs that transit would cause to be "completely unreal."[120] The FRG sought to nail down precise descriptions of who would and would not be allowed transit, insisting that transit be open to all. Bahr further indicated to Kohl that the FRG wanted the lump-sum payment to cover not only the GDR's charge for using the roadways but also the visa costs, not least because sparing travelers the need to pay would make a better " 'optical' impression on the population."[121] Here concern for the "PR dimension" of the results of Bahr and Kohl's work becomes apparent.

An internal Stasi record of a phone report from the talks in progress notes that a leading member of the GDR delegation (most likely Kohl) informed the

Stasi on 4 November that "despite all the problems, we are gaining ground."[122] The SED had made the "tax on profits" more palatable by suggesting it be part of the lump sum that Bonn paid to East Berlin.[123] This suggested the de facto arbitrariness of this charge, because it would seem a priori that the amount would vary yearly depending on the actual profit levels. However, the SED was more interested in guaranteed payments than yearly calculations. Previously, the SED considered its minimum annual lump sum to be DM 160 million a year (as discussed above). In mid-November, it instructed Kohl to raise that minimum to DM 165 million, to include the "tax."[124] It also indicated its willingness to let those who had escaped the GDR to use the transit routes, provided they did not have criminal records (other than those produced by becoming an illegal emigrant).[125]

By the end of the year the two sides had reached agreement on the key issues. As the Soviets had instructed the SED, the provisions of the treaty negotiated with Bonn would be extended to West Berlin. As to the question of who could travel, the final treaty included a "misuse" clause, meaning that the SED did have a legal basis for excluding some travelers, but the conditions under which it could do so were sharply proscribed.[126] The treaty did not prohibit any traveler on the basis of nationality or refugee status. Simply the fact that one had fled the GDR earlier was not sufficient cause to be refused transit. Use of individual autos was permitted. However, those in transit were allowed to stop only at approved rest areas or in case of emergency; a bathroom break on the side of the road would be a punishable crime. As to the question of how much, and how, the GDR would be paid, the two sides agreed on a yearly lump-sum payment. It was payable by 31 March every year until 1975 and amounted to DM 234.9 million, which covered all fees for use of transit ways, the tax on profits, and the cost of transit visas for all travelers.[127]

A delay arose when the three Western powers voiced general objections in late November 1971 that Bahr had made too many concessions; in particular, the three Western powers opposed any "misuse" section at all. Bahr felt that this criticism came unfairly late in the game; it showed that the Western allies had not sufficiently followed the German-German talks.[128] According to Kohl, Bahr reported that he had asked *Falin* to "work on" Rush in this matter, and Falin had agreed.[129] In other words, the West German enlisted his Soviet colleague to put pressure on an American. The highly ironic spectacle of Bahr using Falin to explain aspects of his negotiations to his own nominal allies showed that Bahr's work with Falin in the Group of Three had clearly left him with a close enough working relationship to make such a request. Exactly what Falin told Rush remains unclear, but whatever it was, it worked. The "misuse" clause did appear in the final treaty, despite Western uneasiness. A further delay arose from the need to agree with the West Berlin Senate on some of the details affecting West Berlin particularly.[130] Nonetheless, the two Germanies were able to sign the Transit Accord on 17 December 1971.

Looking back on the rapidity with which the transit agreement was negotiated, FRG delegation member Ulrich Sahm credited it both to Bahr's talents and to desire on the part of the SED to reach an accord.[131] Although Bahr and Kohl had at the beginning of their interaction acted quite coldly toward one another, after negotiating the transit treaty, Bahr saw fit to invite Kohl and his delegation to a small celebration in early 1972 to celebrate. Bahr's invitation to the party, echoing treaty language that called for the most efficient processing of visas and sealed customs containers by the necessary authorities, indicated that the purpose of the evening would be the most efficient possible "unsealing" of sealed containers "constructed for the purpose of carrying alcoholic beverages."[132]

Now the Transit Accord, like the Moscow and Warsaw Treaties, waited upon ratification in West Germany. The Soviets remained as keen as ever to secure this ratification, not least because of worries about other "fronts" in the Cold War. The U.S. announcement in January 1972 of Kissinger's secret talks with the North Vietnamese only exacerbated these worries. Hence, Moscow urged Brandt to push for ratification of the Moscow and Warsaw Treaties in the West German parliament as soon as possible. Parliamentary debate on ratification did, in fact, begin in February 1972, but the outcome was far from certain. The opposition parties, the CDU and CSU, were vehemently opposed to ratification. In an effort to remove Brandt from office before ratification could come to a vote, they decided to call for a vote of no confidence. The date for the vote was set for 27 April 1972. The CDU/CSU opposition coalition hoped to replace Brandt with Rainer Barzel as chancellor.[133] Barzel's success seemed assured; as one historian put it, "Brandt's cause looked hopeless."[134]

Markus Wolf remembered in 1996 that the instructions from Moscow at the time were clear: the SED was to do everything possible to protect Brandt. He was necessary for the ratification of the treaties and, as Brezhnev explained to a meeting of the Warsaw Pact states in January, the Soviet Union viewed the West German recognition of this ratification as indispensable. More importantly, Brezhnev publicly voiced another fear at this point: the USSR wanted to prevent West Germany from gaining access to nuclear weapons in any form.[135] A CDU-led government would be both less likely to ratify and more likely to engage in nuclear cooperation with NATO. Hence, Moscow commanded that a series of measures aimed at strengthening Brandt's position be implemented. So energetic were these efforts that they received a nickname: as Markus Wolf remembered, the week of the vote of no confidence was the so-called "Brandt-schutzwoche," a play on words which in German means roughly both "Fire Safety Week" and "Protect Brandt Week."[136]

"Fire Safety Week" and the Traffic Treaty

Despite the prospect of a no-confidence vote, Bahr continued to try to hammer out practical details of German-German travel. Having completed an accord on transit through GDR territory to West Berlin, he and Kohl now worked on a so-called "traffic treaty" to regulate essentially all other forms of travel between the Germanies. More so than any other treaty produced in the détente and Ostpolitik era, this accord focused on extremely technical issues. It dealt with such mundane matters as, for example, how to coordinate train schedules.[137] Once again, the SED seemed more hesitant than the Soviets about cooperation with the FRG. The SED would, after all, have to live with the immediate consequences of increased travel possibilities. As Kohl complained to Bahr in February 1972, East Berlin sensed an intent on the part of West Germany to "make the borders of the GDR permeable."[138] A Stasi summary of comments made by Bahr shows that he realized he could use Soviet eagerness to pressure the SED. The Stasi report cited Bahr hinting loudly that, were a traffic treaty not to be completed expeditiously, it might complicate the planned ratification proceedings in West Germany.[139] In the face of Nixon's spectacular visit to China, however, the GDR's local concerns paled in comparison to the Soviet worries about the global balance in the Cold War. Nixon arrived in China on 21 February 1972; on 23 February the West German parliament, the Bundestag, began debate on whether or not to ratify "the Eastern treaties," its short-hand term for the Moscow and Warsaw Treaties.

On the day between these two events, 22 February 1972, the SED Politburo took a daring step, designed to help Brandt. The SED announced that it would implement provisions of the Transit Accord on two holiday weekends in the spring of 1972 (Easter and Pentecost), well in advance of its formal ratification.[140] Over a million West Berliners took advantage of the opportunity to visit East Berlin for the first time since 1966 and the rest of the GDR for the first time since 1952. The justification for this measure provided at the Politburo meeting (a vague comment about the improved situation in Europe meriting it) did not mention the China visit or the Bundestag debate, but the timing suggests that the three events are not unrelated. Moreover, Stasi files suggest another reason for the gesture besides sending a political message abroad. The advance implementation served as a dry run for the Stasi security measures that would have to be implemented once the Quadripartite Agreement went into force.[141] Yet another reason was that the issue of "swing credit" had once again come to the fore. East Berlin wanted both to increase the amount of this interest-free credit that it received from the FRG and to receive assurances that it would continue to enjoy this option into the 1980s.[142] In the meeting between Kohl and Bahr on 22–23 March 1972, Bahr mentioned that Bonn would be willing to make these promises only if it received assurances that "the current form of trade between the GDR and the FRG would not change."[143] Neither side went into more detail at this point, however, but the issue would reemerge and play a prominent role in the Basic Treaty negotiations at the end of 1972 (as described in Chapter 6). Finally, another reason became apparent in the name given the gesture by the SED: a "gesture of good will." This name was not as cynical as might be expected. The chance to visit the East did indeed generate good will, which in turn helped improve East-West relations.[144] In short, this gesture, clearly designed to influence the ratification vote, was tactically a smart move on the part of the Politburo.

The military offensive launched by Hanoi on 30 March 1972 dealt a setback to progress on the European front, however. The United States decided to hold the Soviet Union responsible for it and refused Moscow's request to send a message to West German leaders urging ratification of the Eastern treaties.[145] Kissinger informed Bahr on 8 April 1972 that the United States was "reassessing [its] entire Soviet policy" and on 15–16 April the United States retaliated militarily in Vietnam, resulting, among other things, in Soviet loss of life, when four USSR merchant ships in Haiphong harbor were accidentally hit.[146] Kissinger nonetheless went to Moscow on 12 April to begin negotiations for Nixon's visit and to talk about SALT.

The Constructive Vote of No Confidence, 27 April 1972

At their meeting of 12 April, Kohl and Bahr discussed the upcoming vote of no confidence. Kohl informed Bahr that the SED regime would take another step to help Brandt, namely, via a speech by Erich Honecker saying that a CDU-led government would be a hindrance to improving FRG-GDR relations.[147] Kohl also made clear that, after the ratification of the treaties (which presupposed Brandt remaining in office, since the CDU/CSU had made its opposition to ratification clear), the SED would be willing to negotiate a treaty on basic relations between the two Germanies.[148]

A suspenseful week followed, during which the fortunes of the Brandt government hung in the balance. The last couple of days deserve analysis in detail, because they illuminate that the SED clearly had as its motive helping Brandt to survive the vote of no confidence. On 25 April, meeting from 10:00 A.M. until 12:30 P.M., the Politburo decided to take yet more steps to help Brandt. It decided to make concessions in the traffic treaty talks, such as extending its relevant provisions to West Berlin, as had been done with the transit accord.[149] Kohl informed Bahr of this and other concessions in a private conversation at 4:15 P.M. the same day. According to Kohl, Bahr was "very impressed" and suggested that if the two negotiated more or less continuously, it might actually be possible to conclude treaty negotiations before the no-confidence vote in less than 48 hours.[150]

On the morning of the 26th, Erich Honecker reinforced the expressions of the GDR's willingness to help Brandt by meeting personally with Bahr at 9:30 A.M. According to SED documentation, Honecker asked for Bahr's prediction of the vote's outcome, to which Bahr replied that he thought it was too close to call. Bahr commented that the initiative for the vote of no confidence had come not so much from Barzel as from a man Bahr believed to be the rising star of the CDU, the prime minister of the state of Rheinland-Pfalz, Helmut Kohl.[151] Bahr felt sure that the CDU had "bought two or three people" away from Brandt's side but said that there was resistance within the CDU itself that might equalize the matter. The question of whether votes had been for sale has long been debated. A member of the CDU, Julius Steiner, reportedly sold his vote.[152] Markus Wolf stated in 1996 that Steiner was not the only one. Although Wolf refused to name names, he admitted, "Everyone was buying votes. The CDU bought the FDP people, the SPD bought CDU people, we bought people, nobody knows anymore who bought whom."[153] Egon Bahr recalled in his memoirs that he received an offer from the Soviet back channel to provide the SPD with money to purchase votes, which he refused.[154] The Soviets also made a more public gesture when Brezhnev announced that a large number of Germans of Russian extraction could emigrate.[155] Moreover, Kissinger recalled a Soviet request during his visit to Moscow in late April for U.S. help in saving Brandt, remarking, "as if we had any means of doing so."[156] In his conversation with Bahr, Honecker may have been referring to such measures when he hinted that Brandt would win, "not least with our support and thanks to our measures."[157] The SED leader then displayed his willingness to take further steps, albeit small ones, to support Brandt. Honecker indicated that the GDR would be willing to increase hotel space for Western tourists and provide easier conditions for gaining a visa to visit the GDR, including granting them for reasons as mundane as visiting sporting or theatrical events. At the end of their conversation, Honecker emphasized once again the main goal of the SED's efforts: getting the Eastern treaties ratified. The SED chief concluded by telling Bahr "this conversation never happened," with which Bahr concurred.[158]

Leaving Honecker, Bahr then went directly back to negotiations with Kohl, in an attempt to wrap up the traffic treaty. They did so successfully by noon on the 26th. Bahr flew to Bonn to get approval of the treaty so that he could return and announce its conclusion that very same evening in East Berlin. The Soviets contacted Kohl while Bahr was away and added a sweetener of their own, simplifying the process of extending the terms of the treaty to West Berlin.[159]

When Bahr returned to East Berlin much later than expected on the 26th, he told Kohl that the situation in Bonn was "kafkaesque." The upcoming vote of no confidence consumed everyone's attention.[160] Brandt had told Bahr that he would have to get verbal approval of the treaty from the foreign ministry under Scheel and the interior ministry under Genscher. Bahr then scurried around trying to find Scheel and Genscher, both of whom were opposed to it. Bahr told Kohl that he "really had to fight," but that in the end the two ministers agreed to the traffic treaty.[161] Shortly before midnight, Bahr and Kohl announced to the press the successful conclusion of their talks. Before Bahr once again headed back to Bonn for the vote of no confidence, he told Kohl he would say his goodbyes by telegram if his government fell. Brandt went on to survive by only two votes, however, and Kohl and Bahr had more work to do.

The beginning of 1972 revealed much about both SED and Soviet motives. East Berlin sought financial gain, but it also worried about the security risk of greater contact with West Germans. However, when it expressed this fear to Moscow, Moscow made light of East Berlin's worries and instructed the SED to forge ahead. Brezhnev was worried by increasing U.S.-Chinese friendliness and events in Vietnam. The Soviets became especially concerned that East Berlin accommodate Brandt when the specter of a no-confidence vote arose. Such a vote could have ousted Brandt, making ratification impossible and potentially opening the door to closer West German cooperation with the West under a CDU-led government. This explains the fervency of Soviet efforts to protect Brandt during the "Fire Safety Week" of April 1972. The survival of the Brandt government finally made ratification seem to be a real possibility. The West Germans, in turn, hoped to establish some kind of formal treaty on basic relations between the two Germanies. Caught between Moscow and Bonn, the SED placed its hopes in obtaining international political recognition as the best means of asserting itself against both.

Sealing the Bargain in 1972–1973:

The Basic Treaty in the Context

of the International Cold War

The Quadripartite Agreement, the Transit Accord, and the Traffic Treaty were now signed. Brandt had survived the vote of no confidence. Bonn, East Berlin, and their allies could finally turn to long-sought goals: achieving ratification of both the Moscow and Warsaw Treaties and agreeing on a treaty of basic relations between the two halves of divided Germany. Meanwhile, the SED sought international recognition in the form of UN membership for the GDR, if necessary as part of an East/West German dual entry. By the end of 1973, all these goals had been achieved. Explaining why involves exploring the motives of the Soviets and the SED.

The Soviets saw the Moscow Treaty as both a vindication and a guarantee of their sphere of influence. In Moscow's eyes, the accord was a kind of de facto peace treaty to World War II.[1] Moscow also viewed it as a useful hedge against the prospect of German reunification, or against overly close German-American cooperation, which could turn nuclear. All of these implications were extremely important to Moscow at a time when China maintained its threatening stance.

Soviet goals, however, were not always synonymous with SED goals. The SED was trying to achieve as much recognition as possible of the GDR's permanence and legitimacy. The party fought any mention of the term "German nation" in treaties—until Moscow made clear that it would have to change its opinion—because the notion that one nation still existed challenged the GDR's permanence. The party sought UN membership and recognition by as many countries as possible because that enhanced its legitimacy. In short, caught between Soviet and West German eagerness for German-German rapprochement to continue, the SED tried to maximize the legitimization it received via international politics. And if it had to make concessions and put up with the risks of rapprochement, the SED wanted to make sure that it took advantage of the benefits as well—mainly the financial ones.

Ratification and the Brezhnev-Nixon Summit

Once Brandt had survived the no-confidence vote, his first goal—which he shared with Moscow—was to secure ratification of the Moscow and Warsaw Treaties. The Western side of this process has been detailed elsewhere.[2] The East German documents now newly available help explain the sequence of events on the Eastern side.

The pending ratification of the treaty in West Germany appears to have helped the United States to achieve a key foreign policy success: namely, the fact that the U.S. mining and bombing of Haiphong on 9 May, which caused Soviet casualties, did not provoke the Soviets to cancel the summit meeting with Nixon scheduled for two weeks later. Why the Soviets tolerated the U.S. action has remained a mystery.[3] The Soviet ambassador in the United States, Dobrynin, suggested in his memoirs that the Politburo of the CPSU decided to proceed with the summit because "the alternative would amount to handing Hanoi a veto over our relations with America."[4] More recently, William Bundy has revived the notion that the Soviets went ahead with the summit because they did not want to diminish the chances that the West German parliament would ratify the Eastern treaties in its vote on 17 May.[5]

The newly available documents confirm Bundy's argument. Even though Brandt remained in office, the Soviets were still extremely concerned about successful ratification. Moscow repeatedly told the SED that obtaining it was their highest foreign policy priority. These were not empty words; the way that Moscow had supported Brandt when he faced the no-confidence vote bespoke sincerity. Similarly, when the West German CDU/CSU parliamentarians indicated that they could vote for the ratification of the treaties only if the Soviet Union indicated acceptance of both the European Community and the possibility for change in the relations of the two Germanies (implying the possibility of reunification), Moscow quickly complied. In a speech on 20 March 1972, Brezhnev fulfilled these requests.[6] Hence not only the Soviet Union's words but also its actions show that ratification was a high priority.

As for the East Germans, the Stasi kept close tabs on the prospects for ratification, producing summaries of the mood in Bonn and presumably forwarding them to the Soviets.[7] Michael Kohl asked Bahr how he thought the vote would turn out. Bahr replied that the outcome was somewhat uncertain. He told Kohl that the opposition leader Barzel, after losing the vote of no confidence, no longer had any clear idea how his party, the CDU, would vote on ratification and was personally "at the end of his rope."[8] Disarray in the ranks of the CDU did not necessarily ensure ratification, however. As the British ambassador to the FRG pointed out to the Soviet ambassador to the GDR, even though many members of the opposition agreed with the Eastern treaties, they would nonetheless most likely vote against them as a means of opposing Brandt.[9]

As it turned out, the CDU/CSU delegates chose in large part to abstain from the ratification vote on 17 May 1972. Hence, the motion to ratify succeeded. Subsequently, the two Germanies signed the Traffic Treaty on 26 May. This enabled the four powers to put the Quadripartite Agreement into force on 3 June 1972.[10] Finally, Bonn and East Berlin agreed to begin talks about a more fundamental accord that would define the nature of the relationship between the FRG and the GDR.[11]

Now it was the turn of the Western allies to be uneasy. Their discomfort with the expansion of German-German talks from technical to fundamental issues was revealed by the suggestion, made by the Western allies on the day they formally put the Four-Power Accord into force, that there still be quadripartite conversations to accompany the German-German talks.[12] Moreover, Bahr told Kohl that Bonn's efforts to pave the way for Allied acceptance of UN membership for both Germanies had drawn a critical response from the French ambassador. The Frenchman had pointedly asked Bahr "what he got in exchange from the GDR for always standing up for its interests."[13] The three Western powers wanted clear statements that German-German membership in the UN would not affect the rights of the four powers in Germany in any way.[14]

Behind the Scenes at the Brezhnev-Nixon Moscow Summit

Washington in particular had to deal not only with increased German-German rapprochement but also with the upcoming Moscow summit. Brezhnev and Nixon were scheduled to sign various accords. These included the first significant arms control agreements of the Cold War, namely, SALT I and the ABM Treaty.[15] They also included agreements on such diverse topics as wheat sales and repayment for goods delivered to the Soviet Union during World War II.[16] As with the Moscow Treaty, the Soviets viewed these accords as having an importance above and beyond the individual details. Moscow viewed them as an acknowledgment of U.S.-Soviet equality.[17] The USSR was particularly gratified by a vague and idealistic "statement of basic principles" of U.S.-Soviet relations, which Nixon and Kissinger saw as mere rhetorical flourish. As John Lewis Gaddis has pointed out, Nixon and Kissinger's attitude caused them grave difficulties at home. The statement of basic principles "conveyed the false impression that détente meant a cessation of Soviet-American competition everywhere." This impression raised false hopes among the U.S. domestic population, which remained unfulfilled and contributed to the growing sense after Nixon resigned that détente had failed.[18]

The SED archives offer a rare glimpse behind the scenes in Moscow. On a visit to East Berlin after the summit, Gromyko discussed Nixon's visit verbally and provided the SED leaders with a written summary as well.[19] Records of both were kept in the party archive. Taken together, Gromyko's oral commentary and the written summary provide a unique viewpoint at this groundbreaking summit. Assuming that he was being more or less truthful with the SED, these two sources reveal what the primary Soviet concerns were at the time.

Gromyko's written summary noted with satisfaction the American acknowledgment that "we [the Soviets] have more land-based intercontinental ballistic missiles than they do."[20] It stated that the joint U.S.-USSR communiqué issued after the summit constituted public recognition by the United States of the inviolability of the existing borders in Europe.[21] As for current affairs, the Soviets had intentionally avoided discussing China, because they did not want the U.S. delegation "to get the idea that we were disquieted by Nixon's trip to Peking."[22] However, Gromyko's spoken comments to the SED Politburo show that the Chinese visit did in fact weigh heavily on Soviet minds in shaping their summit plans. Indeed, one of the reasons so many accords were signed was to differentiate the Moscow summit from the Peking one. As Gromyko put it, "We did not want just to drink tea and have protocol events as was the case with the Chinese."[23]

Although China had not come up as a topic of discussion at the summit, Vietnam had, but at a time when Gromyko was barred from listening in. Gromyko told the Politburo that Nixon and Kissinger would talk only to Brezhnev and his closest advisers about the war. Since the president and Kissinger had excluded Gromyko's equivalent, Secretary of State William Rogers, from the group, Gromyko was similarly prevented from attending. Gromyko heard about it afterwards, though, and reported that it had been quite contentious. Nixon apparently turned red and then pale with emotion.[24] The written summary transmitted by Moscow to East Berlin gives more details of the conversation about Vietnam that Gromyko did orally. According to the summary, the United States offered to start official talks in Paris with the North Vietnamese. These talks would have as their first goal the establishment of a cease-fire and a prisoner-release program. The United States considered a withdrawal of all its troops within four months possible, if an appropriate agreement could be reached and Vietnamese elections could be held within six months after the conclusion of such an agreement.[25] Moreover, the United States would be willing to tolerate South Vietnamese neutrality and would promise to limit economic and military aid. Were all of these conditions to be met, then the United States saw "a real possibility" that U.S. troops could be completely withdrawn by "September or October of this year," that is, 1972.[26] After the discussion of Vietnam, Nixon reportedly remarked that he was pleased it had been possible to speak openly. He said that Kissinger should use Gromyko as a contact on this issue.[27]

Before coming to East Berlin, Gromyko had visited Bonn. Hence, he was also able to inform the SED of West German reactions to the summit. According to the Soviet foreign minister, Brandt took a positive view of the summit and felt that it echoed his own efforts. However, Gromyko speculated that "had the question of the U.S. presence in Europe been up for discussion . . . then Bonn might have reacted differently." In short, Bonn did not want "a quick withdrawal of U.S. troops."[28] Gromyko speculated aloud that "perhaps Bonn has its own concern about the atomic shield of the U.S., perhaps there is worry that this shield could be weakened." He concluded that the dominant feeling in Bonn nonetheless was optimism, not worry.[29] With regard to German-German relations, Bonn was insisting that UN membership for both the FRG and the GDR be accompanied by the establishment of a treaty of basic relations. Despite the fact that no one in Bonn used the phrase "unity," Gromyko felt that it was a West German ulterior motive to seek unification. In his opinion, it was "obvious that the people in Bonn want to reach some kind of a solution that will create a bridge to 'German unity.' "[30]

Negotiating the Basic Treaty

Worry about unification as the ulterior motive on the part of Bonn underlay the SED's planning for German-German talks on a fundamental treaty of basic relations. To counter it, the SED sought to establish as quickly as possible that East and West Germany should consider each other foreign states. Any mention of special relations between the two could be the beginning of a kind of slippery-slope argumentation that could tend toward unification. For this reason the SED wanted to avoid any mention of "special" or "inner-German" relations.[31]

Exactly how to define the relationship between the German states was but one of the many major issues at stake in the German-German talks. Because of the controversial nature and sheer number of issues involved, negotiations filled six intense months in the second half of 1972. They took place on several levels simultaneously—with groups of technical experts producing detailed drafts of treaty subcomponents as Bahr and Kohl tackled the major issues—and involved complicated legal contortions at nearly every turn. As a result, it is easy to lose sight of the main overarching arguments in the vast sea of paperwork produced. The purpose here is to reveal the interests and motives that determined the conduct of the talks. Concentrating on the most controversial topics serves as a concise method of doing so.[32]

Three questions dominated the negotiations: (1) Did a German nation still exist? (2) What did the lack of a peace treaty for World War II imply for the German situation? and (3) How did one define "German" citizenship? Then, as the two Germanies moved from negotiating to implementing the treaty, three more issues came to the fore: (1) When and how would it be possible for the two Germanies to join the UN? (2) How would the two Germanies manage questions of emigration? and (3) What sums of money would the GDR receive in return for permitting émigrés to leave? Of course these were not separate, unrelated issues; nor were they the only six issues at stake. The negotiators addressed scores of other issues as well—ranging from rights of journalists, to chances for friendly sporting competitions, to the possibility of official GDR visitors attending the Munich Olympic Games in August 1972—but the above-named six issues were central. Moreover, SED documentation makes it clear that the Soviets were actively involved at all points in negotiation on these issues. They provided not only general guidance but also, in the final days of treaty negotiation in October and November 1972, extremely detailed suggestions and instructions.[33]

The National Question

On the question of a common German nation, the SED was clear on what it had to do: deny it completely. The tone of the first round of Basic Treaty talks, on 15 June 1972, immediately turned contentious when this issue arose.[34] The SED's directive to Kohl for the day was simple. It emphasized that he should make clear that the division of Germany was irrevocable and that the border between the two halves was, like all other Cold War borders, final and inviolable.[35] Kohl also sought, as he had in the past, to achieve an exchange of ambassadors and embassies as a means of creating formal, institutional recognition of the separation of the two states from one another.[36] Such institutions would provide de facto what the FRG continually refused to affirm de jure, namely, full legal recognition of the GDR as a separate, foreign state. As Timothy Garton Ash has pointed out, recognition was one of the FRG's most valuable bargaining chips.[37]

Bahr, in a deftly ironic move, replied by quoting official GDR documents to argue that the German nation still existed and hence should be mentioned in the German-German accord.[38] Bahr pointed out that the German nation received mention in the GDR's own constitution. Therefore, he argued, it was clear that the SED regime had "no fear" of the concept of the German nation and would have no problem mentioning it in the treaty.[39] According to Kohl, Bahr went so far as to express his pleasure that East and West Germany had "no difference of opinion" about this central issue.[40]

Kohl did not share Bahr's pleasure. He responded, "There is no more national unity. It was gambled away in two world wars. History has already decided the national question."[41] The SED Politburo was similarly nonplussed. It instructed Kohl to respond to Bahr's rhetorical offensive by pointing out that the GDR's negotiating position was based on the decisions of the eighth SED party congress, not on the constitution.[42] Bahr responded by pointing out—sarcastically but correctly—that the eighth party congress had neither nullified nor superseded the constitution of the GDR.[43] Kohl had no immediate response to this. However, by the next meeting (2–3 August 1972), an SED document noted rumors that the Politburo was preparing to edit the constitution.[44] In 1974, the SED did in fact revise the constitution, making changes whereby all references to a common German nation disappeared.[45]

Bahr's rhetorically combative style hardly served his purpose, namely, overcoming the SED's desire to deny the continued existence of the German nation. His sarcasm did little to make it more palatable. Stasi files also suggest that secret information may have helped to ease the minds of Politburo members in the face of Bahr's rhetorical attack. An internal MfS assessment of West German negotiating intentions in July 1972 found that the government of the FRG was "less concerned with the 'unity of the nation' than with reconciling unification politics with the FRG-GDR treaty."[46] In other words, the FRG was more concerned with the political palatability of the accord within West Germany than with truly reuniting the nation. This view received a kind of confirmation in late August when the Soviets informed Kohl of the remarks of a West German embassy official in Moscow. The official was saying privately that "in the treaty, one does not have to speak directly of the unity of the nation"; it was simply a case of inserting a few "empty words." In reality, "the Brandt Administration knew that too much separated the FRG and the GDR."[47]

Bahr had a private conversation with Honecker on 7 September, just two days after the terrorist killing of Israeli athletes at the Munich Olympics. Honecker began their meeting by expressing regret for the deaths of the Israelis. In light of later findings that strongly suggest that the terrorists received extensive assistance from East Germany, the hypocrisy in Honecker's words becomes apparent; but Bahr did not challenge him at the time. Instead he focused on the matter at hand, emphasizing the need to mention the nation in order to assure that the treaty could withstand a test in Karlsruhe. Honecker assured Bahr of the SED's desire to help where possible and even to provide the SPD-led coalition government with support as it faced elections in the autumn of 1972.[48] Although not regularly scheduled, a vote was going to take place nonetheless, because of a dramatic step planned by Brandt. The West German chancellor had called for another vote of no confidence for 22 September. He intended to lose so as to force a new election. He wanted to do so because the election, by virtue of its timing, would serve effectively as a plebiscite on the treaties he had initialed and brought to ratification in the preceding year. Brandt was hoping for a ringing endorsement. This produced a tricky circularity: although the elections would serve as a means of securing public support for the treaties, the pressure of the upcoming balloting pushed the FRG delegation to secure the treaties as a means of gaining public support.

Despite extensive wrangling, the two sides could not find common ground. Whether or not to mention the nation in the treaty remained an open issue well into October. Brandt and Bahr regarded such a mention as a sine qua non.[49] Without it, not only the opposition and the Supreme Court but also their party's coalition partner, the FDP, would reject the treaty.[50] Although he did not tell the East Germans so, Bahr mentioned to Helmut Schmidt around this time a further concern: Bahr felt that he was in a race against time to reach some kind of agreement before inevitable international recognition of the GDR occurred and undermined the FRG's leverage.[51] Despite all of these concerns, the SED flatly ruled out such a reference.[52]

An internal Politburo assessment at this time reemphasized the SED's motive for opposing a mention of the nation. The East Berlin Foreign Ministry expressed outrage that Bonn would perpetuate "the nationalistic lie of a theoretically still-existing 'unified German nation'" with the dangerous nationalistic consequence that there might still be a "concomitant 'right to self-determination of the German people.'"[53] Erich Honecker personally sent a message to Willy Brandt, via Kohl and Bahr, saying that the West Germans "should give up any hope of having any effect on us as regards the unity of the nation and reunification."[54] Rather than a phrase mentioning unity, the SED expressly sought the opposite: some kind of recognition that the FRG renounced all territorial claims forever. In this, the East Germans enjoyed the hearty backing of the Soviets.[55]

Realizing there was little hope of budging East Berlin, Egon Bahr decided to try his hand in Moscow instead. He arranged to travel to the Soviet Union on 8–10 October on the pretext of wanting to discuss solely FRG-USSR relations.[56] Given that Bonn and Moscow had signed another major pipeline agreement in July (whereby the Soviet Union got both 1.2 million tons of pipeline and, conveniently, DM 1.2 billion in credit with which to pay for it), there did indeed seem to be ongoing matters to discuss.[57] In his memoirs, however, Bahr made clear that his main goal was really to speak to Brezhnev about the German-German talks.[58] Bahr, in a summary written shortly after the meeting, remembered that the Soviets wanted to keep secret the fact that they had discussed the GDR and the Basic Treaty at all.[59] As with the negotiations for the Moscow Treaty, it seems that the Soviets had no desire to inform the SED about their bilateral dealings with Bonn on issues of great import to East Berlin. The Soviet report to the East German Politburo afterwards was vague about what had been said to Bahr. It noted blandly that the USSR would respect the sovereignty of the GDR.[60]

The sequence of events after Bahr's visit suggests, however, that Moscow's regard for GDR sovereignty was not extensive. On the same day he returned from the USSR, 10 October, Bahr had a new compromise to suggest to Kohl. According to Kohl, Bahr proposed that, rather than using the controversial word "nation," the two sides should instead make reference to their difference of opinion about "the national question."[61] Meanwhile, on that same day, the Politburo expressed its thanks to Brezhnev for advice he had given to Honecker.[62] Shortly thereafter the Soviets conveyed in writing to Honecker the exact same suggestion that Bahr had made, that is, to use the term "national question."[63] Finally, an SED directive to Michael Kohl at the end of the month noted specifically that the basis of his negotiation position were agreements made with the Soviet Union.[64] Although no document indisputably links these events, the chronology suggests that they were not unrelated. The compromise solution proposed by both Bahr and the Soviets in fact appeared in the final treaty. The SED, meanwhile, seethed at Bahr's ability to go over its head. According to Bahr's notes from a talk with Kohl, the SED threatened to cease talking about humanitarian issues at all as a result.[65]

Ironically, it might have been possible to get the word "nation" per se into the treaty, had Bahr pursued the matter. As late as 31 October a Soviet consul at the Berlin embassy told Michael Kohl that the SED could, if pushed to the utmost, accept the appearance of the word "nation." Kohl indicated that he would try to avoid this, and the final result shows that he succeeded.[66] In other words, East Berlin was more hard-line than Moscow on this issue. West Germany did strengthen its claim somewhat by insisting that the GDR accept a unilateral statement in the form of a letter, similar to the one given to the USSR at the Moscow Treaty signing, indicating the intent of the West German government to work toward unity by means of free self-determination of the German people.[67]

In other words, although the SED wanted to avoid any mention of the nation at all, it gave in under Soviet pressure and agreed to the weaker formulation "national question." What might the interest of the USSR have been in urging conciliation? There exist indications that, around this time, Moscow had various reasons for nudging the East Germans into a more cooperative mood. At a meeting of the leaders of East Bloc states in the Kremlin on 31 July, Brezhnev had indirectly but repeatedly hinted to Honecker that one should engage the Brandt government constructively. Brezhnev had apparently heard already that Brandt would be calling for new elections and wanted to prevent any risk of a CDU-led government emerging as a result.[68] That the Soviets remained worried about the Chinese at this time as well was shown by the convening of a meeting in Prague to discuss the ongoing conflict.[69] A new level of anxiety arose with the establishment of formal Chinese–West German relations in the wake of the American rapprochement. The FRG foreign minister, Walter Scheel, visited Peking in October 1972 to open formal relations.[70] A Soviet commentary on the event noted that Zhou En-lai had drawn distressing parallels between Chinese and West German attempts to reunite their nations. He had also called into question the durability of the new treaties about Germany.[71]

Meanwhile, the SED had its own reasons apart from Soviet pressure for giving in and allowing the "national question" to be mentioned. It succumbed to the appeal of a windfall in the realm of trade and finance. On the same eventful day of Bahr's return from Moscow, 10 October, a West German economics ministry official in charge of trade with the GDR, Willi Kleindienst, informed an East German trade officer of an attractive offer. Kleindienst announced that he was willing to discuss increasing both the amount of swing credit upon which East Berlin could draw and trade in certain goods that the GDR particularly desired.[72] He held out the possibility that the ceiling on the amount of available swing credit might be lifted to DM 1 billion. Increasing swing credit and trade were both highly sought-after goals in East Berlin. The West Germans left no doubt as to their intentions in making this offer. According to an East German summary passed on to the Soviet embassy, Kleindienst had said clearly that it hoped these proposals "would facilitate finding a solution to the question of the nation in the treaty on the basis of relations between the FRG and the GDR."[73] In other words, the goal of these economic offers was political. The lure of money worked.

The Absence of a Peace Treaty and the Presence of the Four Powers

An issue related to whether or not the German nation should receive mention was the question of whether the lack of a peace treaty for World War II should also be noted. Simply stating the undeniable fact that no peace treaty existed would seem to be unproblematic.[74] However, in the world of treaty negotiation, there is no such thing as an unproblematic reference. Soviet threats to sign a separate peace treaty with the East Germans had served as one of the main components of the crisis over divided Berlin that had led to the construction of the Wall in 1961. Now, however, the roles were reversed. The Western powers sought to call attention to the missing treaty, while the Easterners preferred to downplay it.

Bonn was interested in a mention of the lack of a peace treaty because it would imply that the existing Cold War status quo, inclusive of the German division, might eventually be altered by negotiation of such a treaty. As Bahr put it, he was concerned (according to Kohl) that the agreements between the two Germanies should in no way be construed to preclude any later decisions to "create a unified, democratic and peaceful German state or sign a peace treaty."[75] Bahr quite bluntly explained to Kohl in mid-August that the treaty between the two Germanies "brings no finality with it," saying, "It is not a treaty of division. It does not stand in place of the missing peace treaty. It will not prevent either side from pursuing further the goal of a solution to the national problem."[76]

The SED and the Soviets both wanted to brand the Cold War as permanent. As a result, they fought to avoid any mention of a peace treaty that might bring change. The SED told Bahr that the Moscow Treaty should be viewed as the de facto peace treaty, which had settled the issue of borders for good.[77] The USSR indicated that it would not tolerate any mention of the absence of a peace treaty, because that would imply that the Moscow and Warsaw Treaties were but temporary solutions to key territorial questions.[78] In his memoirs, Bahr recounts that he tried to budge Moscow on this issue during the same visit in which he secured some movement on the national question. However, while the Soviets were willing to compromise on the predominantly German issue of the mention of the nation, Bahr recalled that they were absolutely immovable on the subject of the peace treaty, which more directly affected Moscow's interests.[79] As mentioned before, one of the USSR's key legitimizing strategies was to claim that only communism and Soviet troops could hold back German revanchism. A peace treaty would have robbed Moscow of this argument.

After his return from Moscow, Bahr realized that the Soviets would never budge. He decided to try a more promising tack. Instead of citing the *absence* of a treaty, he began emphasizing the *presence* of the four powers.[80] As he put it, "as long as the four powers have rights [in Germany], the German question is not legally closed."[81] This tactic paralleled that of the three Western allies, who were at the same time discussing the possibility of UN membership for the two Germanies. According to a Stasi summary, the Western powers wanted assurances that UN membership for the Germanies in no way affected the status of the four powers in Germany.[82] By the end of October, Kohl reported that the FRG would probably accept *either* a mention of the missing peace treaty *or* some kind of clear statement of the rights of the four powers.[83] In the end, the two Germanies agreed on a sweeping statement that the Basic Treaty had no impact on previously established treaties and relations, whether these be bilateral or multilateral accords.[84] The wording implied that it did not affect accords with the four powers. A supplemental exchange of letters clarified this point.[85]

The Question of Citizenship

Yet another permutation on the national problem was the question of citizenship. If a "nation" still existed, did Germans on both sides of the border still share a common membership in it?[86] Or were there (as was de facto the case) two kinds of German citizenship, namely, West and East? West Germany, subscribing to the notion of a common German nation, refused to recognize GDR citizenship and automatically bestowed West German citizenship on East Germans who managed to cross the border. The GDR, maintaining that there were two different kinds of citizenships, had long been irritated by this practice.

Hence, logic would suggest that the SED would use the Basic Treaty to tackle this issue. Surprisingly, the SED sought to avoid this tricky topic altogether. Following orders from Moscow, it fought against any mention of citizenship at all.[87] Instead, it sought the inclusion of a vaguely worded statement indicating generally that each side would refrain from applying citizenship laws relating to residents of the other Germany.[88] Indeed, in late October the SED tried to take advantage of the Brandt cabinet's worry about the rapidly approaching election of 19 November to push through its point of view. In a thinly veiled effort to achieve the SED's maximum goals, Honecker sent a message to Bahr through Kohl stating that the SED was not indifferent to the electoral fate of the Brandt government and knew that the conclusion of an agreement would help his chances. Honecker then disingenuously slipped in a comment that the public would still value the treaty even if the question of citizenship (along with that of the nation and the peace treaty) "were left out."[89] In so many words, Honecker was saying that if the FRG were willing to concede these points, the GDR would give it a treaty in time for the elections.

The citizenship issue proved intractable. The FRG insisted that it be mentioned; the GDR insisted that it not be included. On 1 November, Bahr suggested that the FRG make some kind of one-sided statement.[90] What finally emerged was termed a "qualification." The West Germans indicated in their unilateral qualification to the Basic Treaty that they did not consider citizenship to be regulated by the accord. The East Germans included a separate statement indicating their hope that the existence of this treaty would help ease regulation of citizenship questions.[91]

Why did the SED fight so hard against any settlement of the citizenship issue, when it might have used the Basic Treaty to resolve a long-standing point of contention? An internal Stasi assessment of the Basic Treaty (written after it was negotiated but before it was signed) suggested a reason why. The Stasi assessment pointed out that, as long as the issue was not regulated, questions of property belonging to those of disputed citizenship remained open as well. As a result, "the GDR can for the time being continue our measures in this regard (for example, managing the property of those who had fled the republic)."[92] Another reason may have been internal uncertainty about how to handle this issue ideologically. At that time, Honecker was making more and more references to the notion that the GDR needed a "sealing off" or "Abgrenzung" from West Germany, and it may have seemed prudent to leave the question open.[93]

From Negotiation to Implementation:
Human Beings as Bargaining Chips

Although it would be misleading to imply that the Basic Treaty definitively settled any of the open questions between the Germanies, both sides believed that they had reached as much agreement as possible on the three issues described above. These three—mentioning the nation, the absence of a peace treaty, and citizenship—ceased to occupy the foreground of the German-German talks that continued despite the signing of the treaty in 1972. Ostensibly, the 1973 negotiations, which followed seamlessly upon the 1972 talks, were only to discuss remaining technical questions. However, as it developed, they did not confine themselves to minor issues. Instead, these follow-up talks to the Basic Treaty became dominated by three open controversies left over from the negotiations proper. These three open issues had emerged as problems early in the negotiations, but instead of finding resolution, they became only more problematic as both sides moved from negotiating to implementing the accord. These were the questions of UN membership, of human rights, and of trade with and financial transfers between the FRG and GDR.

UN Membership

The SED had pressed for UN membership from the outset. The first page of Kohl's directive for the first day of negotiations made it clear that such membership was one of the GDR's prime motives.[94] Kohl conveyed this to Bahr. At the following meeting, Bahr reported back to Kohl that he had discussed the possibility of UN membership for both Germanies with the three Western allies.[95] The ambassadors, he reported, "had laughed themselves silly" at the GDR's claim that the Western allies could not conceivably have any objection to UN membership for the two Germanies. Rather, he said, they felt that some kind of quadripartite declaration, stating that UN membership in no way diminished the authority of the four powers in Germany, would be necessary before membership.[96] The four powers resumed quadripartite talks over this issue in the fall of 1972.[97]

The FRG wanted to proceed with applications for UN membership only after the Basic Treaty was negotiated.[98] This hesitancy showed that the West Germans recognized where to apply pressure effectively. Not only the SED leaders but also the Soviets were dismayed by this stance. In late August, Brezhnev sent a letter directly to Brandt, hinting that other issues could be more easily negotiated if the Germanies were first allowed to enter the United Nations.[99] Brezhnev and Gromyko also pressed this view shortly thereafter, during their conversations with Kissinger, who visited Moscow in September 1972. (These conversations were precursors to what would become the Conference on Security and Cooperation in Europe and the Mutual Balanced Force Reduction talks.) According to the CPSU summary provided to East Berlin, the Soviets told Kissinger they saw no reason why UN membership for the Germanies should wait until the conclusion of the Basic Treaty. Kissinger's reply showed uncharacteristic consideration for other policymakers. He reportedly demurred because of his worry that even discussing the issue created the risk of friction with the Brandt government.[100] A more likely reason is probably that Kissinger agreed with the stance of the Brandt government.

A *Neues Deutschland* article of 8 November, announcing the initialing of the Basic Treaty, highlighted as its most important merit the fact that both German states had agreed to be guided by the principles of the UN charter.[101] The SED regime thereby showed in public that it valued the prestige of UN affiliation, and it correspondingly continued to press the issue in private. On 12 December, as the two Germanies readied for the signing, Kohl told Bahr that the GDR would not ratify the treaty until it had gained UN membership.[102] On the day of the signing, 21 December, Politburo member Paul Verner personally repeated the threat to Bahr, telling Bahr, "The treaty can go into force only when UN membership is no longer in doubt."[103] This was clearly an issue of great importance to the SED. The party saw UN membership as an important source of legitimization of its own authority. The issue soon became inextricably linked with two even more complex problems: human rights concessions and financial compensation.

Money in Exchange for People

These two issues must be examined in tandem, for they were closely linked. Indeed, the shorthand phrase used to discuss their most common form was "Geld gegen Menschen," or "money in exchange for people." In the 1960s, West Germany had established a practice of essentially buying the freedom of political prisoners and other would-be émigrés from the GDR. By the time the Wall came down, the FRG had spent over DM 3.5 billion to secure the release of roughly 34,000 prisoners and reunite approximately 250,000 families divided by the Wall.[104] Until the time of the Basic Treaty, such dealings occurred primarily along a shadowy back channel. Both West and East German negotiators referred to this channel as the "lawyer level" because of the involvement of attorneys such as Wolfgang Vogel of East Berlin.[105] The Stasi was heavily involved in this matter as well. On the West German side, such dealings were largely the responsibility of the Ministry for Pan-German (later Inner-German) Relations.[106]

From the beginning of the talks, Bahr made clear that the FRG wanted to address thorny human rights issues in the Basic Treaty. In other words, he wanted the topic addressed on an official level of negotiation, as opposed to the lawyer level. Bahr told Kohl at the very first round of Basic Treaty talks on 15 June that the FRG hoped to provide means for 7,000 divided families to reunite. Bonn also sought to increase chances for cross-border marriages and travel.[107] Bahr reportedly said at the next meeting that the FRG would find it difficult to secure domestic approval for any treaty at all if it did not produce some kind of "tangible" improvements in this area.[108] Bahr tried once again, on 16 August 1972, to raise the issue of reuniting families, specifically of allowing minors to emigrate. Kohl indicated that this was a matter for the "highest authority" and would be difficult to resolve.[109] Bahr further wanted to talk about the GDR's infamous "order to shoot" at those trying to flee across the German-German border. Kohl refused to comment.[110]

Bahr continued to press the matter. He sought to include in the treaty an expression of mutual willingness to work on problems arising from the separation of families, engaged couples, and other kinds of dependents. Indeed, at the end of August, Bahr even handed over to Kohl drafts of the precise wording the FRG sought, including prefabricated letters that he hoped to receive from the GDR. These letters spelled out in great detail what rules would govern emigration and travel across the German-German borders, down to specifics of how would-be émigrés should apply. Kohl and his political masters were incensed at having words put into their mouths and returned the documents in a huff.[111] As Kohl put it, "The GDR is, after all, not some conquered country to which terms of a cease-fire can be dictated."[112]

The move smacked of an attempt by the FRG to rush talks in light of the upcoming FRG election. Realizing a tactical error, Brandt conveyed a message via Bahr on 31 August to the effect that the entire package of documents should be forgotten and regarded as nonexistent.[113] He further sought to undo the damage by telling East Berlin that he was trying to reach an agreement *despite* the elections, not because of them. The West Germans announced that they regarded no agreement as preferable to a bad agreement as they faced a federal election.[114] Given the contemporaneous West German press accounts pointing out that Bahr was negotiating with the East Germans to help Brandt negotiate better with West German voters, however, this claim was not entirely convincing.[115]

For its part, the SED regime was concerned about the effects on its citizens of more visits from Westerners, of greater chances to reunite with family members, and of increased opportunity to marry West Germans. In August, the Stasi formulated reasons why divided families should not be allowed to reunite. The MfS was under no obligation to allow them to do so because, in its view, the families themselves were to blame for their division: "Families were torn apart and children were separated from their families because in the vast majority of all known cases the individuals behaved irresponsibly toward their families, in particular toward their children; because they broke down as human beings; and because they engaged in criminal activities and then sought to avoid their due punishment."[116] Clearly, the SED was not willing to be forthcoming on this issue. One of the motives for the SED's stance in its dealings on human rights was worry about increased desire on the part of its population to take advantage of an easing of strictures.[117] Such an easing could potentially lead to the kind of loss in population that the construction of the Wall had been intended to prevent.

The Soviets seem to have shared this concern. In September, Moscow advised the SED to exercise restraint in permitting cross-border marriages. As for the potential opening of more border crossings, Moscow particularly asked East Berlin "to take into account the interests of the Soviet military forces stationed in Germany" (the instructions specially used the name "Germany" and not "GDR") and to seek military consultation on this topic.[118] Also at this time the SED regime began physically installing the border fortifications that had been decided upon earlier, as described in Chapter 5.[119] When asked by Bahr about such fortifications during talks in October, Kohl denied their existence. Bahr said in an interview in 1996 that this was the only time he felt truly deceived by Kohl.[120]

If the SED leaders' actions reveal that on the one hand they feared loss of population, documents show they were motivated on the other hand by a conflicting desire to gain as much as possible in terms of trade and finance. East Berlin had a long list of desiderata. With regard to commerce, the SED hoped to expand German-German trade (a goal that the ratification of the Traffic Treaty on 22 September made more feasible). It wanted a statement guaranteeing this in the Basic Treaty.[121] During the period of German division, trade had remained one of the few significant links between the two Germanies. As Timothy Garton Ash has rightly pointed out, "for the purposes of trade" the FRG and GDR had essentially "recognized each other from the very beginning." This de facto recognition comprised a patchwork of accords set up in the 1950s and 60s. It consisted of what Garton Ash called "four intersecting circles: trade, hard currency transfers to private individuals in the GDR, hard currency transfers to the state, and government-guaranteed credits."[122] The latter offered credit on terms that were extremely advantageous to the SED.[123] West Germany was willing to offer such terms because, as Chancellor Ludwig Erhard had once explained publicly, "it is not 'business,' rather, it is more significantly a means of maintaining a living connection to the people over there."[124] That attitude still governed thinking in the Brandt era. An internal Stasi report on "the opinion of West German government circles about the further development of trade between the GDR and the FRG," one of the few surviving documents from Markus Wolf's office, noted that the extent of trade depended essentially only on the ability of the GDR to deliver goods. As the report summarized, "of primary importance to the FRG is neither the problem of terms of payment" nor the terms of credit, "but rather that there be established via trade significant factors for deepening contacts between the GDR and the FRG."[125]

East Berlin was also specifically interested in increasing the amount of credit it could get from the FRG. In a meeting shortly after he took over, Honecker had promised Brezhnev to start whittling away at the GDR's "mountain of debt."[126] In a conversation with Bahr on 7 September 1972, Honecker mentioned that he wanted negotiations about some kind of payment and "Verrechnungsvertrag," a credit or internal payment arrangement.[127] Honecker also discussed with Bahr his worries about the opposition of the West German Bundesbank to the interest-free swing credit. In 1971, the GDR had taken advantage of this arrangement to the tune of DM 413 million.[128]

Because of these desiderata, the GDR was extremely interested in the Kleindienst proposal of 10 October to exchange financial and trade concessions for use of the word "nation" in the treaty. Kleindienst's offer gave the GDR what it wanted on three fronts. First, it indicated FRG willingness to maintain and even expand swing credit to an unprecedented maximum of DM 1 billion. Second, the proposal offered to continue managing the account via the bookkeeping unit of a "Verrechnungseinheit," or "VE," a notional unit equivalent to both the West German deutsche mark and the East German mark. The VE was, in essence, a means of effecting transactions at an artificial exchange rate of one Eastern mark to one deutsche mark.[129] Third, the Kleindienst proposal suggested expanding trade in industrially produced goods.[130] The SED seized upon this opening and even sought to make progress in the German-German talks conditional upon these proposals being enacted.[131]

In summary, two SED desires—worry about the effects of increased humanitarian concessions and desire to secure economic gain—stood in conflict to one another. The actions of the SED in negotiations suggest that the latter gained the upper hand. East Berlin decided to use humanitarian concessions as bargaining chips. For example, when talks bogged down in late September 1972 over the issue of mentioning the nation, the GDR announced its willingness to issue an amnesty to some prisoners on or about its national day of celebration, 7 October.[132] It also offered to release from GDR citizenship those East Germans who had fled to the West and had become FRG citizens; such a move would enable them to travel back into the East without fear of being repatriated against their will. The Soviet embassy in East Berlin agreed that such a move would give the GDR an edge in negotiations and would also help Brandt as he faced elections.[133] It recommended, however, that the SED remove some wording that justified the appropriation of the property of those who had left the GDR "illegally." As the embassy put it, "It seems to us that this regulation will seriously diminish the positive effect of the planned measure." In other words, too much revelation of SED motives would undercut the public relations bonus of the amnesty in the FRG.[134] The Soviets softened this blow by saying that they had "sympathy" for the desire of the GDR to include such a clause but pointed out quite bluntly that "the question arises as to whether it is useful to raise the issue of property during the electoral campaign in the FRG."[135] The final version of the amnesty took the form of a "law on questions of citizenship," dated 17 October 1972. It effectively released several million West Germans who had originally lived in East Germany from their citizenship there. They could henceforth, like other West Germans, take advantage of the provisions of the new transit and traffic agreements, the latter of which formally went into effect the same day as the new law.[136]

In one of its most cynical moves, the SED also used children as bargaining chips. Michael Kohl made an offer to Bahr in October 1972 to allow roughly 300 children and minors to join family members in the West. SED documents show that Bahr knew this was not a gift. He replied that, "in conjunction with the exit of the children, certain transfer payments probably should be made." Michael Kohl then responded using a term that appeared often in the German-German negotiations: "Junktim," meaning variously package, or deal, or link. Kohl said disingenuously that, while there was no inherent link between the two—that is, between the payments and the children's emigration—the GDR would indeed appreciate it if both events took place simultaneously.[137] He also made it clear in early November that he would be willing to give Bahr a list of the children's names on the day the treaty would be initialed, or accepted as a final draft, awaiting only official signing.[138] The implication was that if there was no treaty, there would be no list. Three hundred and eight minors had become pawns in the negotiating game.

The two sides agreed on a final draft of the Basic Treaty during the first week of November 1972. In the text itself, the topic of human rights received limited mention. Article 7 contained the general statement that both sides would work "to regulate practical and humanitarian questions."[139] Appendices to the treaty further confirmed this intent and included some minor changes.[140] Arrangements for the details of emigration and of payment transfer, however, seem mostly to have taken shape in private conversations between Kohl and Bahr. As promised, Kohl gave Bahr a list of children and minors who would be allowed to emigrate after the final draft of the treaty had been agreed upon.[141] On 10 November the two discussed details of the upcoming emigration. At this time Bahr reportedly pointed out that, if one included all divided families in which the children had been born in 1954 or later, there were actually 1,179 cases in which families remained divided, not just 308. Kohl did not comment on this statement.[142]

The West German Elections and the Signing of the Basic Treaty

The West German parliamentary election of 19 November temporarily pushed all other topics aside. The result showed that Brandt had been correct in assuming he would receive a ringing endorsement for his policies. On election day, a record 91.1 percent voter turnout yielded a clear statement. For the first time in the history of West Germany, the Social Democrats emerged from the balloting with more seats in parliament than the CDU/CSU. A rush of events followed at the end of November. Preliminary talks for what would become the CSCE got underway. Erich Honecker received a unique kind of international recognition by being interviewed in the *New York Times*.[143] And, with the future of the Brandt government seemingly secured, the two Germanies began to make arrangements for the formal signing of the Basic Treaty.

A controversy quickly arose over who would actually sign on the dotted line. Brandt was willing to sign personally, but this created a protocol problem. It was not clear who Brandt's signing partner should be; his nominal equal would be Stoph, but his de facto equal was Honecker. A more significant question was where the signing would take place. Brandt was willing to travel to East Berlin if the SED would allow it. It seems the SED regime was initially willing to entertain this option. The East German foreign ministry representative in the Basic Treaty talks, Karl Seidel, remembered that there were plans to greet Brandt with music, an honor guard, and a motorcade. The goal was to make Brandt's arrival look as much like a visit from a foreign head of state as possible in order to emphasize the separation between the two Germanies.[144] However, such a greeting would essentially have produced the very spectacle that the SED had avoided two years earlier when it had shied away from allowing Brandt to meet

Stoph in East Berlin.[145] Internal Stasi reports suggest that the risk of some kind of overly enthusiastic welcome of Brandt became too great for the SED to stomach, despite the desirability of treating Brandt like a "foreign" dignitary. One MfS report summarized numerous Western media predictions that Brandt would be greeted by the residents of East Berlin in the same way he had been greeted by the residents of Erfurt—with unseemly jubilation.[146] Another noted that the MfS had received word that "there exists the intent to greet him [Brandt] 'properly' in the capital of the GDR."[147]

By mid-December the leaders of the SED had informed Brandt that they would unfortunately all be in Moscow at the end of the month for a celebration of the fiftieth anniversary of the founding of the USSR and hence unable to receive him in East Berlin.[148] Brandt refused to take the obvious hint. Bahr indicated to Kohl on 12 December that Brandt, while sorry he would not have the chance to meet with Honecker, was still thinking of traveling to East Berlin anyway.[149] Flabbergasted, the East German Council of Ministers settled the issue formally: It issued a decree announcing that, in light of the intent of the FRG's representatives "to misuse" their participation in the signing, only the delegation leaders would be invited to sign.[150]

Hence the signatories on 21 December 1972 in East Berlin were Michael Kohl and Egon Bahr. It would be misleading to describe the signing, which was soon overshadowed in the media by the U.S. Christmas bombing of Hanoi, as a joyous occasion and a great triumph.[151] The squabble over who would sign had cast a shadow over the ceremony. Moreover, the treaty itself essentially instituted acceptance of the sad realities of the Cold War.[152] Nonetheless, the merits of the Basic Treaty deserve recognition. Through complex and often contentious talks, the two sides had effectively reached a modus vivendi. With this accord, Bonn and East Berlin recognized that the division of Germany would remain in place for the foreseeable future (even if the FRG avoided including any formal recognition of the GDR as a sovereign state) and established a basis for regulating the practical problems caused by that division. The Basic Treaty also addressed a great range of issues.[153] It formally stated the commitment of both Germanies to the principle of nonviolence in their dealings with one another. It indicated both sides' willingness to try to promote peaceful relations in Europe as a whole. Both Germanies agreed generally to respect each other's autonomy in internal issues. Various appendices indicated more specific intentions, such as to increase trade and ease traffic and postal flows. They also agreed to exchange "permanent representations," or missions, which would essentially be pseudo-embassies. For all its shortcomings, the treaty provided a framework and institutions for resolving German-German conflicts in the future, thereby reducing the chances that such conflicts would escalate.

The limited luster of the Basic Treaty signing was further dimmed by an emerging controversy over the resistance of the SED to following through on the deals it had made on human rights issues. This resistance had become apparent just before the signing. According to Kohl, in a conversation on 12 December, Bahr complained that not all the children on the list were actually being allowed to emigrate. Showing once again that he knew where to apply pressure, Bahr pointed out that the FRG had a sum of about DM 60–70 million " 'on ice,' " but that its release to the GDR was dependent on a satisfactory resolution to the issue of the children's emigration.[154] Kohl responded that some children and minors, as it turned out, did not want to leave. Kohl added that the money the FRG was withholding was rightfully the GDR's, whether or not the children actually emigrated. To explain why, he once again used the term "Junktim," or linkage. He repeated an argument that Bahr had earlier heard personally from Honecker, that the FRG essentially owed the GDR a kind of "child support" payment.[155] This seemed to be intended for children stranded without close relatives in the East. Kohl informed Bahr that the sum of money under discussion was not "the FRG's money, but rather money from those in the FRG who are responsible for paying support to be given to those who are entitled to receive support in the GDR." Kohl complained that the FRG was constructing an unjustified linkage between emigration and payment and was withholding the latter "without any reason or justification."[156] (How the support money was to be distributed to those entitled to it, however, was not discussed.)

In the same conversation, Bahr also complained about the blockage of emigration by certain GDR citizens who had received permission to leave. In some cases these persons had already sold their worldly possessions and sat literally on packed suitcases. Stories of their plight made it into the West German press, where they became colloquially known as the "Kofferfälle," or "suitcase cases."[157] The extent of the problem was made clear in a telegram to Kohl from the head of the West German chancellery, Horst Ehmke. In it, Ehmke complained that there were 2,700 to 3,000 cases in which individuals with exit visas were mysteriously unable to leave.[158]

Bahr addressed this problem by trying to shame the GDR into making concessions. He pointed out that demanding money in exchange for exit visas was not an appropriate action for a respectable state in the international system, which the GDR desperately wanted to be.[159] In other words, Bahr was trying to put an end to the "lawyer level" practice of backroom dealings of money in exchange for exit visas. He felt that, with relations officially normalized, such backroom dealings were unnecessary. SED files show that Bahr in fact made some progress via this route. He succeeded in getting a verbal agreement from a member of the Politburo, Paul Verner, that East Germany "would not make any financial claims in conjunction with the exit of citizens from the GDR."[160] However, Kohl made clear that the GDR still expected to receive at least DM 65 million in "child support" money.[161] Bahr replied he would look into the possibility of transferring the money. Despite these conversations, the blocked emigrations remained a problem well into 1973. Increasing media attention made the issue even more pressing.[162] Kohl reported that Bahr complained again in a contentious meeting at the end of February 1973. Bahr said that it seemed as if the GDR simply wanted to hold out until the FRG ratified the Basic Treaty, presumably in the summer of 1973. Kohl replied that this was not the case; indeed, the SED felt that the FRG should be thankful to the GDR for its forthcoming nature during the recent election campaign.[163]

Historian Heinrich Potthoff has criticized Bahr's handling of the "suitcase cases," saying that Bahr tried too hard to shame the SED into releasing the would-be émigrés by virtue of the argument that it was unseemly for a respectable state to behave otherwise. As Potthoff sees it, Bahr did not make use of the option of exchanging money for people. However, both Bahr's own and SED documents show that while Bahr did try to get the SED leadership to renounce the practice of trading money for people, he remained aware of the importance of cash as an incentive as well. Indeed, at the end of February 1973 Bahr decided to make a wholesale return to prior practice. Bahr told Kohl that he wanted the lawyer level reinstalled (implying he had succeeded in his efforts to have it stop working).[164] Kohl remarked that this was a complete reversal on Bahr's part. Bahr's willingness to return to established practice may have been due in part to sheer physical exhaustion after the exertions of more than two years of negotiating. In early March he became seriously ill and had to be replaced until May 1973 by Horst Grabert, Brandt's head of chancellery.

At the time Grabert took over, some of the 308 minors had emigrated, but Grabert continued to press for resolution of the remaining cases. He also repeated Bahr's request for reinstallation of the back-channel lawyer level.[165] Kohl kept hedging. For his part, he emphasized the SED's desire both to receive payment and to secure promises of UN membership.[166] The problem remained unresolved in late April 1973.[167] In short, it became clear that East Berlin was not receptive to Bonn's offers to reinstitute this back channel, which was the means by which it exchanged visas for money. As Kohl told Grabert in March 1973, "the lawyer level [is] dead."[168] Hence it was not because of Bahr or Bonn but rather because of East Berlin that the lawyer level remained inactive. It seems that the SED, in the spring of 1973, was more interested in having a bargaining chip to secure ratification of the Basic Treaty and UN membership than it was in returning to business as usual. In other words, this seems to have been an occasion where the SED's prime motive was not monetary gain but rather political legitimization. Membership in the United Nations and ratification of the Basic Treaty were important signs of the GDR's ability to act as a legitimate state on the world stage; such recognition could help compensate for a lack of domestic legitimacy.[169] The push for membership also served as a means of subtly expressing pique at Moscow, which preferred to avoid any contention over what it thought to be minor issues such as the timing of UN membership.

The Impact of Soviet Cold War Concerns

In late May, Bahr recovered from his illness and resumed leadership of the West German delegation. By the end of June, he expressed to Kohl his satisfaction that the issue of emigration blockages had been by and large resolved and that "the 'lawyer level' was functioning again" in parallel to the official level.[170] What had happened between the end of April, when the blockage seemed to be an intractable problem, and the end of June?

Some German-German events helped make the SED more conciliatory. Ratification of the Basic Treaty occurred in the West German parliament on 11 May 1973, which meant that one of the SED's goals was fulfilled.[171] However, a Bavarian constitutional challenge to the validity of the treaty immediately shed doubt on its future. Moreover, dual East/West German entry into the UN had not yet happened. In other words, recognition by the international political community was not yet assured. The blockage continued.

In May 1973, SPD parliamentary leader and old Honecker acquaintance Herbert Wehner decided to try his hand personally with the SED leader.[172] He traveled to East Berlin for a visit on 30 May.[173] Was it, as has been claimed, due to Wehner's visit that the emigration problem was resolved?[174] Wehner's visit did have some impact in reinstating the lawyer level, as the work of Potthoff and others has shown.[175] However, Potthoff's assessment of Wehner requires some revision. SED documents from the visit show that criticism of Potthoff's work is justified.[176]

According to the SED files from the visit, Wehner was concerned not only with reinstating the lawyer level; he was also concerned with challenging Bahr. He found some of the negotiating positions of the official level—that is, Bahr's—deleterious to the German-German relationship. During his visit with Honecker, Wehner criticized any attempt to "go behind the GDR's back," by which he seemed to be referring to Bahr's contacts with Moscow. Wehner asserted that Brandt shared this opinion, but that the chancellor unfortunately let himself be swayed "by bad advisers."[177] Wehner expressed sympathy with the view of the SED with regard to payments from the FRG. When Honecker complained that the FRG was holding back on payments until the children had actually emigrated, Wehner criticized his own leaders and responded that "in this regard,

Herbert Wehner (left) and Wolfgang Mischnick (right) meet with Erich Honecker in the GDR on 30 May 1973. (Signatur M 0531/31 N, Bundesarchiv, Koblenz)

the government of the FRG was taking the wrong stance." Wehner himself then used the SED phrase "Junktim" (linkage) to promise that he would get more involved in this issue. He stated that he would actively try to "get this inadmissible linkage removed."[178]

SED documents strongly suggest, however, that one must look beyond German-German politics to find all the factors involved in bringing about an end to the emigration blockages.[179] It was not only the West Germans who were getting the impression that the SED regime was trying to use the would-be émigrés as pawns in its effort to secure Basic Treaty ratification and get the GDR into the United Nations. The Soviets seem to have felt the same way. Surveying the global political perspective from a different level, they had other concerns that they considered to be more important. Détente with the United States had become increasingly problematic, even as MBFR talks began in early 1973. Despite strong internal resistance from Henry Kissinger, the American senator Henry Jackson insisted in late 1972 and early 1973 on linking trade relations with the USSR—specifically the grant of Most Favored Nation (MFN) status—to an easing of restrictions on Jewish emigration.[180] The legislative manifestation was the Jackson-Vanik amendment. As a result, the Soviets did not receive MFN status; officially, they withdrew their request.

Furthermore, throughout the spring of 1973 the Soviets continued to express worry about China to the SED.[181] Only two months before Wehner's May 1973 visit to Honecker, Brezhnev told Willi Stoph, chairman of the East German Council of Ministers, "The Chinese are conducting politics that are dangerous and harmful to us all."[182] He added cryptically, "They are threatening us with reference to the American fleet."[183] Brezhnev then made clear that the Soviets were also worried about the stability of the Brandt government and about the situation in Vietnam, which remained unsettled despite the Paris Accords between the United States and the North Vietnamese. [184] Brezhnev himself argued, "One must support Brandt."[185]

As a consequence of all of these concerns, Brezhnev made it perfectly clear that the SED needed to be more forthcoming in its dealings with the West Germans. Brezhnev told the SED in late March 1973 that the party had to "rethink the issue . . . of allowing families to reunite." Essentially, he created a direct link between the global concerns of the country he headed and the fate of a few hundred families divided by the German-German border. Brezhnev wanted the SED to "prevent any kind of situation from arising which might make things more precarious." He suggested that being more forthcoming would not actually be dangerous for the SED, because it was "an ideologically stable party."[186] Soviet foreign minister Gromyko found it necessary to remind the SED of these concerns in mid-May during a visit to East Berlin with Brezhnev. He told the GDR to re-think its hard-line stance on some details of the German-German entry into the UN. The Stasi summary of his reasoning is quite brief: "take no risks (Chinese)."[187]

A note from Egon Bahr to Willy Brandt at this time reported that, according to Bahr's informants from the Soviet Union, Moscow had given up hope of improving relations with the Chinese.[188] Brezhnev himself, en route to visit Bonn, spoke at length with Honecker about the long list of Soviet geopolitical concerns.[189] As he told Honecker, the most frightening aspect about China was not merely its possession of nuclear weapons; after all, the United States had them as well, and the USSR had its own arsenal. Rather, "the most horrible, frightening and dangerous thing is that the current Maoist leadership has wholly and completely betrayed Marxism-Leninism and will sign a treaty with any old imperialist state, with Bonn and France, with the main goal of harming the Soviet Union."[190] In other words, Brezhnev was more worried about the Chinese because of their hostile intentions than he was about the United States. At the same time, an SED delegation was invited to Moscow and took part in an internal conference on China—only two weeks before Wehner's visit.[191] Then, according to West German documents, while in Bonn in late May, Brezhnev made it clear that he would make emigration possible once again.[192]

Although no single document clearly says so, it is likely that the visit of

Herbert Wehner, less than two weeks later, provided Honecker with a convenient opportunity to accede to Soviet wishes. Honecker could thereby graciously act more forthcoming with the West Germans and make Moscow happy as well. Ironically, it seems that the success of Herbert Wehner—trumpeted as proof that the Germanies could produce significant progress without the involvement of the superpowers—was in fact the result of Soviet pressure. The Soviet Union's global concerns had very real consequences for German-German politics on the domestic and even the individual level.

The Caesura of 1973

For all of these reasons, by the end of June 1973 it was possible to resolve the controversy over emigration blockage (although it would hardly be the last one). Only a handful of open cases remained. Bahr informed Kohl of the transfer of DM 10 million of the "child support" money.[193] Moreover, the Bavarian legal challenge to the Basic Treaty failed in the summer of 1973, and the accord went into force as a result. Also that summer, a Cold War chapter closed with the death of Walter Ulbricht, and another chapter began with the formal opening of CSCE. In the second half of 1973, the FRG negotiated a treaty with Prague similar to the Warsaw accord.[194] Given the momentum produced by these events, the entry of the two Germanies into the UN proceeded with less difficulty than the contentious nature of previous talks about it had suggested it would. In September of 1973, East and West Germany became respectively the 133rd and 134th members of the United Nations.[195] Soon thereafter, questions of German-German relations would take a back seat to dramatic domestic developments in both West Germany and the United States. Brandt would face the exposure of a Stasi agent, Günter Guillaume, on his personal staff; Nixon would endure the revelations of Watergate. In yet another parallel, both leaders would find themselves forced to resign.

Both Michael Kohl and Egon Bahr took advantage of the caesura of 1973 to resign from the wearying task of normalizing German-German relations.[196] Under Michael Kohl, the SED delegation had managed to fulfill its goals of securing payment in return for human rights concessions and of gaining recognition both from the FRG and the world community. It also achieved its priority of avoiding any direct acknowledgment of "Germany" as a united nation. This priority mirrored that of the Soviet Union. The GDR had pushed quite hard to get the Eastern treaties ratified precisely because, in Soviet thinking, they precluded changes to the Cold War status quo, achieved arduously via the Second World War and subsequent superpower confrontation. Under Bahr, the FRG delegation also achieved one of its top priority goals, namely, obtaining some kind of reference to the nation. It also avoided any definite signs that the accord established the division as permanent. Given the difficulties and many points of contention involved, it is not surprising that the Basic Treaty was limited in its achievement. Countless issues remained open, such as questions of citizenship and property ownership. Kohl and Bahr had not reached a resolution, but rather the beginning of a more intense exchange about the issues that divided the Germanies.

Throughout their talks, both Bahr and Kohl had had to take into account the concerns of each other's respective superpower ally. East Berlin in particular had endured micromanagement by Moscow in nearly every aspect of negotiating and implementing the treaty. The Basic Treaty, which regulated German-German local and even individual controversies, thereby became intimately linked to the global Cold War concerns of the Soviet superpower.

Conclusion:

The Costs of Dealing with the Devil

Mit Worten läßt sich trefflich streiten,
Mit Worten ein System bereiten,
An Worte läßt sich trefflich glauben,
Von einem Wort läßt sich kein Jota rauben.

Words can justify us for the fight
And words can make our philosophy right
Thus words ensure our cause is just
From a single word not a jot is lost.
—Goethe, *Faust*

The formal negotiations between the two Germanies drew to a close without any delegation member commenting on just how appropriate the East German gift of *Faust* had been. Perhaps the analogy was simply too unflattering. Yet the course of the East/West German rapprochement shows that it was apt nonetheless. Both Germanies found themselves dealing with the devil in hopes of achieving specific aims.

On the Western end, Brandt and Bahr forsook confrontation and instead used words to fight against the inhumanities of the German division. They found themselves faced with the unpleasant necessity of conversing civilly with dictators, were nearly removed from office by a vote of no confidence because of it, and endured withering press criticism throughout. The particularly vitriolic attacks of the papers owned by Axel Springer at one point prompted Bahr to send an impassioned reply to Springer personally. Bahr wrote that he was unwilling merely to sit by and watch Ulbricht become stronger and the division of Germany become deeper. "To save what can be saved of Germany demands more courage, more fantasy, more work—and the willingness to let oneself be slandered—than simply to cling to some grandiose ideals," he protested to Springer.[1] This cri de coeur summed up the tension Bahr faced throughout his years as a negotiator. On the one hand, he hoped to "save" as much of German unity as possible; on the other, he provided almost full legal recognition of the German division and the GDR through his dealings. The desire to do the former clashed with the need to do the latter; neither he nor Brandt could never fully resolve this contradiction; such was the burden imposed on them by their Faustian bargain.

On the Eastern side, the SED found itself dealing with representatives of a capitalist system that it regarded as ideologically degenerate. The fact that the leaders of the capitalist enemy were also nominally socialists made them more loathsome. It showed that the SPD, by leading such a state, was yet again betraying the interests of workers. On top of all this, the German-German talks created serious tension between both Germanies and their superpower partners. Yet despite all the fears, both sides managed to make many bargains as a result of the détente dialogue.

Finding Answers

This book has explored the SED regime's side of this dialogue. With the details now established, it is time to return to the larger questions posed in the introduction and to gather together the answers that appeared in the course of the narrative. (1) What did the SED and its Soviet backers hope to gain by entering into the German-German conversation? (2) What did they expect to concede in return? (3) How did they go about pursuing their aims, and were those aims ever divergent? (4) What degree of success did they obtain? Most importantly, why do these details matter? What larger insights do these findings yield for our understanding of the structure and development of the Cold War?

(1) What the SED and the Soviets Hoped to Gain

The motives of both East Berlin and Moscow were quite numerous. In reviewing them, it must be kept in mind that the order of priorities shifted back and forth during negotiations. It is clear that at times the SED's main goal was to secure as much economic benefit as possible. The party sought increased trade in desirable goods, easy terms of payment and credit, and direct financial transfers and payments. Although the role of personal venality and corruption in accruing such funds must be kept in mind, the SED's stated intent in seeking such sustenance was to benefit its centralized economic system as a whole. As James McAdams has rightly claimed, a "driving theme" behind both Ulbricht's and Honecker's leadership was the hope of transforming East Germany into "a model of socialist well-being and abundance."[2] Ulbricht hoped to use Western capital and technology to boost the GDR's economic indicators. While no fan of the FRG, Ulbricht seems to have felt that his long years at the top of Communist politics had endowed him both with a knowledge of what the GDR's needs were and an ability to negotiate with the SPD to fill those needs. To the irritation of the USSR, he wanted to make the GDR into a model of socialist economic success. Ulbricht's successor, Erich Honecker, similarly hoped to use income from dealings with West Germany to reduce GDR indebtedness. Both leaders aimed to show that the GDR under the rule of the SED could achieve economic success just as the West had.

However, despite its often eager pursuit of financial benefits, it would be misleading to say that the SED's goals were purely economic. As Timothy Garton Ash has pointed out, the West had primarily two kinds of coin to offer the SED: money and political recognition.[3] On top of this, the party was not always at liberty to decide which coin it preferred; when Moscow expressed a preference, the SED was constrained by it. For example, the SED, following the inclination of the Soviet Union, blocked any kind of progress at the Kassel meeting between Brandt and Stoph. East Berlin did so despite the fact that it had just signed a lucrative postal agreement with the SPD government, knew that other such accords were in the offing, and hoped for an increase in swing credit. Stoph's instructions from the Soviets were clear, though. He should allow progress only if Brandt were willing to recognize the GDR formally on the spot and exchange ambassadors.

This set of instructions was not entirely a losing proposition for the SED. While the party did sacrifice potential financial gains, it at least did so while holding out for another desideratum, formal recognition. The party also thereby demonstrated obedience to the Soviet Union. A similar situation occurred in the 1973 post–Basic Treaty negotiations. At that time, the SED was preventing would-be émigrés from leaving for West Germany. Bonn tried to get them out by reinstituting the so-called "lawyer-level." This level had previously represented a reliable source of income for East Berlin, via exchanging money for visas. The SED rebuffed the attempt, preferring to hold out for concessions on UN membership—that is, the coin of political recognition—which would allow the SED to assert itself more freely not only in response to Bonn but also in response to Moscow. However, the Soviets soon voiced a different preference: in light of rising international tension, they wanted to minimize any potential for conflict in Europe and told East Berlin to let the émigrés go. Obtaining external legitimacy for the GDR was not nearly as important to the Soviets as their own security. As a result, the SED could no longer hold out for the coin of political recognition and had to be satisfied with the more usual form of currency. Once again East Berlin had to subordinate its own interests to Moscow, but it did still manage to gain something in the process.

In short, the actions of the SED during negotiations were guided by a mixture of financial and political motives and constrained by the need to follow Soviet guidance. At times the party's top priority was political recognition, but at other times it was willing to abandon its drive for recognition in favor of securing monetary gain. The most important example of this is the fact that Bonn's refusal to extend formal recognition to the GDR did not prevent the SED from signing the Basic Treaty. Nor did it prevent the SED from accepting hundreds of millions of deutsche marks in swing credit.

The East Berlin Politburo also sought to pay heed to the lessons it had learned from history. SED representatives repeated again and again that they hoped to prevent warfare breaking out in Europe for the third time in the same century. This does not seem to have been a cynical claim. Although the SED did supervise a militaristic regime in a state with a heavily armed border, its interest in preventing World War III seems to have been sincere, given that such a war would most likely include fighting on the soil of the GDR. Many of the SED's leaders had bitter personal memories of war—including Honecker, who had spent years in a concentration camp—and were determined to avoid repetition. Moreover, the desire to prevent massive conflict on the German-German border fit well with the Soviet instructions to avoid confrontation on the Eastern Bloc's European "front." Moscow sought to forestall problems in Europe while dealing with China and the United States. Hence, SED and Soviet professions of interest in Ostpolitik and détente as means of preventing conflict in Europe were not feigned. Both hoped, as did their Western counterparts, that the process of reaching accord on specific points of conflict would help decrease the chances that small-scale conflicts would escalate into larger ones.

(2) What the SED Expected to Concede

In return for the goals it was seeking, what was the SED prepared to concede? The answer is simple: almost nothing. The SED hoped to give away as little as possible. During the initial phase of German-German contacts, it presented the West Germans with a prepared treaty text as a fait accompli and sought its immediate acceptance. Available SED documentation contains no straightforward assessment of "what we should be prepared to concede." Rather, what dominates is evidence of a conviction that the GDR was *entitled* to concessions from the West. East German documents are filled with claims of why the FRG owed the SED fulfillment of its goals: because West Germany had been hostile to the GDR throughout its existence, because West Germans were class enemies, because West Germany was conducting ongoing economic warfare against the

East, because West Germany was withholding "child support money" that rightfully belonged to citizens of East Germany, and so forth.

The SED did, nonetheless, have to pay the piper. It had to make concessions as a result not only of West German but also Soviet pressure on those occasions when there was a divergence between Moscow's and East Berlin's interests. When events Brezhnev desired—such as ratification of the Moscow Treaty—became linked to progress in the German-German talks, he pressured the SED to be more conciliatory than it wanted to be.

(3) How the SED Pursued its Goals

In fact, Soviet dominance was one of the defining characteristics of the way in which the SED conducted negotiations and pursued its goals. The hypothesis advanced by political scientist Hope Harrison—that the East German tail wagged the Soviet dog—does not apply to the détente era.[4] The East German regime conducted its dealings with the West under the direction of the USSR. Moscow issued orders at several critical junctures, and the SED obeyed.[5] When Moscow told the SED to switch the Brandt-Stoph meeting site from East Berlin to Erfurt, it did. When Moscow told East Berlin to "pause" in its conversation with the West, it did. When Moscow indicated that the SED should resume the conversation, it did. When the CPSU dispatched Falin to East Berlin with a message and told the SED to pass the note on to the West Germans, it did. When regular talks between the two Germanies got underway, the SED Politburo routinely gave the directives for Michael Kohl to the CPSU for advance vetting and consulted with top Soviet leaders on all aspects of German-German relations. When Honecker's hard-line stance with regard to émigrés soured the talks at a time of Sino-Soviet tension, Moscow pressured Honecker to act more conciliatory on the issue of family reuniting. He did. In short, the CPSU "micromanaged" the SED throughout the German-German talks.

Moscow's concerns were not the only outside influences on the SED as it conducted German-German talks. A second defining characteristic was the way in which German-German negotiations were interconnected with all of the major détente negotiations and superpower relations as well. Moscow primarily sought ratification of its treaty with West Germany. The West, realizing this, linked the prospects for ratification to progress in the four-power talks in Berlin and the German-German talks. Kissinger, following his principle of linkage, even made U.S.-USSR bilateral contacts dependent on progress in Berlin.

This interconnectedness gave the SED, and Erich Honecker in particular, some leverage, and revealed a paradox inherent in Soviet micromanagement. Moscow's clear desire to control every detail revealed Soviet fears that the details might slip out of their control. The East German Politburo did not disobey the USSR, but the chance that it might do so at a crucial juncture unnerved the Soviets. Once Moscow saw that ratification was dependent on progress in the German-German talks, assurances that the SED could and would make that progress in a way advantageous to Moscow became essential. Since Ulbricht seemed unreliable, Brezhnev finally acted on the Honecker faction's requests to intervene and end internal Politburo squabbling by forcing Ulbricht out. A squabbling Politburo suddenly became less bearable when the satellite had to provide a key part to the complicated puzzle of détente treaties.

Theoretically, Brezhnev could have quieted the Politburo by swatting Honecker down. The fact that he chose to get rid of Ulbricht instead was due not to the particulars of Ulbricht's views on Ostpolitik but rather to the amount of initiative Ulbricht was showing. Before documents were available, many scholars worked on the assumption that Ulbricht's ouster came about because he was *too much opposed* to Ostpolitik and détente.[6] After the archives opened, the first authors to report on this subject swung to the opposite extreme, claiming that Ulbricht was *too much in favor*.[7] Despite their differing answers, all of these authors are asking the same question: What was Ulbricht's stance toward détente and Ostpolitik? The analysis presented here shows that there are more appropriate questions to ask than this one. Ulbricht's attitude toward the West was complex; he saw that there were costs and benefits to rapprochement. For his part, Honecker campaigned against Ulbricht by pointing out the dangers inherent in becoming more interconnected with the West; but once installed in power, Honecker simply continued the talks without any noticeable alteration in tactics or strategy. Most importantly, direction from Moscow was inconsistent. Brezhnev at first played a kind of double game, discouraging FRG-GDR talks while avidly pursuing his own accord with West Germany. Then, when progress in German-German relations became a necessary precondition for ratification of the Soviet–West German accord, he pressured the SED to make both concessions and progress. Hence, the process of examining who was for and who was against Ostpolitik and détente yields a muddled result. Rather, what mattered was the degree of willingness that Ulbricht and Honecker each displayed toward following Moscow's changing guidance on the topic. Moscow was unwilling to tolerate risky initiatives on the part of its German ally. Brezhnev preferred Honecker to Ulbricht because Honecker seemed less likely to take risks on his own. This preference illuminates another defining characteristic of the negotiation process: the tension between taking risks and containing risks. Both superpowers were interested in pursuing détente, despite all the risks it involved. Yet both worried about their respective German allies showing too much initiative in their own contribution—that is, in the talks over Ostpolitik. They wanted to contain risks by keeping close tabs on their respective German partners.

Another characteristic was the tension that arose on those occasions when

SED and Soviet interests diverged. Both Moscow and East Berlin sought to increase security on the European front. However, to the Soviets this meant limiting the potential for conflicts at a time when the USSR faced new challenges from China and the United States. Moscow worried in particular about both Chinese militarism and the potential that the FRG would gain nuclear capabilities of its own. The SED, meanwhile, understood an increase in security to mean protection against the flow of human beings—either a flow of West Germans *into* the GDR, thanks to improved transit and visitation rights; or a flow of East Germans *out* of the GDR, via cooperation with all those new capitalist visitors. In addition, former GDR citizens who had fled to the FRG might return on West German passports and try to reclaim property in the GDR. Hence, East Berlin and Moscow both sought to increase security in Europe, but they did not always agree on what that meant.

An intriguing open question is the extent to which the SED hoped to gain more authority for itself vis-à-vis Moscow by enhancing the GDR's legitimacy via negotiations with the FRG. Voicing such a desire would have been political suicide for any East German leader. Ulbricht came close to doing so when he expressed interest in an economic confederation, or made remarks to the effect that East Germany was a model even for the USSR, or lectured Moscow that it had to take the GDR seriously and not treat it like just another insignificant Soviet state such as Byelorussia. He paid for this perceived arrogance with the loss of his power. Honecker learned the lesson, and made no obvious comments on this topic. The desire of the SED to gain more authority for itself vis-à-vis Moscow seems to have existed, but there is not enough evidence of it to make any decisive statements. What is clear is that when Soviet and SED interests diverged, the Soviets got their way.

(4) What Degree of Success the SED Obtained

From the point of view of the SED, the results of the German-German negotiations were mixed. On the positive side, the SED did secure long sought-after guarantees of an increase in both the amount of swing credit and German-German trade. It also achieved de facto recognition by the West Germans, with whom it exchanged pseudo-embassies and ambassadors. The SED also managed to keep controversial issues out of the Basic Treaty proper. The treaty did not contain the word "nation," nor did it resolve the issue of citizenship nor mention the lack of a peace treaty for World War II. As desired, the GDR became a member of the United Nations. Finally, despite formalization of German-German relations, the SED managed to keep open the back channel for trading exit visas for money.

Hence, at first glance, it would seem that the SED had reason to be completely satisfied. Yet the party had to pay a price as well. It had to endure West German unwillingness to give the GDR full legal recognition and Moscow's unwilling-ness to help the East German regime hold out for more. East Berlin had to tolerate a mention of the "national question" in the Basic Treaty. The entry of East Germany into the UN happened in tandem with that of West Germany, making it seem less justified by virtue of the GDR's status alone. Throughout the negotiation process, the SED had to put up with Soviet micromanagement on nearly all issues.

Finally, implicit in the SED's neediness was an awareness of its own in-stability. Had the economy of the GDR been on a sounder footing, the party would not have needed to seek economic favors from the West. Had the legit-imacy of the SED been more firmly established within the borders of the GDR, the party would not have needed to seek recognition abroad. In other words, the East German regime hoped through contact with the West to enhance its own stability or at least its semblance of stability. However, by doing so, the party put itself into an ideological bind. By beginning a dialogue with the capitalistic devil in hopes of strengthening itself, the SED exposed both weakness and consciousness thereof.

Another downside was that, in return for the concessions it had received, the SED had to tolerate as its part of the bargain increased contacts with the West. Even when such contact was limited to a meeting at the top level—as in Erfurt—an overwhelming public response resulted. The fortifications that Honecker installed on the border during the Basic Treaty talks testify to his concern about its potential permeability. Moreover, the ranks of the Stasi swelled in the 1970s after the implementation of the Ostpolitik treaties.[8] The increase was due largely to the fact that the MfS fulfilled a variety of functions that in West Germany would have been the responsibility of agencies other than the secret service. For example, the increased travel possibilities created a need for more customs and passport agents at border crossings, jobs that were filled by repre-sentatives from the Stasi. The increased number of Western visitors also re-quired more monitoring. Ironically, this meant that Brandt's policies, which had as one of their goals achieving improvements in the living conditions of average East German citizens, inspired an increase in the size of the main apparatus of surveillance and control. This increase nonetheless testifies to insecurity on the part of the SED regime.

Expanding Our Understanding of the Cold War

Challenges Facing Eastern Bloc Leaders

What is the larger significance of the details presented above? They shed light on three aspects of the history of the Cold War. First, the narrative of the East

German Politburo's response to Ostpolitik helps us to better understand the challenges facing the leaders of Eastern Bloc states. Some challenges were internal. It is clear, for example, that Ulbricht faced serious challenges to his policies from within the Politburo. SED documents suggest that Brezhnev faced challenges as well. These findings agree with the assertion of Jonathan Haslam that the heads of Warsaw Pact states were less absolute dictators and more rulers who had to manage the consensus-driven leadership style of the respective politburos.

Ulbricht and Honecker also had to consider the public relations dimension of their actions, despite the lack of an independent press in the GDR. Examples of the need to do so arose again and again during the German-German talks. The SED Politburo wanted to invite Willy Brandt to East Berlin for the first Brandt-Stoph conversation in March 1970, but it rescinded its invitation out of fear of the public response. Then, in planning for a meeting in Erfurt, the SED placed its priority on making a favorable "optical impression" on Western journalists. This preference came at the expense of security; the SED did not establish a highly visible and threatening display of security forces for Brandt's arrival. As a result, citizens of Erfurt felt emboldened to greet Brandt demonstratively. The resulting public relations fiasco showed that the SED's fears of a warm greeting for Brandt in Berlin had been justified. Precisely this fear prevented the SED from inviting Brandt to East Berlin two years later to sign the Basic Treaty. Moreover, during German-German negotiations, the SED in consultation with the Soviets clearly weighed the public relations impact of offers to the FRG. When the SED announced an amnesty in October 1972 as a means of encouraging the Basic Treaty talks, the SED removed a mention of what would happen to the personal property of those who emigrated. It did so because the Soviets suggested that the measure would make a better impression if it did not address that controversial subject. And one of the reasons both Germanies agreed that Bonn would pay East Berlin a lump sum for the privilege of transit through East Germany was that it would make a better impression on the West German population than if every individual traveler had to reach into his or her own wallet.

At first glance it might seem that the SED and the Soviets would have little interest in what public relations impact their actions would have on the citizens of the West. However, the details of the German-German talks show that the SED was ardently interested in securing as much political recognition from outside its borders as possible. From the very beginning of the German-German contacts, it pressed for both full, legal recognition by Bonn and its own induction into the United Nations. Meanwhile, Moscow sought ratification of the Eastern treaties. Obviously, the willingness of Western leaders to provide both recognition and ratification depended in part on the willingness of their respective electorates to tolerate both. Hence, the image of the GDR in the eyes of the West German electorate mattered to the SED and Moscow.

Sensitivity to the public relations dimension of its offers had an interesting linguistic side effect during the German-German talks. Essentially, the SED faced the challenge of acting like a respected member of the international community while simultaneously pursuing mercenary policies such as demanding money for prisoners. Hence, it needed plausible-sounding euphemisms and excuses for receiving payment from the West. Out of this need arose cynical constructions and hollow-sounding euphemisms such as "child support payments." Phrases like this helped maintain a veneer of civility over the process of bartering with human beings for financial gain. The Faustian bargain for the West Germans was that they were required to play along in maintaining the veneer of civility. SED documents show clearly that Bonn, even after attaining its goal of formalizing relations with a treaty, continued to use the euphemisms created by the East German regime and maintain the process of exchanging money for people.

Whether or not the West German government under Brandt's leadership was morally justified in paying this price—in compromising its virtue by exchanging money for people—remains an open question. On the one hand, it is clear that West Germany (not only under Brandt but also afterwards, under CDU-led governments) was party to deals in which human beings were bargaining chips. West Germans got their hands dirty. They had to deal with a government that not only abused human rights within its borders but also seems to have supported terrorist action outside of them as well, most spectacularly at the Munich Olympics. On the other hand, the deals resulted in individuals who wished to leave East Germany gaining permission to do so. As one of the lower-level FRG officials charged with carrying out practical details of financial exchange put it, "You have to remember our feelings at the time." The goal was to get political prisoners freed and families reunited, and the means was trade and hard currency. "What the GDR did with what we gave them was of no importance to me. The important thing was the goal. I would have made a pact with the devil just to get a few poor souls out of jail."[9] In addition, as Bahr recalled, the alternatives seemed limited.[10]

There exists a great deal of literature that either condemns or defends Brandt.[11] The answer to the question of whether his dealings were justified is ultimately a personal moral judgment; it depends on whether one considers the means or the ends more significant.[12] It also depends on the timeframe one uses in judging such dealings. While negotiations may at first be productive, in the long run they can easily become a self-justifying end in and of themselves. In other words, keeping the talks going becomes a long-term goal to which the achievement of the original objectives is subordinated. As Tony Judt has pointed out, democratic leaders can find themselves "allying with disreputable foreign rulers on the 'realist' grounds that they are the people with whom you have to do business, forgetting that in so doing you have deprived yourself of any political leverage over them, because the one thing that matters most to them—how they get and keep power over their subjects—is of no interest to you."[13] On the other hand, the longer-term perspective can also provide a more favorable judgment. Charles Maier has argued that "Hegel's cunning of history rarely acted so deviously" as in the early 1970s when "Western policy makers, intellectuals, and businessmen" entered into talks that helped in the short term to stabilize both the GDR and the Eastern Bloc. Looking back from the perspective of 1997, Maier found that "by subsidizing socialist Fordism, Western banks and states allowed it a new lease on life, but ultimately helped to undermine the bloc."[14] In short, the question of whether the FRG was morally justified in its actions eludes easy answers.

Another challenge that faced both the SED and the Soviets was that of fulfilling ideological goals.[15] Both documents and interviews show the significance of political ideology in the decision-making process of the Warsaw Pact. As historian John Lewis Gaddis asked with regard to the USSR, why would political leaders maintain a clearly faltering command economy or collectivization program if not out of devotion to certain political ideals?[16] The same question could be posed to the SED. Ulbricht clearly hoped to improve the economic health of the GDR. Rather than simply adopting the principles that had produced the "economic miracle" in the other half of Germany, however, he believed that the socialist method of work could produce superior results. In consultation with his chosen experts in socialist economics, he hoped to prove the viability of the ideological system to which he subscribed. For his part, Honecker expressed clear reservations about the ideological perils inherent in dealing with the class enemy. These reservations obviously had a self-serving dimension and were quickly forgotten once Honecker was in charge. But the attacks were cast in ideological terms, which the Honecker faction clearly felt to be an effective way to wound Ulbricht. Moreover, the internal Politburo discussions about Ostpolitik in no way shunned the rhetoric used in public. Rather, there was a striking continuity between the manner in which relations with the West were discussed both internally and externally. Ideological rhetoric was not used merely for show in talking to the FRG; it characterized internal Politburo debates as well.

The need to maintain ideological appearances posed a significant public relations challenge, as the events in Erfurt made clear. Ideological dictators seek to show the world that their citizens share their ideology. As a result, a visit from the head of an ideologically hostile foreign state poses a huge dilemma. On the one hand, heavy-handed police suppression of public expressions of delight at the capitalist leader's presence reveals the bankruptcy of the notion that the public voluntarily subscribes to socialism. On the other hand, too little policing yields exactly the same result.

Parallel Superpower Worries

The findings of this study further show that the superpowers shared a surprising similarity. Moscow and Washington had very different relationships with their German allies, but they experienced similar worries about them. Both the United States and the USSR had to manage relations with a German ally that was a little too interested in changing the status quo for their tastes. In the East, Brezhnev viewed Ulbricht's actions as a challenge to his personal authority and a potential threat to the notion that Soviet preferences should serve at all times as guidelines for the Warsaw Pact nations. He was not opposed to closer contacts with West Germany—indeed, he pursued them himself—rather, he was opposed to letting anyone else manage them. Moscow worried particularly about the unintended consequences of increased contact between the two halves of Germany.[17]

In the West, the United States had similar concerns. Just as Brezhnev disliked Ulbricht, so too did Nixon and Kissinger have serious reservations about both Brandt's person and policies. Nixon and Kissinger also worried that Brandt might unintentionally unleash events he could not control, as he had done on a small scale in Erfurt. Kissinger perceived an ongoing "latent incompatibility between Germany's national aims and its Atlantic and European ties."[18] Throughout the Cold War, U.S. leaders were particularly sensitive to any perception of discord in the American–West German cooperation because it symbolized U.S.-European cooperation as a whole.

This finding brings into question the nature of the relationship between Ostpolitik and superpower détente. Although Nixon and Kissinger did not view it as such, historians and political scientists have treated Ostpolitik as if it were a subset of U.S. détente policies. Political scientist Werner Link, to name but one example, viewed the emergence of Brandt's Ostpolitik as a long process of West German policy gradually accommodating itself to U.S. policy. He has argued that the increased flexibility with regard to the East that characterized the Brandt government brought the FRG into line with the West.[19]

However, the findings of this study suggest that the view of Raymond Garthoff represents a more accurate portrayal of the relationship between Ostpolitik and détente. Garthoff has argued that Ostpolitik fits with détente in terms of practice but not in terms of concept. In practice, détente consisted on the most basic level of four summit meetings, eleven bilateral commissions, and 150 agreements on topics ranging from health to strategic arms limitations (all of which, in his view, deteriorated in the mid-1970s).[20] Ostpolitik in practice consisted of much the same: meetings, agreements, commissions. Indeed, the two were tactically interdependent. The tactics of reaching the superpower agreements depended in part on the production of German-German accords. And the very existence of the GDR strengthened the negotiating position of the Soviet Union. As Heinrich August Winkler has rightly pointed out, "détente depended on the equilibrium between East and West," and this equilibrium rested on the division of Germany.[21]

The difference between détente and Ostpolitik was conceptual rather than practical. Détente served to *reinforce* the status quo equilibrium, by formalizing it with treaties. This is where Garthoff's interpretation becomes important. He has rightly suggested that Ostpolitik differentiated itself from détente by trying to *challenge* the status quo. As shown here, Brandt and Bahr sought via negotiation to restore at least some aspects of the pre–World War II links between the two halves of Germany and its eastern neighbors—in Bahr's words, to save what could be saved of Germany.[22]

Caution is needed at this point. The amount of initiative the Germanies were showing and their desire to reshape the status quo should not be exaggerated. There exists no firm evidence in the East German archives that either Bonn or East Berlin was striving to establish some kind of neutral German entity. There exist only vague hints that Ulbricht may have entertained ideas of an economic confederation of some kind. Scholars on U.S. foreign policy, such as Wolfram Hanrieder, have shown that Washington worried about whether Brandt might have neutrality as his secret goal.[23] If Brandt did have establishing a neutral Germany as an ultimate goal, he kept it secret not only from the public but also from East Berlin.

Indeed, SED documentation suggests that the opposite was the case. The West Germans were quite vocal about their obligations to their alliance partners. Even though Egon Bahr cherished the notion of the unity of the German nation, he did not try to re-create it.[24] Instead, he repeatedly told Michael Kohl that the Western allies and the conservative opposition in the FRG, which favored alliance with the West, hemmed him in and limited what he could accept in negotiations. To repeat but a few examples, during the USSR-FRG talks, the Soviets complained to East Berlin about Bahr's statement that the FRG "considered its 'Ostpolitik' subordinate to its NATO obligations."[25] Implicit in the Soviet complaint was the frustrated desire to wean West Germany away from NATO. Furthermore, in his meetings with Kohl, Bahr repeatedly said that he needed four-power approval for major decisions. Bahr also allowed himself, albeit grudgingly, to be "muzzled" by the three Western allies when they decided that they themselves wanted to deal with the Soviets over transit. Bahr even put the German-German talks into a holding pattern while Kissinger familiarized himself with the issues at hand in order to become more involved.

The East Germans frequently grew exasperated at what they viewed as excessive concern for the sensibility of Western allies. In short, the East German sources show no attempt by the FRG to substitute its connections to the West with some kind of neutral alliance with the GDR. But this does not change the underlying conceptual tension between détente and Ostpolitik as pointed out by Garthoff.

There exists ambiguous evidence on the issue of West Germany's relationship to its European allies specifically, as opposed to its NATO allies as a whole. Timothy Garton Ash has suggested that West Europeans and Americans entertained similar doubts about Ostpolitik. He has argued that the FRG conducted its Ostpolitik as if it were promoting peace on the continent across the East-West divide "in Europe's name," but that it actually had a supplemental and more important goal: it sought to re-acquire power and sovereignty.[26] The evidence yielded by the SED archives does not entirely support this argument. If Brandt hoped to make use of closer cooperation with the GDR as a means of gaining leverage over his European allies, he did not ask the SED explicitly to join him in doing so. In fact, the documents on German-German relations contain astonishingly few references to European relations; the main concerns of both sides were the attitudes of the superpowers.

Bahr did make one leading remark about European security while in Moscow during the USSR-FRG treaty negotiations. According to the Soviets, he had observed that it would be "extremely dangerous to set a goal of dissolving the existing Bloc alliances . . . as long as a European system of security had not yet been created."[27] Hence, there arises the notion that the FRG might be willing to rethink its existing alliances for a more neutral *European*—as opposed to *German*—entity. In essence, this comment suggests the opposite of Garton Ash's claim: that the West Germans were more interested in promoting a neutral Europe than a neutral Germany. However, the evidence is too sketchy to reach any firm conclusions; and the idea remains that a neutral Europe would fall under German leadership in any case. Overall, most documents suggest that the FRG sought to emphasize, rather than diminish, its commitments to its allies. The majority of discussions were characterized by an awareness that existing pacts would be a fact of life for the foreseeable future.

Finally, the worries of the superpowers resembled each other in yet another way. In their dealings in Europe, both superpowers were heavily influenced by concern over issues arising elsewhere in the world. It has been long established in scholarly literature that Nixon and Kissinger linked various U.S. foreign policy initiatives in disparate parts of the globe to one another. Their efforts at détente in Europe were in large part an attempt to establish favorable conditions for a U.S. withdrawal from Vietnam. The new findings presented here suggest that, to an extent not previously appreciated, a similar dynamic was in operation on the Eastern side. Sovietologists such as Michael Sodaro have argued that "there is no conclusive evidence that the Brezhnev leadership sought a comprehensive agreement with Bonn because of the worsening conflict with China."[28] The evidence newly released from the archives refutes Sodaro's thesis. Soviet receptiveness to both détente and Ostpolitik was clearly a function of increasing worry about the Sino-Soviet conflict. Expressions of anxiety about the Chinese appeared early and often in Soviet communications to the East Germans. Repeatedly, the Soviet leaders indicated to East Berlin that they hoped to decrease the chances for conflict on the European front because they considered the threat from China to be more serious than that from the United States. As Brezhnev pointed out to Honecker in 1973, although both the United States and China had nuclear arsenals, Chinese intentions were far more threatening. In fact, worry about China was one of the main reasons the Soviets were willing to abandon an important legitimizing strategy for the Warsaw Pact—namely, the argument that it was a defense against West German revanchism. Ostpolitik accords were the beginning of the end for that strategy, but Moscow was willing to let it go. In short, Henry Kissinger's courting of China turned out to be extremely beneficial for the Western negotiating stance regarding détente in Europe.

As a result, the global concerns of the Soviet superpower had direct consequences for the resolution of German-German squabbles, down to the level of decisions about individual émigrés. Brezhnev told Honecker in no uncertain terms that, because of Soviet concerns about China, East Berlin needed to be more forthcoming with regard to several hundred cases of families who wished to reunite. He therefore established a direct link between international and individual worries.

The Local and the Global

This link exemplifies the third way in which a study of German-German relations can expand our understanding of the Cold War: it reveals the tight interconnection between local and global politics.[29] On the one hand, the international context strongly shaped the German-German decision-making process. On the other, the often individual questions dividing the two halves of Germany shaped international events.

During the middle years of the Cold War—a time often viewed as a highwater mark of bipolar superpower politicking—worry about developments in divided Germany remained a key component of Soviet foreign policymaking.[30] Out of this worry arose Moscow's ardent interest in the ratification of the Moscow Treaty. In his memoirs, Henry Kissinger registered surprise at just how often he was able to use Brezhnev's interest in the Moscow Treaty to gain leverage over the Soviets.[31] Kissinger remained continually amazed by the significance that Moscow accorded to this treaty with a "rump state" that had no nuclear arsenal whatsoever.[32] Any of the other accords under negotiation at the same time—such as SALT—might have been more logical choices as top priority. The clear interest Moscow had in getting a treaty with West Germany ratified was, in essence, an interest in reinforcing the Cold War status quo of the early 1970s. In Soviet eyes, it provided a measure of security on the European front as tensions with China remained high. It also sealed the division of Germany and confirmed the borders that the Soviets felt they had achieved at great expense during the war. As an important added bonus, the cooperation with the FRG carried with it the unspoken implication that Bonn might be willing to cooperate on other issues, perhaps even to the detriment of NATO.

The weight that the Soviets assigned not only to the Moscow Treaty but also to the process of regulating open questions about the German division as a whole suggests strongly that scholars of the bipolar era need to devote more consideration to German issues. English-language scholarship about the Cold War has focused primarily on bipolar issues. Meanwhile, German scholarship on the same time period has often explored German-German relations as independent from the international context, looking for examples of the two Germanies regulating conflict without superpower involvement. This is not to suggest that such approaches were misguided; much fruitful scholarship resulted. Now, however, the opening of previously inaccessible archives shows that both approaches are incomplete. Arguments over what were essentially municipal questions of access from one half of Berlin to the other demonstrably influenced superpower relations. And global concerns such as the Sino-Soviet conflict determined the fate of German children who wanted to reunite with their families. In other words, the solutions reached to local—and even individual—questions of German-German relations often had their origins in Soviet concern over issues of global importance, and vice versa.

Historical writing on Cold War Europe needs to show an awareness of these links between the local and the global levels, because, as in Goethe's masterpiece *Faust,* the deals and the bargains took place on many levels. Ironically, just as Faust met with a surprisingly peaceful fate due to the unexpected intervention of angelic higher powers, so too did the division of Germany come to a pacific end because of unanticipated larger events. Rather than concluding in suffering, the Faustian bargain and the German division both dissolved in the face of greater forces. The painless ending was all the more surprising since the GDR in particular and the bipolar structure of the Cold War in general appeared to have achieved lasting stability just before they vanished entirely.

The analysis presented here has taken advantage of the windfall of East German sources to highlight cracks in this historical facade of stability. It has explored the insecurities engendered within and between the East German and

Soviet regimes by the challenge of Ostpolitik and détente. If this book may claim to offer any larger wisdom for political history as a whole, it is perhaps that scholars proclaiming the discovery of stability in political entities should keep the words of Goethe in mind:

Denn alles, was entsteht
Ist wert, daß es zugrunde geht
For all that comes to birth
Is fit for overthrow, as nothing worth.

Note on Sources: The Bureaucracy of Evil

The essay below addresses the challenge of working with the paperwork produced by the bureaucracy of a dictatorship. It reveals the scholarly infrastructure of this book and is intended to help those considering future reading or perhaps future research. First, there is an overview of the primary sources and methodology. Technical details about these primary sources, such as archival locations and call numbers, may be found in the Bibliography listings. Next, the most relevant books and articles of secondary literature are summarized. These works, along with many others, are addressed in detail in the endnotes to the book, and full citations are given in the Bibliography as well.

Primary Sources

Eastern

The sources for this study came primarily from files in the former SED party and GDR state archives (the party-state distinction is much clearer in the archives than it ever was in reality).[1] When I was conducting my research, these materials were located respectively in Berlin and Potsdam. The archives of the Ministry for State Security (usually abbreviated in official documents to MfS, or Stasi—located in Berlin, Dresden, and Leipzig—provided significant evidence as well.[2] The party, state, and Stasi archives opened to researchers only after the fall of the Berlin Wall; often I found that I was the first Western scholar to use a particular collection of documents.[3]

The most important East German file groups were the following: notes from Politburo meetings in East Berlin, the official GDR transcripts from the German-German negotiating rounds, matching secret transcripts from Stasi surveillance, and GDR preparatory papers for each negotiating round. These papers were scattered between the party, state and Stasi archive; usually each archive contained some but not all of a collection, making cross-checking between the three archives mandatory.

Equally important was the extensive correspondence between not only the SED and West Germany but also between the SED and the CPSU. Most of the latter is in a collection with the bland name of the "General Department." The SED borrowed this name from the Soviets. Its blandness concealed the significance of the department's work, namely, the coordination of relations between East Berlin and Moscow.[4] Hence the "General Department" records were among the most informative of all collections and were especially rich in Soviet documents.

Essentially the only East German documentary collection that was not available was the archive of the East German Ministry for Foreign Affairs, which is now in possession of the West German Foreign Ministry. The latter ministry decided to impose a thirty-year hold on documents. My request for an exception to this rule was denied. However, as eminent political scientist Wilhelm Bruns pointed out in his extensive survey of GDR foreign relations, foreign policy was not made in the ministry but rather in the party headquarters.[5] Hence the lack of these sources—many of which exist as copies in party files—is not particularly worrisome.

Soviet sources were much more problematic. Files of the CPSU Politburo, Comintern, and International Department of the Central Committee were notionally "open" at the time of research. In reality, as Soviet scholar Jonathan Haslam explained, hardly any worthwhile files were actually obtainable. As he put it, "when an entry appears on the agenda connected with foreign policy, defense, or intelligence matters, the reader is referred to 'O[sobaiia] P[apka]'—special file. This category of documents—the highest category of secrecy—is not normally available to researchers, certainly not to foreigners. And since the key policy decisions were taken by the Politburo, we are denied access to the crucial sources."[6] The archives of the foreign ministry were closed for this time period, and the defense ministry and KGB archives were closed full stop. In other words, practically speaking very few documents of importance were available at the time of research. In light of this, and considering the extensive number of Soviet documents available in SED files, I decided that the effort and expenditure needed to conduct research in Moscow would not be worth the extra documents it would yield. This decision necessarily colors the character of this book. This study should be viewed as a history of the East German interaction with the Soviet Union, not a history of Soviet decision-making.

Some sources were not available; other sources simply did not exist. As with any historical era, the paper trail is incomplete. To cite but one example, during the détente era there existed a complex web of "back channels." These included but were not limited to: one between Brandt and Brezhnev, one between Bahr and Kissinger, and one between the lawyers who handled the details of the exchange of émigrés for some kind of payment. Because of their secretive nature, they left few written documents, although the Bahr archive does contain a surprising amount of correspondence with Kissinger. The influence of the back channels had to be factored in nonetheless, largely via interviews with participants.

Of course, interviews helped to assess more than just the role of back channels.[7] They often supplied a sense of atmosphere and personality as well. However, they were less useful for reconstructing details. For the book, I either verified detailed claims made in interviews with documents, or indicated where it was not possible to do so, by making clear that the statement was the interviewee's own interpretation.

Western

The most significant Western documents were drawn from Willy Brandt's and Egon Bahr's papers, which are open to users with some restrictions via the Friedrich Ebert Foundation in Bonn.[8] The Bahr Depositorium is particularly useful; it includes copies of documents Bahr kept from not only the German-German but also the West German–Soviet negotiations. Since Bahr, as the confidante of the West German head of the government (Brandt) actually conducted the talks personally, these documents are much more useful than, say, the official records of SALT negotiations, which make little sense without a knowledge of the secret dealings of the confidante (Kissinger) of the U.S. leader (Nixon).[9]

So, despite the fact that official FRG and allied documents were closed at the time of research, it was still possible to create a credible sketch of the Western point of view as well.[10] Interviews with Western politicians, along with materials from the private papers of Helmut Schmidt in Hamburg, the U.S. National Security Archive in Washington, and photos from the Bundesarchiv in Koblenz helped to flesh out the sketch. As a result, this study provides one of the first documented assessments of both German-German and four-power efforts at détente, via the Strategic Arms Limitations Talks (SALT) and the quadripartite negotiations, since the East Germans received copies of Soviet files on these negotiations.[11] What was not possible to assess was the debate and in-fighting within the West German government over the implementation of Ostpolitik; research in the official files of various West German ministries and offices would be necessary to produce this assessment. Such a study is one of the biggest historiographical desiderata for this era.

Reading the Paperwork of Repression

Working with these new East German materials provided the rare opportunity, as historian Klaus Hildebrand once said, "of clearing previously uncatalogued territory, in order to make it manageable and contribute to its gradual cultivation."[12] With opportunity, however, came challenges. The first challenge was to assess to what extent the documents of dictators reflected reality. Certainly any reader would be unwise to take the contemporaneous reports in the main party and GDR newspaper, *Neues Deutschland* ("New Germany"), as accurate descriptions of events. Does the same apply to the internal party documents, or, as the Protestant minister Ulrich Schröter put it with regard to the MfS, "can a repressive apparatus by definition produce only 'false files'?"[13]

Some "false files" do in fact exist in the SED archives. An incident involving Walter Ulbricht after he was ousted from power proves this. After his "resignation," Walter Ulbricht continually tried to play an active role in policymaking, to the annoyance of Honecker and others. As described by researcher Jochen Stelkens, he became so annoying that the Politburo found it necessary to reprimand him, primarily at a Politburo meeting on 26 October 1971.[14] The Politburo file from this meeting contains what is ostensibly a word-for-word stenographic protocol. It includes a litany of complaints about Ulbricht, primarily his personal arrogance, his tendency to bypass the party in formulating economic policy, and his unfortunate habit of patronizing Brezhnev.[15] Hermann Axen remembered in particular Ulbricht's unfortunate comment to Brezhnev that the GDR would expect wholehearted cooperation with the Soviet Union because East Germany was, after all, not just some insignificant Soviet region like Byelorussia. Axen recalled his feelings at the time: "I wished I could just sink into the ground. That was a sign of national arrogance"—one of the ultimate sins of the communist brotherhood.[16]

However, this file is highly suspect. There exist, in addition to the so-called "stenographic protocol," copies of the original version from which it was produced. In other words, the "protocol" seems to have been edited and doctored. This suggests that such editing may have happened to other "stenographic protocols" as well.

Hence researchers must be aware that there are altered files in the archives. However, any good historian knows that all sources must be approached cautiously, so the fact that there are misleading papers in the SED archive is hardly unique. On the whole, I agree with Heinrich Potthoff that SED files "are characterized . . . by a high degree of reliability, because they were meant for the inner power circle."[17] In other words, the internal documents, since they were produced for a small circle of the top leaders of the party who had to make decisions based on them, were not as spurious as the newspapers and other publications of the period. Historian Roger Engelmann, a member of the internal research unit of the Stasi archive, has also subscribed to this view. He has argued that, although the Stasi in particular did have a tendency to convey information to the SED in the most favorable possible light, MfS files nonetheless represent sources of high quality.[18] Those documents that were altered were edited as they were passed down the hierarchy of power.[19] Hence, this problem can be addressed in part by reading documents from the *top* of the hierarchy, that is, from the Politburo. In short, such doubts are no reason to avoid the SED files altogether. Rather, researchers must make clear that an awareness of their potential ambiguity informs any analysis.

One way to maintain such an awareness is to try to establish, and then bear in mind, what the specific problems with a documentary collection might be. For example, it is clear that Erich Honecker, after assuming power, selectively destroyed some of Walter Ulbricht's files.[20] In addition, Honecker actively sought to increase the circulation of remaining files that cast Ulbricht in an unfavorable light. One of the most often cited sources in current GDR research is a selective compilation of papers from the late 1960s and early 1970s, which Honecker himself culled from both his own and Ulbricht's files. Honecker had these documents typed up, bound in faux calf-leather (hence the collection's nickname, the "calf-leather volume" or, in German, "Kalbslederband") and distributed for a limited time period to fellow Politburo members in 1989.[21] Why he did so was not clear; presumably Honecker wanted to remind his peers of his own skill in backroom maneuvering (which led to the ouster of Ulbricht) at a time when he sensed rebellion in the ranks. Portions of it were published by Peter Przybylski, but Przybylski created titles for documents and made other changes not justified by the originals; hence, the original documents have been cited in this study.[22] In any event, this bound collection is a useful but problematic source, since documents were clearly selected tendentiously to improve Honecker's image.

Another challenge was the necessity of maintaining an awareness of the peculiar nature of Stasi documents on détente. They differ from MfS surveillance of private life in several regards, but one deserves particular emphasis: the Stasi was listening to top-level negotiators who knew they were under observation. The two lead negotiators, Bahr for the FRG and Michael Kohl for the GDR, indicated this awareness at various points. The fact that both men assumed that their so-called "private conversations" were "on the air" adds a layer of complexity to their talks, similar to that described in the chapter "Ketman" of Czesław Miłosz's brilliant book *The Captive Mind*.[23] As Miłosz put it,

> [I]t is hard to define the type of relationship that prevails between people in the East otherwise than as acting, with the exception that one does not perform on a theater stage but in the street, office, factory, meeting hall, or even the room one lives in. . . . Acting in daily life differs from acting in the theater in that everyone plays to everyone else, and everyone is fully aware that this is so.[24]

Miłosz named this practice "Ketman" after a term from Islamic philosophy. The word describes the actions of someone trying to "keep silent about one's true convictions."[25] This was considered a desirable activity, because "he who is in possession of truth must not expose his person, his relatives or his reputation to the blindness, the folly, the perversity of those whom it has pleased God to place and maintain in error."[26] Miłosz found this to be a surprisingly accurate description of the way people spoke to each other in Eastern Europe under Soviet hegemony. Although Miłosz was thinking of interactions between two Easterners, the description is an apt one for the Bahr-Kohl "private" conversations as well, since both assumed that they were acting not only for each other but for Stasi microphones as well. Hence, the influence of this assumption on their conversation with each other must be borne in mind when reading accounts of their "one-on-one" talks. Records of Kohl's remarks exist not only in the form of these conversations with Bahr but also in personal summaries of his impressions of each negotiating round, which he delivered after nearly every meeting to his political masters in the SED Politburo.

Yet another kind of research challenge emerged not from the documents themselves but rather from the archive rules—specifically the Stasi archive guidelines. The extremely strict laws governing use of the MfS archive mean that researchers cannot consult *any finding aids whatsoever*. As a result, one must *guess* where there might be interesting documents—without knowledge of how the millions of Stasi documents are divided or catalogued—and request them from an assigned case worker who in most cases is not an archivist. When this guesswork does result in relevant files being delivered, the case worker must first vet them and decide whether or not they are suitable for release, a decision that often ends in the negative, in which case the researcher is not informed about the withheld papers.[27] On top of this, the Stasi archive has not yet finished cataloguing its holdings. Hence, there may be many more documents on the topic of this book, both known and unknown to archival staff, in the archive of the East German Ministry for State Security.[28] In the course of my research, I essentially created a finding aid for myself, which I have reproduced in the Bibliography.

Finally, I faced a personal challenge in reading the SED and Soviet paperwork of repression. On the one hand, there was the difficulty of following the advice of law professor Siegfried Mampel that *ratio* had to take precedence over *emotio*, no matter how distressing the bureaucracy of evil might become. On the other hand, I wanted to avoid the notion that "tout comprendre, c'est tout pardonner"—to understand is to forgive.[29] The reader will have to decide to what extent I have succeeded in doing both.

Methodology

To deal with the content of these documents and interviews, I used the methodology of archivally based political history combined with interviews and oral history. The amount of material available on this topic was enormous (the German-German negotiations alone produced thousands of pages of transcripts). In an effort to make the amount of reading manageable, I imposed strict limits on the breadth of the topic. My focus was on the impact of Ostpolitik and détente on the political elite of the GDR and on the relationship of that elite with the Soviet Union. The East German archives show, quite unsurprisingly, that the real political elite in East Germany was not the East German government.[30] Rather, power rested with the *party* organizations, namely, the CPSU Politburo for the most significant decisions and the SED Politburo for the rest. Therefore the SED Politburo members, their actions, and their relations to their Soviet colleagues serve as the focus of this study.[31]

This book does not attempt to evaluate GDR public attitudes toward Ostpolitik. A serious attempt to ascertain public opinion in a dictatorship would have required not only a different methodology but also different sources than those employed here. Such a study remains a hole in the literature that needs to be filled. This study has instead focused on elite decision-making as newly revealed by formerly secret archives.

Overview of Secondary Literature

Even before these archives opened—indeed, while politicians were still at work—détente and Ostpolitik inspired a great deal of scholarly assessment. Numerous titles are cited in both the narrative and endnotes. It may be helpful, however, to those seeking further reading to provide an overview of the most relevant academic literature here.[32] In the interest of brevity, this overview highlights scholarship dating from after the opening of Eastern bloc sources, although the insights of many authors who wrote before 1989 remain worthwhile reading.[33] Given that the literature on Cold War German-German relations is so large, I will focus on three subgroups of the relevant literature that I found most helpful in preparing this study.[34]

First, a large amount of energy has been devoted to investigating the largely West German issue of whether or not Brandt's policy of engagement with the East was appropriate, both in terms of its constitutionality and its morality. Shortly after unification, social scientists such as Jens Hacker and Konrad Löw argued that it was not.[35] This point of view is now, however, most strongly associated with the name of Timothy Garton Ash. His 1993 treatise, *In Europe's Name: Germany and the Divided Continent*, examined Ostpolitik both in theory and in practice from 1969 until 1989, with copious references to the 1949–1969 period as well.[36] Garton Ash found that "the idea of liberalisation through stabilisation, with its behaviourist core of relaxation through reassurance, was always flawed."[37] Rather, he argued, the accommodating attitude of the West German government toward the Socialist Unity Party (SED) created the opposite, namely, a stabilization of the GDR without liberalization. Garton Ash came to the conclusion that, as a result, Ostpolitik discouraged those who sought reforms, encouraged those in power to continue with business as usual, and thereby hindered and delayed the protest process, which eventually produced the revolutions of 1989. Since the publication of Garton Ash's book, Klaus Schroeder and Jochen Staadt have taken Garton Ash's criticism even further. They have suggested that, following the lead of politicians trying to make the best of geopolitical realities, scholars did the same with the image of the GDR.[38] Schroeder and contributors to his 1994 book *Geschichte und Transformation des SED-Staates: Beiträge und Analysen* argued that West German commentators overestimated the positive aspects of socialist life and downplayed the role of terror in the dictatorship.[39] The other side of this argument has been most eloquently presented by Peter Bender. In a second edition of his book *Neue Ostpolitik* (*New Ostpolitik*) published in June 1995, Bender used Garton Ash's own words to contradict him. Bender argued that

> neither Brandt nor Schmidt nor Kohl was so naive as to believe that stabilization would bring liberalization; but all three knew that it would be in no one's interest if the GDR, kept alive by Moscow, became fatally ill. Past experience had shown that failing communist regimes began to use violence and sealed themselves off from the outside world. So the government of the FRG chose to concentrate on a long-term strategy.[40]

The policy of change through rapprochement proved itself in the nonviolent revolution that resulted, Bender suggested. Similar praise tempered the otherwise negative assessment of Ostpolitik in the study of the collapse of the Berlin Wall by Philip Zelikow and Condoleezza Rice. They found that Ostpolitik established both a history of negotiating and a network of personal contacts, which bore fruit in the speedy diplomatic agreement over German unification in 1990.[41] The authors on both sides of this debate have one key commonality: while they may or may not draw on Eastern sources, they focus on providing a critique or a defense of the actions of West Germans. This is a valid undertaking, but it is not the goal of the present study.

Second, there does exist a body of scholarship that examines the Cold War from the East German point of view.[42] The most relevant works for this book are those studies which address Ostpolitik as part of a larger survey of GDR history, or en route to explaining 1989.[43] The most prominent books in this group are Charles Maier's *Dissolution: The Crisis of Communism and the End of East Germany*, James McAdams's *Germany Divided*, and Hans-Hermann Hertle's German-language writings on the collapse of the Berlin Wall.[44] Another particularly worthwhile study is Jeffrey Kopstein's investigation of the entire existence of the GDR in his study of its economic decline, *The Politics of Economic Decline in East Germany, 1945–1989*.[45]

Finally, there do exist some studies focused specifically on the history of the GDR in the years of Ostpolitik. Those most relevant to the topic of this book are the following: Monika Kaiser's detailed study of the ouster of SED leader Walter Ulbricht in 1971;[46] Jochen Staadt's book on the SED's Westpolitik, or "Western policies," which he saw to be a counterweight to West German initiatives;[47] Heinrich Potthoff's two edited collections of documents on German-German relations from 1969 onward, which contain both Eastern and Western sources;[48] and two booklets by Detlef Nakath that specifically address German-German negotiations in the 1970s. In one, Nakath attempted a reconstruction of the meetings in Erfurt and Kassel between the two postwar German heads of government; in the other, a reconstruction of a few Basic Treaty negotiating sessions.[49] What the present study offers this body of GDR-focused scholarship is an expansion of the field of focus. This study places the East German view of Ostpolitik into the international context of superpower competition.

Indeed, one of the main findings of the analysis presented here is that the actions of the SED can be understood only in conjunction with those of the Soviet Union and the three Western allies as they tried to negotiate their own détente accords. Hence, the final body of scholarship to which this study contributes is that which addresses the history of superpower relations. Works such as William Bundy's *Tangled Web*, Raymond Garthoff's massive *Détente and Confrontation*, W. R. Smyser's *From Yalta to Berlin*, and the writings by and about Henry Kissinger have offered initial scholarly assessments of the Cold War.[50] This study expands upon these works by documenting the role that divided Germany played in superpower decision-making in the détente era. For this reason, the findings described here should be of use not only to Germanists but also to scholars whose primary interest is in the international conduct of the Cold War.

In closing, I would like to devote a special mention to a book that greatly facilitated the production of this volume. I often relied on *The Longman Companion to Cold War and Détente 1941–91*. This compilation of key dates, terms, and events, edited by John W. Young, was an invaluable help. Since the Cold War connected events in many disparate locales around the globe, it is difficult to remember exactly who did what when to whom in every country simultaneously. Many a time Young's volume helped me to find the correct date or leader's name in no time at all. Readers contemplating their own research projects should make this paperback volume their first purchase.[51]

Notes

Abbreviations

This list explains the abbreviations used in the endnotes. For more details about the nature and characteristics of the various collections cited (particularly the Stasi sources), see the Bibliography. Some less used and self-explanatory abbreviations (such as the shortening of "Sonderablage Stoph" to "Stoph" or "Büro Kohl" to "Kohl" on second reference) are not included.

Abt.	Abteilung (Department)
Allg. Abt.	Allgemeine Abteilung (General Department, i.e., the SED archival collection that holds records of GDR-Soviet correspondence)
BA-V	Bundesarchiv-Abteilung V (Federal Archive, Department V, i.e., the former GDR state archive)
BStU	Bundesbeauftragter für die Unterlagen des ehemaligen Staatssicherheitsdienstes der DDR (Federal Commissioner for the Files of the Former State Security Service of the GDR, i.e., Stasi Archive)
EBD	Egon Bahr Depositorium
FES	Friedrich Ebert Stiftung
Gen.	SED abbreviation for "Genosse" (Comrade)
HM	Hauptamtlicher Mitarbeiter ("official coworker" of the Stasi)
HS PA	Helmut Schmidt Privatarchiv
HV A	Hauptverwaltung Aufklärung (main administration, surveillance, i.e., Markus Wolf's department)
IM	Inoffizieller Mitarbeiter ("unofficial coworker" of the Stasi)
IntVer	Abt. Internationale Verbindungen (Department for International Relations, i.e., the department of the SED Central Committee that kept records from German-German negotiations)
"Kalbslederband"	This is a collection of papers that Erich Honecker had stored in his private steel office storage case ("Panzerschrank"). In 1989, he took out these papers and had them bound in artificial "Kalbsleder," or calf-leather. Hence the volume has the nickname "Kalbsleder-band," or "calf-leather volume." Unfortunately, the pages of the "Kalbslederband" are not numerated. As it is a bound volume with fixed pages, however, one can number the pages oneself from the first page to the end (page 171). Hence the page numbers cited from this volume (identified as "my page no.") are the result of my own numbering; they may be easily used to find a page in the bound volume by counting forward from the first page.
MfAA	Ministerium für Auswärtige Angelegenheiten (East German Ministry for Foreign Affairs)
MfS	Ministerium für Staatssicherheit (Ministry for State Security, i.e., Stasi; see Bibliography for list of departments)
NG	Niederschrift aus dem Gedächtnis (protocol written from memory, akin to a "memcon" in U.S. parlance)

Pz	Panzerschrank (private filing cabinet)
SAPMO	Stiftung-Archiv der Parteien und Massenorganisationen der DDR (Foundation/Archive of the Parties and Mass Organizations of the GDR, i.e., the former SED archive)
SdM	Secretariat des Ministers (minister's office)
SN	Stenografische Niederschrift (stenographic protocol)
SPK	Staatliche Plan Kommission (State Planning Commission, i.e., the central authority for economic planning in the GDR)
StS	Staatssekretär (state secretary, *not* equivalent to U.S. secretary of state)
WHY	*White House Years*, first volume of Henry Kissinger's memoirs
WVS	Warschauer Vertragsstaaten (Warsaw Treaty States, East German abbreviation for states of the Warsaw Pact)
VdM	Vorsitzender des Ministerrates. SED files tend to use full titles on nearly every single reference. Hence "Willi Stoph" is usually referred to as "Vorsitzender des Ministerrates der DDR Willi Stoph (Chairman of the Council of Ministers of the GDR Willi Stoph)." This has been abbreviated to "VdM Willi Stoph" throughout.
vorl.	vorläufig (temporary)
ZA	Zentrales Archiv (Central Archive)
ZAIG	Zentrale Auswertungs- und Informationsgruppe (Central Assessment and Information Group)
ZK	Zentralkomitee (Central Committee)

Note on Usage

1. Henry Kissinger, *WHY* (Boston: Little, Brown, 1979), 97; Charles S. Maier, "West Germany as Subject . . . and Object," *Central European History* 11 (Dec. 1978): 384. See also the suggestion of two political scientists that one should refer to East Germany as part of an "informal empire": Alexander Wendt and Daniel Friedheim, "Hierarchy under Anarchy: Informal Empire and the East German State," *International Organization* 49 (Autumn 1995): 689–722.

2. The author thanks Peter Jukes for his help in rendering the poetry of *Faust* into English. Excerpts from *Faust* are taken from the 1887 edition, reprinted by Reclam Verlag (Stuttgart, 1986). The translations given here were informed by, and in part drawn from, the Philip Wayne English-language edition (London: Penguin, 1949).

Introduction

1. Letter from Brandt to Stoph, 25 March 1970, in DC20-I/2-1341 (Ministerrat) BA-V. Goethe was apparently a topic of conversation at various points during the day as well. He was discussed both during the lunch—see "Vermerk über Gespräche während des Mittagessens, das der VdM am 19.3.1970 für den Bundeskanzler der BRD und Mitglieder seiner Delegation gab," p. 5, in DC20-4682 (Stoph), BA-V—and at the end of the day; see "Vermerk über die Begleitung des westdeutschen Bundeskanzlers auf der Rückfahrt von Erfurt und die Verabschiedung des Bundeskanzlers am Grenzkontrollpunkt Gerstungen," 20 March 1970, p. 29, in DC20-4681 (Stoph), BA-V.

2. Indeed, Walter Ulbricht seems to have believed that West Germans had lost the

right to say they spoke in Goethe's language. As he announced at the thirteenth plenary session of the Central Committee in June 1970, "Man kann . . . nicht mehr von der Gemeinsamkeit der deutschen Sprache sprechen. Zwischen der traditionellen deutschen Sprache Goethes, Schillers, Lessings, Marx und Engels, die von Humanismus erfüllt ist, und der vom Imperialismus verseuchten und von den kapitalistischen Monopolverlagen manipulierten Sprache besteht eine große Divergenz."("One can no longer speak of the commonality of the German language. A large divergence now exists between the traditional German language of Goethe, Schiller, Lessing, Marx, and Engels and the manipulated language that has been corrupted by imperialism and manipulated by capitalistic, monopolistic publishers.") In IV 2/2/408 (ZK), SAPMO, on the page with the handwritten page number 175.

3. "Die DDR öffnete Goethes Sarkophag, Geheimaktion im November 1970," *Frankfurter Allgemeine Zeitung*, 18 March 1999, 1.

4. The East German archives show, quite unsurprisingly, that real political power in East Germany was in the hands of the Politbüro, not the state apparatus. For further discussion of the power structure of the GDR, see A. James McAdams, *Germany Divided: From the Wall to Reunification* (Princeton: Princeton University Press, 1993).

5. This assertion differs from the argument advanced by Hope Harrison in 1993 that, in the early 1960s, Ulbricht did do a certain amount of "wagging." She argued that Khrushchev felt forced by Ulbricht into building the Wall; see Hope M. Harrison, "Cold War International History Project: Ulbricht and the Concrete 'Rose,' New Archival Evidence" on the Dynamics of Soviet-East German Relations and the Berlin Crisis, 1958–1961" (Washington, D.C.: Woodrow Wilson International Center for Scholars, Working Paper No. 5, May 1993): 7. Further details on specific documents are available in Hope M. Harrison, "Inside the SED Archives: A Researcher's Diary," *Cold War International History Project Bulletin* 2 (Fall 1992): 20, 28–32; and Hope M. Harrison, "The Berlin Crisis and the Khrushchev-Ulbricht Summits in Moscow, 9 and 18 June 1959," *Cold War International History Project Bulletin* 11 (Winter 1998): 204–17.

6. One of the main reasons European powers were willing to enter into what became World War I was their fear that, were they to wait, their enemies might become too powerful to defeat in the future. On this topic, see David Herrmann, *The Arming of Europe and the Making of the First World War* (Princeton: Princeton University Press, 1996).

7. John Lewis Gaddis, *Strategies of Containment: A Critical Appraisal of Postwar American National Security Policy* (Oxford: Oxford University Press, 1982), 286.

8. Alexander Wendt and Daniel Friedheim, "Hierarchy under Anarchy: Informal Empire and the East German State," *International Organization* 49 (Autumn 1995): 689–722.

9. Robert H. Jackson and Carl Rosberg draw a useful distinction between "empirical" sovereignty or legitimacy, which is conferred by an electorate, and "juridical" sovereignty, which is conferred by other states and does not require empirical sovereignty as a precondition. See Jackson and Rosberg, "Why Africa's Weak States Persist: The Empirical and the Juridical in Statehood," *World Politics* 35 (1982): 1–24. See also Robert H. Jackson, *Quasi-States: Sovereignty, International Relations, and the Third World* (New York: Cambridge University Press, 1990). Another significant book on this subject is Stephen Krasner, *Sovereignty: Organized Hypocrisy* (Princeton: Princeton University Press, 1999).

10. Timothy Garton Ash, *In Europe's Name: Germany and the Divided Continent* (New York: Vintage, 1993), chap. 3.

11. The phrasing of this sentence comes from Paul Rabinow, ed., *The Foucault Reader*

(New York: Pantheon, 1984). On the theme that one must study the Communist leadership élite as well as the life of the masses, see Martin Malia's introduction to the English translation of Stéphane Courtois et al., *Le livre noir du Communisme: The Black Book of Communism*, translated by Jonathan Murphy and Mark Kramer (Cambridge: Harvard University Press, 1999). Malia argues that "the central issue in Communist history is not the Party's ephemeral worker 'base'; it is what the intelligentsia victors of October later did with their permanent coup d'etat, and so far this has scarcely been explored" (x).

12. Charles S. Maier, *Dissolution: The Crisis of Communism and the End of East Germany* (Princeton: Princeton University Press, 1997), 47.

13. One could envision the kind of attempts that Ian Kershaw made to discern public opinion in the Nazi period being attempted for East Germany as well. See Ian Kershaw, *Popular Opinion and Political Dissent in the Third Reich: Bavaria 1933–1945* (Oxford: Clarendon Press, 1983); *The "Hitler Myth": Image and Reality in the Third Reich* (Oxford: Oxford University Press, 1987); and *The Nazi Dictatorship: Problems and Perspectives of Interpretation*, 3d ed. (London: Edward Arnold, 1993).

14. McAdams, *Germany Divided*, 11.

15. Peter H. Merkl, *German Foreign Policies, West & East* (Santa Barbara, Calif.: Clio, 1974), 133.

16. This phrase appears in the Politburo instructions for Willi Stoph before his meeting with Willy Brandt in Kassel in May 1970. "Grundsatzerklärung des VdM der DDR, Genosse Willi Stoph, beim Zusammentreffen mit dem Bundeskanzler der BRD, W. Brandt, in Kassel," 1–2, in J IV 2/2A/1.438–39 (Politbüro), SAPMO.

17. N. Edwina Moreton, *East Germany and the Warsaw Alliance: The Politics of Détente* (Boulder, Colo.: Westview, 1978), 5.

18. Peter Pulzer, *German Politics, 1945–1995* (Oxford: Oxford University Press, 1995), 127.

19. Tony Judt, "Counsels on Foreign Relations," *New York Review of Books*, 13 August 1998, 54.

20. John Lewis Gaddis's study of postwar American foreign policy, *Strategies of Containment*, begins with the Faust metaphor. He points out that, during World War II, "collaboration with the Soviet Mephistopheles helped the United States and Great Britain achieve victory over their enemies in a remarkably short time and with surprisingly few casualties, given the extent of the fighting involved." Gaddis also cites an old Balkan proverb that President Roosevelt would use as justification for cooperating with Stalin: " 'My children, it is permitted to you in the time of grave danger to walk with the devil until you have crossed the bridge.' " Gaddis, *Containment*, 3.

21. For more information on debates within West Germany over Ostpolitik, see Dennis L. Bark and David R. Gress, *A History of West Germany*, 2d ed. (Oxford: Blackwell, 1993), which is divided into Vol. 1, *From Shadow to Substance, 1945–1963*, and Vol. 2, *Democracy and Its Discontents, 1963–1991*; and David F. Patton, *Cold War Politics in Postwar Germany* (London: Macmillan, 1999).

Chapter One

1. Alexander George, "The 'Operational Code': A Neglected Approach to the Study of Political Decision-Making," *International Studies Quarterly* 12 (June 1969): 190–222. The quotation is taken from John Lewis Gaddis, *Strategies of Containment: A Critical Appraisal of Postwar American National Security Policy* (Oxford: Oxford University Press, 1982): viii–ix.

2. Jack Snyder, "East-West Bargaining Over Germany: The Search for Synergy in a Two-Level Game," in *Double-Edged Diplomacy: International Bargaining and Domestic Politics,* edited by Peter B. Evans, Harold K. Jacobson, and Robert D. Putnam (Berkeley: University of California Press, 1993), 118.

3. The secondary literature about the time period 1945–1969 is more extensive on the Western side, with the consequence that this historical review is better informed for the West than for the East, but an attempt has been made to counter this tendency by citing key Eastern documents where possible. Readers looking for further reading on the pre-1969 history of the Germanies have a range of choices. Probably the most detailed account of the Cold War history of West Germany is K. D. Bracher, Theodor Eschenburg, Joachim C. Fest, and Eberhard Jäckel, eds., *Geschichte der Bundesrepublik Deutschland,* 5 vols. (Stuttgart: Deutsche Verlags-Anstalt, 1983–1986). See also Dennis L. Bark and David R. Gress, *Democracy and Its Discontents, 1963–1991,* Vol. 2 of *A History of West Germany,* 2d ed. (Oxford: Blackwell, 1993). For a concise introduction to the history of both Germanies, see Henry Ashby Turner Jr., *Germany from Partition to Reunification* (New Haven: Yale University Press, 1992).

4. Timothy Garton Ash, *In Europe's Name: Germany and the Divided Continent* (New York: Vintage, 1993), 317.

5. The literature on the immediate postwar period in Germany is vast. Readers interested in further information might want to start with recent publications and then use their bibliographies for further guidance. See Carolyn Eisenberg, *Drawing the Line: The American Decision to Divide Germany, 1944–1949* (Cambridge: Cambridge University Press, 1996); Klaus-Dietmar Henke, *Die amerikanische Besetzung Deutschlands* (Munich: Oldenbourg, 1995); and Norman Naimark, *The Russians in Germany: A History of the Soviet Zone of Ocupation, 1945–1949* (Cambridge: Harvard University Press, 1995).

6. For more information on the role of the SED in the history of German socialism and communism, see Eric D. Weitz, *Creating German Communism, 1890–1990: From Popular Protests to Socialist State* (Princeton: Princeton University Press, 1997).

7. Turner, *Partition,* 65–73.

8. For basic information on 1953, see Arnulf Baring, *Der 17. Juni 1953,* 2d ed. (Stuttgart: Deutsche Verlags Anstalt, 1983). For accounts written after the opening of the East German archives, see Manfred Hagen, *DDR-Juni '53* (Stuttgart: Steiner, 1992); Armin Mitter and Stefan Wolle, *Untergang auf Raten* (Munich: Bertelsmann, 1993); and Ilko-Sascha Kowalczuk, Armin Mitter, and Stefan Wolle, eds., *Der Tag X, 17. Juni 1953* (Berlin: Links, 1995). See also Egon Bahr, *Zu meiner Zeit* (Munich: Karl Blessing, 1996) 78–81, on the role of RIAS in the uprising. For an interesting account of the U.S. reaction to the 1953 uprising, as well as footnotes that serve as good bibliographic guides, see Christian Ostermann, " 'Die Ostdeutschen an einen langwierigen Kampf gewöhnen': Die Vereingten Staaten und der Aufstand vom 17. Juni 1953," *Deutschland Archiv* 3 (May/June 1997): 350–68.

9. Bahr, *Zu meiner Zeit,* 157. Here, presumably, are the seeds of what critics would later claim was his overly statist approach, i.e., one that ignored citizens' movements in favor of ruling elites.

10. Turner, *Partition,* 83–84.

11. Turner, *Partition,* 87–88.

12. For the draft of an order to seal the border, see "Beschluß des Ministerrates der Deutschen Demokratischen Republik," J IV 2/202/107, Büro Walter Ulbricht, SAPMO. For maps indicating where transit lines would be cut, see the file J IV 2/202/177, Büro Walter Ulbricht, SAPMO.

13. For basic historical information on the construction of the Berlin Wall, see (to

name but a few works) Hermann Weber, *DDR: Grundriß der Geschichte* (Hannover, Ger.: Fackelträger, originally published 1976; new ed. 1991), Hermann Weber, *Die DDR 1945– 1990* (München: Oldenbourg, 1993), or Peter Bender, *Die "Neue Ostpolitik" und Ihre Folgen: Vom Mauerbau bis zur Vereinigung* (originally published May 1986; 2d ed., München: Deutscher Taschenbuchverlag, Feb. 1995). See also Hope M. Harrison, "Cold War International History Project: Ulbricht and the Concrete 'Rose': New Archival Evidence on the Dynamics of Soviet-East German Relations and the Berlin Crisis, 1958– 1961," Working Paper No. 5, Woodrow Wilson International Center for Scholars, Washington, D.C., 1993; Michael Lemke, *Die Berlinkrise 1958 bis 1963: Interessen und Handlungsspielräume der SED in Ost-West Konflikt* (Berlin: Akademie, 1996); and A. James McAdams, *Germany Divided* (Princeton: Princeton University Press, 1993).

14. Hans-Hermann Hertle, *Chronik des Mauerfalls: Die dramatischen Ereignisse um den 9. November 1989* (Berlin: Links, 1996), 28–38.

15. Brandt had spent many years in Berlin local politics, and his tenure as mayor lasted from 1957 to 1966. For autobiographical and biographical information about Brandt, see Willy Brandt, *My Life in Politics* (New York: Viking, 1992), and Barbara Marshall, *Willy Brandt: A Political Biography* (Oxford: Macmillan, 1997).

16. Brandt, *My Life in Politics*, 4–5.

17. East Germany reportedly expected only 30,000 people to petition for passes; instead an estimated 1.2 million did. See Bender, *"Neue Ostpolitik,"* 131. Bahr called the first Passierscheinabkommen "ein riesengroßer kleiner Erfolg" ("A great big giant little success"). Bahr, *Zu meiner Zeit*, 164.

18. А. А. Громыко, *Ламятное* Кн. 1.-2-е (Москва: изгательство политической литературы, 1990), 63. An abridged, one-volume version of Gromyko's memoirs is available in English: Andrei Gromyko, *Memoirs* (New York: Doubleday, 1989).

19. Roger Engelmann and Paul Erker, *Annäherung und Abgrenzung* (Oldenbourg: München, 1993), 165.

20. Heinrich Potthoff (among others) finds that the Passierscheinabkommen of 1963 "became a model for how practical improvements in daily life could be reached through agreements with the Communist system in the other half of Germany" ("wurde zum Modell für das mühselige Unterfangen, konkrete Verbesserungen für die Menschen durch Vereinbarungen mit dem kommunistischen System im anderen Teil Deutschlands zu erreichen"). Heinrich Potthoff, *Bonn und Ost-Berlin 1969–1982* (Bonn: Dietz, 1997), 19.

21. This strategy is reminiscent of Karl Deutsch's model of European integration, in which small-scale functional cooperation can "spill over" into deeper political cooperation and eventually identity change. Thanks to Tim Snyder and Jeffrey Kopstein for pointing this out.

22. Andreas Vogtmeier, *Egon Bahr und die deutsche Frage: Zur Entwicklung der sozialdemokratischen Ost-und Deutschlandpolitik vom Kriegsende bis zur Vereinigung* (Bonn: Dietz, 1996), 61. See also GDR diplomat Karl Seidel's comments that the two precursors to Ostpolitik, in the view of the East Germans, were the Pass-Agreements between the government of the GDR and the Senate of West Berlin and Bahr's speech to the Evangelische Akademie in Tutzing. Karl Seidel, "Erste Schritte auf dem Weg zu normalen Beziehungen zwischen der Deutschen Demokratischen Republik und der Bundesrepublik Deutschland. Persönliche Erinnerungen an die deutsch-deutschen Verhandlungen Anfang der siebziger Jahre," in Detlef Nakath, ed., *Deutschlandpolitiker der DDR erinnern sich* (Berlin: Fides, 1995), 100.

23. For information on the Pass-Agreements in both 1963 and after, see Engelmann and Erker, *Annäherung*. On German-German trade before 1969, see Garton Ash, *In*

Europe's Name, 152–62; Maria Haendcke-Hoppe-Arndt, "Interzonenhandel/Innerdeutscher Handel," in Deutscher Bundestag, ed., *Deutschlandpolitik, innerdeutsche Beziehungen und internationale Rahmenbedingungen*, Vol. 5 of *Materialien der Enquete-Kommission "Aufarbeitung von Geschichte und Folgen der SED-Diktatur in Deutschland,"* (Baden-Baden/Frankfurt a.M.: Nomos Verlag/Suhrkamp Verlag, 1995); and Karl-Heinz Schmidt, *Dialog über Deutschland: Studien zur Deutschlandpolitik von KPdSU und SED (1960–1979)* (Baden-Baden: Nomos, 1998), 27. On deal-making to secure the release of prisoners, see Rainer Barzel, *Es ist noch nicht zu spät* (Munich: Droemer Knaur, 1976), 31–42; Ludwig A. Rehlinger, *Freikauf: Die Geschäfte der DDR mit politisch Verfolgten 1963–1989* (Frankfurt: Ullstein, 1991); and Craig R. Whitney, *Spy Trader: Germany's Devil's Advocate and the Darkest Secrets of the Cold War* (New York: Random House, 1993).

24. For a history of German-agreements before the 1960s, see Ernest D. Plock, *The Basic Treaty and the Evolution of East-West German Relations* (Boulder, Colo.: Westview, 1986).

25. Bark and Gress, *Democracy and Its Discontents*, 100–101. On this topic see also Joseph Held, ed., *The Columbia History of Eastern Europe in the Twentieth Century* (New York: Columbia University Press, 1992). The GDR instituted an "Ulbricht Doctrine" in reaction to the Hallstein Doctrine in February 1966. According to this doctrine, the GDR would not normalize relations with West Germany until it established diplomatic relations with the GDR; see Rudolf Morsey, *Die Bundesrepublik Deutschland: Entstehung und Entwicklung bis 1969* (München: Oldenbourg Verlag, 1990), 94.

26. Klaus Hildebrand, *Von Erhard zur Großen Koalition 1963–1969*, Vol. 4, *Geschichte der Bundesrepublik Deutschland*, edited by K. D. Bracher, Theodor Eschenburg, Joachim C. Fest, and Eberhard Jäckel (Stuttgart: Deutsche Verlags-Anstalt, 1984), 187–88. On the peace note, see also Klaus Schroeder, *Der SED-Staat: Geschichte und Strukturen der DDR* (Munich: Bayerische Landeszentrale für Politische Bildungsarbeit, 1998), 192.

27. Raymond Garthoff, *Détente and Confrontation: American-Soviet Relations from Nixon to Reagan*, rev. ed. (Washington, D.C.: Brookings Institution, 1994), 125.

28. Potthoff, *Bonn und Ost-Berlin*, 19.

29. On Kiesinger, see Bark and Gress, *Democracy and Its Discontents*, 98; see also Morsey, *Bundesrepublik*, 94. On the various uses of the word "Ostpolitik," see Note on Sources.

30. See Willi Stoph's files on his correspondence with Kiesinger in DC20-4539/41 (Stoph), BA-V. See also A. James McAdams, "The New Diplomacy of the West German Ostpolitik," in *The Diplomats, 1939–1979*, edited by Gordon A. Craig and Francis L. Loewenheim, (Princeton: Princeton University Press, 1994), 547.

31. Morsey, *Bundesrepublik*, 95; see also Potthoff, *Bonn und Ost-Berlin*, 20.

32. The political scientist Boris Meissner views the so-called "Budapest Appeal" as an indicator of the sincerity of Soviet interest in détente. Boris Meissner, "Das Entspannungskonzept der Hegemonialmacht: Entspannungsbegriff und Entspannungspolitik aus der Sicht der Sowjetunion," in Hans-Peter Schwarz and Boris Meissner, eds. *Entspannungspolitik in Ost und West* (Cologne: Carl Heymanns, 1979), 11. Ultimately, this appeal was to result in the conference that produced the Helsinki accords of 1975. Kissinger attributed the fact that the European Security Conference ever happened at all to unparalleled Soviet doggedness. As he put it, "the idea of a European Security Conference had been a staple of East-West discussions for a decade and a half." He continued: "Communist policy is often described as diabolically clever, complicated, following well-thought-out routes toward world domination. This was not my impression. On the contrary, I found Soviet diplomacy generally rigid; nor is subtlety the quality for which

Soviet diplomacy will go down in history.... But Soviet diplomacy has one great asset. It is extraordinarily persevering; it substitutes persistence for imagination.... So it was to some extent with the idea of the European Security Conference. Disparaged in the Fifties, rejected in the Sixties, it finally began to gain acceptance with the passing years by default, as it were." Henry Kissinger, *WHY* (Boston: Little, Brown, 1979), 412–13.

33. Morsey, *Bundesrepublik*, 98.

34. Bark and Gress, *Democracy and Its Discontents*, 107–8.

35. Kissinger, *WHY*, 99.

36. On Bahr's work in the Foreign Ministry's planning staff (Planungsstab), see Vogtmeier, *Bahr*, 98–104; and Bahr, *Zu meiner Zeit*, 224–47. Bahr stated that "Ohne die drei Jahre der Großen Koalition wäre der Grundriß für die Ostpolitik nicht entworfen worden; er erlaubte den unmittelbaren Start zur operativen Umsetzung im Kanzleramt, scheinbar aus dem Stand; denn das Gebäude auf dem Reißbrett war öffentlich nicht bekannt" (247) (in brief, these years spent planning allowed him to hit the ground running once Brandt became chancellor). Bahr also stressed the importance of his work in the APAG (Atlantic Policy Advisory Group), the political planning group of NATO (224). Because of this preparatory work, Bahr maintained that policies that seemed to appear suddenly at the beginning of Brandt's time in office had in fact been prepared during the Große Koalition: "Was draußen überstürzt aussah, erschien im Kanzleramt oft quälend langsam" ("What seemed rushed to outsiders seemed unbearably slow to those of us in the chancellery") (279). The Foreign Ministry was not the only institution rethinking approaches to the East; in August 1968, in the time period of the Grand Coalition, the Deutsche Gesellschaft für Auswärtige Politik also produced a study on the issue of "Anerkennung der DDR." Perhaps it should not come as a surprise to find that a copy of this report is preserved in the Stasi Archive: " 'Anerkennung der DDR: Die politische und rechtliche Problematik,' Deutsche Gesellschaft für Auswärtige Politik, Studiengruppe für Internationale Sicherheit," pp. 144–216, in Rechtsstelle 1001, ZA, BStU.

37. Kissinger, *WHY*, 99.

38. The chances that Brandt could become chancellor outright—that is, of his party's winning an absolute majority in elections—were slim, so a coalition partner would be required. Contemporaneous changes within another major West German party, the liberal FDP, made the chances of such an alliance with the SPD more likely. Walter Scheel replaced Erich Mende as party leader at the nineteenth party congress in January 1968, a switch that meant that the FDP would look more favorably on the efforts of Brandt and Bahr. See Vogtmeier, *Bahr*, 119. Mende had reportedly grown tired of pressure from within his own party for a more flexible attitude toward the GDR. See Hildebrand, *Von Erhard*, 282.

39. Peter G. Boyle, *American-Soviet Relations: From the Russian Revolution to the Fall of Communism* (London: Routledge, 1993), 160.

40. John W. Young, *The Longman Companion to Cold War and Détente, 1941–91* (New York: Longman, 1993).

41. Quoted in Bender, "*Neue Ostpolitik*," 83. Détente scholar Raymond Garthoff argued that De Gaulle issued this call because he failed to make France an alternative center of power to the superpowers. Garthoff, *Détente*, 11. On DeGaulle, see also J. P. D. Dunbabin, *The Cold War: The Great Powers and Their Allies* (London: Longman, 1994), 272–73.

42. Zdeněk Mlynář, *Nachtfrost: Erfahrungen auf dem Weg vom realen zum menschlichen Sozialismus* (Cologne: Europäische Verlagsanstalt, 1978), 300–301. According to Mlynář, Brezhnev made these comments at a meeting of the Czech leadership with the

Politburo of the CPSU in Moscow on 26 August 1968. Translation in text is by the author, but the book is also available in English: Zdeněk Mlynář, *Nightfrost in Prague: The End of Humane Socialism* (New York: Karz, 1980).

43. In his book *In Europe's Name*, Garton Ash referred to the FRG's tendency to go through Moscow to produce concessions in East Berlin as the practice of "working the triangle" (83 and chap. 3, titled "Bonn-Moscow-Berlin").

44. Bahr, *Zu meiner Zeit*, 157.

45. Vortrag von Prof. Dr. Werner Link, in Deutscher Bundestag, ed., *Deutschland- politik, innerdeutsche Beziehungen und internationale Rahmenbedingungen*, 442.

46. Christopher Andrew and Oleg Gordievsky, *KGB: The Inside Story of Its Foreign Operations from Lenin to Gorbachev* (New York: HarperCollins, 1990), 489.

47. H. Weber, *DDR: Grundriß der Geschichte*, 104.

48. Bark and Gress, *Democracy and Its Discontents*, 174. On this point, see also Monika Kaiser, *Machtwechsel von Ulbricht zu Honecker: Funktionsmechanismen der SED-Diktatur in Konfliktsituationen 1962 bis 1972* (Berlin: Akademie, 1997), 278.

49. "Stenografische Niederschrift der Beratung der sechs Bruderparteien in Dresden am Sonnabend, dem 23. März 1968," p. 2, in J IV 2/201/777 (ZK), SAPMO. The file J IV 2/201/778 contains a continuation of this document as well. On the significance of the Dresden meeting, see Kieran Williams, *The Prague Spring and Its Aftermath: Czechoslo- vak Politics 1968–1970* (Cambridge: Cambridge University Press, 1997), 71–75.

50. "Information über die Moskauer Besprechung am 8. Mai 1968," Berichterstatter Hermann Axen, p. 20, in J IV 2/201/787 (ZK), SAPMO. See also "Stenografische Nie- derschrift der führender Repräsentanten sozialistischer Länder 14/15.07.68," J IV 2/201/790 (ZK), SAPMO, particularly Ulbricht's comment on p. 41: "Es geht doch nicht nur um die tschechoslowakische Frage, es geht um eine große internationale Auseinan- dersetzung" ("It is not just a question of Czechoslovakia; it is a matter of great interna- tional debate").

51. The most useful investigation of the GDR's military role in the Prague invasion is Rüdiger Wenzke, *Die NVA und der Prager Frühling 1968: Die Rolle Ulbrichts und der DDR- Streitkräfte bei der Niederschlagung der tschechoslowakischen Reformbewegung* (Berlin: Links, 1995). For more general studies of Prague, see Jan Pauer, *Prag 1968: Der Einmarsch des Warschauer Paktes* (Bremen: Edition Temen, 1995); Lutz Prieß, Vaclav Kural, and Manfred Wilke, *Die SED und der "Prager Frühling" 1968: Politik gegen einen "Sozialismus mit menschlichem Antlitz"* (Berlin: Akademie, 1996); and Williams, *Prague Spring*.

52. Kaiser claims that the new leadership in Prague was not feared but rather was warmly welcomed by Ulbricht and that the only real point of contention was the Czech- oslovak press criticism of various SED Politbüro members. Kaiser, *Machtwechsel*, 288. For this analysis, she relied heavily on the transcript of the Dresden meeting (J IV 2/201/777), which does not unequivocally support her claim, and on interviews with former Politbüro member Peter Florin and Ulbricht's former economic adviser Wolfgang Berger.

53. Kaiser, *Machtwechsel*, 300.

54. "Information über die Moskauer Besprechung am 8. Mai 1968," p. 25.

55. Wenzke, *NVA*, 100.

56. Ibid., 158, but the entire chapter "21. August 1968—Der Anteil der DDR und der NVA an der Invasion," pp. 115–59, is worth reading for its carefully nuanced answer to the question, did the NVA participate in the Prague invasion? Wenzke comes to the con- clusion that, since intent to intervene was clearly present, the number of East German troops who actually set foot on Czechoslovak soil is not important. Here is how Wenzke phrases this point in his own words: "für die politische, moralische, und juristische

Beurteilung der Teilnahme der DDR und ihrer Streitkräfte ist es jedoch weitgehend unerheblich, wieviel Soldaten der NVA nun im wahren Sinne des Wortes einmarschiert waren. Die Führung des ostdeutschen Staates hatte sich von Anfang an mitschuldig an der Unterdrückung der Reformbewegung gemacht. Sie trägt auf Grund ihrer Integration in die Vorbereitung und Durchführung der militärischen Intervention die politische und militärische Mitverantwortung. Die Haltung und die Aktivitäten der NVA waren eindeutig gegen die Souveränität der CSSR gerichtet und verletzten Völkerrecht" (158–59).

57. Pauer, *Prag 1968*, 385.

58. McAdams, *Germany Divided*, 72.

59. Wenzke, *NVA*, 69.

60. For more information on Ulbricht's economic policies, see Martin McCauley, *The German Democratic Republic since 1945* (London: Macmillan, 1983).

61. Rainer Weinert, "Wirtschaftsführung unter dem Primat der Parteipolitik," 291, in Theo Pirker, M. Rainer Lepsius, Rainer Weinert, and Hans-Hermann Hertle, eds., *Der Plan als Befehl und Fiktion: Wirtschaftsführung in der DDR* (Opladen: Westdeutscher Verlag, 1995). According to Weinert, high-level SED supporters of NÖS included Erich Apel, Wolfgang Berger, Helmut Koziolek, Claus Krömke, Günter Mittag, and Herbert Wolf.

62. Hans-Hermann Hertle, *Der Fall der Mauer: Die unbeabsichtigte Selbstauflösung des SED-Staates* (Opladen: Westdeutscher Verlag, 1996), 23.

63. Weinert, "Wirtschaftsführung," 292–93.

64. Hertle, *Fall der Mauer*, 24.

65. See, for example, the specific amounts of various raw goods requested in the 13 April 1970 letter from Ulbricht and Stoph to Brezhnev in DC20-4455 (Stoph), BA-V.

66. Hertle, *Fall der Mauer*, 21, 35; and Kaiser, *Machtwechsel*, 403. See also Jeffrey Kopstein, *The Politics of Economic Decline in East Germany, 1945–1989* (Chapel Hill: University of North Carolina Press, 1997).

67. Kaiser, *Machtwechsel*, 378.

68. "Stenografische Niederschrift der Besprechnungen anläßlich des Freundschaftsbesuches der Partei- und Regierungsdelegation der DDR in der Sowjetunion vom 7. bis 14. Juli 1969," p. 22 of "Zweiter Beratungstag: Dienstag, 8. Juli 1969 (Genosse Breshnew eröffnet die zweite Besprechung im Moskauer Kreml um 10.30 Uhr)," in J IV 2/201/819 (IntVer), SAPMO. Quoted in Kaiser, *Machtwechsel*, 306.

69. The quotation here comes from a document with no title, dated 28.7.1970, in "Kalbslederband," my page 30. (See Note on Sources for description of this source.)

70. Hertle, *Fall der Mauer*, 26. On the Valuta-Mark, see Armin Volze, "Ein großer Bluff? Die Westverschuldung der DDR," *Deutschland Archiv* 5 (Sept./Oct. 1996): 701–13.

71. Jochen Staadt, *Die geheime Westpolitik der SED 1960–1970: Von der Gesamtdeutschen Orientierung zur sozialistischen Nation* (Berlin: Akademie, 1993), 210–11; and Weinert, "Wirtschaftsführung," 289. The discussion in "Fritz Schenk im Gespräch mit Gerhard Schürer. Günter Mittags Rolle in der DDR-Wirtschaft," *Deutschland Archiv* 6 (June 1994): 633–37, suggests that Apel was the true author of NÖS, along with Günter Mittag, which might help to explain why he would be particularly disappointed by its failings.

72. See the section "Der Weg in die Verschuldung (1971–1980)" in Hertle, *Fall der Mauer*, 34–42.

73. Melvin Croan argued that Erfurt and Kassel showed "Ulbricht's reluctance to engage in constructive negotiations," but the analysis below will show that in fact the reluctance stemmed from the Soviets and Ulbricht's opposition within the Politburo. See Melvin Croan, *East Germany: The Soviet Connection* (Beverly Hills: Sage, 1976), 25–26.

74. Christian F. Ostermann, "New Evidence on the Sino-Soviet Border Dispute, 1969–1971," *Cold War International History Project Bulletin* 6/7 (Winter 1995/96): 187.

75. Arnulf Baring also discussed its importance in his 1982 book *Machtwechsel: Die Ära Brandt-Scheel* (Stuttgart: Deutsche Verlags-Anstalt, 1982), 235–36.

76. "Übersetzung aus dem Russischen," no descriptive heading but first line "Vom 20. bis 23. August hielt sich eine Delegation der SPD mit dem stellvertretenden Vorsitzenden der Partei und Vorsitzenden der SPD-Fraktion im Bundestag, Schmidt, sowie seinen Fraktions-Stellvertreterns Möller und Franke in Moskau auf," p. 5 in J IV 2/202/89 (Büro Ulbricht), SAPMO.

77. Document without title or date, first sentence reads "2 марта 1969 г. на острове Даманский . . . ," in J IV 2/202/359 (Allg. Abt.), SAPMO.

78. Document without title, handwritten date 13 March 1969, note at top "Inf. an GS Betr.: sowjetisch-chines. Beziehungen," in J IV 2/202/359 (Allg. Abt.), SAPMO.

79. Garthoff, *Détente*, 228–42. On the same topic, less useful but still interesting is Richard Nixon, *The Memoirs of Richard Nixon* (New York: Grosset & Dunlap, 1978).

80. Garthoff, *Détente*, 233.

81. Ostermann, "Sino-Soviet," 188. In his 1994 book *Diplomacy*, Henry Kissinger suggested that the Soviets were most likely the provocateurs, because "the skirmishes invariably took place near major Soviet supply bases and far from Chinese communications centers—a pattern one would expect only if the Soviet forces were in fact the aggressors." Kissinger, *Diplomacy* (New York: Simon and Schuster, 1994), 722. For Soviet descriptions of skirmishes in 1969, see the various summaries passed on to East Berlin in J IV 2/202/359 (Allg. Abt.), SAPMO.

82. "Авантюристический Курс Пекина," *Pravda*, 28 Aug. 1969, 2–3. See also Garthoff, *Détente*, 237.

83. Kissinger, *WHY*, 183. He was most likely referring to the following: "А война, если бы она вслыхнула в нынешних условиях, лри существующей технике, смертоносном оружии и современных средствах его доставки, не оставила бы в стороне ни один континент" (roughly, "Should war break out under today's conditions, with today's technology, deadly weapons, and modern means of delivery, it would not restrict itself to one continent"). *Pravda*, 28 Aug. 1969, 3.

84. Harrison Salisbury, *War between Russia and China* (New York: Norton, 1969). On Soviet attitudes, see also the RAND study by Thomas W. Wolfe, *Soviet Military Power and European Security*, (Los Angeles: RAND Corporation, 1966).

85. Kissinger, *Diplomacy*, 722–24.

86. Garthoff, *Détente*, 239.

87. Document given to Honecker by Norden, 16 September 1971, in J IV 2/202/542 (Allg. Abt.), SAPMO. First line of document reads, "Den Gepflogenheiten folgend, hält es das ZK der KPdSU für erforderlich, über den Stand der sowjetisch-chinesischen Beziehungen in jüngster Zeit zu informieren"; original of the quoted passage is as follows: "Nach dem Treffen der Regierungschefs der UdSSR und der VRCh, das auf unsere Initiative am 11. September 1969 stattfand, kam es zu einem gewissen Fortschritt in der Normalisierung der staatlichen Beziehungen . . . Etwas vergrößert hat sich unser Handel mit China . . . Wir sind der Auffassung, daß auch weiterhin Bemühungen zur Normalisierung der sowjetisch-chinesischen Beziehungen unternommen werden müssen." Raymond Garthoff, a leading specialist on détente, has reached a similar conclusion. According to Garthoff, "the precipitous plunge in Sino-Soviet relations that began after Czechoslovakia was arrested by October 1969, but within a context of continuing mistrust and hostility." Garthoff, *Détente*, 241.

88. Garthoff, *Détente*, 19. See also Keith L. Nelson, *The Making of Détente: Soviet-*

American Relations in the Shadow of Vietnam (Baltimore: John Hopkins University Press, 1995), 45; and Robin Edmonds, Soviet Foreign Policy 1962–1973: The Paradox of Super Power (London: Oxford University Press, 1975).

89. Egon Bahr, Vermerk, 14 October 1969, summarizing conversation with Henry Kissinger on 13 October, in 439, EBD, FES. On the complicated nature of the relationship between Kissinger and Bahr, see Stephan Fuchs, "Dreiecksverhältnisse sind immer kompliziert": Kissinger, Bahr und die Ostpolitik (Hamburg: Europäische Verlagsanstalt, 1999).

90. Gaddis, Containment, 275.

91. Kissinger, WHY, 128–29.

92. For the text of Nixon's remarks during his visit to Berlin, see James Mayall and Cornelia Navari, eds., The End of the Post-War Era: Documents on Great-Power Relations 1968–1975 (Cambridge: Cambridge University Press, 1980), 27–29. See also "Remarks at the Siemens Factory, West Berlin, 27 February 1969," Document 82 in The Public Papers of the Presidents of the United States: Richard Nixon, Vol. 1, 1969 (Washington D.C.: U.S. Government Printing Office, 1971), 157. There Nixon remarked, "No unilateral move, no illegal act, no form of pressure from any sources will shake the resolve of Western nations to defend their rightful status as protectors of the people of free Berlin."

93. Document without title or date, first sentence reads "2 марта 1969 г. на острове Даманский . . . ," p. 3, in J IV 2/202/359 (Allg. Abt.), SAPMO. Wjatscheslaw Keworkow also emphasized the importance of this skirmish in influencing Soviet thinking at the time. Keworkow, Der geheime Kanal (Berlin: Rowohlt, March 1995), 44.

94. Garthoff, Détente, 274. He adds that on 11 March, "in a most unusual step, the Soviet ambassador in Bonn briefed Chancellor Kiesinger on the clash."

95. See Kissinger's account of his talks with the North Vietnamese in Kissinger, WHY, 441–48. See also Boyle, American-Soviet Relations, 166.

96. Gaddis, Containment, 298.

97. On the centrality of Vietnam to the Nixon administration, see Stephen E. Ambrose, Nixon: The Triumph of a Politician, 1962–1972 (New York: Simon and Schuster, 1989), 233; and Garthoff, Détente, 13.

98. Bahr recalls in Zu meiner Zeit, 122, that Nixon actually referred to him as "Brandt's Kissinger."

99. Kissinger, WHY, 138. See Kissinger's further account of his dealing with Dobrynin in WHY, 112–14. Kissinger recounts that he first met Dobrynin on the fringes of a reception for the director of a Soviet research institute. This director was, according to Kissinger, "endlessly ingenious in demonstrating how American rebuffs were frustrating the peaceful, sensitive leaders in the Kremlin, who were being driven reluctantly by our inflexibility into conflicts that offended their inherently gentle natures" (112). See also the account of the Kissinger-Dobrynin channel from the other side: Anatoly Dobrynin, In Confidence: Moscow's Ambassador to America's Six Cold War Presidents (1962–1986) (New York: Random House, 1995).

100. Kissinger, WHY, 140.

101. On establishing this channel, see Bahr's "Nur für W.B. und H.E.," no date, in 439, EBD, FES.

102. For discussions of the significance of the Bahr-Kissinger channel, see Kissinger, WHY, 410–12; Bahr, Zu meiner Zeit, 262, in which he reports that he and Kissinger used the Marines as go-betweens; and Bahr's "Nachwort" in Keworkow, Kanal, 274.

103. Kissinger indeed praised Rush for conducting complex negotiations without the knowledge of his nominal employer, the State Department; see Kissinger, WHY, 807–9. For an account of the first time the Soviet ambassador received Rush after he was named

ambassador to Germany and head of the U.S. military administration in West Berlin, see "Information über die Unterredung mit dem Botschafter der USA in der BRD, Kenneth Rush," 15 October 1969, in J IV 2/202/136 (Büro Ulbricht), SAPMO.

104. On the secret channel from Brandt to Brezhnev, see Keworkow, *Kanal*; and Bahr, *Zu meiner Zeit*, 263.

105. For an example of this, see Kissinger, *WHY*, 532.

106. For a detailed analysis of Brandt's assumption of power, see Baring, *Machtwechsel*; and Heinrich Potthoff, *Im Schatten der Mauer: Deutschlandpolitik 1961 bis 1990* (Hamburg: Propyläen, 1999). See also Bahr's description of September 1969: Bahr, *Zu meiner Zeit*, 269.

107. On the making of Brandt's Regierungserklärung, see Ordner 115, EBD, FES.

108. Gottfried Niedhart discusses the origins of Brandt's thinking in Brandt's time as mayor of divided Berlin: see Niedhart, "Ostpolitik: The Role of the Federal Republic of Germany in the Process of Détente," in Carola Fink, Philipp Gassert, and Detlef Junkert, eds., *1968: The World Transformed* (New York: Cambridge University Press, 1998).

109. The historian James McAdams has made the insightful point that Brandt's new tack toward the East should be viewed as an attempt to regularize, rather than normalize, relations with the GDR. McAdams is right to point out that there was little normal about the relations between the two postwar Germanies either before or after Brandt's time in office. However, since the term "normalization" is more common, I use it here. McAdams, "New Diplomacy," 538. On the early days of Brandt's chancellorship, see also McAdams, *Germany Divided*, 79.

110. "Regierungserklärung von Bundeskanzler Brandt vom 28. Oktober 1969 (Auszug)," in Ingo von Münch, ed., *Dokumente des geteilten Deutschland*, vol. 2, *Seit 1968* (Stuttgart: Kröner, 1974), 167–69.

111. Potthoff, *Bonn und Ost-Berlin*, 22.

112. Bark and Gress, *Democracy and Its Discontents*, 169.

113. Heinrich August Winkler, "Rebuilding of a Nation: The Germans Before and After Unification," *Daedalus* 123 (Winter 1994): 109. As Winkler put it, "The East-West Treaties went hand in hand with a reversal of the domestic political fronts concerning the national question. During the Adenauer era, the moderate political Right had pursued a policy of supranational integration, while the moderate Left had proclaimed the primacy of German unity. Compared with the Empire and the Weimar Republic, this was a complete volte-face of position between the Left and the Right."

114. For an account of Bahr's early years, his career in Berlin, and the beginnings of his relationship with Willy Brandt, see Bahr, *Zu meiner Zeit*. For information on later years, see Dettmar Cramer, *gefragt: Egon Bahr* (Bornheim: Dagmar Zirngibl, 1974); and Vogtmeier, *Bahr*.

115. Not all press coverage was negative, of course. *Der Spiegel* frequently endorsed government policies. For example, Rudolf Augstein once defended Brandt against criticism by saying that his opponents should tell the world what *they* would do to maintain the "Zusammengehörigkeit" of Germans on both sides of the German-German border; see Rudolf Augstein, "Dulles oder Nichts?" *Der Spiegel*, 23 March 1970, 26.

116. In the literature about foreign policymaking during the Nixon era, there exists disagreement over whether Nixon or Kissinger was the shaping force. This study subscribes to the view advanced by William Bundy in his study of Nixonian foreign policy, namely, that in the early years Nixon set the direction but that Kissinger managed implementation because "negotiations bored Nixon and fascinated Kissinger, whose enthusiasm was not always matched by his skill." Bundy postulates that, as domestic difficulties increasingly consumed Nixon, Kissinger became solely responsible. See Wil-

liam Bundy, *A Tangled Web: The Making of Foreign Policy in the Nixon Presidency* (New York: Hill and Wang, 1998), 511, and passim.

117. For those interested in further biographical details about Henry Kissinger, there is an immense amount of biographical and autobiographical information available. See, to name just a few prominent examples in alphabetical order: Bundy, *Tangled Web*; William Burr, ed., *The Kissinger Transcripts: The Top-Secret Talks with Beijing and Moscow* (New York: New Press, 1998); Seymour Hersh, *The Price of Power: Kissinger in the Nixon White House* (New York: Summit, 1983); Walter Isaacson, *Kissinger: A Biography* (New York: Simon & Schuster, 1992); Kissinger, *WHY*; Henry Kissinger, *Years of Upheaval* (Boston: Little, Brown, 1982); Henry Kissinger, *Years of Renewal* (New York: Simon & Schuster, 1999); and Robert Schulzinger, *Henry Kissinger: Doctor of Diplomacy* (New York: Columbia University Press, 1989).

118. Hersh, *Price of Power*, 417.

119. Gaddis, *Containment*, 335.

120. Gregory L. Freeze, ed., *Russia: A History* (Oxford: Oxford University Press, 1997), 372–73.

121. See Jonathan Haslam, "Russian Archival Revelations and Our Understanding of the Cold War," *Diplomatic History* 21 (Spring 1997): 226. On the topic of Andropov's role in shaping foreign policy, see Keworkow, *Kanal*; and Dobrynin, *In Confidence*, 210. On the Soviet Politburo generally, see Michael S. Voslensky, *Sterbliche Götter: Die Lehrmeister der Nomenklatura* (Vienna: Straube, 1989).

122. Keworkow, *Kanal*, 64–71. Keworkow claims that Gromyko used to compare German Social Democrats to "Vertreterinnen des ältesten Gewerbes der Welt" ("representatives of the oldest profession in the world") (69). It seems in some ways as if the Gromyko/Andropov relationship to Brezhnev resembled the Bahr/Wehner relationship to Brandt (with Gromyko/Bahr focused on securing change through the opposing superpower capital and Andropov/Wehner seeing the key in German-German dealings), although it would be unwise to push the comparison between the relationships between Soviet and West German politicians too far.

123. For an in-depth look at the SED pre-1968, see Peter Christian Ludz, *Parteielite im Wandel: Funktionsaufbau, Sozialstruktur und Ideologie der SED-Führung* (Opladen: Westdeutscher Verlag, 1968). See also Deutscher Bundestag, ed., *Machtstrukturen und Entscheidungsmechanismen im SED-Staat und die Frage der Verantwortung*, vol. 2 of *Materialien der Enquete-Kommission "Aufarbeitung von Geschichte und Folgen der SED-Diktatur in Deutschland,"* (Baden-Baden/Frankfurt a.M.: Nomos Verlag/Suhrkamp Verlag, 1995). For basic information about how the SED functioned on a day-to-day basis, see the account by Hans Modrow, which describes mainly the time period of his own experience (in the second half of the Cold War) but gives a sense of what the party was probably like in the earlier period as well: Hans Modrow, ed., *Das Große Haus: Insider berichten aus dem ZK der SED* (Berlin: Edition Ost, 1994).

124. For background information, see Norbert Podewin, *Walter Ulbricht: Eine neue Biographie* (Berlin: Dietz, 1995). The Podewin book is somewhat problematic for this time period, however, because of the author's sources: he quotes *Stern* magazine's reproductions of SED documents rather than the original documents. For the time after 1962, see also Kaiser, *Machtwechsel*. Kaiser rightly pointed out that Podewin erred when he claimed that the Kassel meeting of Willi Stoph and Willy Brandt took place without Soviet influence or approval; see Kaiser, *Machtwechsel*, 362.

125. He reportedly did so, for example, in a speech at the Twenty-fourth Party Congress of the CPSU in Moscow. There he talked about his participation in the Fourth Comintern Congress of 1922: "bei dem Lenin am 13. November gesagt hatte, daß Kom-

munistern lernen, lernen und nochmals lernen müßten" "at which Lenin had said on the 13th of November that Communists must learn, learn, and learn more"). The suggestion was that the Russians still had much to learn, presumably from the example of the GDR. Ulbricht is quoted in Wolfgang Pfeiler, "Alternativen der Deutschlandpolitik unter Breshnew und Andropow," in Heiner Timmermann, ed., *Dikaturen in Europa im 20. Jahrhundert—der Fall DDR* (Berlin: Duncker & Humblot, 1996), 647.

126. McAdams, *Germany Divided*, 6.

127. Bark and Gress found that "ideologically Ulbricht took an increasingly independent course . . . following the Wall." They point out, "This was astounding to those who remembered his slavish loyalty to Stalin and his use of terror to destroy all rivals, including anyone who advocated even minimal independence from Moscow." Bark and Gress, *Democracy and Its Discontents*, 174.

128. For the early history of the FDJ, see Ulrich Mählert, *Die Freie Deutsche Jugend 1945–1949* (Paderborn, Ger.: Schöningh, 1995).

129. The leading scholars of Soviet intelligence, KGB expert Christopher Andrew and former KGB agent Oleg Gordievsky, find that Markus Wolf's work represented a significant exception to the rule that, by the Brezhnev era, Soviet espionage was more successful in the developing world than in the West. See Andrew and Gordievsky, *KGB*, 513.

130. Markus Wolf, *Spionagechef im geheimen Krieg* (München: List, 1997), 244. The Wolf memoirs also appeared in English: Markus Wolf with Anne McElvoy, *Man without a Face* (New York: Random House, 1997). However, the English and German versions differ substantially; see M. E. Sarotte, "Under Cover of Boredom: Review Article of Recent Publications on the East German Ministry for State Security, or Stasi," *Intelligence and National Security* 12 (October 1997): 196–210. The longer, German version is used here (and translated by the author), except in those cases where a quotation appeared only in the English version.

131. Author's interview with Wolf, 6 June 1996.

132. Political scientist Stephen Sestanovich has argued that Soviet nonproliferation policy in the 1960s "was an attempt to turn China and West Germany from ownership of nuclear weapons," adding, "This was perhaps the main project of Soviet foreign policy in the transitional years of the late Cold War and its resolution did much to set the outlines of the period that followed." Sestanovich, "Nuclear Proliferation and Soviet Foreign Policy, 1957–1968. The Limits of Soviet-American Cooperation" (Ph.D. diss., Harvard University, 1971), 357.

133. "J. W. Andropow zur Einschätzung der Lage," 17 November 1969, pp. 1–5, quote on 1, in SdM 1473, ZA, BStU. On this document, see also K.-H. Schmidt, *Dialog über Deutschland*, 211.

134. "J. W. Andropow zur Einschätzung der Lage," 1.

135. Ibid., 2.

136. Ibid.

137. Ibid., 3.

138. Ibid., 4.

139. See "1. Stellungnahme zur Lage in Westdeutschland und der Regierungserklärung der Bonner Regierung/Berichterstatter: Gen. Norden," J IV 2/2A/1.399 (Politbüro), SAPMO, which states: "Dem Politbüro der KPdSU wird vorgeschlagen, daß am 19.11.69 eine Konsultation des Genossen Ulbricht mit Genossen Breshnew über die weitere Taktik gegenüber der Bonner Regierung und dem Westberliner Senat erfolgt" ("It is proposed to the CPSU Politburo that Comrade Ulbricht meet with Comrade Brezhnev to consult on the further tactics with regard to the Bonn government and the West Berlin Senate").

140. A letter from Ulbricht to Brezhnev confirms the rescheduling of the Central Committee meeting. Letter dated 20 November 1969, J IV 2/202/346 (Büro Ulbricht), SAPMO.

141. "Unkorrigiert Rohübersetzung," 13 November 1969, (message from Brezhnev delivered via Abrasimov), J IV 2/202/274 (Büro Ulbricht), SAPMO.

142. A letter from Ulbricht to Brezhnev confirms the plans of the SED delegation to travel to Moscow for this meeting. Letter dated 20 November 1969, J IV 2/202/346 (Büro Ulbricht), SAPMO. Ulbricht's preparatory notes for his own report at this meeting are in "Gedanken für die Aussprache mit der Parteiführung der KPdSU (am 2. Dezember 1969)," J IV 2/202/1125 (Büro Ulbricht), SAPMO. These preparatory notes seem to contain a skeptical view of Brandt's new initiatives, saying "Die Veränderungen in der westdeutschen Bundesrepublik sind nicht als Machtwechsel, sondern nur als Regierungswechsel einzuschätzen" ("The changes in the West German Federal Republic should not be interpreted as a fundamental shift of power, but rather simply as a change of government") (p. 1)—implying that the left-of-center Brandt government would simply follow the policies of its right-of-center predecessors. What appear to be excerpts from this meeting are in a document without title, dated 2.12.69, in the "Kalbslederband."

143. Document without title, dated 2 December 1969, "Kalbslederband," my page 14. See also, in the "Kalbslederband," a document identified only as "Döllnsee 1969," my pages 9–13, which seems to have been written about the same time and expresses similar sentiments to those described here.

144. Document dated 2.12.69, "Kalbslederband," my page 14.

145. "Kalbslederband," my page 15.

146. An archival copy of a draft treaty, which seems to be the document referred to by Brezhnev, does indeed ask for "official representations—called missions" rather than embassies. See "3. Entwurf: Vertrag über die Aufnahme gleichberechtigter Beziehungen ohne jegliche Diskrimineirung zwischen der Regierung der Deutschen Demokratischen Republik und der Regierung der Bundesrepublik Deutschland," part 3 of "Konzeption für Verhandlungen mit der westdeutschen Koalitionsregierung Brandt/Scheel," pp. 185–89, quote on 189, in SdM 1839, ZA, BStU. There exist several documents with either this or similar titles, not only in this file but also in party archive files, which seem to be successive drafts of the same document. Since most have no date or author indicated, it is not possible to ascertain with certainty which version of the draft treaty Brezhnev was referring to in his comments of 2 December 1969.

147. Document dated 2 December 1969, "Kalbslederband," my page 17.

148. Handwritten document with "WU-Döllnsee" at top, pp. 6 and 7, Vorl. SED 41656 (Büro Honecker), SAPMO. The original shows that Ulbricht also said: "*Also* ich schlage vor eine Änderung der Taktik eine Änderung gegenüber früher. Ich bin für eine neue Westpolitik, ja für eine neue Westpolitik (Nicht für Presse) ["*Therefore*: I propose a chnage in tactics, a change in contrast to what has come before. I am for a new 'Westpolitik,' yes, for a new 'Westpolitik' (Not for the press)"]. In Kaiser, *Machtwechsel*, the author claimed (plausibly) that these handwritten notes, in Honecker's hand, are from the "außerordentliche Politbürositzung" of 30 October 1969. As she points out on p. 327, there exist twelve pages of handwritten notes, of which only the first four are reproduced in the "Kalbslederband."

149. "Konzeption für Verhandlungen mit der westdeutschen Koalitionsregierung Brandt/Scheel," p. 188, SdM 1839, ZA, BStU.

150. "Stenografische Niederschrift des Treffens führender Persönlichkeiten sozialistischer Länder Anfang Dezember 1969 in Moskau," p. 133, J IV 2/2A/1.406 (Politbüro), SAPMO.

151. "Diskussionsrede auf der 12. Tagung des ZK der SED, 12/13.12.69," p. 36, J IV/202 (Büro Honecker), SAPMO.

152. This impression is strengthened by a remark in the memoirs of Hermann Axen to the effect that, at a 1969 meeting, Ulbricht said that there was a need to talk to China. It is not clear from Axen's memoirs when in 1969 this meeting took place—although from context it could have been the December 1969 meeting in Moscow—nor is it clear precisely what Ulbricht meant. See Hermann Axen with Harald Neubert, *Ich war ein Diener der Partei* (Berlin: Edition Ost, 1996), 312.

153. The final versions (letter from Ulbricht to Heinemann, 17 December 1969, and "Entwurf Vertrag über die Aufnahme gleichberechtigter Beziehungen zwischen der Deutschen Demokratischen Republik und der Bundesrepublik Deutschland") are in DC20-4678 (Stoph), BA-V.

154. Copies of Ulbricht's letter and draft treaty are in DC20-4678 (Stoph), BA-V. A copy of the treaty is also in J IV 2/202/103 (Büro Ulbricht), SAPMO, along with an account of how the letter was actually delivered ("Bericht über die Übergabe der Botschaft des Vorsitzenden des Staatsrates der Deutschen Demokratischen Republik an den Bundespräsidenten der westdeutschen Bundesrepublik"). Numerous published copies exist as well; see "Schreiben des Vorsitzenden des Staatsrates der Deutschen Demokratischen Republik, Ulbricht, an Bundespräsident Heinemann vom 17. Dezember 1969," in von Münch, *Dokumente*, 169–72, and Seidel, "Erste Schritte," in Nakath, *Deutschlandpolitiker der DDR erinnern sich*, 103.

155. Heinemann's response to Ulbricht is in DC20-4678 (Stoph), BA-V, also reprinted in von Münch, *Dokumente*, 172–73.

156. The "außerordentliche Sitzung" ("special session") of the Politbüro was held on 22 December 1969. See J IV 2/2/1259 and J IV 2/2A/1.412 (Politbüro), SAPMO.

157. Letter from Brandt to Stoph, 22 Jan. 1970, in DC20-I/2-1341 (Ministerrat), BA-V. Stoph's reply of 11 Feb. 1970 is in the same file, as are further Stoph-Brandt letters or telegrams. See also "Antwort des Bundeskanzlers der BRD, Willy Brandt, an den VdM der DDR, Willi Stoph, vom 18.2.1970 (Fernschreiben)" in DC20-4678 (Stoph), BA-V. See also Seidel, "Erste Schritte," 103.

158. Wolf, *Spionagechef*, 247.

159. Ibid.

160. Bark and Gress, *Democracy and Its Discontents*, 165.

161. Gordon Craig and Alexander George, *Force and Statecraft: Diplomatic Problems of Our Time* (New York: Oxford University Press, 1983), 257; and Bark and Gress, *Democracy and Its Discontents*, 169–70. This agreement was much criticized at the time by hawks in the United States.

162. On the beginnings of SALT, see Nelson, *Making of Détente*.

163. Letter from Brandt to Kosygin, 19 November 1969, reprinted in Keworkow, *Kanal*, 50–53, quote on 50; see also 69–70.

164. See files in Bahr's papers on the background to this meeting, in 434, EBD, FES. For the story of establishing this secret channel from the Soviet side, see Keworkow, *Kanal*. See also the author's review of this book in Sarotte, "Under Cover of Boredom."

165. Keworkow, *Kanal*, 57. The original German conversation summarized in the main text is as follows: Bahr asked, "Herr Lednew, sind Sie ganz sicher, daß die Leute, die Sie hierher geschickt haben, über genügend Einfluß verfügen, um sich mit der Klärung so globaler Probleme zu befassen?" Answer: "Ganz sicher, denn es geht um Brezhnev."

166. See "Nachwort" by Egon Bahr in Keworkow, *Kanal*, 271–74.

167. Letter from "Heinz Lathe," one of the cover names used by messengers, 22 Jan. 1970, in 434, EBD, FES.

168. Bahr, "Nachwort," in Keworkow, *Kanal*, 275.

169. Ibid., 276.

170. See note from Bahr to Kissinger, 30 December 1969, 439, EBD, FES; and Bahr, *Zu meiner Zeit*, 283.

171. For a summary of the Gromyko-Allardt conversation, conveyed to GDR Foreign Minister Otto Winzer by the Soviet ambassador in Berlin, Pjotr Abrasimov, see letter from Winzer to Ulbricht, Stoph, Honecker, and Axen, 11 December 1969, "Botschafter Abrassimow informiert am 11.12.1969 Genossen Winzer über das Gespräch des Aussenministers der UdSSR, Genossen Gromyko, mit dem westdeutschen Botschafter Allardt in Moskau vom 8.12.1969," in J IV 2/202/332 (Büro Ulbricht), SAPMO. See also Ulrich Sahm, *"Diplomaten taugen nichts:" Aus dem Leben eines Staatsdieners* (Düsseldorf: Droste, 1994), 279; and Benno Zündorf, alias Antonius Eitel, *Die Ostverträge* (Munich: C. H. Beck, 1979), 243.

172. The Soviets proposed talks on this topic to the United States on 12 September 1969, and the three Western allies agreed to them on 16 December 1969. On the initial maneuvering between these two dates, see the following sources: "*Vermerk* Botschaftsrat Genosse Hotulew informierte am 16.10.1969 Genosse Staatssekretär Dr. Kohl anhand einer schriftlichen Aufzeichnung über ein Telegramm des Genossen Gromyko," in IV 2/2.035/118 (Büro Axen), SAPMO; Arthur G. Kogan, "The Quadripartite Berlin Negotiations," Research Project No. 1035 (Secret; declassified 4 Apr. 1994 via Freedom of Information Act (FOIA) Request No. 9305297), Office of the Historian, Bureau of Public Affairs, Department of State, Sept. 1977, pp. 51–54, in Box 26, Nuclear History/Berlin Crisis, National Security Archive, Washington, D.C. (Kogan provides a summary of the initiatives and also the text of the tripartite statement delivered to Moscow on 16 December 1969); Garthoff, *Détente*, esp. 137; a letter from Ulbricht to Stoph, 9 Feb. 1970, passing on to Stoph what seems to be a Soviet reply to the West, in DC20-4460, BA-V.

173. "Information über ein Gespräch mit dem Botschafter der USA in der BRD, K. Rush" 12 December 1969, in J IV 2/202/136 (Büro Ulbricht), SAPMO.

174. "Information über ein Gespräch mit dem Botschafter der USA in der BRD, K. Rush," p. 8.

175. "Übersetzung aus dem Russischen," 17 Feb. 1970, in SdM 1471, ZA, BStU. As this document points out, these exercises became known at the time to the West German intelligence service (BND).

176. Reprinted in Keworkow, *Kanal*, 51.

177. Ibid., 59.

178. On this topic of Western allied anxiety about West Germany, Gordon Craig, Alexander George, and Peter Pulzer's assessments of Brandt's initial moves deserve reconsideration, because documents now available confirm their views. Craig and George praised Brandt for never forgetting "that he could negotiate successfully with the Soviet Union and its allies only if he operated from a position of strength based upon his NATO connection." Craig and George, *Force and Statecraft*, 258. Similarly, Peter Pulzer has argued that Ostpolitik attempted to provide an opening to Moscow while maintaining loyal ties to Washington. Peter Pulzer, *German Politics, 1945–1995* (Oxford: Oxford University Press, 1995), 110.

Chapter Two

1. Gerhard Naumann and Eckhard Trümpler, *Von Ulbricht zu Honecker: 1970 Krisenjahr* (Berlin: Dietz, March 1990), 16–20.

2. Henry Kissinger, *WHY* (Boston: Little, Brown, 1979), 805–6.

3. Accounts of these four meetings (Moscow, Erfurt, Berlin, and Kassel) exist already, but few rest on primary sources or emphasize their mutual interactions. A notable exception is Timothy Garton Ash, *In Europe's Name: Germany and the Divided Continent* (New York: Vintage, 1993). There do exist accounts on each individual set of talks. On Erfurt and Kassel, and based on primary sources, there is the pamphlet by Detlef Nakath, *Erfurt und Kassel: Zu den Gesprächen zwischen dem BRD-Bundeskanzler Willy Brandt und dem DDR-Ministerratsvorsitzenden Willi Stoph im Frühjar 1970* (Berlin: Forscher- und Diskussionskreis DDR-Geschichte, 1995). On the Quadripatite talks, but written before documentation was available, there are Honoré M. Catudal, *The Diplomacy of the Quadripartite Agreement on Berlin: A New Era in East-West Politics* (Berlin: Berlin Verlag, 1978); Honoré M. Catudal, *A Balance Sheet of the Quadripartite Agreement on Berlin: Evaluation and Documentation* (Berlin: Berlin Verlag, 1978); and David M. Keithly, *Breakthrough in the Ostpolitik: The 1971 Quadripartite Agreement* (Boulder, Colo.: Westview, 1986). Additionally, the secret internal U.S. State Department history of the Berlin talks is now available; see Arthur G. Kogan, "The Quadripartite Berlin Negotiations," Research Project No. 1035, September 1977, released 4 April 1994 via FOIA Request #9305297, Box 26, Nuclear History/Berlin Crisis, National Security Archive, Washington, D.C.

4. For an overview of Bahr's time in Moscow, see Andreas Vogtmeier, *Egon Bahr und die deutsche Frage* (Bonn: Dietz, 1996), 128–33. Specifically on the first round, see Egon Bahr, *Zu meiner Zeit* (Munich: Karl Blessing, 1996), 284–338.

5. On the secret channel, see Chapter 1 and Wjatscheslaw Keworkow, *Der geheime Kanal* (Berlin: Rowohlt, March 1995).

6. Author's conversation with Bahr, 14 Nov. 1997, Vienna.

7. Bahr, *Zu meiner Zeit*, 284.

8. Arnulf Baring, *Machtwechsel: Die Ära Brandt-Scheel* (Stuttgart: Deutsche Verlags-Anstalt, 1982), 264–65. According to Baring, Brandt and Scheel also doubted that the man-on-site in Moscow, West German ambassador Helmut Allardt, was the right man for the job.

9. See files 391, 392, and 429, EBD, FES.

10. This insight sprang from both common sense and experience; as Timothy Garton Ash puts it, "the failure of Foreign Minister Schröder's 'policy of movement' . . . [showed] that Bonn could not hope to develop closer ties with East European states without Moscow's assent." Garton Ash, *In Europe's Name*, 84.

11. Dennis L. Bark and David R. Gress, *Democracy and Its Discontents*, vol. 2 of *A History of West Germany*, 2d ed. (Oxford: Blackwell, 1993), 169–70.

12. "Protokoll über den deutsch-sowjetischen Meinungsaustausch," 30 Jan. 1970, in 392, EBD, FES.

13. "*Inoffizielle Übersetzung*," describing conversation from 30 Jan. 1970, p. 94, in DC20-4460 (Stoph), BA-V.

14. Ibid., 95.

15. Ibid., 96.

16. In a conversation with Walter Ulbricht on 24 February, Gromyko informed him that the issue of border recognition was the most important issue of the talks. Cited in Detlef Nakath, "Gewaltverzicht und Gleichberechtigung: Zur Parallelität der deutsch-sowjetischen Gespräche und der deutsch-deutschen Gipfeltreffen in Erfurt und Kassel im Frühjahr 1970," *Deutschland Archiv* 2 (Mar./Apr. 1998): 205.

17. Document without title, dated 6 Feb. 1970, first line reads "Während der neuen Zusammenkunft mit Bahr am 3. Februar im MfAA der UdSSR," p. 98, in DC 20-4460 (Stoph), BA-V.

18. Document without title, 6 Feb. 1970, p. 99.

19. Document without title, handwritten date at top "1970," first line reads "6 февраля с.г. министр иностранных дел СССР принял статссекретаря Бара по его просьбе," in J IV 2/20.1/6 (Allg. Abt.), SAPMO.

20. Document without title or date, handwritten "Übersetzung Umlauf PB" at top, first line reads "13 февраля с.г. Председатель Совета Министров СССР А.Н. Косыгин лринял статссекретаря ведомства федерального канцлера ФРГ З. Бара по его просьбе," in J IV 2/20.1/6 (Allg. Abt.), SAPMO. What appears in all likelihood to be a translation of this document exists in a different archive: See "Übersetzung aus dem Russischen," p. 103, in DC20-4460 (Stoph), BA-V.

21. "Übersetzung aus dem Russischen," p. 104.

22. Ibid.

23. Ibid., p. 106.

24. Bahr, *Zu meiner Zeit*, 304.

25. Kogan, "Quadripartite," 66. For evidence of the further development of this trend, see the various summaries that Bahr sent the three Western allies concerning the status of his negotiations with the GDR in 445, EBD, FES.

26. Bahr, *Zu meiner Zeit*, 305. Arnulf Baring has argued, "Bahr hatte die Verständigungsschwierigkeiten unterschätzt, die schon bei Vokabular begannen. Man buchstabierte sich gegenseitig die Worte, mußte beträchtliche Zeit und Mühe darauf verwenden, einander die Bedeutung von Begriffen zu erläutern." ("Bahr had underestimated how much difficulty the two sides would have in understanding each other. They essentially used differing vocabularies, had to spell out words to each other, had to put a great deal of time and effort into simply making the meaning of concepts clear.") Baring, *Machtwechsel*, 281.

27. Author's conversation with Valentin Falin, 14 Nov. 1996, Vienna. In his memoirs, Falin also detailed worries on the part of the Polish leader Gomułka about the USSR-FRG negotiations; see Valentin Falin, *Politische Erinnerungen* (München: Knaur, 1995), 84–85.

28. Letter from Bahr to Brandt, written in Moscow on 7 March 1970 and hand-carried back by Herr Sanne, in 429B, EBD, FES.

29. "Übersetzung aus dem Russischen," 12 Mar. 1970, p. 2, in J IV 2/202/82 (Büro Ulbricht), SAPMO.

30. "Gipfeltreffen," *Der Spiegel*, 23 March 1970, 25.

31. Gordon Craig and Alexander George, *Force and Statecraft: Diplomatic Problems of Our Time* (New York: Oxford University Press, 1983), 252.

32. Bark and Gress, *Democracy and Its Discontents*, 176.

33. Author's conversation with Falin, Vienna, 14 November 1997.

34. Kissinger, *WHY*, 532.

35. The West Germans published portions of this correspondence at the time and in subsequent documentations issued by the Bundesministerium für innerdeutsche Beziehungen. A 1980 collection also included some of the official statements from Erfurt and Kassel as well; see the documents provided in Bundesministerium für innerdeutsche Beziehungen, ed., *Zehn Jahre Deutschlandpolitik: Die Entwicklung der Bezehungen zwischen der Bundesrepublik Deutschland und der Deutschen Demokratischen Republik 1969–1979* (Bonn: Bundesministerium, Feb. 1980). The analysis below draws mainly from unpublished primary documents rather than published, however.

36. Letter from Brandt to Stoph, 22 Jan. 1970, p. 1, in DC20-4678 (Stoph), BA-V.

37. Letter from Stoph to Brandt, p. 1, in J IV 2/2A/1.418 (Politbüro), SAPMO. This

version is actually a draft, which left the date of the meeting open. By the time of the final version [in DC20-4678 (Stoph), BA-V, and approved at the Politbüro meeting of 10 Feb. 1970, in J IV 2/2A/1.421 (Politbüro), SAPMO], Stoph had requested a meeting for either 19 or 26 February.

38. Kissinger, *WHY*, 532.

39. "*Vertraulich,*" 16 Feb. 1970, p. 2, in J IV 2/202/358 (Büro Ulbricht), SAPMO.

40. Ibid., p. 4.

41. Ibid., p. 7.

42. Kissinger, *WHY*, 532.

43. Telegram from Brandt to Stoph, 18 Feb. 1970, p. 84, in DC20-4678 (Stoph), BA-V. On Brezhnev's pressure to alter Ulbricht's draft, see the discussion in Chapter 1.

44. Kissinger, *WHY*, 532. A document summarizing internal SED reactions to Brandt's suggestion of lower-level delegations wondered, "Vielleicht ist das seitens Bonn eine Taktik, um die Verhandlungen selbst zu verhindern?" ("Perhaps this is a tactic of Bonn's, one designed to hinder the negotiations themselves?") The SED seems at this point to have wanted the talks as soon as possible. See "Meinungen und Stimmungen im Zusammenhang mit den technischen Vorgesprächen zur Vorbereitung des vom VdM der DDR, Genosse Stoph, vorgeschlagenen Treffens mit Brandt," (identified in catalogue as being from Feb. 1970), p. 1, in J IV 2/2J/2883 (IntVer), SAPMO.

45. Kissinger, *WHY*, 532.

46. On the details of the Quadripartite Negotiations, see the internal state department history, Kogan, "Quadripartite." Details on the initial offers appear on p. 62.

47. Kissinger, *WHY*, 530.

48. For example, Tagesordnungspunkt 7 of J IV 2/2A/1.426/27 (Politbüro), SAPMO, describes the problems in agreeing on how Brandt would depart.

49. "Information über Vorbereitungen für eine provokatorische Ausnutzung eines evtl. Besuches von Brandt beim VdM der DDR, Gen. Willi Stoph," undated, p. 1, in SdM 1471, ZA, BStU.

50. Ibid., p. 2.

51. "Stenografische Niederschrift des Gesprächs des Genossen Walter Ulbricht mit dem Genossen Andrej Gromyko im Amtssitz des Staatsrates in Berlin," 24 Feb. 1970, in J IV 2/201/1108 (Büro Ulbricht), SAPMO.

52. Letter from Willy Brandt to Willi Stoph, 8 Mar. 1970, in DC20-4678 (Stoph), BA-V. There was also a question about the suitability of Brandt using Allied air corridors to land at an East Berlin airport; the author is grateful to Prof. Helga Haftendorn for pointing this out.

53. Gromyko had the message for the SED leadership conveyed by the Soviet ambassador in East Berlin, Pjotr Abrasimov, to the East German foreign minister, Otto Winzer, who in turn passed it on in the form of a letter to Ulbricht. Letter from Otto Winzer to Walter Ulbricht, Willi Stoph, Erich Honecker, and Hermann Axen, 11 Mar. 1970, p. 1, in J IV 2/202/82 (Büro Ulbricht), SAPMO. A secret telegram from Bahr in Moscow to Scheel and Brandt on 12 Mar. 1970 stated "treffen mit stoph sicher" ("meeting with Stoph definite"), implying that there had been some doubt about the matter which had been resolved in Moscow. See Bahr's telegram, 12 Mar. 1970, in 392, EBD, FES. In a private, handwritten note to Brandt on the same day, Bahr noted that "Man hat hier Stoph '*gezwungen,*' das Treffen zu machen" ("Stoph has been forced to agree to the meeting"). In 429B, EBD, FES.

54. See J IV 2/2A/1.426/27 (Politbüro), SAPMO; according to Tagesordnungspunkt 7, as of the date of the Politbüro meeting (10 Mar. 1970), the site under discussion was

still Berlin. However, a "Vorlage für das Politburo" with the date 11 March 1970 (it was not uncommon to include paperwork from after the Politburo meeting into the preceding file) mentions Erfurt as a site.

55. Ulrich Sahm was at this point a foreign ministry official working in Brandt's chancellery. See Sahm's autobiography for details of the lower-level talks: Ulrich Sahm, *"Diplomaten taugen nichts:" Aus dem Leben eines Staatsdieners* (Düsseldorf: Droste, 1994), 251–60. Sahm recollects that, from the Klosterstraße meeting site, he could see the building that had been his father's office from 1931 to 1935: the Rotes Rathaus.

56. Letter from Winzer, 11 Mar. 1970, p. 2.

57. Raymond Garthoff, *Détente and Confrontation: American-Soviet Relations from Nixon to Reagan*, rev. ed. (Washington, D.C.: Brookings Institution, 1994), 286.

58. While the SED files do not resolve this issue, they do in small part help to shed light on the extent to which North Vietnam received aid from the Soviet Union. A summary of Soviet aid to North Vietnam from May 1966 states that, up until 1965, the Soviets gave their Vietnamese allies weaponry and support materials worth 200 million rubles, and then signed four agreements in 1965 to increase that amount dramatically. See "Die sowjetische militärische und wirtschaftliche Hilfe für Vietnam (Kurze Übersicht)" 20 May 1966, in J IV 2/202/248 (Büro Ulbricht), SAPMO.

59. Stephen J. Morris, "The Soviet-Chinese-Vietnamese Triangle in the 1970s: The View from Moscow," Working Paper No. 25, Woodrow Wilson International Center for Scholars, Washington, D.C., April 1999, p. 40.

60. Anatoly Dobrynin, *In Confidence: Moscow's Ambassador to America's Six Cold War Presidents (1962–1986)* (New York: Random House, 1995), 248. (See also the review of Dobrynin's memoirs by Vladislav M. Zubok, "A Messenger to Moscow," *Diplomatic History* 22 (Winter 1998): 149–53.) For scholarly assessment of the uneasy nature of the Soviet–North Vietnamese relations, see Ilya V. Gaiduk, "The Vietnam War and Soviet-American Relations, 1964–1973: New Russian Evidence," *Cold War International History Project Bulletin* 6/7 (Winter 1995/1996): 232, 250–58; and Morris, "Triangle." See also the work of Keith Nelson, who has addressed this issue from existing secondary literature: Nelson, *The Making of Détente: Soviet-American Relations in the Shadow of Vietnam* (Baltimore: John Hopkins University Press, 1995).

61. See DC20-4679 (Stoph), BA-V, for various documents fixing details of the meeting.

62. "Information an das Politbüro des ZK," summary of Sekretariat des ZK meeting on 25 Mar. 1970, p. 2 in J IV 2/2J/2901 (IntVer), SAPMO (emphasis in original).

63. Befehl Nr. 12/70, 13 Mar. 1970, p. 2, in Dok.-Nr. 100614, ZA, BStU. The order determining later coverage of the Kassel talks called it "Konfrontation II"; see Befehl Nr. 17/70, 11 May 1970, and Dok.-Nr. 100614, in ZA, BStU. That consultation with the Soviets occurred is confirmed in "Bericht über die Maßnahmen zur Absicherung des Treffens zwischen dem VdM der DDR, Gen. Willi Stoph, und dem Kanzler der westdeutschen Bundesrepublik, Willy Brandt, am 19.3.1970 in Erfurt," p. 2, in J IV 2/3A/1866 (Sekretariat), SAPMO, in which Mielke informed Honecker of cooperation with the "Leiter der Gruppe der sowjetischen Tschekisten in der DDR, Gen. Generalleutnant Fadekin" and the "Oberkommandierender der Gruppe sowjetischer Streitkräfte in der DDR, Gen. Generaloberst Kulikow."

64. Brandt's delegation consisted of the following (in official listings for the Erfurt meeting, their titles were given in short version as follows; this avoided the indelicacy of giving Franke's full title, which was at that time Bundesminister für innerdeutsche Beziehungen): Bundesminister Egon Franke, Parlamentarischer Staatssekretär Wolfram Dorn, Staatssekretär Conrad Ahlers, Ministerialdirektor Dr. Ulrich Sahm, Ministerialdirigent Jürgen Weichert, along with various technical experts and stenographers. The

GDR delegation consisted of VdM Willi Stoph, Minister für Auswärtige Angelegenheiten Otto Winzer, Staatssekretär beim Ministerrat Dr. Michael Kohl, Staatssekretär
im Ministerium für Auswärtige Angelegenheiten Günther Kohrt, Stellvertreter des
Leiters des Büros des Ministerrates Dr. Gerhard Schüßler, Abteilungsleiter im Ministerium für Auswärtige Angelegenheiten Dr. Hans Voß. Official lists in "Ablaufplan," pp.
87–98, in DC20-4679 (Stoph), BA-V.

65. Comments of Genosse Bräutigam, 1. Sekretär der Bezirksleitung Erfurt at the
Sitzung des Sekretariats des Zentralkomitees on 25 March 1970, Stichwort-Protokoll,
p. 7 in J IV 2/3A/1866 (Sekretariat), SAPMO.

66. Gerhard Naumann and Eckhard Trümpler, *Der Flop mit der DDR-Nation 1971*
(Berlin: Dietz, 1991), 45.

67. Even the internal Stasi analysis of what went wrong in Erfurt fails to explain why
this lapse occurred, finally chalking it up to lack of cooperation between various units
charged with coordinating security. See "Information über die provokatorische Demonstration zu Beginn des Treffens des VdM der DDR, Willi Stoph, und des Bundeskanzlers
der Bundesrepublik, Willy Brandt, in Erfurt," pp. 153–61 in SdM 1832, ZA, BStU.
Accompanying cover note, pp. 151–52, is dated 23 Mar. 1970.

68. Western journalists were able to talk to the crowds across the barricades, or as a
caption on photos of Erfurt in the SED files put it, "Die Aufnahme zeigt, daß bereits vor
dem Durchbruch westliche Reporter Einfluß auf die Passanten ausüben." [The people
indicated as passersby were standing approximately ten deep behind a barricade near
Brandt's hotel.] In J IV 2/3A 1866, Bd. 1 (Sekretariat), SAPMO. Captions are under
copies of photos from Erfurt (no page numbers).

69. "Information über die provokatorische Demonstration," p. 159.

70. Letter and accompanying report sent by Erich Mielke to Erich Honecker on
30 Mar. 1970, both initialed by Honecker on same date. Letter: Mielke to Honecker,
30 Mar. 1970, Tgb.-Nr. VMA/130/70. Report: "Bericht über die Maßnahmen zur Absicherung des Treffens zwischen dem VdM der DDR, Gen. Willi Stoph, und dem Kanzler
der westdeutschen Bundesrepublik, Willy Brandt, am 19.3.1970 in Erfurt," 30 Mar.
1970, Anlage zu VM/A/130/70, pp. 1–17. Both in J IV 2/3A/1866, Bd. 1 (Sekretariat),
SAPMO. Quotations are from the report, pp. 14–15.

71. See Brandt's own accounts of the Erfurt meeting in Willy Brandt, *Begegnungen
und Einsichten: Die Jahre 1960–1975* (Hamburg: Hoffmann & Campe, 1976); and Brandt,
My Life in Politics (New York: Viking, 1992).

72. Author's interview with Wolf, 6 June 1996.

73. "Bericht über die Maßnahmen zur Absicherung des Treffens," p. 15.

74. Author's interview with Görner, 7 June 1996.

75. "Stenografische Niederschrift des Gesprächs des VdM der DDR, W. Stoph, mit
dem Bundeskanzler der BRD, W. Brandt, in Erfurt, 19. März 1970," (hereafter "SN
Erfurt"), p. 31, in J IV 2/201/831 (IntVer), SAPMO. Portions of this document are
published as Document 1 in Heinrich Potthoff, *Bonn und Ost-Berlin 1969–1982: Dialog
auf höchster Ebene und vertrauliche Kanäle Darstellung und Dokumente* (Bonn: Dietz,
1997).

76. "SN Erfurt," p. 11.

77. Ibid., p. 20.

78. Ibid., p. 21.

79. Ibid., p. 30.

80. Ibid., p. 41.

81. Ibid., p. 36.

82. Ibid., pp. 42–43.

83. Ibid., p. 44.

84. "Vermerk über Gespräche während des Mittagessens, das der VdM am 19.3.1970 für den Bundeskanzler der BRD und Mitglieder seiner Delegation gab," p. 2, in DC20-4682 (Stoph), BA-V.

85. Ibid., p. 4.

86. Letter from Brandt to Stoph, 25 Mar. 1970, in DC20-I/2-1341 (Ministerrat), BA-V. As mentioned in the Preface, Goethe was apparently a topic of conversation at various points during the day. He was discussed both during the lunch at Erfurt (see "Vermerk über Gespräche während des Mittagessens," p. 5) and at the end of the day; see "Vermerk über die Begleitung des westdeutschen Bundeskanzlers auf der Rückfahrt von Erfurt und die Verabschiedung des Bundeskanzlers am Grenzkontrollpunkt Gerstungen," 20 Mar. 1970, p. 29, in DC20-4681 (Stoph), BA-V .

87. "Niederschrift der wichtigsten Probleme, die im persönlichen Gespräch mit dem westdeutschen Bundeskanzler Brandt am 19.3.1970 in Erfurt behandelt wurden," p. 332, in DC20-4680 (Stoph), BA-V. Ulbricht sent a copy of this to Brezhnev; see his letter to Brezhnev of 1 Apr. 1970, in J IV 2/202/103 (Büro Ulbricht), SAPMO.

88. See "Niederschrift der wichtigsten Probleme," pp. 318–332, and "Brandt, 21.40 (ungenaue Wiedergabe)," in J IV 2/201/831 (IntVer), SAPMO.

89. "Interview des VdM der DDR, Willi Stoph, zum Abschluß des Treffens in Erfurt vom 19.3.1970," p. 4, in DC20-4682 (Stoph), BA-V.

90. Ibid., p. 4.

91. "Demonstration des Vertrauens zu Partei und Regierung," *Neues Deutschland,* 20 March 1970, 2.

92. Monika Kaiser, *Machtwechsel von Ulbricht zu Honecker: Funktionsmechanismen der SED-Diktatur in Konfliktsituationen 1962 bis 1972* (Berlin: Akademie, 1997), 460.

93. Comments of Genosse Bräutigam, pp. 1–3 in J IV 2/3A/1866 (Sekretariat), SAPMO.

94. Comments of Genosse Sorgenicht at the Sitzung des Sekretariats des Zentralkomitees on 25 Mar. 1970, Stichwort-Protokoll, p. 11, in J IV 2/3A/1866 (Sekretariat), SAPMO.

95. Comments possibly from Genosse Sorgenicht in ibid., p. 13.

96. "Beschluß des Politbüros vom 28.4.1970 zu den Vorkommnissen am 19.3.1970 in Erfurt," pp. 3–4, in IV 2/1/407 (ZK), SAPMO.

97. Markus Wolf, *Spionagechef im geheimen Krieg* (Munich: List, 1997), 250; and author's interview with Wolf, 6 June 1996.

98. Wolf, *Spionagechef,* 250.

99. Jens Gieseke, *Die hauptamtlichen Mitarbeiter des Ministeriums für Staatssicherheit,* unnumbered volume in *MfS Handbuch: Anatomie der Staatssicherheit, Geschichte Struktur Methoden,* edited by Klaus-Dietmar Henke, Siegfried Suckut, Clemens Vollnhals, Walter Süß, and Roger Engelmann (Berlin: BStU, Aug. 1995), 41. See also Helmut Müller-Enbergs, *Inoffizielle Mitarbeiter des Ministeriums für Staatssicherheit: Richtlinien und Durchführungbestimmungen,* 2d ed., (Berlin: Links Verlag, 1996), 49 (Vol. 3 of *Wissenschaftliche Reihe des Bundesbeauftragten für die Unterlagen des Staatssicherheitsdienstes der ehemaligen Deutschen Demokratischen Republik,* edited by Abteilung Bildung und Forschung).

100. Letter from Klaus Dieter Arndt to Helmut Schmidt, 28 Apr. 1970, in HS Privatpolitisch, 1970, Bd. 7, HS PA.

101. Ibid.

102. Ibid.

103. Quoted in Stephen E. Ambrose, *Nixon: The Triumph of a Politician, 1962–1972* (New York: Simon and Schuster, 1989), 386.

104. Author's interview with Wolf, 6 June 1996.

105. Ibid. On the topic of the growing division between Honecker and Ulbricht, see Kaiser, *Machtwechsel*; and Norbert Podewin, *Walter Ulbricht: Eine neue Biographie* (Dietz: Berlin, 1995).

106. Ulbricht requested consultation with the Soviets in two letters: Ulbricht to Brezhnev, 1 Apr. 1970 and 4 May 1970, both in J IV 2/202/103 (Büro Ulbricht), SAPMO.

107. This document survives in the "calf-leather volume," or "Kalbslederband," circulated by Erich Honecker to fellow Politburo members in 1989. For a description of this problematic source, see Note on Sources.

108. "Kalbslederband" document with date 15 May 1970 and first heading "L. I. Breshnew," my p. 19.

109. "Kalbslederband" document with date 15.5.1970 and first heading "L. I. Breshnew," my pp. 21–24. Heinrich Potthoff mistakenly suggests that this notion originated in East Berlin; see Potthoff, *Im Schatten der Mauer* (Hamburg: Propyläen, 1999), 89–90.

110. On the scandal surrounding the publication of the Bahr paper, see Baring, *Machtwechsel*, 311–13; Bark and Gress, *Democracy and Its Discontents*, 181; and Bahr, *Zu meiner Zeit*, 324–25.

111. Richard Löwenthal, *Vom kalten Krieg zur Ostpolitik* (Stuttgart: Seewald Verlag, 1974): 81–89.

112. In 1996, Egon Bahr speculated on who might have given these papers to the press. He said that it must have been the Moscow Botschaftsrat Immo Stabreit. See Bahr, *Zu meiner Zeit*, 325. Stabreit's denial, in a letter to the editor of *Spiegel* on 23 Sept. 1996, showed that even twenty-five years later the resentment of Foreign Office officials at having to take a back seat to Bahr in the most important diplomatic developments of the day had not abated: "Herr Bahr selbst weiß sehr gut, daß es nicht die Beamten des Auswärtigen Amtes waren, die sich im Interesse einer politischen Sache souverän über Vorschriften, Regeln und Usancen sowie sonstigen Formelkram hinwegsetzen zu können glaubten" ("Mr. Bahr knows very well that it was not the officials of the Foreign Ministry who believed themselves to be so sovereign that they could safely ignore guidelines, prescriptions, nuances, and other formal trivialities in the interest of a political goal")—the implication being clearly that Bahr did.

113. Documents from this group, the "Kontaktausschuß," are in 404, EBD, FES. See also Benno Zündorf, alias Antonius Eitel, *Die Ostverträge* (Verlag C. H. Beck: München, 1979), 184.

114. Garthoff, *Détente*, 1129.

115. Also on 4 May, thirty-seven college presidents signed a letter to Nixon, asking him to show his determination to end the war promptly (Ambrose, *Nixon*, 350). Furthermore, on 8 May, thirteen of Henry Kissinger's former colleagues from the Harvard faculty visited him and soundly criticized his policies in Vietnam. Kissinger says that the rejection of his policies by his former colleagues "completed my transition from the academic world to the world of affairs." Kissinger, *WHY*, 515.

116. Nelson, *Making of Détente*, 82.

117. James E. Cronin, *The World the Cold War Made: Order, Chaos, and the Return of History* (New York: Routledge, 1996).

118. As historian Stephen Ambrose noted, "The big news in Europe, relatively unnoticed by most Americans in the late sixties and the beginnings of the seventies because

of American preoccupation with Southeast Asia, was the development of détente." Ambrose, *Nixon*, 385.

119. Wolfram Hanrieder, *Germany, America, Europe: Forty Years of German Foreign Policy* (New Haven: Yale University Press, 1989), 199.

120. Ibid., 200.

121. Ibid. Hanrieder is not alone in his opinion; for example, Geir Lundestad agrees that one of the main reasons the United States supported European integration was that it furthered the "double containment" of both Germany and Russia. See Geir Lundestad, *"Empire" by Integration: The United States and European Integration, 1945–1997* (New York: Oxford University Press, 1998), 4.

122. They apparently echoed concerns voiced by British premier Harold Wilson and French premier George Pompidou during their own respective visits to Nixon in January and February 1970. See Kissinger, *WHY*, 420–22, in particular 422: "Like all his colleagues, he [Pompidou] claimed that he trusted Brandt but feared that Brandt's policies might unleash nationalistic tendencies that would prove impossible to contain." The French seem to have been particularly worried by the specter of reunification raised at Erfurt.

123. Ambrose, *Nixon*, 386.

124. Hanrieder, *Germany, America, Europe*, 199.

125. Kissinger, *WHY*, 411.

126. Ibid., 409.

127. Ibid., 411.

128. Space constraints prevent a fuller exploration of French attitudes toward Ostpolitik here, but a good deal of secondary literature on this topic exists already. To cite a few studies: (a) Alfred Grosser points out that "il y a bien inquiétude" in Paris over Brandt's Eastern initiatives, "et irritation aussi"; that is, Paris was both worried and irritated about losing its importance as an intermediary between Bonn and Warsaw and Moscow. See Alfred Grosser, *Affaires Exterieures: La Politique de la France 1944–1989* (Saint-Amand, Fr.: Flammarion, 1989): 244. (b) Pompidou worried about both the spotlight focused on Willy Brandt, with whom his relations were "difficiles," and the implications for France's trading position in the East; see Louis Muron, *Pompidou* (Mesnil-sur-l'Estrée, Fr.: Flammarion, 1994): 288. (c) For a book-length assessment of French attitudes toward Ostpolitik, see Andreas Wilkens, *Der unstete Nachbar: Frankreich, die deutsche Ostpolitik und die Berliner Vier-Mächte-Verhandlungen, 1969–1974* (Munich: Oldenbourg, 1990). (d) For its part, the SED assumed that the French, because of their worry about the possibility of unification, would be interested in friendly relations with the GDR. The GDR "overestimated" its own importance in French foreign policy, because France did not in fact succumb to the temptation to use the GDR as a kind of "lever" in its relations with the FRG. See F. Sirjacques-Manfrass, "Die Rolle Frankreichs aus der Sicht der DDR und Frankreichs Haltung zur Wiedervereinigung," in Heiner Timmermann, ed., *Diktaturen in Europa im 20. Jahrhundert—Der Fall DDR* (Berlin: Duncker & Humblot, 1996).

129. William Burr, ed., *The Kissinger Transcripts: The Top Secret Talks with Beijing and Moscow* (New York: New Press, 1998), 37.

130. Georges-Henri Soutou, *L'alliance incertaine: Les rapports politico-stratégiques franco-allemands, 1954–1996* (Paris: Fayard, 1996), 319. As he further argued: "Les craintes de Georges Pompidou quant aux conséquences à long terme de l'Ostpolitik ont probablement largement contribué à façonner sa politique allemande, europénne et occidentale. . . . Il craignait un départ des troupes américaines d'Europe (ce fut chez lui une obsesion constante) qui pourrait conduire à un accord Germano-soviétique. L'Allemagne

pourrait alors se trouver réunifiée, neutralisée, mais disposant d'armes nucléaires: la pire des situations possible pour la France! La seule défense possible était d'ancrer l'Allemagne dans une Europe occidentale solide, de façon à ce qu'elle ne sorte pas du cadre européen et ne conduise pas à un condominium germano-soviétique" (319–20). (In essence, Pompidou feared the long-term consequences of Ostpolitik, particularly the possibility of a unified, neutral Germany that possessed nuclear weapons.)

131. John W. Young, *Cold War Europe, 1945–1991: A Political History*, 2d ed. (London: Arnold, 1996), 259.

132. Author's conversation with Bahr, 13 Nov. 1997. See also Bahr, *Zu meiner Zeit*, 107.

133. Historians and political scientists continue to argue over whether or not the "Stalin Note" of 1952 represented a serious offer. Rolf Steininger thinks that it did; see Steininger, *Eine vertane Chance die Stalin-Note vom 10. März 1952 und die Wiedervereinigung* (Berlin: Dietz, 1985). However, this view has not been widely accepted.

134. Hanrieder, *Germany, America, Europe*, 199.

135. Kissinger, *WHY*, 410.

136. "Erklärung von Botschafter Rush, 26.3.1970," p. 2, and letter from Otto Winzer to Walter Ulbricht, Willi Stoph, Erich Honecker, and Hermann Axen, 26 Mar. 1970, both in J IV 2/202/137/9 (Allg. Abt.), SAPMO. The Winzer letter forwarded "die Übersetzung des Wortlautes der Rede, die der sowjetische Botschafter, Genosse Abrassimow" ("the translation of the text of the speech that the Soviet ambassador, Comrade Abrasimov, had delivered") at the Four Power round of that day.

137. Information about these meetings may also be found in J IV 2/202/137/9 (Allg. Abt.), SAPMO.

138. "Stellungnahme zu möglichen Vorschlägen und taktischen Manövern der westdeutschen Delegation," Anlage 5 in J IV 2/2A/1.441 (Politbüro), SAPMO.

139. "Information über westdeutsche Vorstellungen für das Gespräch Brandts mit Genossen Stoph am 21.5.1970 in Kassel," 20 May 1970, p. 94, in SdM 1473, ZA, BStU. See also "Information über die Reaktion der Bevölkerung im Hinblick auf das Treffen in Kassel," 20 May 1970, pp. 134–141, in SdM 1471, ZA, BStU.

140. "Stellungnahme zu möglichen Vorschlägen und taktischen Manövern der westdeutschen Delegation," p. 4.

141. "Hinweise für das Verhalten während des Aufenthaltes auf dem Territorium der BRD," pp. 153, 155, in DC20-4683 (Stoph), BA-V.

142. "Vorschlag über Maßnahmen zur Sicherstellung des Treffens am 21. Mai 1970," p. 85, in DC20-4683 (Stoph), BA-V.

143. GDR specialist David Childs has rightly pointed out that the GDR could have done worse: it could have canceled Kassel entirely but chose not to do so. Clearly, interest in better relations with the FRG remained. See David Childs, *The GDR: Moscow's German Ally* (London: Unwin Hyman, 1988), 81.

144. See Catudal, *Diplomacy*, 110. This settlement also covered mail in transit through the GDR to other East European countries. It contained a promise on the part of the GDR to increase the number of telephone lines between the two Germanies from thirty-four to seventy-four, as well as an increase in telex lines from nineteen to thirty-five; SED dilatoriness in actually installing them would remain a problem, as will be discussed in subsequent chapters. See also Karl Seidel, "Erste Schritte auf dem Weg zu normalen Beziehungen zwischen der Deutschen Demokratischen Republik und der Bundesrepublik Deutschland. Persönliche Erinnerungen an die deutsch-deutschen Verhandlungen Anfang der siebziger Jahre," in Detlef Nakath, ed., *Deutschlandpolitiker der DDR erinnern sich* (Berlin: Fides, 1995), 107.

145. Catudal, *Diplomacy*, 109.

146. Author's interview with Görner, 7 June 1996.

147. Seidel, "Erste Schritte," 105. For the detailed SED organization plan for the meeting, see J IV 2/2J/2962 (IntVer), SAPMO. See also Nakath, *Erfurt and Kassel*.

148. Seidel, "Erste Schritte," 105.

149. "Stenografische Niederschrift über das Gespräch des VdM der DDR, W. Stoph, mit dem Bundeskanzler der BRD, W. Brandt, in Kassel, 21. Mai 1970," p. 5, in J IV 2/201/840 (IntVer), SAPMO. Portions of this document are published as Document No. 4 in Potthoff, *Bonn und Ost-Berlin*. See also J IV 2/201/845 (IntVer), SAPMO, on the topic of the protests.

150. "Nazistischer Terror, Flaggenschändung und wüste Ausschreitungen—das steckte hinter Bonns Gerede von Frieden, Freiheit und Menschlichkeit," *Neues Deutschland*, 22 May 1970, 1.

151. "Stenografische Niederschrift über das Gespräch des VdM der DDR, W. Stoph, mit dem Bundeskanzler der BRD, W. Brandt, in Kassel, 21 Mai. 1970," p. 6.

152. "Erklärung des VdM der DDR, W. Stoph beim Treffen mit dem Bundeskanzler der BRD, W. Brandt in Kassel, 21. Mai 1970," in J IV 2/2J/2964 (IntVer), SAPMO.

153. The complete text is in "Stenografische Niederschrift über das Gespräch des VdM der DDR, W. Stoph, mit dem Bundeskanzler der BRD, W. Brandt, in Kassel, 21. Mai 1970." The points listed here are numbers 3, 4, 5, 6, 10, 11, 15, and 16.

154. "Telefonische Mitteilung des VdM Willi Stoph über sein Gespräch unter 4 Augen mit W. Brandt (durchgegeben am 21.5.1970 um 12.30 Uhr)," in DC20-4667 (Stoph), BA-V. Records of other personal conversations may be found in "Vermerk über Gespräche des Genossen Dr. Kohl mit Staatssekretär Conrad Ahlers während des Treffens der Regierungschefs der DDR und der BRD in Kasssel am 21. Mai 1970," pp. 46–51, and "Vermerk über Gespräche des Genossen Dr. Kohl mit dem Parlamentarischen Staatssekretär im Bundesministerium des Innern, Wolfram Dorn, während des Treffens der Regierungschefs der DDR und der BRD in Kassel am 21. Mai 1970," pp. 52–53, in SdM 1474, ZA, BStU.

155. See "Vier-Augen-Gespräche des Herrn Bundeskanzlers mit dem VdM der DDR, Herrn Stoph, in Kassel am 21. Mai 1970," in HS privat Pz DDR 1966–74, Bd. I, HS PA. Also published as part of Document 3 in Potthoff, *Bonn und Ost-Berlin*.

156. Cover page of *Der Spiegel*, 25 May 1970. The MfS had code-named the coverage of Erfurt "Konfrontation," that of Kassel "Konfrontation II."

157. Abt. Westdeutschland [MfAA], "Erste Einschätzung des Treffens zwischen dem VdM der DDR, Willi Stoph, und dem Bundeskanzler der BRD, Willy Brandt, am 21. Mai 1970 in Kassel," p. 28, in SdM 1870, ZA, BStU.

158. Ibid., p. 28.

159. Ibid., p. 30.

160. "Auszug aus einem IM-Bericht," p. 34, in SdM 1830, ZA, BStU.

161. See, e.g., Nelson, *Making of Détente*, 96; and Young, *Cold War Europe*, 259.

162. "Bemerkungen zu den Beziehungen zwischen der DDR und der BRD Rede von Walter Ulbricht auf der 13. Plenartagung des ZK der SED," 9 June 1970, p. 40 in FBS/363-Film 15136 (Nachlaß Ulbricht), SAPMO. See also the ZK files from the 13. Plenum, particularly IV 2/1/408 (ZK), SAPMO.

163. Hermann Axen with Harald Neubert, *Ich war ein Diener der Partei* (Berlin: Edition Ost, 1996), 312–13.

164. Karl-Heinz Schmidt also concluded that the Soviets were against a continuation of the Brandt-Stoph meetings. See Schmidt, *Dialog über Deutschland: Studien zur Deutschlandpolitik von KPdSU und SED (1960–1979)* (Baden-Baden: Nomos, 1998).

Chapter Three

1. Available sources shed light on these conflicts to varying degrees. Compared to the documentation open on the Eastern side, there is relatively little available on internal West German in-fighting. However, the East German archives provide an unexpected amount of information about both Soviet and U.S. worries. They also provide a good deal of information on internal SED disagreements, although in an indirect fashion. Politburo meetings were not transcribed, so it is difficult to reconstruct exactly what was said. Instead, a summary of all decisions was produced afterwards and filed with supporting paperwork. In other words, Politburo files contain the kind of preparatory papers the members had read and a record of the decisions taken but no text of the actual conversation or debate. There are rare exceptions to this general statement; occasionally the handwritten notes of a participant at a meeting appear in files, and the meeting of 26 October 1971 was transcribed. (See Note on Sources for a description of this meeting.)

2. Peter Bender, *Episode oder Epoche? Zur Geschichte des geteilten Deutschlands* (Munich: dtv, Apr. 1996), 104.

3. Cover note to Ulbricht of 8 Aug. 1970 (author not known), attached to the 7 Aug. 1970 "Studie über die Verhandlungen zwischen der UdSSR und der BRD," in J IV 2/202/82 (Büro Ulbricht), SAPMO. The cover note indicates that the "Studie" had been written by two of "our" foreign ministry bureaucrats, suggesting that the author of the cover note may be Otto Winzer, the foreign minister. The authors of the study were Karl Seidel, head of Abt. BRD of the Foreign Ministry, and Genosse Dr. Bock, head of the Grundsatzabteilung.

4. Historians are not much better off than the unhappy SED bureaucrats charged with writing the report; documentary sources are limited. However, it is possible to expand on existing historiography on the Moscow Treaty by taking account of both the reports on the meeting that survive in Bahr's papers and the wealth of Eastern memoirs that have become available since the collapse of the Berlin Wall. The memoirs of Bahr's KGB back-channel contact Kevorkov and those of Soviet diplomats Yuli Kvizinski and Anatoly Dobrynin are particularly informative.

5. Michael Sodaro, *Moscow, Germany, and the West from Khrushchev to Gorbachev* (Ithaca: Cornell University Press, 1990), 135.

6. Egon Bahr, *Zu meiner Zeit* (Munich: Karl Blessing, 1996), 308.

7. Wjatscheslaw Keworkow, *Der geheime Kanal* (Berlin: Rowohlt, Mar. 1995), 73.

8. SED Politburo member Hermann Axen remembered that, after dropping the demand for full legal recognition, Brezhnev told Ulbricht, "Daß man aber die BRD noch zur Anerkennung zwingen werde" ("that one would still force the FRG into recognition"). Hermann Axen with Harald Neubert, *Ich war ein Diener der Partei* (Berlin: Edition Ost, 1996), 281. See also Bahr, *Zu meiner Zeit*, 309.

9. See Hans-Dietrich Genscher, *Erinnerungen* (Berlin: Siedler Verlag, 1995), 192; and review of the English translation, *Rebuilding a House Divided* (New York: Broadway, 1998), by Philip Zelikow, "After the Wall," *New York Times Book Review*, 1 Mar. 1998, 33.

10. Valentin Falin stated in his memoirs that he helped to write the letter; see Falin, *Politische Erinnerungen* (Munich: Knaur, 1995), 107–9. On this letter, see also Arnulf Baring, *Machtwechsel: Die Ära Brandt-Scheel* (Stuttgart: Deutsche Verlags-Anstalt, 1982), 342–43; Bahr, *Zu Meiner Zeit*, 319; and Dennis L. Bark and David R. Gress, *Democracy and Its Discontents*, vol. 2 of *A History of West Germany*, 2d ed. (Oxford: Blackwell, 1993), 183.

11. Julij A. Kwizinskij, *Vor dem Sturm: Erinnerungen eines Diplomaten* (Berlin: Siedler, 1993), 231. Gromyko's comments to this effect at the meeting of the Supreme Soviet of

the USSR about the treaty became problematic when the West German government requested a stenographic transcript of this meeting (presumably to prove to FRG domestic opposition that the unity note had in fact received official Soviet attention). Kvizinski recalled that Soviet diplomat Valentin Falin convinced a furious Gromyko to take such comments out of the highly edited "transcript" that was given to the West Germans. This incident, while minor in its impact at the time, merits mention because it should serve as a major warning for scholars attempting to use new sources from the Eastern Bloc. This is not the only case where a "stenographic transcript" was in fact a selectively edited version of events. SED documents bear evidence of it in a couple of other cases (see Note on Sources for a discussion of this topic), and it can be assumed that more successful—i.e., undetectable—cases of alteration exist as well.

12. The full German-language text of the treaty may be found in Auswärtiges Amt, ed., *Außenpolitik der Bundesrepublik Deutschland: Dokumente 1949 bis 1994* (Cologne: Verlag Wissenschaft und Politik, 1995), 337–40.

13. Ibid., 337.

14. Ibid., 338.

15. For a detailed discussion of both the Bahr Paper and the Moscow Treaty, see Benno Zündorf (pseudonym for Antonius Eitel, aide to Bahr), *Die Ostverträge* (Munich: C. H. Beck, 1979), 27–61. Zündorf compares the Bahr Paper with the final treaty; ironically, a similar document drawing the same comparison exists in German translation from the Russian in "Vereinbarung über die Absichten der Seiten," 27 Aug. 1970, in J IV 2/202/334 (Büro Ulbricht), SAPMO.

16. I am grateful to Tim Snyder for pointing this out to me.

17. Keworkow, *Kanal*, 87–88.

18. "Договор между Союзом Советских Социалистических Республик и Федеративной Республикой Германии," *Pravda*, 13 Aug. 1970, 1.

19. As political scientist Karl Birnbaum has pointed out, Moscow sought as a result to emphasize the "static qualities" of the treaty; in other words, it sought to emphasize its endorsement of the Cold War borders and political realities. The West Germans, for their part, preferred to emphasize the "dynamic aspects." See Karl E. Birnbaum, *East and West Germany: A Modus Vivendi* (Lexington, Mass.: Lexington Books, 1973), 9.

20. Zündorf, *Die Ostverträge*, 61.

21. Richard Löwenthal, "Faktoren und Perspektiven der sowjetischen Westpolitik," in *Sowjetpolitik der 70er Jahre*, edited by Richard Löwenthal and Heinrich Vogel (Stuttgart: Kohlhammer), 30.

22. For a discussion about the role that fear of close German cooperation with NATO, particularly the possibility of nuclear cooperation, played in the first half of the Cold War, see Marc Trachtenberg, *A Constructed Peace: The Making of the European Settlement 1945–1963* (Princeton: Princeton University Press, 1999).

23. "Auszug aus dem Dolmetscher-Protokoll über das Gespräch des Herrn Bundeskanzler mit dem Generalsekretär des ZK der KPdSU, Breschnjew, am 12. August 1970, von 15.30–19.30 Uhr," p. 5, in HS privat Pz UdSSR 1968–74, HS PA. The Western summary of the same conversation contains a similar remark. See "Dolmetscher-Protokoll über das Gespräch des Herrn Bundeskanzlers mit dem Generalsekretär des ZK der KPdSU, Breschnjew, am 12. August 1970 von 15.30–19.30 Uhr," p. 7, in 429A, EBD, FES.

24. Wolfram Hanrieder, *Germany, America, Europe: Forty Years of German Foreign Policy* (New Haven: Yale University Press, 1989), 201.

25. "Protokoll Nr. 27/70 der außerordentlichen Sitzung des Politbüros des ZK der SED am 8. Juni 1970," in J IV 2/2A/1.449 (Politbüro), SAPMO.

26. Notes from the day after contain only some of the details of the treaty. See

"Vorlage an das Politbüro des ZK der SED," J IV 2/2A/1.459 (Politbüro), SAPMO. See also "Ein Erfolg für alle, die für Entspannung und Frieden sind" and "Persönliche Verschlußsache," in J IV 2/2A/1.461 (Politbüro), SAPMO.

27. Author's conversation with Falin, 14 Nov. 1997, Vienna.

28. "Zu den Gesprächen Gen. L. I. Breshnew," 20 Aug. 1970, pp. 7–8, in vorl. SED 41656 (Büro Honecker), SAPMO; this file contains Honecker's partly handwritten and partly typed notes, from which the "Kalbslederband" was typed and assembled. The same document and phrases appear in "Kalbslederband," my pp. 39–41 (quotes on my p. 38). The tone of the document suggests that "ich" is Brezhnev and that Honecker was recording Brezhnev's words as spoken.

29. In contrast to the Moscow negotiations, the quadripartite talks are extremely well documented in SED files. The Soviets provided East Berlin with summaries, and in some cases transcripts, of nearly all meetings in 1970. Perhaps they did so because, in essence, little of significance happened.

30. Zündorf, *Die Ostverträge*, 125.

31. Henry Kissinger, *WHY* (Boston: Little, Brown, 1979), 823.

32. For a detailed overview of the talks, see Honoré M. Catudal, *The Diplomacy of the Quadripartite Agreement on Berlin: A New Era in East-West Politics* (Berlin: Berlin Verlag, 1978) and Catudal, *A Balance Sheet of the Quadripartite Agreement on Berlin: Evaluation and Documentation* (Berlin: Berlin Verlag, 1978).

33. "Information über das Treffen der Botschafter der vier Mächte am 9. Juni 1970 zu Fragen, die mit Westberlin zusammenhängen," 10 June 1970, pp. 1–2 in J IV 2/202/137 (Allg. Abt.), SAPMO. The same document is also available on pp. 142–53 in SdM 1834, ZA, BStU.

34. "Information über das Treffen der Botschafter der vier Mächte am 9. Juni 1970 zu Fragen, die mit Westberlin zusammenhängen," p. 2.

35. Ibid., pp. 8–9. The historical debating continued into fifth quadripartite meeting, on 30 June; see "Information über das Treffen der Botschafter der UdSSR, der USA, Großbritanniens und Frankreichs im Rahmen des Meinungsaustausches über Westberlin am 30. Juni 1970," 13 July 1970, pp. 9–10 in J IV 2/202/138 (Allg. Abt.), SAPMO.

36. "Erklärung des amerikanischen Botschafters vom 21. Juli," p. 15 in DC20-4403 (Stoph), BA-V. Another copy of this document exists in J IV 2/202/138 (Allg. Abt.), SAPMO.

37. Ibid., p. 18.

38. "Ansprache des Botschafters der UdSSR in der DDR P. A. Abrassimow am 30. September 1970," p. 63, in DC20-4403 (Stoph), BA-V.

39. "Über das Zusammentreffen der Botschafter der Vier Mächte in Westberlin am 4. November," pp. 84–85, in DC20-4403 (Stoph), BA-V.

40. Catudal, *Diplomacy*, 130.

41. "Information über das Treffen der Botschafter der Vier Mächte in Westberlin am 16.11.1970," p. 97, in DC20-4403 (Stoph), BA-V.

42. "Information über das Treffen der Botschafter der Vier Mächte über Westberlin am 10. Dezember 1970," p. 6, in SdM 1834, ZA, BStU.

43. For more information on the more famous Cuban crisis and its links to Berlin, see Aleksandr Fursenko and Timothy Naftali, *"One Hell of a Gamble": Khrushchev, Castro, and Kennedy, 1958–1964* (New York: Norton, 1997).

44. Kissinger, *WHY*, 632–52. I disagree with the assessment of Keith L. Nelson, *The Making of Détente: Soviet-American Relations in the Shadow of Vietnam* (Baltimore: John Hopkins University Press, 1995), 132, that Cienfuegos was a "regional and relatively unimportant" incident; rather, I feel that the beginnings of détente lent international

significance to any such one-sided move. See also Philip Nash, *The Other Missiles of October: Eisenhower, Kennedy, and the Jupiters, 1957–1963* (Chapel Hill: University of North Carolina Press, 1997), 172, which states that Nixon's response to hearing about Cienfuegos was to consider restationing Jupiter missiles in Turkey!

45. Kissinger, *WHY*, 831.

46. The four summaries of French-Soviet bilateral contacts are from conversations on 8 June 1970, in J IV 2/202/137 (Allg. Abt.), SAPMO; on 1 Oct. 1970, in J IV 2/202/139 (Allg. Abt.), SAPMO; on 17 Feb. 1971, in DC20-4403 (Stoph), BA-V, and in J IV 2/202/140 (Allg. Abt.), SAPMO; and sometime between 25 May and 2 June 1971, in DC20-4400 (Stoph), BA-V, and J IV 2/202/504 (Allg. Abt.), SAPMO. There are also three summaries of U.S.-Soviet bilateral talks from conversations on 2 Sept. 1970, in DC20-4403 and J IV 2/202/138 (Allg. Abt.), SAPMO; 18 Jan. 1971, in DC20-4403 and J IV 2/202/140 (Allg. Abt.), SAPMO; and 31 May 1971, in DC20-4403 and J IV 2/202/504 (Allg. Abt.), SAPMO. Finally, there are notes about a Soviet meeting with the West Berlin mayor in "Information über ein Gespräch mit dem Regierenden Bürger-meister Westberlins K. Schütz am 7. Oktober 1970," pp. 68–84, in SdM 1834, ZA, BStU.

47. "ИНФОРМАЦИЯ о беседе с послом Франции в ФРГ Ж. СОВАНьЯРГОМ 1 октября 1970 года," p. 5, in J IV 2/202/139 (Büro Ulbricht), SAPMO.

48. Ibid., p. 1.

49. See the summary written by Hermann Axen, 1 July 1970, "Betr.: Gespräch mit dem französichen Außenminister Maurice Schumann in Paris," in J IV 2/202/1363 (Büro Ulbricht), SAPMO.

50. On this topic, see Peter G. Boyle, *American-Soviet Relations: From the Russian Revolution to the Fall of Communism* (London: Routledge, 1993), 167; Kissinger, *WHY*, 698–99; and Nelson, *Détente*, 88.

51. Kissinger, *WHY*, 698–708.

52. Ibid., 552. Kissinger thought that Nixon's interest in a summit came from his hope of paralyzing antiwar agitators "by a dramatic peace move."

53. Anatoly Dobrynin, *In Confidence: Moscow's Ambassador to America's Six Cold War Presidents (1962–1986)* (New York: Random House, 1995), 218.

54. Ibid., 221.

55. Ibid., 226.

56. Arthur G. Kogan, "The Quadripartite Berlin Negotiations," Research Project No. 1035 (Secret; declassified 4 Apr. 1994 via FOIA Request No. 9305297), Office of the Historian, Bureau of Public Affairs, Department of State, Sept. 1977, p. 233, in Box 26, Nuclear History/Berlin Crisis, National Security Archive, Washington, D.C.

57. Kissinger, *WHY*, 800.

58. Catudal, *Diplomacy*, 140.

59. Kwizinskij, *Vor dem Sturm*, 239.

60. Kissinger, *WHY*, 805. The latter comment begs the question, why did he ask his staff to do so?

61. Ibid., 801–10.

62. Ibid., 828.

63. Walter Isaacson, *Kissinger: A Biography* (New York: Simon & Schuster, 1992), 324; and Kissinger, *WHY*, 810.

64. In an interview with the author on 21 May 1996, Bahr argued that the "group of three" was the driving force behind the quadripartite agreement. There was little paper-work produced by the group, given its unofficial nature, but telegrams that passed between Bahr and Kissinger do survive and confirm Bahr's assertions about the signifi-cance of this group. See the various telegrams and other documents in 439, EBD, FES. For

further material on cooperation between West Germany and the Western allies, see also files 386A and 386B, EBD, FES.

65. Kwizinskij, *Vor dem Sturm*, 240.

66. Boyle, *American-Soviet Relations*, 168.

67. Raymond Garthoff, *Détente and Confrontation: American-Soviet Relations from Nixon to Reagan*, rev. ed. (Washington D.C.: Brookings Institution, 1994), 170. For further information on the SALT talks, see Kissinger's memoirs and those of the lead U.S. negotiator, Gerard Smith, *Doubletalk: The Story of the First Strategic Arms Limitation Talks* (New York: Doubleday, 1980).

68. One finds this view, for example, in Hans-Adolf Jacobsen, Gert Leptin, Ulrich Scheuner, and Eberhard Schulz, eds., *Drei Jahrzehnte Außenpolitik der DDR* (Munich: R. Oldenbourg Verlag, 1979). See also Melvin Croan, *East Germany* (Beverly Hills, Calif.: Sage, 1976); he argues on pp. 26–27 that Erfurt and Kassel showed that Ulbricht did not want to negotiate with the West. See also a more recent example, a RAND report on East Germany written by a team of expert scholars in 1990. This team found that the key difference between Ulbricht and Honecker was that the latter embraced the task of negotiating with the West but the former shrank from it. Ronald D. Asmus, J. F. Brown, and Keith Crane, *Soviet Foreign Policy and the Revolutions of 1989 in Eastern Europe* (Santa Monica: RAND, 1991), 93–94.

69. A. James McAdams, *Germany Divided* (Princeton: Princeton University Press, 1993), 89.

70. Author's interview with Wolf, 6 June 1996.

71. Ibid.; see also Markus Wolf, *Spionagechef im geheimen Krieg: Erinnerungen* (Munich: List, 1997), 254. Axen made a remark to this effect in response to an interviewer's question; see Axen with Neubert, *Ich war ein Diener der Partei*, 311–12. James McAdams saw the difference between Ulbricht's interest in potentially reunifying Germany (under socialism) and Honecker's interest in two sharply divided states as one source of Honecker's appeal to the Soviets as a replacement for Ulbricht; see McAdams, *Germany Divided*, 93.

72. Wolfgang Berger, "Als Ulbricht an Breshnew vorbeiregierte," *Neues Deutschland*, 23–24 Mar. 1991, Ausgabe B, 13. Wolfgang Berger was Ulbricht's prime adviser on economic issues at this time, especially regarding dealings with the FRG. On Berger, see Monika Kaiser, *Machtwechsel von Ulbricht zu Honecker: Funktionsmechanismen der SED-Diktatur in Konfliktsituationen 1962 bis 1972* (Berlin: Akademie, 1997), 400.

73. See the discussion of Kaiser's view on Ulbricht and the Prague invasion in Chapter 1.

74. An otherwise insightful analysis of the ouster of Ulbricht, offered by Jochen Stelkens in his master's thesis and published as an article in the *Vierteljahrshefte für Zeitgeschichte*, does not sufficiently address the development of opposition in 1970. See Jochen Stelkens, "Machtwechsel in Ost-Berlin: Der Sturz Walter Ulbrichts 1971," *Vierteljahrshefte für Zeitgeschichte* 4 (Oct. 1997): 503–33.

75. Kaiser has plausibly suggested the evolution of a kind of "double leadership," in which Honecker exploited Ulbricht's absenteeism from the Secretariat to establish a rival leadership base for himself. Kaiser, *Machtwechsel*, 460. She estimates that by early 1970, Ulbricht had not attended a Secretariat meeting in ten years. Ibid., 371.

76. Tagesordnungspunkt 7 states that the "Argumentation zu Fragen des Außenhandels mit Westdeutschland" was "bestätigt" (confirmed) with some changes, in J IV 2/2A/1.446 (Politbüro), SAPMO. The "Argumentation" itself is actually an extensive series of documents and appendices in J IV 2/2A/1.448 (Politbüro), SAPMO.

77. Vorlage für das Politbüro, undated, "Betr.: Fragen der Außenwirtschaftsbezie-

hungen der DDR zu Westdeutschland sowie die Schulden- und Schadensersatzverpflichtungen der BRD gegenüber der DDR," in J IV 2/2A/1.448 (Politbüro), SAPMO.

78. "Dokumentation I," 28 May 1970, p. 5, in J IV 2/2A/1.448 (Politbüro), SAPMO.

79. "Anlage C, Schulden und Schadensersatzverpflichtungen der BRD gegenüber der DDR," p. 3, in J IV 2/2A/1.448 (Politbüro), SAPMO.

80. "Dokumentation I," pp. 5–6.

81. Ibid., p. 8.

82. "Anlage D, Weiteres Vorgehen zur Auseinandersetzung mit der BRD und zur Durchsetzung der Forderungen der DDR auf Begleichung der Schulden und Regelungen der Schadensersatzverpflichtungen durch die BRD," in J IV 2/2A/1.448, (Politbüro), SAPMO.

83. Ulbricht had explained in a letter to the Politburo that he would not be able to take part in the next meeting due to an operation. Ulbricht to Politbuoro, 21 June 1970, in J IV 2/2A/1.450 (Politbüro), SAPMO.

84. "Instruktion zur Durchsetzung der politischen und ökonomischen Interessen der DDR in den Außenwirtschaftsbeziehungen der DDR mit der BRD und der selbständigen politischen Einheit Westberlin," Vorlage für das Politbüro, 19 June 1970, J IV 2/2A/1.450 (Politbüro), SAPMO.

85. Ibid., p. 3. Similar sentiments can also be found in "Zur Entwicklung des imperialistischen Systems in der Bundesrepublik Analyse und Prognose" undated but probably from July 1970, in DC20-4451 (Stoph), BA-V.

86. "Instruktion zur Durchsetzung," p. 3.

87. Ibid., p. 8.

88. Jeffrey Kopstein, "Ulbricht Embattled: The Quest for Socialist Modernity in the Light of New Sources," *Europe-Asia Studies* (formerly *Soviet Studies*) 46 (1994): 597–616, argues that Honecker and Stoph in particular were worried that Ulbricht, in a misguided attempt to catch up with the West, would take the country deep into debt in order to buy the necessary equipment (610).

89. See "Niederschrift über die Beratung des Genossen Walter Ulbricht mit Genossen Tichonow am 25. Juni 1970", at which Günter Mittag, head of the State Planning Commission Gerhard Schürer, and Ulbricht's economic adviser Wolfgang Berger were present on the GDR side, and Pjotr Abrasimov on the Soviet side, in DE1 (Bln) VA-Nr. 56128 (SPK), BA-V.

90. Ibid., p. 5.

91. Ibid., pp. 5–6. Tikhonov later succeeded Kosygin as prime minister.

92. Tagesordnungpunkt 1, J IV 2/2A/1.451 (Politbüro), SAPMO.

93. Tagesordnungpunkt 2, "Fragen der Arbeitsweise des Politbüros und des Sekretariats des ZK," 1 July 1970, J IV 2/2A/1.452 (Politbüro), SAPMO.

94. Kaiser, *Machtwechsel*, 372–74.

95. Kaiser's source for this conclusion is a portion of an interview that Abrasimov gave to a West German journalist after the fall of the Wall. According to it, Abrasimov had a recollection that Ulbricht had tried to dismiss Honecker at some point, but he could not place the date. Kaiser maintains that an "examination yields beyond doubt the result that this event took place at the beginning of July 1970," but she fails to explain what her examination comprised and offers no independent confirmation. Kaiser, *Machtwechsel*, 371. Kaiser also cited a conversation with former Politburo member Werner Eberlein. According to Kaiser, Eberlein originally thought that Abrasimov's comment was a "slip of the tongue," but Kaiser added that after she explained to him her "thesis based on the study of the documents," Eberlein agreed that Abrasimov must have been right. Unfor-

tunately, Kaiser does not specify on which documents she had based her thesis but instead cites only the interview. See Kaiser, *Machtwechsel*, 373 fn. 8.

96. Tagesordnungspunkt 1, 7 July 1970, J IV 2/2A/1.453 (Politbüro), SAPMO.

97. "Den Rechtsblock in der Bundesrepublik gemeinsam schlagen!" *Neues Deutschland*, 17 July 1970, 3–4. On this speech, see also Norbert Podewin, *Walter Ulbricht: Eine neue Biographie* (Dietz: Berlin, 1995), 423; and Stelkens, "Machtwechsel," 527.

98. Tagesordnungspunkt 5, 28 July 1970, J IV 2/2A/1.457 (Politbüro), SAPMO.

99. Untitled document, dated 28 July 1970, in vorl. SED 41656 (Büro Honecker), SAPMO. This is the handwritten file from which the "Kalbslederband" (see description in Note on Sources) was produced; this citation appears on my p. 26 of the Kalbslederband. (Since the document in 41656 does not contain page numbers, the page numbers from the "Kalbslederband" are given in the following citations. Peter Przybylski also published this document, giving it—without justification—the title "Protokoll einer Unterredung zwischen L. I. Breschnew und Erich Honecker am 28. Juli 1970," in *Tatort Politbüro*, Vol. 1, *Die Akte Honecker* (Berlin: Rowohlt, 1991), 280–88. While it is likely that the transcript records a Honecker-Brezhnev conversation, it is not certain, and the document does not bear the title Przybylski gave it. Because of this and other discrepancies between the documents and Przybylski's reproductions of them, the citations below come from the original documents (the handwritten version in 41656 and the typed version in the Kalbslederband).

100. Untitled document dated 28 July 1970, in vorl. SED 41656 (also "Kalbslederband," my p. 26).

101. Ibid. (also "Kalbslederband," my p. 26).

102. Ibid. (also "Kalbslederband," my p. 26).

103. Ibid. (also "Kalbslederband," my p. 29).

104. Ibid. (also "Kalbslederband" my p. 27).

105. Ibid. (also "Kalbslederband" my p. 27).

106. Ibid. (also "Kalbslederband" my p. 30).

107. Ibid. (also "Kalbslederband" my p. 30).

108. Author's interview with Wolf, 6 June 1996. There were also articles about Brandt's visit on page 1 of *Pravda* on the two proceeding days; "О предстоящем приезде в Советский Союз федерального канцлера Федеративной Республики Германии В. Брандта," *Pravda* (11 Aug. 1970), 1; and "Приезд в Москву Вилли Брандта," *Pravda*, 12 Aug. 1970, 1. Wolf also recounts this story in his 1997 memoirs; see Wolf, *Spionagechef*, 252–53.

109. "Zu den Gesprächen Gen. L. I. Breshnew" 20 Aug. 1970, which exists both in a handwritten version in Büro Honecker/SAPMO files (vorl. SED 41656) and in a typed version in the "Kalbslederband."

110. "Zu den Gesprächen Gen. L. I. Breshnew" 20 Aug. 1970 in vorl. SED 41656, p. 1.

111. Ibid., pp. 14–15.

112. Brezhnev refers to this meeting in a letter to Ulbricht of 21 Oct. 1970, in J IV 2/2J/3164 (Büro Ulbricht), SAPMO.

113. "Vermerk über die gemeinsame Besprechung der Delegation des ZK der KPdSU mit der Delegation des ZK der SED am 21.8.1970, Moskau," in "Kalbslederband," my p. 52. (Peter Przybylski also published this document, giving it the title "Aus einem geheimen Vermerk . . . ," in *Tatort Politbüro*, Vol. 1, *Die Akte Honecker* (Berlin: Rowohlt, 1991), 289–96.) On the significance of Ulbricht's comment as a sign of his arrogance, see also Kaiser, *Machtwechsel*, 395; and Stelkens, "Machtwechsel," 520.

114. "Vermerk über die gemeinsame Besprechung der Delegation des ZK der KPdSU

mit der Delegation des ZK der SED am 21.8.1070, Moskau," in "Kalbslederband," my p. 43.

115. Ibid., my p. 45.

116. Tagesordnungspunkt 3, 8 Sept. 1970, J IV 2/2A/1.463 (Politbüro), SAPMO.

117. Willi Stoph and Günter Mittag, "Vorlage für das Politbüro des ZK der SED, Betr.: Beschlußentwurf zur Analyse über die Plandurchführung im 1. Halbjahr 1970," Anlage "Beschlußentwurf," p. 1, in J IV 2/2A/1.463 (Politbüro), SAPMO.

118. Rede Walter Ulbrichts zum Thema "Durchführung des Volkswirtschaftsplanes 1970 und die Vorbereitung der Investitionen für 1971," Beratung des Sekretariats des ZK der SED mit den 1. Sekretären der Bezirksleitungen und den Vorsitzenden der Räte der Bezirke am 21.9.1970," in NY4182-782 (Nachlaß Ulbricht), SAPMO.

119. Ibid., p. 3.

120. Ibid., p. 20.

121. Ibid., p. 1.

122. "Zur Eröffnung des Parteilehrjahres 1970/71, Rede Erich Honeckers, am 14. September 1970 in Dresden," pp. 66–78, in J IV/218 (Büro Honecker), SAPMO.

123. "Rede zur Eröffnung des Parteilehrjahres 1970/71 in Erfurt, 25.09.70," p. 87, in J IV/219 (Büro Honecker, Reden und Vermerke), SAPMO.

124. For example, a letter from Brezhnev to Ulbricht shortly after Honecker's Erfurt speech, on 16 October, echoed Honecker's concerns. See Л. Брежнев В. Ульбрихту, 16 Oct. 1970, in J IV 2/202/347 (Büro Ulbricht), SAPMO. German translations (with the date 21 Oct. 1970 typed on top, which seems to be either the date of receipt or translation) exist in that same file as well as in J IV 2/2J/3164 (Büro Ulbricht) and in the "Kalbslederband," my pp. 54–62.

125. Author's interview with Wolf, 6 June 1996. One is reminded of the question, "Wer regiert in Berlin?" ("Who is in charge in Berlin?").

126. "Vermerk über ein Gespräch mit dem Leiter der 3. Europäischen Abteilung des sowjetischen Außenministeriums, Genossen Falin, am 27.10.1970," in J IV 2/202/82 (Büro Ulbricht), SAPMO.

127. A later document refers to the "mit Genossen Falin selbst abgestimmten mündlichen Mitteilung an Brandt vom 29.10.1970" ("oral message for Brandt, agreed to with Comrade Falin himself on 29 October 1970"). See "Vermerk über die Konsultation des Ministers für Auswärtige Angelegenheiten der DDR, Genossen Otto Winzer, mit dem Minister für Auswärtige Angelegenheiten der UdSSR, Genossen A. Gromyko, am 11.1.1971 in Moskau," p. 14, in J IV 2/202/136 (Büro Ulbricht), SAPMO.

128. "Vermerk über ein Gespräch mit dem Leiter der 3. Europäischen Abteilung des sowjetischen Außenministeriums, Genossen Falin, am 27.10.1970," Anlage, p. 1.

129. Ibid., p. 2.

130. Wolf, Spionagechef, 259.

131. The text of the message as delivered differs hardly at all from the draft message as delivered by Falin. The only difference of significance is that the message delivered to Brandt contained the statement that all agreements should be "auf Grund der allgemeinen völkerrechtlichen Normen" ("on the basis of the general legal norms"), as opposed to Falin's draft, which mentioned only "allgemeinen Normen" ("general norms"). The quotation in text is from Falin's draft; a copy of the message as delivered to Brandt is in DC-20, Ministerrat, I/4 (Präsidium des Ministerrates) PM 02-137/V.1/70 Prot. 04.11.70, BA-V.

132. "Am 29.10.1970 fand in der Zeit von 11.45-12.05 Uhr ein Gespräch zwischen Bundeskanzler Willy Brandt und dem persönlichen Beauftragten des Vorsitzendes des

Ministerrates der DDR, Genosse Prof. Dr. Herbert Bertsch, stellv. Leiter des Presseamtes beim Vorsitzenden des Ministerrates der DDR, im Bundeskanzleramt statt," in J IV 2/2J/3183 (IntVer), SAPMO. This document was published as Document No. 5 in Heinrich Potthoff, *Bonn und Ost-Berlin 1969–1982* (Bonn: Dietz, 1997).

133. Ibid., pp. 2–3.

134. Ibid., p. 3.

135. Ibid., pp. 1–2. For Western views of the Bertsch visit, see Ulrich Sahm, *"Diplomaten taugen nichts": Aus dem Leben eines Staatsdieners* (Düsseldorf: Droste, 1994), 279; and Zündorf, *Die Ostverträge*, 181.

136. Note from Bahr to Kissinger, 3 Nov. 1970, in 439, EBD, FES. Original reads: "Der Schritt der DDR [not specified but seems to mean reopening of talks] ist von den Sowjets veranlaßt worden."

137. See the correspondence in J IV 2/2J/3206 (IntVer), SAPMO.

138. "Brief des Genossen Walter Ulbricht an den Generalsekretär des ZK der KdSU, Genossen L. I. Breshnew," approved by Politbüro im Umlauf 13.11.1970, in J IV 2/2A/1.478 (Politbüro), SAPMO, in response to Л. Брежнев В. Ульбрихту, 16 Oct. 1970.

139. Wolf, *Spionagechef*, 247.

Chapter Four

1. Biographical details on Michael Kohl come from his Kaderakte (Party file): IV 2/11/v5370 (Abt. Kaderfragen), SAPMO. Kohl was born on 28 Sept. 1929 and died on 4 July 1981. For personal recollections of Kohl, see Karl Seidel, "Erste Schritte auf dem Weg zu normalen Beziehungen zwischen der DDR und der BRD. Persönliche Erinnerungen an die deutsch-deutschen Verhandlungen Anfang der siebziger Jahre," in *Deutschlandpolitiker der DDR erinnern sich*, edited by Detlef Nakath (Berlin: Fides, 1995).

2. Kohl reportedly wrote his doctoral thesis on the position of China in the international system, with reference to the problem of Taiwan. In his thesis, he defended a "one state" view, in which Taiwan was part of China. However, as head of the GDR delegation, he had to defend not only the notion of two states but later two nations. Author's interview with Görner, 7 June 1996.

3. Since documentary sources convey specific details more readily than an overall sense of atmosphere, interviews with those who participated in the talks on both sides help to supplement documents by reconstructing a sense of personalities and attitudes. The following delegation members were interviewed for this study: from the West German delegation, Egon Bahr, Hans-Otto Bräutigam, Antonius Eitel, Günter Gaus, and Ulrich Sahm; from the East German delegation, Gunter Görner and Karl Seidel. Kurt Nier declined a request to be interviewed.

4. No interview with Michael Kohl was possible because he died in 1981 at the age of fifty-one.

5. Egon Bahr, *Zu meiner Zeit* (Munich: Karl Blessing, 1996), 373.

6. Author's interview with Bahr, 21 May 1996.

7. Ibid.

8. M. E. Sarotte, "Spying Not Only on Strangers: Documenting Stasi Involvement in Cold War German-German Negotiations," *Intelligence and National Security* 11 (Oct. 1996): 765–79.

9. Helmut Müller-Enbergs, ed., *Inoffizielle Mitarbeiter des Ministeriums für Staatssicherheit: Richtlinien und Durchführungsbestimmungen*, Vol. 3 of *Wissenschaftliche Reihe*

des Bundesbeauftragten für die Unterlagen des Staatssicherheitsdienstes der ehemaligen Deutschen Demokratischen Republik, edited by Abteilung Bildung und Forschung (Berlin: Links Verlag, 1996), 7. This volume is a good basic source for information about IMs.

10. For further information about IM classification, see ibid., chap. 3. For information on the Stasi in general, see the various works reviewed in M. E. Sarotte, "Under Cover of Boredom: Review Article of Recent Publications on the East German Ministry for State Security, or Stasi," *Intelligence and National Security* 12 (Oct. 1997): 196–210.

11. Author's interview with Wolf, 6 June 1996.

12. Ibid. Wolf added that, in cases where someone who had been an IM earlier on reached a position of prominence, they would then cease work as an IM. However, out of force of habit, sometimes their old IM code name would still be used in paperwork. Wolf seemed to be suggesting that Kohl had been "Koran" in the past and that the name simply continued to be used on paperwork, but he did not say so outright. Another lawyer in the GDR delegation, the legal expert Günter Görner, seconded Wolf's comments in an interview in 1996. Görner said that Kohl not only had a "relationship of trust" with the MfS but also that it was in fact necessary that he have such a relationship. Had he not, explained Görner, he would not have lasted long as the delegation leader of the GDR. Author's interview with Görner, 7 June 1996.

13. Indeed, in a 1992 interview Wolf claimed he would go so far as to say "that the *détente* between East and West Germany was only possible because of the role of the security services," noting, "Without us to confirm the genuineness of the other side's intentions, the negotiations would never have got off the ground." Quoted in Anne McElvoy, *The Saddled Cow: East Germany's Life and Legacy* (London: Faber and Faber, 1992), 110. Hans-Hermann Hertle, *Chronik des Mauerfalls: Die dramatischen Ereignisse um den 9. November 1989* (Berlin: Links, 1996) points out that, in questions of emigration and travel, the Innenministerium of the GDR essentially functioned "als nachgeordnete Behörde des MfS" ("as a subsidiary of the Stasi") (50).

14. For information on secret dealings to secure exit visas for would-be émigrés, see the history written by a West German participant in the dealings, Ludwig A. Rehlinger, *Freikauf: Die Geschäfte der DDR mit politisch Verfolgten 1963–1989* (Frankfurt: Ullstein, 1991). For information about the East German side, see Craig R. Whitney, *Spy Trader: Germany's Devil's Advocate and the Darkest Secrets of the Cold War* (New York: Random House, 1993). Deals to "purchase" exit visas for GDR citizens also fell partly in the competency of the notorious GDR money launderer Alexander Schalck-Golodkowski; see Wolfgang Seiffert and Norbert Treutwein, *Die Schalck-Papiere: DDR-Mafia zwischen Ost und West* (Munich: Quick Verlag, 1991), 154; and Peter-Ferdinand Koch, *Das Schalck-Imperium lebt: Deutschland wird gekauft* (München: Piper, 1992), 112.

15. For basic information on Markus Wolf's "HVA," or Hauptverwaltung Aufklärung, as well as on the MfS in general, see David Childs and Richard Popplewell, *The Stasi: The East German Intelligence and Security Service* (London: Macmillan, 1996); Karl Wilhelm Fricke, *MfS intern: Macht, Strukturen, Auflösung der DDR-Staatssicherheit Analyse und Dokumentation* (Cologne: Wissenschaft und Politik, 1991); Hubertus Knabe, *Die "West-Arbeit" des MfS und ihre Wirkungen: Bericht des BStU an die Enquete-Kommission des Deutschen Bundestages "Überwindung der Folgen der SED-Diktatur im Prozeß der deutschen Einheit* (Berlin: BStU, 1998); and Peter Siebenmorgen, *"Staatssicherheit der DDR: Der Westen im Fadenkreuz der Stasi* (Bonn: Bovier, 1993). Also useful is Deutscher Bundestag, ed., *Das Ministerium für Staatssicherheit—Seilschaften, Altkader, Regierungs- und Vereinigungskriminalität,* Vol. 8 of *Materialien der Enquete-Kommission 'Aufarbeitung von Geschichte und Folgen der SED-Diktatur in Deutschland* (Baden-Baden/Frankfurt a.M.: Nomos Verlag/Suhrkamp Verlag, 1995).

16. Author's interview with Seidel, 25 March 1996.

17. See Sarotte, "Spying Not Only on Strangers," 769–70. On HMs, see Jens Gieseke, *Die hauptamtlichen Mitarbeiter des Ministeriums für Staatssicherheit*, unnumbered volume in *MfS Handbuch: Anatomie der Staatssicherheit, Geschichte Struktur Methode* (Berlin: BStU, Aug. 1995).

18. Author's interview with Görner, 7 June 1996. What is not yet clear is whether or not there were any MfS operatives in the West German delegation (or indeed operatives for the West German secret service, BND, on either side). Stasi archivists have concluded that there is no information on Egon Bahr, Antonius Eitel, Günter Gaus, or Ulrich Sahm. For Hans-Otto Bräutigam, there are documents that show that he was the subject of eavesdropping in the 1980s. See M. E. Sarotte, "Nicht nur Fremde ausspioniert: MfS-Dokumente zu den deutsch-deutschen Verhandlungen Anfang der siebziger Jahre," *Deutschland Archiv* 3 (May/June 1997): 409.

19. Sarotte, "Spying Not Only on Strangers," 770.

20. Notes dated 30 Aug. 1971, "Vergleich zwischen dem offiziellen und inoffiziellen Material der Unterredung Kohl-Bahr vom 26.8.71," pp. 38–39, in SdM 233, ZA, BStU.

21. Author's interview with Seidel, 25 March 1996.

22. Christopher Andrew and Oleg Gordievsky, *KGB: The Inside Story of Its Foreign Operations from Lenin to Gorbachev* (New York: HarperCollins, 1990), 37.

23. Hans Modrow, who headed the SED briefly during the revolutionary period in 1989–90 and was often touted as the GDR's Gorbachev, recollected in 1994 that Honecker and Mielke used to meet weekly. According to Modrow, "Außenpolitik" (foreign policy) was one of their usual topics of conversation. Hans Modrow, ed., *Das Große Haus: Insider berichten aus dem ZK der SED* (Berlin: Edition Ost, 1994), 55–56.

24. In an interview in 1992 with French author Maurice Najman, Markus Wolf addressed the topic of Stasi influence on the formation of Ostpolitik in the following way: "Il serait absurde de nier que les informations et les analyses que nous produisions (sur l'importance de l'Ostpolitik de Brandt . . .) aient influencé la politique de la diréction du SED. D'ailleurs, c'était là leur fonction" (in essence, it would be silly to deny that the analyses produced by his office affected policymaking). However, the advice of the MfS was not always followed; in Wolf's words, "Ce pouvoir politique du HvA n'était qu'indirect et ne pouvait s'exercer que sur la direction du Parti . . . via Mielke." Wolf did admit, "Il y avait aussi un autre canal: mes connexions avec les services secrets soviétiques. J'ai utilisé au maximum ce chemin." He concluded, however, that "le HvA ne pouvait pas jouer de rôle politique indépendant." Najman, *L'oeil de Berlin: Entretiens de Maurice Najman avec le patron des services secrets est-allemands* (Paris: Editions Balland, 1992), 208. For further discussion on the question of the subordinate relationship of the MfS to the SED, see Siegfried Suckut and Walter Süß, eds., *Staatspartei und Staatssicherheit: Zum Verhältnis von SED und MfS* (Berlin: Links Verlag, 1997), Vol. 8 of *Wissenschaftliche Reihe des Bundesbeauftragten für die Unterlagen des Staatssicherheitsdienstes der ehemaligen Deutschen Demokratischen Republik*, edited by Abteilung Bildung und Forschung; see in particular Siegfried Suckut, "Generalkontrollbeauftragter der SED oder gewöhnliches Staatsorgan? Probleme der Funktionsbestimmung des MfS in den sechziger Jahren," 151–67.

25. It is difficult to produce a "full list" of either delegation, since both delegations picked up new members and shed old ones in the course of the talks. What follows is an alphabetical list of the most significant members of each delegation over the course of the talks from 1970 to 1973 and their positions at the time. The mainstays of the GDR delegation, all using the title "Comrade," were Hans Bernhardt, the deputy leader of the Abt. BRD of the East German Foreign Ministry (MfAA); Alwin Brandt, identified in the

negotiating rounds only as a passport and visa expert but in fact an HM from the MfS, as discussed above; Gerhard Breitbarth, Kohl's personal aide; Heinz Gerber, identified in the negotiations only as a traffic expert but also working as an IM for the MfS; Gunter Görner, from the Abt. Rechts- und Vertragswesen of the MfAA; Helmut Nacke, identified only as a customs expert but working as an HM for the MfS; Kurt Nier, head of the Abt. Nordeuropa of the MfAA; and Karl Seidel, head of the Abt. BRD of the MfAA. On the West German side were Hans-Otto Bräutigam, from the Auswärtiges Amt; Antonius Eitel, Bahr's personal aide; Ulrich Sahm, representing the federal chancellery; and Jürgen Weichert, representing the Ministerium für inner-deutsche Beziehungen.

26. Author's interview with Bräutigam, 7 Mar. 1996.

27. Ibid.; and author's interview with Eitel, 20 Sept. 1996.

28. See his autobiography, Ulrich Sahm, *"Diplomaten taugen nichts": Aus dem Leben eines Staatsdieners* (Düsseldorf: Droste, 1994).

29. Author's interview with Eitel, 20 Sept. 1996.

30. Author's interview with Bräutigam, 7 Mar. 1996; seconded in author's interview with Seidel, 25 Mar. 1996.

31. Author's interview with Seidel, 25 Mar. 1996.

32. Author's interview with Bräutigam, 7 Mar. 1996.

33. "Erwägungen zur Frage eines Meinungsaustausches mit der BRD über die Beziehungen zwischen der DDR und der BRD," 17 Nov. 1970, sent by Otto Winzer to Walter Ulbricht, 18 Nov. 1970, with a cover note stating that it had been written "entsprechend Deinem Auftrag," in J IV 2/202/105 (Büro Ulbricht), SAPMO. This offer also indicated that East Germany was ready from the outset to talk about basic questions, in contrast to the assertion published by Benno Zündorf, alias Antonius Eitel, that the GDR was not interested in speaking generally about normalization in the initial phase of talks. See Benno Zündorf, *Die Ostverträge* (Munich: C. H. Beck, 1979), 183.

34. Author's interview with Görner, 7 June 1996.

35. Hans-Hermann Hertle, "Die Diskussion der ökonomischen Krisen in der Führungsspitze der SED," in *Der Plan als Befehl und Fiktion: Wirtschaftsführung in der DDR*, edited by Theo Pirker, Rainer M. Lepsius, Rainer Weinert, and Hans-Hermann Hertle (Opladen, Ger.: Westdeutscher Verlag, 1995), 311.

36. Author's interview with Görner, 7 June 1996.

37. Ibid.

38. Author's interview with Seidel, 25 Mar. 1996. Seidel recalled that they even proofread Kohl's summaries of his one-on-one talks for the Politburo. On the West German side, however, Hans-Otto Bräutigam recalled that as the Kohl-Bahr conversations got longer, Bahr's summaries of them for the delegation got shorter (from author's interview with Bräutigam and confirmed by Bahr). In response to Bräutigam's remark, Bahr in a 1996 interview defended himself by saying that, since many of the one-on-one conversations he had with Kohl repeated early ones and made no progress, he saw no need to go beyond abbreviated reports, such as, "On the topic of the nation, nothing new."

39. Author's interview with Seidel, 25 Mar. 1996.

40. A nearly complete set of stenographic protocols and Kohl's summaries of "private" conversations with Bahr exist in the collection called Abt. Internationale Verbindungen (IntVer) at SAPMO. Since real authority rested with the Politburo and, above that, with Moscow, this Abteilung does not seem to have had an influence on the conduct of the talks. Rather, it seems merely to be home to its files. The collection is, however, not complete and needs to be supplemented with files from BA-V (the old Potsdam collection) and BStU. The file for the first meeting is "Stenografische Niederschrift des

Meinungsaustausches zwischen Genossen Dr. Kohl und Egon Bahr im Hause des Minis-terrates der DDR" (hereafter SN Kohl-Bahr), in J IV 2/201/1165 (IntVer), SAPMO.

41. The squabbling was over whether or not the day's meeting had come about as a result of the Bertsch delegation's (i.e., Falin's) message of 29 October or because of earlier efforts by the FRG.

42. SN Kohl-Bahr, 27 Nov. 1970, 4.

43. Ibid., 5.

44. Ibid., 22.

45. Ibid., 43. Similar remarks may be found in the West German match to this docu-ment, the "Protokoll des ersten Gesprächs StS Bahr-StS Dr. Kohl, Ost-Berlin, Haus des Ministerrats, 27. November 1970, 10.00-13.00 Uhr," 30 Nov. 1970, p. 6, in 375A, EBD, FES.

46. SN Kohl-Bahr, 27 Nov. 1970, 10.

47. Ibid., 21.

48. Ibid., 23. Similar remarks are in the West German counterpart to this document: "Protokoll des ersten Gesprächs StS Bahr-StS Dr. Kohl," 8.

49. SN Kohl-Bahr, 27 Nov. 1970, 61.

50. Ibid., 57–58.

51. East German written summaries of these one-on-one conversations were pro-duced afterwards. It seems that these reports were often written by Kohl, even though he is referred to in the third person; interviews with Seidel and Görner have confirmed this. (The Stasi archive includes summaries based on bugging, but these usually are identified as such.)

52. "Niederschrift aus dem Gedächtnis über interne Gespräche mit Bahr am 27.11.1970," (hereafter NG Kohl), J IV 2/201/1165 (IntVer), SAPMO. This file actually contains two such summaries; the other is "Erster Bericht (Gedächtnisniederschrift) über das Gespräch zwischen Staatssekretär Dr. Kohl und Staatssekretär Bahr am 27. November 1970 im Hause des Ministerrates." It is not clear who wrote this second summary.

53. See also Bahr, *Zu meiner Zeit*, 357.

54. NG Kohl, 27 Nov. 1970, 3–5. For a rather poignant summary of the trip from East Berlin to Bonn, see Seidel, "Erste Schritte."

55. NG Kohl, 27 Nov. 1970, 2.

56. "Vermerk, Bonn, den 27. November 1970," 2, in 375A, EBD, FES. Bahr noted, "Eine beträchtliche Unsicherheit ist sowohl bei dem Gesprächspartner wie bei der Position der DDR zu spüren. Sie wird besonders deutlich, wenn einer klaren positiven Stellungnahme zu den Moskauer Intentionen ausgewichen wird" (in essence, Bahr noted uncertainty on the part of the opposite side, especially when discussing Moscow's intentions).

57. "StS Bahr, Betrifft: Erster Meinungsaustausch BRD-DDR (Kurze Zusammen-fasung)," 27 Nov. 1970, p. 2, in 375A, EBD, FES.

58. "Langer Atem," *Der Spiegel*, 30 Nov. 1970, 34.

59. SN Kohl-Bahr, 27 Nov. 1970, 3.

60. See Bahr's discussion of his ongoing battle for better press coverage in Bahr, *Zu meiner Zeit*.

61. See the "Stenografische Niederschrift des Politischen Beratenden Ausschusses der Staaten des Warschauer Vertrages in Berlin, dem 2. Dezember 1970," in J IV 2/2A/1.484 (Politbüro), SAPMO.

62. "Überarbeitete Rede des Genossen Breshnew auf der Beratung des Politischen Beratenden Ausschusses der WVS am 2.12.1970 in Berlin," p. 4, in J IV 2/2A/1.484 (Politbüro), SAPMO. What exactly "überarbeitet" (literally, "worked-over") means in

this context is not apparent. This word was often used to imply a translation that had been proofread and streamlined, but it is not clear if that is the case here. On this linkage, see also Karl-Heinz Schmidt, *Dialog über Deutschland: Studien zur Deutschlandpolitik von KPdSU und SED (1960–1979)* (Baden-Baden: Nomos, 1998), 275.

63. "Überarbeitete Rede des Genossen Breshnew auf der Beratung des Politischen Beratenden Ausschusses der WVS am 2.12.1970 in Berlin," 4. In an interview in 1996, Valentin Falin recollected that this was a key development in Soviet dealings with West Germany. Author's interview with Falin, 17 May 1996.

64. A large file on establishing this linkage survives in Bahr's papers in 146A Mappe 2, EBD, FES. See also Honoré M. Catudal, *The Diplomacy of the Quadripartite Agreement on Berlin: A New Era in East-West Politics* (Berlin: Berlin Verlag, 1978), 144.

65. "Überarbeitete Rede des Genossen Breshnew auf der Beratung des Politischen Beratenden Ausschusses der WVS am 2.12.1970 in Berlin," 13.

66. Ibid., n.p.

67. The full text of the German-language version of the treaty may be found in Auswärtiges Amt, ed., *Außenpolitik der Bundesrepublik Deutschland: Dokumente 1949 bis 1994* (Cologne: Verlag Wissenschaft und Politik, 1995), 340–42. For analysis of the treaty, see Bahr, *Zu meiner Zeit*, 338–44; Dennis L. Bark and David R. Gress, *Democracy and Its Discontents 1963–1991*, Vol. 2 of *A History of West Germany*, 2d ed. (Oxford: Blackwell, 1993), 188; Barbara Marshall, *Willy Brandt: A Political Biography* (Oxford: Macmillan, 1997), 71–72; and Zündorf, *Die Ostverträge*, 62–91.

68. Robert Bideleux and Ian Jeffries, *A History of Eastern Europe: Crisis and Change* (London: Routledge, 1998), 563.

69. An English-language version of the treaty may be found in J. A. S. Grenville and Bernard Wasserstein, eds., *The Major International Treaties since 1945: A History and Guide with Texts* (London: Methuen, 1987), 195–96.

70. Marshall, *Willy Brandt*, 72. On the significance of Brandt's gesture, see also Peter Bender, *Die "Neue Ostpolitik" und Ihre Folgen: Vom Mauerbau bis zur Vereinigung*, 2d ed. (Munich: dtv, Feb. 1995), 182.

71. Henry Kissinger, *WHY* (Boston: Little, Brown, 1979), 797. For more information on Poland, see Garton Ash, *In Europe's Name*.

72. The author is grateful to Tim Snyder for pointing this out.

73. Henry Kissinger, *Years of Upheaval* (Boston: Little, Brown, 1982), 57.

74. It is difficult to analyze this controversy because there exist several versions of these remarks in the files. Nearly all versions bear evidence of editing by various persons (including Ulbricht himself). The most useful version is that entitled "stenographic transcript"; see "Stenogramm (redigiert) auf der 14. Tagung 11.12.70," with "von Genossen Walter Ulbricht" added in pen, in IV 2/1/415 (ZK), SAPMO. However, heavy editing in various handwritings covers this so-called "transcript" as well. In an interview in 1996, Hermann Axen claimed that he, along with fellow Politburo member Paul Verner, had been responsible for the task of editing out offensive portions of Ulbricht's closing remarks. Hermann Axen with Harald Neubert, *Ich war ein Diener der Partei* (Berlin: Edition Ost, 1996), 312.

75. "Stenogramm (redigiert) auf der 14. Tagung 11.12.70," 277.

76. Note from Stoph, 17 Dec. 1970, "Ich bin nicht dafür, das Schlußwort zu veröffentlichen, da es nicht in Übereinstimmung mit den Beschlüssen steht," p. 217, in IV 2/1/415 (ZK), SAPMO. On the report of 8 September 1970, see Chapter 4.

77. Verner to Ulbricht, Hausmitteilung, 17 Dec. 1970, in IV 2/1/415 (ZK), SAPMO; the notes from Axen, Hager and Halbritter, Lamberz, Sindermann and Norden are in the same file. Norden seems to have gotten the date wrong by one day.

78. Axen to Ulbricht, Hausmitteilung, 17 Dec. 1970, in IV 2/1/415 (ZK), SAPMO.

79. Axen repeated this complaint in his memoirs: Axen with Neubert, *Diener der Partei*, 310.

80. Monika Kaiser, *Machtwechsel von Ulbricht zu Honecker: Funktionsmechanismen der SED-Diktatur in Konfliktsituationen 1962 bis 1972* (Berlin: Akademie, 1997), 285, 371.

81. Axen with Neubert, *Diener der Partei*, 308.

82. Ulbricht to the Politburo, 17 Dec. 1970, p. 244, in IV 2/1/415 (ZK), SAPMO. On this letter, see also Jochen Stelkens, "Machtwechsel in Ost-Berlin: Der Sturz Walter Ulbrichts 1971," *Vierteljahrshefte für Zeitgeschichte* 4 (Oct. 1997): 507; and Peter Przybylski, *Die Akte Honecker*, Vol. 1 of *Tatort Politbüro* (Berlin: Rowohlt, 1991), 105.

83. "Zur Korrektur der Wirtschaftspolitik Walter Ulbrichts auf der 14. Tagung des ZK der SED 1970," in "Kalbslederband," my pp. 97–122.

84. Ibid., my p. 97.

85. Bahr reminded Kohl that, in a "gentleman agreement [sic]," the GDR had in early 1970 agreed to install a certain number of telephone lines between the two halves of Berlin but had failed to do so. The GDR was supposed to receive in return DM 30 million in the form of a transfer payment to the East German postal authority. See Bahr, "Vermerk," 30 Dec. 1970, in 375A, EBD, FES. According to Catudal, the GDR had specifically agreed to install 150 telephone lines in exchange for DM 30 million but had not done so. Catudal, *Diplomacy*, 144–46.

86. Bundesministerium für innerdeutsche Beziehungen, ed., *Zehn Jahre Deutschlandpolitik: Die Entwicklung der Beziehungen zwischen der Bundesrepublik Deutschland und der Deutschen Demokratischen Republik 1969–1979* (Bonn: Bundesministerium, Feb. 1980), 87.

87. Quoted in the East German "NG über interne Gespräche mit Bahr am 23. Dezember 1970," p. 2, in J IV 2/201/1166 (IntVer), SAPMO; mentioned in the West German summary, "Vermerk," 30 Dec. 1970, 2.

88. In both the West German "Zusammenfassender Bericht," 23 Dec. 1970, in 375A, EBD, FES; and the East German "Stenografische Niederschrift des Meinungsaustausches zwischen Genossen Dr. Kohl und Egon Bahr am 23. Dezember 1970 im Hause des Ministerrates der DDR," (hereafter SN Bahr-Kohl, 23 Dec. 1970) in J IV 2/201/1166 (IntVer), SAPMO. The directive is in Hermann Axen's "Vorlage für das Politbüro des ZK, Betrifft: Zweites Gespräch des Genossen Dr. Kohl mit dem Staatssekretär Bahr," 16 Dec. 1970, in J IV 2/2A/1.489 (Politburo), SAPMO.

89. In both the West German "Zusammenfassender Bericht" 2; and SN Bahr-Kohl, 23 Dec. 1970, 11.

90. SN Bahr-Kohl, 23 Dec. 1970, 29.

91. "Information über die Konsultation des Stellv. des MfAA, Genossen Ewald Moldt, im MfAA der UdSSR am 6. und 7. Januar 1971," in J IV 2/202/187 (Büro Ulbricht), SAPMO.

92. Kissinger's memoirs show that this complaint was justified; indeed, Kissinger remarks that he was pleased by the slow progress. See Kissinger, *WHY*, 532.

93. "Vermerk über die Konsultation des Ministers für Auswärtige Angelegenheiten der DDR, Genossen Otto Winzer, mit dem Minister für Auswärtige Angelegenheiten der UdSSR, Genossen A. Gromyko, am 11.1.1971 in Moskau," p. 3, in J IV 2/202/136 (Büro Ulbricht), SAPMO.

94. Ibid., 8.

95. Ibid., 12.

96. Henry Kissinger, *Diplomacy* (New York: Simon & Schuster, 1994), 736.

97. Information about this offer is contained in a note from two and half years later.

See document without title, dated 18 June 1973, circulated to the Politburo, in J IV 2/202/542 (Allg. Abt.), SAPMO.

98. "Information," 6 Apr. 1971, in J IV 2/202/359 (Büro Ulbricht), SAPMO.

99. Michael Kohl, "Vermerk über ein Gespräch mit Genossen Falin auf dem Weg zum Flugplatz am 12.1.1971," p. 3, in J IV 2/202/135 (Büro Ulbricht), SAPMO. According to Kohl, Falin said, "Genosse Gromyko und er hätten manchmal den Eindruck, daß wir den Begriff der völkerrechtlichen Anerkennung zu eng und vielleicht ein wenig zu formal sehen würden. Genosse Gromyko habe gestern bereits dargelegt, daß im Grunde genommen die in den Moskauer Absichtserklärungen festgelegten Punkte einer völkerrechtlichen Anerkennung der DDR gleichkämen" (in essence, Falin and Gromyko felt that the SED was interpreting the concept of full legal recognition too narrowly). Gromyko repeated these same two points—that the most important task was to get the Moscow and Warsaw Treaties ratified, and that the Moscow Treaty implied recognition of the GDR—in another conversation with Winzer on 10 February 1971. See "Niederschrift über das Gespräch zwischen dem Minister für Auswärtige Angelegenheiten der DDR, Genossen Otto Winzer, und dem Minister für Auswärtige Angelegenheiten der UdSSR, Genossen A. A. Gromyko, am 10.2.1971," in DC20-4400 (Stoph), BA-V.

100. In both the West German "Zusammenfassung," 15 Jan. 1971, p. 2, in 375A, EBD, FES; and the East German "Bericht über das Treffen von Genossen Dr. Kohl mit Staatssekretär Bahr am 15.1.1971 in Bonn," p. 4, in J IV 2/201/1167 (IntVer), SAPMO.

101. "Bericht über das Treffen von Genossen Dr. Kohl mit Staatssekretär Bahr am 15.1.1971 in Bonn," 9.

102. Ibid., 1. However, a follow-up note from Bahr indicates that the GDR installed only some, not all, of the promised lines, and the issue was not entirely resolved; see Bahr's "Vermerk," 27 Jan. 1971, in 375A, EBD, FES.

103. "Bericht über das Treffen von Genossen Dr. Kohl mit Staatssekretär Bahr am 15.1.1971 in Bonn," 9.

104. Bahr, "Nur für den Bundeskanzler," 15 Jan. 1971, p. 2, BD 375A, EBD, FES. As Bahr noted, "Dies ist in Wahrheit die grösste Schwenkung, die DDR in den letzten Monaten vorgenommen hat. Wir sollten darauf eingehen. Falin führt sich gut ein" (in essence, this is a significant opportunity, of which Bonn should take advantage).

105. Kissinger, WHY, 802.

106. As mentioned in Chapter 3.

107. Kissinger, WHY, 802.

108. "Niederschrift des Gespräches des Botschafters der UdSSR in der DDR mit dem Botschafter der USA in der BRD Rush am 18. Januar 1971," p. 137, in DC20-4403 (Stoph), BA-V.

109. Reinhold Andert and Wolfgang Herzberg, ed., Der Sturz: Erich Honecker im Kreuzverhör (Berlin: Aufbau-Verlag, 1990), 271.

110. A copy exists in the calf-leather volume. Indeed, it is remarkable that Honecker would have placed a copy of the letter there, given that it proves he is guilty of what within the party was the serious crime of factionalism. As former SED leader Hans Modrow put it, the party taught that "Einheit und Geschlossenheit" ("unity and closed ranks") were "höchstes Gebot" ("of the utmost importance"), thanks to the "Erfahrungen der verhängisvollen [sic] Wirkung von Fraktionsbildungen in der Tätigkeit der KPD der Weimarer Republik" (in essence, the unhappy past expriences when factions arose). Modrow, Das Große Haus, 68.

111. Axen even stated in his memoirs that Abrasimov in fact initiated the idea of sending a letter. Axen, Diener der Partei, 322. SED files neither prove nor disprove this.

On this letter, see also Przybylski, *Akte Honecker*, 110 (Przybylski reprints the letter on 297–303); and Stelkens, "Machtwechsel," 507–10.

112. Letter to Brezhnev, 21 Jan. 1971, signed by Hermann Axen, Gerhard Grüneberg, Kurt Hager, Erich Honecker, Günter Mittag, Horst Sindermann, Willi Stoph, Paul Verner, Erich Mückenberger, Herbert Warnke, Werner Jarowinsky, Werner Lamberz, and Günter Kleiber, in "Kalbslederband," my p. 141.

113. Ibid., my p. 142. Although Brezhnev did not say so in the letter, this kind of accusation implied that Ulbricht was in the company of pariahs like Trotsky.

114. Ibid., my p. 143.

115. Ibid.

116. Ibid. In the "Kalbslederband," this document is followed by another document which, although it has no title or date, seems to be notes from a conversation with Brezhnev making many of the same points made in the letter. See "Zu einigen Fragen," "Kalbslederband," 147–51.

117. "Stenografische Niederschrift der Unterredung zwischen Genossen Dr. Michael Kohl und Egon Bahr am 26. Januar 1971," p. 6, in J IV 2/201/1168 (IntVer), SAPMO.

118. In both the West German "Protokoll des 4. Gesprächs StS Bahr/StS Dr. Kohl, Ost-Berlin, Haus des Ministerrates, 26 January 1971, 10.00 Uhr bis 12.00 Uhr," p. 11, in BD 375 A; and the East German "Stenografische Niederschrift der Unterredung zwischen Genossen Dr. Michael Kohl und Egon Bahr am 26. Januar 1971," 30.

119. "NG über interne Gespräche mit Bahr am 26. Januar 1971," pp. 7–8, in J IV 2/201/1168 (IntVer), SAPMO.

120. Kissinger, *WHY*, 810.

121. For documentation on the 15. ZK-Tagung (fifteenth plenary session of the SED Central Committee), see IV 2/1/419-22 (ZK), SAPMO.

122. Stelkens, "Machtwechsel," 510. Ulbricht had requested the visit in the USSR himself; see his letter to Brezhnev in J IV 2/202/349 (Büro Ulbricht), SAPMO, arranging his stay in Barwicha from 8 February until 6 March 1971.

123. Kissinger, *WHY*, 825–26.

124. Letter from Ulbricht to Brezhnev, 12 Mar. 1971, p. 85, in NY4182/1206 (Nachlaß Ulbricht), SAPMO.

125. "Встреча товарищей Л.И. Брежнева и В. Ульбрихта," *Pravda*, 15 Mar. 1971, 1.

126. Stelkens also asserts that Ulbricht and Brezhnev spoke while Ulbricht was in the USSR but provides only secondary works as sources. Stelkens, "Machtwechsel," 510.

127. Anatoly Dobrynin, *In Confidence: Moscow's Ambassador to America's Six Cold War Presidents (1962–1986)* (New York: Random House, 1995), 217.

128. Keith L. Nelson, *The Making of Détente: Soviet-American Relations in the Shadow of Vietnam* (Baltimore: John Hopkins University Press, 1995), 101.

129. Kissinger, *WHY*, 707.

130. William Burr, ed., *The Kissinger Transcripts: The Top Secret Talks with Beijing and Moscow* (New York: New Press, 1998), 41.

131. Kissinger, *WHY*, 707.

132. "Information," 6 May 1971, in J IV 2/202/358 (Büro Ulbricht), SAPMO.

133. "Information für die Leiter der Delegationen der Bruderparteien zum XXIV. Parteitag der KPdSU über den Stand der sowjetisch-chinesischen Beziehungen," 8 Apr. 1971, p. 4, in J IV 2/202/358 (Büro Ulbricht), SAPMO. This document also noted, on p. 2, that the Chinese were contesting 4,000 kilometers of the border.

134. See Beschlußprotokoll, J IV 2/2A/1.506 (Politburo), SAPMO. See also Stelkens, "Machtwechsel," 511.

135. "Прибытие зарубежных делегаций," *Pravda*, 30 Mar. 1971, 1.

136. "Выступление товарища Вальтера Ульбрихта," *Pravda*, 1 Apr. 1971, 7.

137. Ulbricht's handwritten notes from XXIV. Parteitag of the KPdSU, p. 161, in NY4182/1206 (Nachlaß Ulbricht), SAPMO.

138. See the materials from the 16. ZK-Tagung (sixteenth plenary session of the SED Central Committee) in IV 2/1/424 (ZK), SAPMO.

139. Letter from the SED Politburo to Brezhnev, 27 Apr. 1971, in "Kalbslederband," my p. 152.

140. See Punkt 2 in the Tagesordnung of 27 Apr. 1971 in J IV 2/2A/1.510 (Politbüro), SAPMO.

141. Stelkens has claimed that on 12 April Brezhnev finally had the fateful talk with Ulbricht that the Honecker faction had requested in January. See Stelkens, "Machtwechsel," 511.

142. "Встреча в ЦК КПСС," *Pravda*, 13 Apr. 1971, 1.

143. Axen with Neubert, *Diener der Partei*, 314.

144. Markus Wolf, *Spionagechef im geheimen Krieg: Erinnerungen* (Munich: List Verlag, 1997), 256–57.

145. Kaiser, *Machtwechsel*, 436–38; see esp. 436 fn. 203. She refers to his "letztendlich freiwilligen Rücktritt" ("by the end voluntary resignation") on 438.

146. See the Note on Sources for a description of Ulbricht's ongoing attempts to make policy.

147. Even Raymond Garthoff, arguably the most thorough scholar of the détente period, has subscribed to this opinion. See Garthoff, *Détente and Confrontation: American-Soviet Relations from Nixon to Reagan*, rev. ed. (Washington D.C.: Brookings Institution, 1994), 138.

148. The view of Ulbricht as anti-Ostpolitik survived the fall of the Wall and the opening of the East German archives; see, for example, W. R. Smyser, *From Yalta to Berlin* (New York: St. Martin's, 1999), 252; and Marshall, *Willy Brandt*, 73. For the opposite view, see Kaiser, *Machtwechsel*; and Stelkens, "Machtwechsel," 503–33.

149. Stelkens concludes that, while there is no evidence that Ulbricht was thinking about a political confederation, there are numerous hints that he was thinking of an economic one. Stelkens, "Machtwechsel," 529.

150. The importance of this characteristic was also noted by Erhart Neubert, who assesses the impact within the GDR on opposition movements of Honecker's rise to power. As Neubert put it, "Honecker brach auch Ulbrichts Experimente ab, partielle Selbständgkeit gegenüber der Sowjetunion zu praktizieren, und band die DDR trotz wirtschaftlicher Schwierigkeiten wieder deutlicher an die UdSSR" (in short, Honecker ended experimentation with partial independence and toed Moscow's line). See Neubert, *Geschichte der Opposition in der DDR 1949–1989* (Bonn: Bundeszentrale für politische Bildung, 1997), 203.

151. Bahr to Kissinger, 5 May 1971, in 439, EBD, FES. Bahr asked Kohl if the talks would proceed as planned despite the change in leadership, and Kohl answered in the affirmative. See Egon Bahr, "Vermerk," 24 May 1971, in 375A, EBD, FES.

Chapter Five

1. "16. Tagung des Zentralkomitees der SED," *Neues Deutschland*, 4 May 1971, 1. On this point, see also Hans-Hermann Hertle, *Der Fall der Mauer: Die unbeabsichtigte Selbstauflösung des SED-Staates* (Opladen, Ger.: Westdeutscher Verlag, 1996), 20.

2. One aspect of Honecker's leadership that resembled that of Ulbricht's was his method of dominating his nominal equals, the Politbüro members. As Markus Wolf remembered in 1991, just after assuming power Honecker employed a more collegial method of leadership, including consultation on important decisions. This method evaporated, however, over the course of his time in power. See Markus Wolf, *Im eigenen Auftrag* (Munich: Schneekluth, 1991), 28.

3. Actual implementation was delayed until September 1972. See M. E. Sarotte, "Vor 25 Jahren: Verhandlungen über den Grundlagenvertrag," *Deutschland Archiv* (Nov./Dec. 1997): 905, fn. 25.

4. Hans-Hermann Hertle, *Chronik des Mauerfalls: Die dramatischen Ereignisse um den 9. November 1989* (Berlin: Links, 1996), 29–32. It was for the installation of these mines that Politburo members were tried in the mid-1990s. See Peter Jochen Winters, "Wie souverän war die DDR?" *Deutschland Archiv* 2 (Mar./April 1996): 170–72.

5. On Nixon's opening to China, see Kissinger's memoirs, along with Anatoly Dobrynin, *In Confidence: Moscow's Ambassador to America's Six Cold War Presidents (1962–1986)* (New York: Random House, 1995); John H. Holdridge, *Crossing the Divide: An Insider's Account of the Normalization of U.S.-China Relations* (Lanham, Md.: Rowman & Littlefield, 1997); and Walter Isaacson, *Kissinger: A Biography* (New York: Simon & Schuster, 1992), to name just a few.

6. Herbert Dittgen, "Die Ära der Ost-West-Verhandlungen und der Wirtschafts- und Währungskrisen (1969–1981)," in Klaus Larres and Torsten Oppelland, eds., *Deutschland und die USA im 20. Jahrhundert: Geschichte der politischen Beziehungen* (Darmstadt, Ger.: Wissenschaftliche Buchgesellschaft, 1997), 189.

7. For a more detailed overview of the quadripartite negotiations than is presented here, see the two-volume work by Honoré Catudal, which is useful but not based on primary sources. See Honoré M. Catudal, *The Diplomacy of the Quadripartite Agreement on Berlin: A New Era in East-West Politics* (Berlin: Verlag, 1978); and Catudal, *A Balance Sheet of the Quadripartite Agreement on Berlin: Evaluation and Documentation* (Berlin: Verlag, 1978).

8. Henry Kissinger, *WHY* (Boston: Little, Brown, 1979), 801–5.

9. "Material von Genossen Honecker, 9.2.71, Original Englisch-Text und Original Übersetzung," pp. 175–193, quote on 189, in SdM 1835, ZA, BStU.

10. Ibid., 190.

11. "Information über das Treffen der Botschafter der vier Mächte zum Meinungsaustausch über Westberlin am 8.2.1971," p. 169, in SdM 1835, ZA, BStU.

12. "Information über das Treffen der Botschafter der vier Mächte über Westberlin am 18. Februar 1971," p. 184, in DC20-4403 (Stoph), BA-V.

13. Ibid., 181.

14. In both the West German "Zusammenfassung," 17 Feb. 1971, p. 2, in 375A, EBD, FES; and the East German "NG über interne Gespräche mit Bahr am 17. Februar 1971," pp. 5–9, in J IV 2/201/1170 (IntVer) SAPMO.

15. "Anlage Nr. 5," p. 70, in J IV 2/2/1325 (Politbüro), SAPMO.

16. In both the West German "Zusammenfassung," 17 Feb. 1971, p. 3, in 375A, EBD, FES; and the East German "Stenografische Niederschrift der Unterredung zwischen Genossen Dr. Michael Kohl und Bahr am 17. Februar 1971 im Hause des Ministerrates in Berlin," pp. 20–21, in J IV 2/201/1170 (IntVer), SAPMO.

17. The transcript of this conversation in the Stasi archive comes from "Department 26," which was the Stasi department responsible for acoustical surveillance—i.e., bugging. See Abt. 26, "Am 8. März 1971 fand eine Unterredung zwischen Herrn Kohl (K) und Herrn Bahr (B) statt," p. 259, in SdM 1837, ZA, BStU. On this incident, see also

M. E. Sarotte, "Spying Not Only on Strangers: Documenting Stasi Involvement in Cold War German-German Negotiations," *Intelligence and National Security* 11 (Oct. 1996): 768. The accuracy of the document is confirmed by Bahr's papers; the details provided by the Stasi transcript are in agreement with a shorter summary of the same conversation in Bahr's own papers. See Egon Bahr, "Zusammenfassung betr. Gespräch Bahr/Kohl am 8. März 1971 in Ostberlin im Hause des Ministerrats," 8 Mar. 1971, in 375A, EBD, FES.

18. Abt. 26, "Am 8. März 1971 fand eine Unterredung . . . ," 260.

19. Ibid., 259.

20. Ibid., 261. On the topic of Bahr and Kohl's awareness of surveillance, see the Note on Sources.

21. Author's interview with Bahr, 21 May 1996.

22. Ibid.

23. Kissinger, *WHY*, 832–33.

24. Michael Kohl, "Vermerk über ein Gespräch mit den Genossen Kwizinski und Hotulew," 28 May 1971, p. 297, in SdM 1837, ZA, BStU. When asked in 1996 about the attitude of the three Western powers to the German-German talks, Bahr's former aide Antonius Eitel replied, "Besorgt bis sehr vorsichtig, oder vorsichtig bis besorgt. . . . Mit der Brandt'schen Ostpolitik waren die nicht so ganz glücklich. Kissinger macht daraus kein Hehl" (in short, they were concerned and not very happy about it). Author's interview with Eitel, 20 Sept. 1996.

25. "Information über die Sitzung der Botschafter der Viermächte im Rahmen der Westberlin-Verhandlungen vom 9.3.1971," p. 199, in DC20-4403 (Stoph), BA-V.

26. Ibid., 199.

27. Kissinger, *WHY*, 826–27.

28. "Vorlage für das Politbüro des ZK der SED," 15 Mar. 1971, pp. 245–49, in SdM 1837, ZA, BStU. Also, it seems that the Soviets often provided written comments on the directive that the Politburo planned to give to Kohl. Although no complete record of these commentaries exist, they appear often enough to suggest that they were a regular feature of SED-CPSU correspondence. See, for example, "Bemerkung der Freunde" ("Freunde" being a euphemism for Soviets), no date, pp. 320–22, also in SdM 1837.

29. "Entwurf der Vereinbarung," 24 Mar. 1971, Anlage 2, pp. 215–16, in DC20-4403 (Stoph), BA-V.

30. Ibid., 210.

31. "Информация о встрече послов четырех держав в рамках переговоров по западному Берлину 26 марта 1971 г.," p. 96, in SdM 1835, ZA, BStU.

32. In both the East German "Stenografische Niederschrift der Unterredung zwischen Genossen Dr. Michael Kohl und Egon Bahr am 31. März 1971 im Hause des Minister-rates in Berlin," in J IV 2/201/1173 (IntVer), SAPMO; and the West German version, "Protokoll des 10. Gespräches StS Bahr/StS Dr. Kohl, Berlin, Haus des Ministerrates der DDR, 31. März 1971 19.50 bis 13.15 Uhr," p. 29, in 375A, EBD, FES. The West German version names the study written by the young Kohl as follows: "Michael Kohl, *Mehr-staatlichkeit Deutschlands und Wiedervereinigung*, Staat und Recht 1957" and cites pp. 843 and 846 from it.

33. Hertle, *Chronik*, 29.

34. Egon Bahr, "Zusammenfassung betr. Gespräch Bahr/Kohl am 30 April 1971 im Bundeskanzleramt in Bonn," 30 Apr. 1971, p. 1; and Bahr, "Vermerk," 30 Apr. 1971, p. 1, both in 375A, EBD, FES. Original quotation from the latter: "Ich habe mit dem Hinweis auf die mehrfachen Brände geantwortet, die durch Raketen der DDR auf dem Gebiet der BRD verursacht worden sind. Im übrigen sei es schwer zu verstehen, warum nicht einmal ein Wort des Bedauerns zu hören sei, wenn—unabhängig davon, warum und wie

die Lage an unserer Grenze sei—ein Mensch zu dauerndem Schaden käme oder ver-
blute." ("I replied by mentioning the many small fires on FRG soil that are caused by
GDR projectiles. On top of this, it is difficult to understand why one hears not a single
word of regret when—regardless of how and why a situation on the border arises—a
human being sustains severe injuries or bleeds to death.")

35. In both the East German "NG über interne Gespräche mit Staatssekretär Bahr am
30. April 1971 in Bonn," p. 6, in J IV 2/201/1174 (IntVer), SAPMO; and the West
German: Bahr, "Vermerk," 30 Apr. 1971, 1–2.

36. Quotation comes from the East German "NG über ein persönliches Gespräch mit
Staatssekretär Bahr am 21.05.71," p. 8, in J IV 2/201/1175 (IntVer), SAPMO. A similar
sentiment is expressed in the West German summary of the same conversation: Bahr,
"Vermerk," 27 May 1971, p. 4, in 375, EBD, FES.

37. Kissinger, WHY, 714–16, 817.

38. Brezhnev's announcement came as the Mansfield Amendment, which sought to
limit funding for the U.S. military presence in Europe, was being debated. The Soviet
announcement caused the defeat of the amendment, because it seemed inappropriate to
make one-sided reductions if the Soviets were willing to negotiate bilateral ones. Exactly
why Brezhnev made such an announcement on 14 May has been a puzzle ever since.
Kissinger saw in it a sign of the rigidity of Soviet foreign policy-making; he argued that
the speech had probably been prepared in advance, to help move the Berlin talks along.
William Bundy challenged this notion and suggests that the Soviets in some way saw the
U.S. presence in Europe as a necessary evil, preferable to German leadership, and in fact
were against the Mansfield Amendment because it would have reduced the U.S. role in
NATO. As Bundy put it, "The Soviet Union was only moderately concerned by the
existence of a new German Army *within NATO and under U.S. leadership*, but if the U.S.
presence was lessened, it feared a resurgent German nationalism." See William Bundy, *A
Tangled Web: The Making of Foreign Policy in the Nixon Presidency* (New York: Hill and
Wang, 1998), 258.

39. Kissinger says the three started meeting on 10 May 1971 (Kissinger, WHY, 828).
Similarly, Bahr referred to the first meeting in a secret note to Kissinger on 11 May 1971,
439, EBD, FES. The group's work was expedited by Falin's ability to bypass Gromyko and
deal directly with the top Soviet leadership in Moscow. However, Bahr felt that the
Gromyko-Falin rivalry did sometimes cause delays; see Bahr's note to Kissinger on
30 June 1971, in 439, EBD, FES. According to Keworkow, Falin had been sent into a kind
of honorable exile in Bonn because he and Gromyko had so much difficulty working
together at the Foreign Ministry in Moscow. Wjatscheslaw Keworkow, *Der geheime
Kanal* (Berlin: Rowohlt, Mar. 1995), 92. Hence, Gromyko must have been especially
nonplussed when Falin's role in Bonn became increasingly important.

40. Author's interview with Bahr, 21 May 1996. Bahr's papers contain some telegrams
to Kissinger concerning the work of this group; see 439, EBD, FES. Even the official State
Department historian charged with writing an account of the four-power negotiations—
who did so, producing a study of over 800 pages—did not know about the secret negotiating levels. He found out about them only after completing his survey, thus undercutting
its value significantly. See Arthur G. Kogan, "The Quadripartite Berlin Negotiations,"
Research Project No. 1035, (Secret; declassified 4 Apr. 1994 via FOIA Request No.
9305297), Office of the Historian, Bureau of Public Affairs, Department of State, Sept.
1977, p. ii, in Box 26, Nuclear History/Berlin Crisis, National Security Archive, Washington, D.C. Indeed, Kissinger's determination to bypass the State Department had an unintended consequence: he used naval channels to communicate, and careful monitoring of
these channels (in what was essentially domestic espionage) meant that the U.S. Joint

Chiefs of Staff could inform themselves about the dealings being conducted in this way. See Isaacson, *Kissinger*, 324. Some relevant documents may be viewed on the Internet: The Richard Nixon Library and Birthplace Foundation, Transcripts of Newly Released White House Tapes, release date 25 Feb. 1999, pp. 27–31, at www.nixonfoundation.org.

41. See for example, the secret note from Kissinger to Bahr, 24 May 1971, in 439, EBD, FES.

42. Author's interview with Bahr, 21 May 1996.

43. "Vermerk über ein Gespräch des Genossen Dr. Kohl mit dem Botschaftsrat der sowjetischen Botschaft, Genossen Hotulew, am 1. Juni 1971," 1 June 1971, p. 286, in SdM 1837, ZA, BStU.

44. As a result of the lack of documentation, it is difficult to follow the chain of decision-making in the quadripartite talks from this point on, since the paperwork from the official level became insignificant, and the secret channel produced almost none.

45. Author's interview with Falin, 17 May 1996.

46. Brandt had had Bahr tell Kissinger along the secret channel that he hoped for "zügige Verhandlungen" ("speedy negotiations") with any pause over the summer but he was to be disappointed. Top Secret note from Bahr to Kissinger, 24 May 1971, in 439, EBD, FES.

47. Kissinger, *WHY*, 829.

48. Ibid.

49. Ibid., 816–17.

50. Document without title, dated 10 May 1971, initialed by Erich Honecker and passed on to Willi Stoph, in DC20-4400 (Stoph), SAPMO.

51. For an erudite discussion of the role that nuclear weapons played in Soviet foreign policymaking, see Jonathan Haslam, *The Soviet Union and the Politics of Nuclear Weapons in Europe 1969–1987: The Problem of the SS-20* (London: Macmillan, 1989).

52. Kissinger, *WHY*, 817. Raymond Garthoff, *Détente and Confrontation: American-Soviet Relations from Nixon to Reagan*, rev. ed. (Washington D.C.: Brookings Institution, 1994), 166–67, points out that the flap over the 20 May announcement was highly informative for the Soviets and that they in fact were very forthcoming on some minor related matters at the time. As Garthoff surmised, the Soviets gained valuable insight from the spat between Kissinger and Smith; as he put it, "What the Soviet leadership had learned about Nixon, Kissinger, and the American administration was worth far more than quibbling over any details." Garthoff is seconded by William Bundy, who has argued that deception was a dominant characteristic of Nixon and Kissinger's foreign policy-making. See Bundy, *Tangled Web*, xiii.

53. Kissinger, *WHY*, 820.

54. Ibid., 822.

55. Ibid., 821. On this point, see also Isaacson, *Kissinger*, 323.

56. Kissinger, *WHY*, 830.

57. "Information über das Gespräch P. A. Abrassimows mit dem französischen Botschafter in der BRD J. Sauvagnargues," no date but based on context, the meeting took place in late May or early June 1971, p. 221, in DC20-4400 (Stoph). The French ambassador's complaint—mentioned to Abrasimov in "Information über das Treffen des Botschafters der UdSSR in der DDR P. A. Abrassimow mit dem Botschafter der USA in der BRD K. Rush am 31. Mai d.J.," pp. 277–78, DC20-4403 (Stoph), BA-V—was most likely about Rush's intention to return to the United States to speak with Nixon in June. However, it seems that the Soviets knew not to place too much emphasis on French expressions of discontent with their allies. As Yuli Kvizinski, Abrasimov's aide in the four-power talks, explained to Michael Kohl during one of what were presumably several

Soviet consultations on the progress of the Four Power talks, "Die französische Seite tritt zwar . . . in Worten außerordentlich liebenswürdig und verständigungsbereit auf, verfolgt aber im Grunde genommen ganz hart das Ziel, ihre Position als Besatzungsmacht in Westberlin abzusichern." ("The French side gives the appearance of being extremely affectionate and accommodating, but in reality the French are pushing hard for their goal of guaranteeing their position as an occupying power in West Berlin.") In Kohl, "Vermerk über ein Gespräch mit den Genossen Kwizinski und Hotulew," p. 296.

58. Note from Bahr to Kissinger, 22 July 1971, in 439, EBD, FES.

59. Gromyko and Falin lingered "incognito" in East Berlin to be on hand for the final days. See Egon Bahr, *Zu meiner Zeit* (Munich: Karl Blessing, 1996), 368; Julij Kwizinskij, *Vor dem Sturm: Erinnerungen eines Diplomaten* (Berlin: Siedler, 1993), 246–47; and Keworkow, *Kanal*, 96–97.

60. For an English-language text of the final treaty, see J. A. S. Grenville and Bernard Wasserstein, eds., *The Major International Treaties since 1945: A History and Guide with Texts* (London: Methuen, 1987), 196–98. For a Russian-language version, see Министерство иностранных дел СССР, Министерство иностранных дел ГДР. *Уетырехстороннее соглашение по Западному Верлину и его реализация 1971–1977 гг. Документы* (Москва: Издательство политической литературы, 1977), 8–11. See also Bahr, *Zu meiner Zeit*, 364.

61. For an analysis of the terms of the treaty, see Garthoff, *Détente*, 138–41; and Benno Zündorf, alias Antonius Eitel, *Die Ostverträge* (Munich: C. H. Beck, 1979), 117–74.

62. As late as 30 July, however, the USSR refused to allow citizens of West Berlin to hold West German passports, a sine qua non for the West Germans, who were ostensibly not part of the negotiations. See "Information über das Treffen der Botschafter der Viermächte im Rahmen der Verhandlungen über Westberlin am 30. Juli 1971," in file "Informationen an Erich Honecker," J IV/J/1 (Büro Honecker), SAPMO. As Bahr recounted in his memoirs, the FRG managed to secure these passports via their own back-channel contacts to Brezhnev. Bahr, *Zu meiner Zeit*, 365.

63. Cited in Kogan, "Berlin Negotiations," 824. In German, the difference was "sind suspendiert worden" instead of "sind außer Kraft gesetzt worden."

64. Kissinger, *WHY*, 832.

65. David M. Keithly, *Breakthrough in the Ostpolitik: The 1971 Quadripartite Agreement* (Boulder, Colo.: Westview, 1986), 199.

66. Adam B. Ulam, *Expansion and Coexistence: Soviet Foreign Policy 1917–1973*, 2d ed. (New York: Praeger, 1974), 755.

67. Garthoff, *Détente*, 139.

68. Seymour Hersh, *The Price of Power: Kissinger in the Nixon White House* (New York: Summit, 1983), 421.

69. Peter Pulzer, *German Politics 1945–1995* (Oxford: Oxford University Press, 1995), 127.

70. This observation was made by Ambassador John Kornblum, who took part in both negotiations, in a speech at the Aspen Institute in Berlin, 11 Dec. 1998. For more information on the subsequent history of the Quadripartite Agreement, see Gerhard Wettig, *Das Vier-Mächte-Abkommen in der Bewährungsprobe* (Berlin: Berlin Verlag, 1981).

71. Keith L. Nelson, *The Making of Détente: Soviet-American Relations in the Shadow of Vietnam* (Baltimore: Johns Hopkins University Press, 1995), 102. See also Hersh, *Price of Power*, 420.

72. Philip Zelikow and Condoleezza Rice, *Germany Unified and Europe Transformed: A Study in Statecraft* (Cambridge: Harvard University Press, 1995), 59.

73. For description of the visit, see "Vermerk über Gespräch mit Breschnew während der Fahrt von Simferopol nach Oreanda am Abend des 16. September 1971," written by Brandt in Oreanda on 17 Sept. 1971, in 430, EBD, FES. See also Willy Brandt, *Begegnungen und Einsichten* (Hamburg: Hoffmann & Campe, 1976), 459–71; and Keworkow, *Kanal*, 101–3.

74. Peter H. Merkl, *German Unification in the European Context* (University Park: Pennsylvania State University, 1993), 59.

75. "Direktive für das Auftreten des Beauftragten der Regierung der DDR in der am 26. August 1971 beginnenden Phase der Verhandlungen mit dem Beauftragten der Regierung der BRD," in J IV 2/2A/1.533 (Politbüro), SAPMO.

76. Ibid., 4, section titled "Anlage 2: Vertrag zwischen der DDR und der Bundesrepublik über Fragen des Verkehrs." The draft also mentions that these fees should be paid "in Form jährlicher Pauschalsummen" ("in the form of an annual lump sum") (p. 5).

77. "Vorlage für das Politbüro des ZK der SED, Betr. Beschluß über die Pauschalierung der Straßenbenutzungsgebühr und der Steuerausgleichsabgabe," 15 Sept. 1971, p. 1, in I J IV 2/2A/1.539 (Politbüro), SAPMO.

78. Ibid., 3. In September of 1971 the GDR and FRG also reached agreements on postal and radio transmission rights, which provided an additional source of income. On these agreements, see Ernest D. Plock, *The Basic Treaty and the Evolution of East-West German Relations* (Boulder, Colo.: Westview, 1986).

79. "Beschluß über die Pauschalierung," 4.

80. Ibid., 6.

81. A transcript of Kohl and Bahr's conversation, which seems to have been typed up after bugging their talk, exists in the Stasi archive. See "Unterhaltung der Herren Dr. Kohl (K) und Bahr (B) am 27. August 1971 in Berlin," 26 Aug. 1971 (note that the date of the conversation is most likely an error because otherwise this protocol was produced the day before the conversation took place), p. 57, in SdM 233, ZA, BStU. The West German documentation from the same day contains similar comments; see "Protokoll des 16. Gespräches StS Bahr/StS Dr. Kohl, Ostberlin, Hause des Ministerrates, 26. August 1971, 14.55 bis 15.50 Uhr," 26 Aug. 1971, p. 2, in 375B, EBD, FES. See also "NG über interne Gespräche mit Staatssekretär Bahr am 26. August 1971 in Berlin," pp. 7–8, in J IV 2/2J/3629 (IntVer), SAPMO.

82. "Unterhaltung der Herren Dr. Kohl (K) und Bahr (B) am 27. August 1971 in Berlin," 67, and the same in "NG über interne Gespräche mit Staatssekretär Bahr am 25. August 1971 in Berlin," 7–8.

83. "Niederschrift über persönliche Unterredungen mit Staatssekretär Bahr am 9. Sept. 1971," p. 2, in J IV 2/2J/3649 (IntVer), SAPMO. On the spat over translations, see also Karl Seidel, "Erste Schritte auf dem Weg zu normalen Beziehungen zwischen der Deutschen Demokratischen Republik und der Bundesrepublik Deutschland. Persönliche Erinnerungen an die deutsch-deutschen Verhandlungen Anfang der siebziger Jahre," in Detlef Nakath, ed., *Deutschlandpolitiker der DDR erinnern sich* (Berlin: Fides, 1995), 114–16.

84. "Vergleich zwischen dem offiziellen und inoffiziellen Material der Unterredung Kohl-Bahr vom 26.8.1971," 30 Aug. 1971, p. 38, in SdM 233, ZA, BStU. This document compares the official materials from the Bahr-Kohl talks (i.e., the stenographic protocols of the official talks and Kohl's notes from conversations with Bahr) with "unofficial" material, which seems to mean typed protocols produced from acoustic surveillance. The document notes that missing from the "official" materials was "die Bemerkung Bahrs, daß die Lage sich so verändert habe, daß jetzt die vier Mächte auf die Verhandlungsergebnisse der 'kompetenten deutschen Stellen' warten und ihre weiteren Pläne u.a.

(Europäische Sicherheits-Konferenz, Truppenreduzierung in Europa, SALT-Gespräche) vom Ergebnis der deutschen Verhandlungen zumindest terminlich beeinflußt werden." ([Missing was] "Bahr's comment that that situation was much changed. Now, the four powers are waiting for the results of the negoations of the 'responsible German authorities' [as opposed to the other way around]. The four powers' future plans (including but not limited to CSCE, reduction of troops in Europe, SALT talks) will, at the very least, have their timing affected.")

85. Document without title with note at top saying it is a translation, 16 Sept. 1971, initialed by Erich Honecker on 17 Sept. 1971, first line reads "Den Gepflogenheiten folgend, hält es das ZK der KPdSU für erforderlich, über den Stand der sowjetisch-chinesischen Beziehungen in jüngster Zeit zu informieren," in J IV 2/202/542 (Allg. Abt.), SAPMO.

86. Ibid., 2.

87. Ibid., 4.

88. Ibid., 9–10. The Soviets argued that on several occasions friendly Chinese gestures toward the United States had encouraged U.S. aggression in Vietnam. In their view, a conversation that Mao Zedong had had with the U.S. journalist Edgar Snow in 1965 (in which Mao indicated that China would not intervene in the Vietnamese conflict) had emboldened the United States to bombard North Vietnam. A similar situation arose when the United States invaded Laos after another Snow interview. Now, in the Soviets' view, the invitation to Nixon to visit China had emboldened the United States to extend the Vietnamese conflict.

89. In a note informing the SED of this decision, the Soviets claimed that they did so because the growth of Soviet military and economic strength had forced the realization on the United States that there was no way around Moscow in future policymaking. The Soviets did not mention the U.S. rapprochement with China. See "Information des Gen. Gorinowitsch am 9. Oktober 1971," in J IV 2/202/571 (Allg. Abt.), SAPMO.

90. Kissinger, WHY, 770.

91. See Tagesordnungspunkt 4, Politbüro meeting of 6 July 1971, "Maßnahmen zur Erhöhung der Sicherheit und Ordnung an der Staatsgrenze der DDR zur BRD," and the supporting documentation in J IV 2/2A/1.524 (Politburo), SAPMO. On this measure, see also Winters, "Wie souverän war die DDR?" for information about the trial that Politbüro members later faced for mining the border; and Klaus Schroeder, Der SED-Staat: Geschichte und Strukturen der DDR (Munich: Bayerische Landeszentrale für Politische Bildungsarbeit, 1998), 213–15.

92. Präsidium des Ministerrates, "Beschluß über Maßnahmen zur Erhöhung der Sicherheit und Ordnung an der Staatsgrenze der DDR zur BRD und zu WESTBERLIN vom 8. September 1971," p. 241, in SdM 2392, ZA, BStU.

93. Ibid., 242.

94. See Jochen Staadt, Die geheime Westpolitik der SED 1960–1970: Von der gesamtdeutschen Orientierung zur sozialistischen Nation (Berlin: Akademie, 1993); and "Gedankenführung auf der konstituierenden Sitzung der Westkommission am 9. September 1971," in IV A 2/10.02/1 (Westabteilung), SAPMO.

95. See Tagesordnungspunkt 10, "Maßnahmen zur Sicherung der Rechte der DDR gegenüber den möglichen Ansprüchen anderer Staaten aus dem in der DDR befindlichen Vermögen von Berechtigten dieser Staaten und zur Sicherung der Vermögensansprüche der DDR gegenüber diesen Staaten," in J IV 2/2A/1.539 (Politbüro), SAPMO.

96. Brezhnev's talk with Brandt may have produced some new instructions to the SED. The Politburo meeting of 5 October expressed thanks to Brezhnev for his report about his recent meeting with Brandt and stated its agreement with the positions Brezhnev

took. See Tagesordnungspunkt 2, meeting of 5 Oct. 1971, in J IV 2/2A/1.543 (Politbüro), SAPMO. For West German documentation on this meeting, see "Zussamenfassung," 6 Oct. 1971, in 375B, EBD, FES.

97. See Chapter 4 and "Vorlage für das Politbüro des ZK der SED, Betr.: Fortsetzung der Verhandlungen des Genossen Dr. Kohl mit Staatssekretär Bahr am 6. Oktober 1971," in J IV 2/2A/1.543 (Politburo), SAPMO. See also "Bericht über den Ablauf," p. 3, DC20-5547 (SeKo), BA-V. The three experts added to the delegation were Alwin Brandt, Heinz Gerber, and Helmut Nacke.

98. "Unterhaltung der Herren Dr. Kohl (K) und Bahr (B) am 27. August 1971 in Berlin," p. 56.

99. It seems that the reports the Stasi agents filed fell mostly into the domain of the HV A; hence, their files have disappeared or been destroyed. However, a (unfortunately rather uninformative) report from Heinz Gerber, code-named "Mehlhorn," on meetings at the beginning of October has survived. See "Verhandlungen am 6.10. u. 8.10.71," pp. 1–5, in Hauptabteilung XIX, ZA, BStU.

100. The extensive legal details and their implications have been analyzed elsewhere. See, for example, I. D. Hendry and M. C. Wood, *The Legal Status of Berlin* (Cambridge: Grotius, 1987), chap. 8; and the two-volume work by Catudal, *Diplomacy* and *Balance Sheet*. Here the focus is on the controversial issues that do the most to illuminate SED and Soviet motives in, and worries about, the negotiating process.

101. Debate on this point was especially heated at the meeting of 3–4 November 1971. See "Stenografische Niederschrift der Verhandlung (27. Treffen) zwischen Genossen Dr. Michael Kohl und Egon Bahr am 2. und 4. November 1971 im Bundeskanzleramt in Bonn," in J IV 2/201/905 (IntVer), SAPMO. See also the West German version, "Protokoll der Delegationssitzung anlässlich der 27. Begegnung von StS Bahr/StS Dr. Kohl, Bonn, Bundeskanzleramt, am 3. November 1971," and the "Fortsetzung" of 4 November, in 376A, EBD, FES.

102. "Stenografische Niederschrift der Verhandlungen (22. Treffen) zwischen Genossen Dr. Michael Kohl und Egon Bahr am 6. Oktober 1971 im Hause des Ministerrates," pp. 53–54, in J IV 2/201/901 (Int Ver), SAPMO.

103. Bahr expressed his objection to this measure at a meeting on 27–28 October. See "Zusammenfassender Bericht über die Verhandlungen zwischen Staatssekretär Dr. Kohl und Staatssekretär Bahr am 27./28.10.1971," in J IV 2/2J/3740 (IntVer), SAPMO.

104. "Vorlage für das Politbüro des ZK der SED," 11 Oct. 1971, p. 2, in J IV 2/2A/1.545 (Politbüro), SAPMO.

105. "Stenografische Niederschrift der Verhandlung zwischen Dr. Kohl und Bahr im Hause des Ministerrates der DDR, 27/28 Okt. 1971," pp. 26–29, in J IV 2/201/904 (IntVer), SAPMO.

106. "NG über ein persönliches Gespräch mit Staatssekretär Bahr am 8. Oktober 1971 in Bonn," p. 3, in J IV 2/2J/3694 (IntVer), SAPMO.

107. "Stenografische Niederschrift der Verhandlungen (22. Treffen) zwischen Genossen Dr. Michael Kohl und Egon Bahr am 6. Oktober 1971 im Hause des Ministerrates," p. 39.

108. Egon Bahr, "Vermerk," 20 November 1971, in 376B, EBD, FES.

109. The SED term for this tax was "Steuerausgleichsabgabe." See the East German version, "Zusammenfassender Bericht über die Verhandlungen zwischen Genossen Staatssekretär Dr. Kohl und Staatssekretär Bahr am 13. und 14. Oktober 1971 in Berlin," pp. 10–11, in J IV 2/2J/3706 (IntVer), SAPMO; and the West German, "Zusammenfassung," 14 Oct. 1971, p. 4, in 376A, EBD, FES.

110. "Zusammenfassender Bericht über die Verhandlungen zwischen Genossen

Staatssekretär Dr. Kohl und Staatssekretär Bahr am 13. und 14. Oktober 1971 in Berlin," p. 11. See also the West German version, "Protokoll (Fortsetzung)," 14 Oct. 1971, p. 26, in 376A, EBD, FES.

111. "Stenografische Niederschrift der Verhandlungen (22. Treffen) zwischen Genossen Dr. Michael Kohl und Egon Bahr am 6. Oktober 1971 im Hause des Ministerrates," p. 10.

112. "NG über persönliche Unterredungen mit Staatssekretär Bahr am 14. Oktober 1971 in Berlin," 14 Oct. 1971, p. 2, in J IV 2/2J/3706 (IntVer), SAPMO.

113. Hermann Axen and Otto Winzer, "Vorlage für das Politbüro des ZK der SED, Betr. Konsultation des Genossen O. Winzer mit Genossen A. A. Gromyko," 18 Oct. 1971, p. 2, in J IV 2/2A/1.547 (Politbüro), SAPMO.

114. "Gedanken für einleitende Ausführungen des Genossen Winzer bei der Konsultation mit dem sowjetischen Außenminister, Genossen Gromyko," no date, p. 2, in J IV 2/2A/1.547 (Politburo), SAPMO.

115. GDR foreign minister Otto Winzer provided Erich Honecker with a summary of their meeting on 21 October. See letter from Winzer and "Bericht über die Konsultation" between Winzer and Gromyko, 20 Oct. 1971, in J IV 2/2A/1.549 (Politbüro), SAPMO.

116. "Bericht über die Konsultation," p. 7a.

117. Ibid., 14.

118. Hermann Axen and Otto Winzer, "Vorlage für das Politbüro des ZK der SED," 2 Nov. 1971, in J IV 2/2A/1.551 (Politburo), SAPMO.

119. "Zusammenfassender Bericht über die Verhandlungen zwischen Staatssekretär Dr. Kohl und Staatssekretär Bahr am 27./28.10.71 in Berlin," p. 2, in J IV 2/2J/3740 (IntVer), SAPMO. In the West German version, Bahr mentions that this tax came as a surprise for the West and that he would prefer to discuss it with Kohl in their private conversation; however, his summary of the private conversation does not mention it. See "Protokoll der Delegationssitzung anlässlich der 16. Begegnung von StS Bahr/StS Dr. Kohl, Ostberlin, Haus des Ministerrats, am 27. Oktober 1971," 27 Oct. 1971, p. 15, in 376A, EBD, FES.

120. "NG über persönliche Unterredungen mit Staatssekretär Bahr am 3. und 4. November 1971 in Bonn," p. 7, in J IV 2/2J/3760 (IntVer), SAPMO.

121. Ibid., 2. The West German documentation of this conversation does not contain this quotation but does note that the subject was discussed; see Bahr, "Vermerk," 4 Nov. 1971, pp. 2–3, in 376A, EBD, FES.

122. Abt. 26, "Bericht," 5 Nov. 1971, p. 227, in SdM 1837, ZA, BStU.

123. "NG über eine persönliche Unterredung von Dr. Michael Kohl mit Staatssekretär Bahr am 28.10 in Berlin," pp. 1–2, in J IV 2/2J/3747 (IntVer), SAPMO.

124. Otto Winzer, "Vorlage für das Politbüro des ZK der SED," 8 Nov. 1971, pp. 1–2, in J IV 2/2A/1.552 (Politbüro), SAPMO. It actually instructed Kohl to ask for DM 170 million in the hopes of receiving DM 165 million.

125. Ibid., 2.

126. Article 16 of the treaty is the "misuse clause," or "Mißbrauchsklausel." See Ingo Von Münch, ed., Dokumente des geteilten Deutschland, 2 vols. (Stuttgart: Kröner, 1976), 130–31.

127. Agreement on the sum of DM 230 million emerged at the 10–13 November 1971 meeting, then modified slightly, to DM 234.9 million, for the final treaty. See "Zusammenfassender Bericht über die Verhandlungen zwischen Staatssekretär Dr. Kohl und Staatssekretär Bahr vom 10. bis 13. November 1971," in J IV 2/2J/3774 (IntVer), SAPMO; and Article 18 of the treaty, in Von Münch, Dokumente, 132–33.

128. They had this feeling despite the fact that they received some form of consulta-

tion or report after all negotiating rounds, according to author's interviews with Eitel (20 Sept. 1996) and Bahr (21 May 1996).

129. "NG über persönliche Unterredungen mit Staatssekretär Bahr am 18. November 1971," in J IV 2/2J/3790 (IntVer), SAPMO. The West German summary (i.e., Bahr's summary) of this conversation does mention that the three Western allies wanted time to assess the German-German accord but contains no mention of Falin. See Bahr, "Vermerk," 20 Nov. 1971, p. 4, in 376B, EBD, FES.

130. This produced some late-night negotiating; see "NG über die Zusammenkunft mit Staatssekretär Bahr am 3.12 (22.15 Uhr) bis 4.12.1971 (2.30 Uhr)," in J IV 2/2J/3826 (IntVer), SAPMO.

131. Ulrich Sahm, "Diplomaten taugen nichts": Aus dem Leben eines Staatsdieners (Düsseldorf: Droste, 1994), 286.

132. A copy of the invitation is in Sahm, Diplomaten, 287. The original wording was "Artikel 3: Entplombung. Im Interesse der einfachsten, schnellsten und sichersten Abwicklung des Abends werden die zuständigen Stellen darauf hinwirken, daß solche Behältnisse, die nach ihrem Bautyp zur Beförderung von alkoholischen Getränken bestimmt sind, in größtmöglichem Umfang geöffnet, und, soweit es der Zustand der Beteiligten zuläßt, in andere Behältnisse umgefüllt werden."

133. There exist several accounts of the vote of no confidence. See, for example, Karl Dietrich Bracher, Wolfgang Jäger, and Werner Link, Republik im Wandel 1969–1974: Die Ära Brandt (Stuttgart: Deutsche Verlags-Anstalt, 1986), 67–72. See also Dennis L. Bark and David R. Gress, Democracy and Its Discontents, vol. 2 of A History of West Germany, 2d ed. (Oxford: Blackwell, 1993), 208–11; and Arnulf Baring, Machtwechsel: Die Ära Brandt-Scheel (Stuttgart: Deutsche Verlags-Anstalt, 1982), 416–24.

134. Bark and Gress, Democracy and Its Discontents, 209.

135. "Stenografische Niederschrift," Tagung Politisch Beratender Ausschuß in Prague, 25–26 January 1972, pp. 14–16, in J IV 2/202/526 (Allg. Abt.), SAPMO. On the issue of West Germany gaining nuclear weapons, see Marc Trachtenberg, A Constructed Peace: The Making of the European Settlement 1945–1963 (Princeton: Princeton University Press, 1999).

136. Author's interview with Wolf, 6 June 1996.

137. For the details of this treaty, see Von Münch, Dokumente, 247–301.

138. "Zusammenfassender Bericht über die Verhandlungen zwischen Genossen Staatssekretär Dr. Kohl und Staatssekretär Bahr am 2./3. Februar 1972 in Bonn," p. 2, in J IV 2/2J/3950 (IntVer), SAPMO.

139. "Information über Äußerungen von Staatssekretär Bahr zu den Verhandlungen mit der DDR," p. 64, in HV A 382, ZA, BStU.

140. See the documentation to Tagesordnungspunkt 2, "Geste des guten Willens der DDR," in the Politbüro meeting of 22 Feb. 1972 in J IV 2/2A/1.577 (Politbüro), SAPMO.

141. The MfS order for the start of the operation is in "Befehl Nr. 5/72," Dok.-Nr. 100724, in ZA, BStU. See also Dok.-Nr. 100729 for further details.

142. The amount of "swing," or interest-free, credit available to the GDR, was set at DM 200 million from 1962 until 1968; after that it rose to DM 360 million in 1969, DM 440 million by the end of 1970 (after a midyear increase), DM 585 million by 1972, and DM 620 million by 1972. See Bundesministerium für innerdeutsche Beziehungen, ed., Zehn Jahre Deutschlandpolitik: Die Entwicklung der Bezehungen zwischen der Bundesrepublik Deutschland und der Deutschen Demokratischen Republik 1969–1979 (Bonn: Bundesministerium, Feb. 1980), 29. Thereafter, the yearly sum increased in the following manner: 1976–79, DM 400 million; 1980–89, DM 525 million; planned for 1990–99, DM 860 million. Seidel, "Erste Schritte," 118.

143. "NG über persönliche Unterredungen mit Staatssekretär Bahr am 22. und 23. März 1972 in Bonn," p. 8, in J IV 2/2J/4012 (IntVer), SAPMO. However, this issue is not mentioned in Bahr's summary of the same conversation; see Bahr's "Vermerk," 25 Mar. 1972, in 377A, EBD, FES.

144. As Bahr put it, he was anxious to see how the terms he and Kohl had agreed upon would work in practice. Bahr found that they "were not bad at all." The German-German talks had finally yielded a benefit for the broader population, and Bahr was clearly pleased, not least by a positive media response. See both the West German "Protokoll der Delegationssitzung anlässlich der 38. Begegnung der Staatssekretäre Bahr/Dr. Kohl am 5. April 1972 in Bonn, Bundeskanzleramt, von 10,40 Uhr bis 1300 Uhr," p. 1, in 377B, EBD, FES; and the East German "Stenografische Niederschrift der Verhandlungen (38. Treffen) zwischen Genossen Dr. Michael Kohl und Egon Bahr über einen Verkehrsvertrag am 5. und 6. April im Bundekanzleramt in Bonn," p. 4, in J IV 2/201/1143 (IntVer), SAPMO.

145. Kissinger, WHY, 1114.

146. Ibid., 1122.

147. "NG über persönliche Unterredungen zwischen Genossen Dr. Michael Kohl und Staatssekretär Egon Bahr, 12. April 1972," in J IV 2/2J/4032 (IntVer), SAPMO. Honecker did deliver a speech on 18 April 1972 in Sofia, which was less hard-line than usual and retreated from a demand for full legal recognition of the GDR by the FRG. On this speech, see Plock, Basic Treaty, 63.

148. "Auszug aus der Rede des Ersten Sekretärs des ZK der SED, Erich Honecker, am 18. April 1972 in Sofia," in J IV 2/2A/1.589 (Politbüro), SAPMO. The Bundesausschuß of the CDU had stated on 24 January 1972 that the CDU would refuse to confirm the treaties. See Bracher, Jäger, and Link, Ära Brandt, 213.

149. See Tagesordnungspunkt 3 at the meeting of 25 April 1972, in J IV 2/2A/1.589 (Politbüro), SAPMO.

150. "NG über eine persönliche Unterredung mit Staatssekretär Bahr am 25.4.1972, 16.15 bis 16.50 Uhr," p. 3, in J IV 2/2J/4055 (IntVer), SAPMO. The West German protocol notes that Bahr "dankte der DDR-Delegation für die konstruktive Art der Mitarbeit in der Schlussphase" ("thanked the GDR's delegation for their constructive cooperation in the end phase"). "Protokoll der 41. Verhandlung der Staatssekretär Bahr/Dr. Kohl in Ostberlin, Haus des Ministerrates, am 25./26. April 71," p. 4, in 378A, EBD, FES.

151. "Vermerk über einen vertraulichen Empfang von Staatssekretär Egon Bahr beim Ersten Sekretär des ZK der SED, Genossen Erich Honecker," p. 1, in J IV 2/2J/4057 (IntVer), SAPMO. This document has also been published by Heinrich Potthoff as Document No. 6 in Bonn und Ost-Berlin 1969–1982 (Bonn: Dietz, 1997). What seems to be Bahr's account of the same conversation appears in Bahr, Zu meiner Zeit, 389–91.

152. Wolf stated in his memoirs that he approved an expenditure to purchase Steiner's vote but thinks that he may not have been the only one and that Steiner may have gotten paid twice. See Markus Wolf, Spionagechef im geheimen Krieg: Erinnerungen (Munich: List, 1997), 261. See also Horst Ehmke, Mittendrin (Berlin: Rowohlt, 1994), 157; and Bracher, Jäger, and Link, Ära Brandt, 112–13.

153. Author's interview with Wolf, 6 June 1996.

154. Bahr, Zu meiner Zeit, 382–83.

155. Keworkow, Kanal, 108–10.

156. Kissinger, WHY, 1150.

157. "Vermerk über einen vertraulichen Empfang von Staatssekretär Egon Bahr beim Ersten Sekretär des ZK der SED, Genossen Erich Honecker," p. 2.

158. Ibid., 5.

159. "NG über persönliche Unterredungen mit Staatssekretär Bahr am Abend des 26. und Morgen des 27.4.1972," p. 3, in J IV 2/2J/4056 (IntVer), SAPMO. According to the West German protocol, Kohl informed Brandt that the regulations could be extended to West Berlin on the 26th as well; see "Protokoll (Fortsetzung)," 27 Apr. 1972, 378A, EBD, FES.

160. "NG über persönliche Unterredungen mit Staatssekretär Bahr am Abend des 26. und Morgen des 27.4.1972," p. 5.

161. Ibid., 1.

Chapter Six

1. William Bundy sees this as the reason the Soviets were interested in CSCE as well. According to his account, they hoped to achieve the maximum result, namely, "full ratification and legitimization of Soviet control of the Eastern European countries, the recognized 'sphere of influence' for which Stalin had striven in the war and immediate postwar years." Bundy, *A Tangled Web: The Making of Foreign Policy in the Nixon Presidency* (New York: Hill and Wang, 1998), 247.

2. See, for example, Dennis L. Bark and David R. Gress, *Democracy and Its Discontents 1963–1991*, vol. 2 of *A History of West Germany* (Oxford: Blackwell, 1993), 211–14; and Karl Dietrich Bracher, Wolfgang Jäger, and Werner Link, *Republik im Wandel 1969–1974: Die Ära Brandt* (Stuttgart: Deutsche Verlags-Anstalt; and Mannheim: F. A. Brockhaus, 1986), 206–13. The latter includes (on p. 210) a copy of the "Gemeinsame Erklärung des Bundestags zu den Ostverträgen, 17. Mai 1972," which served the purpose of stating explicitly what the West German parliament believed to be implicit in the treaties.

3. Henry Kissinger, *WHY* (Boston: Little, Brown, 1979), 1179.

4. Anatoly Dobrynin, *In Confidence: Moscow's Ambassador to America's Six Cold War Presidents (1962–1986)* (New York: Random House, 1995), 248.

5. As Bundy puts it, "Brandt's carefully developed policy and its coming up for final Bundestag approval at that crucial moment saved the summit. At the moment of truth, stabilizing the situation in Germany, completing a new European order, and ensuring Soviet control of the Eastern European nations for as far ahead as the eye could see were more important to the Soviet Union than 'international solidarity.'" Bundy, *Tangled Web*, 321.

6. Bracher, Jäger, and Link, *Ära Brandt*, 209.

7. See "Information über die Einschätzung der Situation in Bonn durch führende Politiker," 5 May 1972, pp. 188–191, and "Information über Auseinandersetzungen in der Westberliner SPD im Zusammenhang mit der Ratifizierung der Verträge zwischen der BRD und der Sowjetunion bzw. der Volksrepublik Polen," pp. 32–26, both in HV A 383, ZA, BStU.

8. "NG über ein Gespräch unter vier Augen mit Staatssekretär Bahr anläßlich der Paraphierung des Verkehrsvertrages, 12. Mai 1972," p. 5, in J IV 2/2J/4091 (IntVer), SAPMO.

9. "Information über ein Gespräch mit dem Botschafter Großbritanniens in der BRD, R. Jackling," 15 May 1972 report of conversation on 12 May 1972, in DC20-4406 (Stoph), BA-V.

10. Honoré M. Catudal, *The Diplomacy of the Quadripartite Agreement on Berlin: A New Era in East-West Politics* (Berlin: Berlin Verlag, 1978), 275. For a copy of the formal act of 3 June 1972, see Bundesministerium für innerdeutsche Beziehungen, ed., *Zehn Jahre Deutschlandpolitik: Die Entwicklung der Beziehungen zwischen der Bundesrepublik*

Deutschland und der Deutschen Demokratischen Republik 1969–1979 (Bonn: Bundesministerium, Feb. 1980), 188–89. The Stasi was responsible for the details of implementing the agreements on transit and access. See Befehl Nr. 20/72, 2 June 1972, in Dok.-Nr. 100725, ZA, BStU; and pp. 199–241 in SdM 2399, ZA, BStU.

11. "NG über persönliche Unterredungen mit Staatssekretär Bahr anläßlich der Unterzeichnung des Verkehrsvertrages, 26. Mai 1972," in J IV 2/2J/4118 (IntVer), SAPMO.

12. "Information über ein Treffen des sowjetischen Botschafters mit dem amerikanischen Botschafter in der BRD, M. Hillenbrand," 17 Aug. 1972, mentions this suggestion from 3 June 1972, in DC20-4406 (Stoph), BA-V.

13. "NG über ein persönliches Gespräch mit Staatssekretär Bahr im Bundeskanzleramt in Bonn am 31. Mai 1972 von 17.30 bis 19.00," p. 8, in J IV 2/2J/4127 (IntVer), SAPMO. This comment is not recorded in the West German version: Egon Bahr, "Vermerk," 31 May 1972, in 378A, EBD, FES.

14. "NG über ein persönliches Gespräch mit Staatssekretär Bahr im Bundeskanzleramt in Bonn am 31. Mai 1972 von 17.30 bis 19.00," 5.

15. For a quick overview of the Moscow summit, see Peter G. Boyle, *American-Soviet Relations: From the Russian Revolution to the Fall of Communism* (London: Routledge, 1993), 169–73. For more detailed assessments of not only the Moscow summit but also the process of arms control negotiation, see Raymond Garthoff, *Détente and Confrontation: American-Soviet Relations from Nixon to Reagan*, rev. ed. (Washington, D.C.: Brookings Institution, 1994), esp. 181–213; Walter Isaacson, *Kissinger: A Biography* (New York: Simon & Schuster, 1992), 425–28; Kissinger, *WHY*, chap. 28; and Gerard Smith, *Doubletalk: The Story of the First Strategic Arms Limitation Talks* (New York: Doubleday, 1980).

16. The deal on grain sales turned out to be one of which the USSR would make copious use. Already by July of 1972, Moscow realized that the harvest would be disastrous. See "Vermerk über ein Gespräch mit Genossen Kossygin am 12.7.1972," p. 182, in DC20-4406 (Stoph), BA-V. As pointed out by historian Gregory L. Freeze, agriculture was "the Achilles heel of the Soviet Prometheus." Indeed, reports Freeze, Brezhnev oversaw economic decline in the USSR on all fronts: "Whereas national income rose 5.9 per cent per capita in 1966–70, thereafter it fell sharply, bottoming out at 2.1 per cent in 1981–85. GNP followed a similar trajectory: 6 per cent in the 1950s, 5 per cent in the 1960s, 4 per cent from 1970–78, and 2 per cent in subsequent years. This corresponded, predictably, to a decrease in the rate of growth in investment capital."Gregory L. Freeze, ed., *Russia A History* (Oxford: Oxford University Press, 1997), 373–74.

17. William Burr, ed., *The Kissinger Transcripts: The Top Secret Talks with Beijing and Moscow* (New York: New Press, 1998), 32.

18. John Lewis Gaddis, *Strategies of Containment: A Critical Appraisal of Postwar American National Security Policy* (Oxford: Oxford University Press, 1982), 318–19.

19. A written overview of comments made by Gromyko exists under the title "Ausführungen des Genossen Andrej Gromyko, Minister für Auswärtige Angelegenheiten der UdSSR am 5. Juni 1972 im Hause des ZK der SED," in IV 2/2.035/55 (Büro Axen), SAPMO. Its authorship is unclear but it is in the files of Hermann Axen, the Politburo member who was nominally designated as the foreign policy expert. In his comments, Gromyko referred to a written summary that the SED had already been given. While there is no summary in the same file as the overview of his comments, another file contains the document to which Gromyko most likely referred, namely, document without title, 6 June 1972, in J IV 2/202/571 (Allg. Abt.), SAPMO. This document exists in both German and Russian versions.

20. Document without title, 6 June 1972, 4.

21. Ibid., 10.

22. Ibid., 15.

23. "Ausführungen des Genossen Andrej Gromyko, Minister für Auswärtige Angelegenheiten der UdSSR am 5. Juni 1972 im Hause des ZK der SED," 41.

24. Ibid., 47.

25. Document without title, 6 June 1972, 12.

26. Ibid., 13.

27. "Ausführungen des Genossen Andrej Gromyko, Minister für Auswärtige Angelegenheiten der UdSSR am 5. Juni 1972 im Hause des ZK der SED," 47.

28. Ibid., 36–37.

29. Ibid., 36.

30. Ibid., 38.

31. Michael Kohl, "Vermerk," 13 June 1972, pp. 47–50, in Rechstelle 120/1, ZA, BStU. Kohl sought (and received) Soviet approval for this stance.

32. Readers interested in an overview of the entire Basic Treaty should see Benno Zündorf, alias Antonius Eitel, *Die Ostverträge* (Munich: Beck, 1979), 211–319; and Ernest D. Plock, *The Basic Treaty and the Evolution of East-West German Relations* (Boulder, Colo.: Westview, 1986). For a text of the treaty, see Bundesministerium für innerdeutsche Beziehungen, *Zehn Jahre Deutschlandpolitik*, 205–16.

33. Many of these are preserved in the file SdM 1837, ZA, BStU.

34. "Stenografische Niederschrift des Meinungsaustausches zwischen Staatssekretär Dr. Michael Kohl und Staatssekretär Egon Bahr über die Herstellung nomaler [*sic*] Beziehungen zwischen der DDR und der BRD," 15 June 1972, p. 2, in J IV 2/201/1145 (IntVer), SAPMO (hereafter SN Bahr-Kohl, 15 June 1972). Portions of this document are published as Document No. 7 in Heinrich Potthoff, *Bonn und Ost-Berlin 1969–1982: Dialog auf höchster Ebene und vertrauliche Kanäle Darstellung und Dokumente* (Bonn: Dietz, 1997). See also the West German version, "Protokoll der Delegationssitzung anlässlich der 1. Begegnung von StS Bahr/StS Kohl im Meinungsaustausch über das Grundverhältnis BRD/DDR, in Ostberlin, Haus des Ministerrats, am 15. Juni 1972, 10.00 bis 13.00 Uhr," in 378A, EBD, FES (hereafter West German "Protokoll").

35. "Direktive für das Auftreten des Genossen Dr. Kohl beim Meinungsaustausch mit Staatssekretär Bahr am 15./16. Juni 1972," in J IV 2/2A/1.602 (Politbüro), SAPMO.

36. SN Bahr-Kohl, 15 June 1972, pp. 15–16.

37. Timothy Garton Ash, *In Europe's Name* (New York: Random House, 1993), 162–76.

38. See the West German "Protokoll," 15 June 1972, 28–29.

39. SN Bahr-Kohl, 15 June 1972, 62a. See also the West German "Protokoll," pp. 28–29, which contains a similar comment.

40. SN Bahr-Kohl, 15 June 1972, 62a. Bahr relied heavily on the constitution of the GDR in this kind of rhetorical skirmish, but he also used other GDR documents as well. See, for example, "Stenografische Niederschrift des Meinungsaustausches zwischen Staatssekretär Dr. Michael Kohl und Staatssekretär Egon Bahr über die Herstellung normaler Beziehungen zwischen der DDR und der BRD," 21–22 June 1972, p. 83, in J IV 2/201/1146 (IntVer), SAPMO, in which he quoted a letter written by Otto Winzer in February 1966 calling for an end to the division of Germany and the establishment of a confederation. See also the East German ("Stenografische Niederschrift des Meinungsaustausches zwischen Staatssekretär Dr. Michael Kohl und Staatssekretär Egon Bahr über die Herstellung normaler Beziehungen zwischen der DDR und der BRD," 28 June 1972, in J IV 2/201/1147 [IntVer], SAPMO) and West German ("Protokoll der Delega-

tionssitzung anlässlich der 3. Begegnung der Staatssekretär Bahr/Kohl im Meinungsaustausch über einen Grundvertrag zwischen den beiden deutschen Staaten in Ost-
berlin, Haus des Ministerrats, am 28. Juni 1972," in 378B, EBD, FES) documents from
28 June 1972, when Bahr's rhetorical attack dominated the entire meeting.

41. SN Bahr-Kohl, 15 June 1972, 69. The West German protocol does not contain this
quotation but indicates that Kohl began using historical references as a counterargument
to Kohl's point; see "Protokoll" p. 30, in 378, EBD, FES.

42. "Vorlage für das Politbüro," 26 June 1972, p. 9, in J IV 2/2A/1.605 (IntVer),
SAPMO.

43. SN Bahr-Kohl, 28 June 1972, p. 46, in J IV 2/201/1147 (IntVer), SAPMO; also in
the West German "Protokoll" of the same date, p. 21, in 378B, EBD, FES.

44. "Vermerk über ein Gespräch mit Dr. Sanne am 3. August 1972 in Bonn," p. 2, in
DC20-5585 (SeKo), BA-V.

45. On the 1974 changes to the GDR constitution, see Hermann Weber, *Die DDR
1945–1990* (Munich: Oldenbourg, 1993), 80–81. In his memoirs, Bahr wrote that he
believed his comments during the negotiations were in part causative. Historian Heinrich Potthoff argued that Bahr's belief was completely unfounded. The chronological
sequence of events nonetheless suggests strongly that there may be a connection. See
Egon Bahr, *Zu meiner Zeit* (Munich: Karl Blessing, 1996), 401; and Heinrich Potthoff,
"Eine zweite Etappe der Deutschlandpolitik," *Deutschland Archiv* 1 (Jan./Feb. 1997): 116.

46. "Information über die westdeutschen Vorstellungen zum Inhalt eines Vertrages
über die grundsätzliche Regelung der Beziehungen zwischen DDR und BRD," p. 151, in
Rechtsstelle 120/2, ZA, BStU.

47. "Vermerk von Michael Kohl für Erich Honecker, Willi Stoph, Paul Verner, Hermann Axen, Erich Mielke, und Peter Florin," 25 Aug. 1972, p. 213, in Rechtsstelle 120/3,
ZA, BStU. In a 1994 article, historian Heinrich August Winkler offered a kinder interpretation of the FRG's stance on this issue, pointing out that the Social Democrats under
Willy Brandt had realistically decided that "the consequences of partition must be rendered more bearable through dialogue with the [GDR] . . . and the overall coherence of
the nation must take precedence over the restoration of a German nation state." See
Heinrich August Winkler, "Rebuilding of a Nation: The Germans Before and After
Unification," *Daedalus* 123 (Winter 1994): 109.

48. Accounts from both sides of the conversation survive. See both the East German
"Vermerk über ein Gespräch des Genossen Erich Honecker mit Staatssekretär Bahr am
7. September 1972," in IV 2/1/460 (ZK), SAPMO; and Bahr's account of the conversation in "Vermerk Gespräch mit Honecker am 7.9.1972 in seinem Büro," in 380A, EBD,
FES. Heinrich Potthoff published both as "Gespräch Bahr-Honecker am 7. September
1972 (Berlin-Ost)," Document No. 9 in Potthoff, *Bonn und Ost-Berlin*. The 1999 Oscar-
winning documentary film *One Day in September* provides interview evidence that
strongly suggests East German complicity in the terrorist activities of 5 September 1972.

49. See both the West German "Zusammenfassung Betr. Meinungsaustausch Bahr/
Kohl am 28.6.1972 in Ost-Berlin," pp. 1–2, in 378B, EBD, FES; and the East German
"Zusammenfassender Bericht über den Meinungsaustausch zwischen Genossen Staatssekretär Dr. Kohl und Staatssekretär Bahr am 28. Juni 1972 in Berlin," pp. 1–2, in J IV
2/2J/4174 (IntVer), SAPMO.

50. As Bahr tried to explain to Kohl, the Brandt government needed certain phrases
that would be "verfassungskonform." See "NG über persönliche Unterredungen mit
Staatssekretär Bahr am 30. und 31. August 1972," p. 8, in J IV 2/2J/4289 (IntVer),
SAPMO.

51. Letter from Egon Bahr to Helmut Schmidt, 18 Apr. 1972, in HS privat Pz Innen-

politik, Bd. 4, 1972, HS PA. Bahr's intent in writing this letter was to give Schmidt some suggestions for ideas that he might discuss in a forthcoming meeting with Henry Kissinger.

52. For example, see "NG über persönliche Unterredungen mit Staatssekretär Bahr am 28. Juni 1972," p. 5, in J IV 2/2J/4174 (IntVer), SAPMO, in which Kohl told Bahr, "für uns eine Aufnahme des Themas Nation in den Vertrag nicht in Frage käme" ("in our view, there is no chance of mentioning the issue of the nation in the treaty").

53. "Vorlage für das Politbüro des ZK der SED," prepared by the MfAA, 14 July 1972, p. 2, in J IV 2/2A/1.611 (Politbüro), SAPMO.

54. "NG über persönliche Unterredungen mit Staatssekretär Bahr am 16. August 1972," 17 Aug. 1972, p. 5, in J IV 2/2A/1.615 (Politbüro), SAPMO.

55. Document without title, dated 25 Sept. 1972, from content appears to be Soviet commentary on the SED directive for the next round of Kohl-Bahr talks, p. 2, in J IV 2/20.1/30 (Allg. Abt.), SAPMO.

56. Bahr let Kohl know on very short notice that he was going to the Soviet Union, which seems to have come as an unpleasant surprise to Kohl. See "Vermerk über zwei Gespräche mit dem Persönlichen Referenten von Staatssekretär Bahr, Dr. Eitel, am 30. September und 4. Oktober 1972," 4 Oct. 1972, in J IV 2/2J/4330 (IntVer), SAPMO. A Stasi transcript of part of the conversation on 4 October exists, probably produced by bugging the room; see "Bericht über das Gespräch zwischen den Herren Dr. Kohl (K) und Eitel (E) vom 4.10.1972," 4 Oct. 1972, pp. 184–85, in Rechtsstelle 120/5, ZA, BStU. This file also contains other documentation from the same date. See also Bahr, *Zu meiner Zeit*, 416–17, where Bahr claims that Honecker was apparently so infuriated by Bahr's trip that he arrogantly called Brezhnev and demanded to know what was going on. For further information on the West German side about Bahr's visit, see Arnulf Baring, *Machtwechsel: Die Ära Brandt-Scheel* (Stuttgart: Deutsche Verlags-Anstalt, 1982), 491.

57. On the Soviet-West German agreement of July 1972, see Bark and Gress, *Democracy and Its Discontents*, 170.

58. For Bahr's account of the trip, see Bahr, *Zu meiner Zeit*, 416–20.

59. "Betr. Verhandlungen mit der DDR über einen Grundvertrag; hier: Besuch StS Bahr in Moskau und laufende Runde der Verhandlungen Bahr/Kohl," in 431A, EBD, FES.

60. Document without title, dated 12 Oct. 1972, initialed by Erich Honecker on the same date, from content appears to be a summary of Bahr visit to Moscow, in J IV 2/202/493 (Allg. Abt.), SAPMO.

61. Bahr told Kohl that he had also discussed this compromise with Willy Brandt, Hans-Dietrich Genscher, and Walter Scheel. According to the summary that Kohl wrote up afterwards, Genscher and Scheel were opposed to it. Indeed, Genscher wrote in his memoirs that, throughout the Ostpolitik negotiations, he paid special attention to questions that touched on the prospects of unification. See Hans-Dietrich Genscher, *Erinnerungen* (Berlin: Siedler, 1995), 189. However, Scheel was about to leave on his trip to China; after his departure, Bahr was able to convince those who remained. See Michael Kohl, "Bahr im persönlichen Gespräch am 10.10," p. 1, in J IV 2/2J/4340 (IntVer), SAPMO.

62. See Beschlußprotokoll, 10 Oct. 1972, in J IV 2/2A/1.629 (Politbüro), SAPMO.

63. "Überlegungen der sowjetischen Seite zur Interpretation der sog. Frage der Nation bei den Grundlagenvertragsverhandlungen zwischen der DDR und der BRD," initialed by Erich Honecker on 26 Oct. 1972, in J IV 2/20.1/30 (Allg. Abt.), SAPMO. The Soviets suggested that Kohl accept the formulation "исходя из исторических условий и несмотря на различия во взглядах ГДР и ФРГ по принципиальным вопросам, в том числе

по вопросу о нации," which translates into German as "ausgehend von den historischen Gegebenheiten und ungeachtet der unterschiedlichen Auffassungen der DDR und der BRD zu grundsätzlichen Fragen darunter zur nationalen Frage," into English as "proceeding from the historical facts and without regard to the different views of the GDR and the FRG on fundamental questions, including the national question." This formulation is practically identical to that which actually appeared in the final treaty (changes shown in italics to emphasize the small differences): "ausgehend von den historischen Gegebenheiten und *unbeschadet* der unterschiedlichen Auffassungen *der Bundesrepublik Deutschland und der Deutschen Demokratischen Republik* zu grundsätzlichen Fragen, darunter zur nationalen Frage" ("Proceeding from the historical facts and *without prejudice* to the different views of the *Federal Republic of Germany and the German Democratic Republic* on fundamental questions, including the national question").

64. Peter Florin and Michael Kohl, "Vorlage für das Politbüro des ZK der SED," 30 Oct. 1972, in J IV 2/2A/1.635 (Politbüro), SAPMO, notes that "Grundlinie für die Verhandlungsführung des Genossen Kohl bleiben die in Übereinstimmung mit der sowjetischen Seite am 25.9 und 10.10. sowie am 24.10.1972 abgestimmten Direktiven" ("basis for the conduct of the negotiations by Comrade Kohl remain the directives agreed upon with the Soviet side on 25 September, 10 October, and 24 October").

65. Egon Bahr, "Vermerk," 12 Oct. 1971, in 378B, EBD, FES.

66. See "Vermerk über ein Gespräch mit Genossen Botschaftsrat Dr. Beletsky am 31. Oktober 1972, 9.00 Uhr," p. 101, in SdM 1837, ZA, BStU.

67. Bahr proposed this in early November; see "Stand der Verhandlungen mit der BRD," 4 Nov. 1972, p. 2, in J IV 2/2J/4388 (IntVer), SAPMO. (Some documents from the negotiations of 1–4 November also appear in Potthoff, *Bonn und Ost-Berlin*.) Bahr's proposal and the final letter were largely similar, indicating the intent of the FRG "auf einen Zustand des Friedens in Europa hinzuwirken, in dem das deutsche Volk in freier Selbstbestimmung seine Einheit wiedererlangt" ("to work toward a situation of peace in Europe, a situation in which the German people, in free self-determination, achieve unity once again"). For the final version, see Bundesministerium für innerdeutsche Beziehungen, *Zehn Jahre Deutschlandpolitik*, 206–7.

68. "Stenogramm des Freundschaftstreffens führender Vertreter der kommunistischen und Arbeiterparteien der sozialistischen Länder," 31 July 1972, in the Crimea, in IV 2/1/460 (ZK), SAPMO. Published as "Treffen der Ostblockführer am 31. Juli 1972 auf der Krim," Document No. 8 in Potthoff, *Bonn und Ost-Berlin*.

69. The meeting apparently took place at the beginning of July. Honecker wrote a brief follow-up note to Brezhnev about it on 24 August 1972 but did not illuminate what had been discussed. See letter from Honecker to Brezhnev, 24 Aug. 1972 (note typed on top reads "Zur internen Beratung der China-Frage") and appendix Выводы in J IV 2/202/542 (Allg. Abt.), SAPMO.

70. Bahr indicated to Kohl on 14 September that the FRG would shortly be establishing diplomatic relations with China; see "Vermerk für Erich Honecker, Willi Stoph, Hermann Axen, Erich Mielke, Otto Winzer, Peter Florin, Oskar Fischer," from Michael Kohl, 15 Sept. 1972, p. 1, in DC20-5590 (Stoph), BA-V.

71. How the Soviets knew this information is not revealed. See document without title, with "Information des ZK der KPdSU" and handwritten date 7 December 1972 at top, which refers to Scheel's visit to China in October 1972, in J IV 2/202/542 (Allg. Abt.), SAPMO.

72. Document without title, handwritten date of October 1972, in J IV 2/20.1/6 (Allg. Abt.), SAPMO (hereafter Kleindienst proposal) states that "Der Bevollmächtigte der BRD für Fragen des Handels mit der DDR Kleindienst (Ministerium für Wirtschaft und

Finanzen)" ("the plenipotentiary of the FRG for questions of trade with the GDR, Kleindienst [Ministry for Economics and Finance]") passed on this announcement on 10 October, which the East Germans then relayed to the Soviets.

73. Kleindienst proposal, 2. The swing credit never actually made it to a billion deutschmarks; the maximum reached was DM 850 million in the late 1980s. See Maria Haendcke-Hoppe-Arndt, "Interzonenhandel/Innerdeutscher Handel," in *Deutschland-politik, innerdeutsche Beziehungen und internationale Rahmenbedingungen*, Vol. 5 of *Materialien der Enquete-Kommission "Aufarbeitung von Geschichte und Folgen der SED-Diktatur in Deutschland*," edited by Deutscher Bundestag, (Baden-Baden/Frankfurt a.M.: Nomos Verlag/Suhrkamp Verlag, 1995), 1567.

74. Indeed, on 30 August, Bahr tried to convince Kohl using just this argument. See "NG über persönliche Unterredungen mit Staatssekretär Bahr am 30. und 31. August 1972," 9. Honecker showed some sympathy for it in a conversation with Bahr: see "Vermerk Gespräch mit Honecker am 7.9.1972 in seinem Büro," p. 10, in 380A, EBD, FES. Honecker also recommended that the two Germanies not try to address every open issue in the treaty proper; the SED leader felt that many issues could be addressed in supplementary protocol notes or letters exchanged on the day of the signing. What he did not add was that such appendices enjoyed an uncertain status; they would clearly be inferior to the treaty proper, but it was not clear by how much.

75. Quotation from the East German SN Bahr-Kohl, 15 June 1972, 22.

76. Quotation from the East German "Stenografische Niederschrift der Verhandlungen zwischen Staatssekretär Dr. Michael Kohl und Staatssekretär Egon Bahr über die Herstellung normaler Beziehungen zwischen der DDR und der BRD," p. 9, in J IV 2/2J/4259 (IntVer), SAPMO. The West German "Protokoll der Delegationssitzug anlässlich der 5. Begegnung der Staatssekretäre Bahr/Kohl zum Vertrag über die Grundlagen des Verhältnisses zwichen den beiden Staaten (1. Verhandlung) in Ostberlin im Hause des Ministerrates am 16. August 1972," p. 2, in 378B, EBD, FES, contains the summary of Bahr's comments to the effect that "Beide Staaten wollen die Perspektiven eines Friedensvertrages und einer Wiedervereinigung offenhalten" ("both states want to keep up the prospects of a peace treaty and reunification"), a claim with which the DGR side would surely have disagreed if it had known about it.

77. "Vermerk über das persönliche Gespräch mit Staatssekretär Bahr am 27.9.1972," p. 1, in DC20-5592 (SeKo), BA-V. See also the discussion of the topic offered by noted Soviet scholar Robin Edmonds in his *Soviet Foreign Policy 1962–1973: The Paradox of Super Power* (London: Oxford University Press, 1975), 93.

78. Document without title, dated 11 Oct. 1972, identified in catalogue as "Darlegungen der Moskauer Genossen zu den von Genossen Erich Honecker übermittelten Überlegungen für die weiteren Verhandlungen mit der BRD sowie der Entwurf der Direktiven für Genossen Michael Kohl, 10. Okt. 1972," p. 1, in J IV 2/2J/4339 (IntVer), SAPMO. What is perhaps a sign of internal conflict in Moscow over this issue appears in the Stasi archive. Five days earlier, the MfS received Russian-language suggestions for formulating a mention of the missing peace treaty; see untitled document from 6 Oct. 1972, p. 248, in Rechtsstelle 120/7, ZA, BStU. The document suggests the following formulations: "исходя из того, что мирного договора нет (или: принимая во внимание отсутствие мирного договора." These suggestions translate into German as "Ausgehend davon, daß es keinen Friedensvertrag gibt (oder: in Anbetract des fehlens eines Friedensvertrages)", into English as "Proceeding from the fact that there is no peace treaty (or: in consideration of the lack of a peace treaty)." The 11 October document, as well as Bahr's memoirs, suggest however that the willingness to make such a mention had evaporated by the time of Bahr's visit.

79. Bahr, *Zu meiner Zeit*, 419.

80. Note from Bahr to Brandt and Scheel, 27 Oct. 1972, in 445, EBD, FES.

81. "NG über eine persönliche Unterredung mit Staatssekretär Bahr am Vormittag des 12. Oktober 1972," p. 20, in J IV 2/2J/4341 (IntVer), SAPMO. In his summary of this conversation, Bahr mentioned that the issue of the peace treaty reference came up but did not go into details. See Egon Bahr, "Vermerk Betrifft: Persönliche Gespräche mit StS Kohl am 10., 11. und 12. Oktober 1972," 12 Oct. 1972, in 379, EBD, FES.

82. "Information über die Einschätzung des Verlaufs der Botschaftergespräche der vier Mächte vom 23.10. bis 6.11.1972 über die gemeinsame Erklärung zum UNO-Beitritt der DDR und der BRD," p. 44, in Rechtsstelle 0127, ZA, BStU.

83. "Zusammenfassender Bericht über die Verhandlungen zwischen Genossen Staatssekretär Dr. Kohl und Staatssekretär Bahr vom 24. bis 26. Oktober 1972 in Bonn," p. 2, in J IV 2/2J/4373 (IntVer), SAPMO. Bahr repeated this point clearly on 1 November 1972, according to Kohl. See "Bericht über ein Gespräch zwischen Genossen Dr. Kohl und Staatssekretär Bahr am 1. November 1972 (von 14.00 bis 16.45 im Hause des Ministerrates der DDR)," p. 3, in J IV 2/2J/4382 (IntVer), SAPMO. A sign of just how intimately involved the Soviets were in the details of the German-German negotiations survives in the Stasi archive. While Kohl and Bahr were discussing a mention of the four powers' rights, Beletzky from the Soviet embassy called with Soviet suggestions for wording. See "Anruf des Gen. Beletzky am 1.11.1972, 16.15 Uhr," p. 15, in Rechtsstelle 120/7, ZA, BStU.

84. Appeared as Article 9 of the Basic Treaty. See Bundesministerium für innerdeutsche Beziehungen, *Zehn Jahre Deutschlandpolitik*, 206.

85. See "Briefwechsel vom 21. Dezember 1972 mit dem Wortlaut der Noten der Regierung der Bundesrepublik Deutschland und der Regierung der Deutschen Demokratischen Republik zu Artikel 9 des Vertrages," Bundesministerium für innerdeutsche Beziehungen, *Zehn Jahre Deutschlandpolitik*, 210–11.

86. For an introduction to the cultural history approach to answering this question, see Erica Carter, "Culture, History and National Identity in the Two Germanies since 1945," 432–53, and John Breuilly, "The National Idea in Modern German History," 556–94, both in Mary Fulbrook, ed., *German History since 1800* (New York: St. Martin's, 1997).

87. Document without title, dated 11 Oct. 1972, p. 2, in J IV 2/2J/4339 (IntVer), SAPMO.

88. "Zusammenfassender Bericht über die Verhandlungen zwischen Staatssekretär Dr. Kohl und Staatssekretär Bahr vom 26.–28. September 1972 in Berlin," p. 6, in J IV 2/2J/4321 (IntVer), SAPMO.

89. "Abschrift 16.10.72 Gen. Honecker zur Übermittlung an Sts. Bahr," p. 145, in SdM 1837, ZA, BStU.

90. "Bericht über ein Gespräch zwischen Genossen Dr. Kohl und Staatssekretär Bahr am 1. November 1972 (von 14.00 bis 16.45 im Hause des Ministerrates der DDR)," 9. Bahr's summary of the same conversation, written three days later, does not mention this suggestion; see Egon Bahr, "Vermerk," 4 Nov. 1972, in 379, EBD, FES.

91. See "Vorbehalt zu Staatsangehörigkeitsfragen durch die Bundesrepublik Deutschland," in Bundesministerium für innerdeutsche Beziehungen, *Zehn Jahre Deutschlandpolitik*, 207.

92. "Hinweise zu Problemen im Zusammenhang mit dem Vertrag über die Grundlagen der Beziehungen der DDR mit der BRD," p. 2, in ZAIG 4635, ZA, BStU.

93. The author is grateful to James McAdams for pointing this out.

94. "Direktive für das Auftreten des Genossen Dr. Kohl beim Meinungsaustausch mit Staatssekretär Bahr am 15./16. Juni 1972."

95. Egon Bahr, "Vermerk Betrifft: Persönliches Gespräch mit Herrn Kohl am 21. Juni 1972 in Bonn, Bundeskanzleramt," p. 3, in 378A, EBD, FES.

96. "NG über persönliche Unterredungen mit Staatssekretär Bahr am 21. und 22. Juni in Bonn," pp. 6–7, in J IV 2/2J/4155 (IntVer), SAPMO.

97. Various summaries and protocols from the four-power meetings about a joint statement concerning German entry into the UN have survived in the Stasi archive. See "Information über die Einschätzung des Verlaufs der Botschaftergespräche der vier Mächte vom 23.10. bis 6.11.1972 über die gemeinsame Erklärung zum UNO-Beitritt der DDR und der BRD," 19 Dec. 1972, pp. 44–52, in Rechtsstelle 0127, ZA, BStU. See also the numerous records in SdM 1836. In SAPMO, see the papers in J IV J/2 (Büro Honecker), SAPMO. The files from Mielke's office contain various documents from these talks, conveyed to East Berlin by Moscow. One minor but interesting aspect of these documents is a cover note specifically stating that Kohl does not know that the MfS is in possession of this material. The MfS seems to have wanted to keep secrets even from its own. See half-slip of paper, "Teilinformation zur Beratung der vier Botschafter—übergeben von Genossen Beletzky am 3.11.1972, vormittag," p. 40 in SdM 1836, ZA, BStU.

98. Bahr informed Kohl on 13 September that he himself had told Kissinger that the FRG would cease to oppose the GDR's receiving observer status at the UN once the Basic Treaty was signed. Bahr said that Kissinger agreed and said that the United States would act similarly. See "NG über persönliche Unterredungen mit Staatssekretär Bahr am 13. und 14. September 1972," p. 7, in J IV 2/2J/4301 (IntVer), SAPMO. On the GDR attitude, see SN Bahr-Kohl, 28 June 1972, 16.

99. Portions of Brezhnev's letter to Brandt, an unofficial version of which arrived in Bonn in early August and an official version on 22 August 1972, are reprinted in Baring, *Machtwechsel*, 477–79.

100. Document without title, handwritten note at top "Information des ZK der KPdSU," initialed by Erich Honecker on 18 Sept. 1972, p. 4, in J IV 2/202/571 (Allg. Abt.), SAPMO.

101. "Beschluß des Politbüros des ZK der SED und des Ministerrates der DDR," *Neues Deutschland*, 8 Nov. 1972, 1.

102. "NG über persönliche Unterrednungen mit Staatssekretär Bahr am 12. Dezember 1972," 2.

103. "Vermerk über ein Gespräch des Mitglieds des Politbüros des ZK der SED Genosse Paul Verner mit dem Bundesminister Egon Bahr am 21.12.72", p. 5, in J IV 2/2J-4483 (IntVer), SAPMO.

104. Hans-Hermann Hertle, *Chronik des Mauerfalls: Die dramatischen Ereignisse um den 9. November 1989* (Berlin: Links, 1996), 45.

105. The original German term for "lawyer level" was "Anwaltsebene." On Vogel, see Craig R. Whitney, *Spy Trader: Germany's Devil's Advocate and the Darkest Secrets of the Cold War* (New York: Random House, 1993).

106. See the memoirs of the state secretary in the ministry responsible for the operative management of the dealings: Ludwig A. Rehlinger, *Freikauf: Die Geschäfte der DDR mit politisch Verfolgten 1963–1989* (Frankfurt: Ullstein, 1991). The FRG usually tried to pay in kind rather than in cash; on the means by which the GDR turned the goods back into cash, see Thomas Kleine-Brockhoff and Oliver Schröm, "Das Kirchengeschäft B," *Die Zeit*, 28 Aug. 1992.

107. See both the West German "Protokoll," 15 June 1972, 15–16; and the East German "Zusammenfassender Bericht über den Meinungsaustausch zwischen Staats-

sekretär Dr. Kohl und Staatssekretär Bahr am 15. Juni 1972," p. 6, in J IV 2/2J/4148 (IntVer), SAPMO.

108. "Von Bahr am 22. Juni 1972 entwickelte Vorstellungen der BRD zu Regelungen auf bestimmten Sachgebieten," p. 1, Anlage to "Zusammenfassender Bericht über den Meinungsaustausch zwischen Staatssekretär Dr. Kohl und Staatssekretär Bahr am 21. und 22. Juni 1972 in Bonn," in J IV 2/2J/4155 (IntVer), SAPMO.

109. Egon Bahr, "Vermerk Betr.: Persönliche Gespräche mit StS Kohl am 16. und 17. August 1972 in Ostberlin," 17 Aug. 1972, pp. 4–5, in 378B, EBD, FES. The German-language original of the exchange described above is as follows: "Zum Thema der Kinder erklärte er am 16.8., er hätte berichtet, sei aber nicht in der Lage, schon etwas sagen zu können. Ich habe ihm darauf erklärt, auch ich selbst würde nun keine Möglichkeit mehr sehen, eine öffentliche Auseindersetzung darüber zurückzuhalten, und ihn dringend gebeten, mit seinen zuständigen Stellen noch einmal zu sprechen. Er kam dann von sich aus am Abend darauf zurück. Er habe mit der höchsten möglichen Stelle gesprochen. Es handle sich um ein sehr schwieriges Probem. Die Sache werde sorgfältigst überprüft" (4–5).

110. See the West German version, ibid., 6; and the East German version, "NG über persönliche Unterredungen mit Staatssekretär Bahr am 16. August 1972," 17 August 1972, p. 14–15, in J IV 2/2A/1.1615 (Politbüro), SAPMO. Bahr also raised the issue of reuniting families again on 12 October; see "NG über eine persönliche Unterredung mit Staatssekretär Bahr am Vormittag des 12. Oktober 1972."

111. See "Vermerk," 30 Aug. 1972, and attachments, in J IV 2/2J/4289 (IntVer), SAPMO.

112. "NG über persönliche Unterredungen mit Staatssekretär Bahr am 30. und 31. August 1972," 14. The West German files from the same dates do not contain clear references to this sequence of events: see the various papers in 378B, EBD, FES.

113. Ibid., 19; and "Zusammenfassender Bericht über die *offiziellen* Verhandlungen zwischen Genossen Staatssekretär Dr. Kohl und Staatssekretär Bahr am 30./31. August 1972 in Bonn," p. 4, in J IV 2/2J/4289 (IntVer), SAPMO.

114. Document without title, date received 7 Sept. 1972, accompanied by cover note reading "Punkte, die von BAHR vorgetragen wurden und die er noch an anderer Stelle vorträgt," pp. 162–64, in Rechtsstelle 120/4, ZA, BStU. Bahr repeated this point clearly on 1 November 1972, according to Kohl: "Bericht über ein Gespräch zwischen Genossen Dr. Kohl und Staatssekretär Bahr am 1. November 1972 (von 14.00 bis 16.45 im Hause des Ministerrates der DDR)," 2.

115. "In Berlin die obligate Zwischenkrise?" *Der Spiegel*, 6 Nov. 1972, 23.

116. Document without title, handwritten note "zurück 18.08.72" on cover sheet, p. 2, in ZAIG 4634, ZA, BStU. The original German-language MfS quotation reads as follows: "Familien auseinandergrissen [*sic*] bzw. Kinder von ihren Eltern getrennt wurden, weil in der großen Mehrzahl aller bekannten Fälle sich Menschen gegenüber ihren Familienangehörigen, vor allem auch gegenüber ihren Kindern verantwortungslos verhielten, weil sie menschlich versagten, weil manche von ihnen kriminell in Erscheinung traten und sich ihrer gerechten Bestrafung entzogen." It should be noted that, according to GDR law, any attempt to flee East Germany was considered a criminal act, called "Republikflucht" (literally, "Republic-flight").

117. This worry received expression in a speech that Mielke gave and afterwards had distributed in written form to all MfS district branches. See the "Referat vor der Dienstkonferenz," 16 Nov. 1972, in Dok.-Nr. 102219, ZA, BStU.

118. Document without title, dated 25 September 1972, from content appears to be

Soviet commentary on the SED directive for the next round of Kohl-Bahr talks, p. 3, in J IV 2/20.1/30 (Allg. Abt.), SAPMO.

119. The document calling for fortifications is from a year earlier; see "Einige Fragen der Verwirklichung der Direktive des Sekretariats des Zentralkomitees vom 16. August 1961 an der Staatsgrenze West" (this document was approved by the Politbüro on 6 July 1971), p. 14, in J IV 2/2A/1.524, (Politbüro), SAPMO. According to a summary of the Politbüro meeting on 23 January 1973, "Bericht über die Durchführung der Direktive des Sekretariats des ZK zur weiteren Arbeit im Grenzgebiet an der Staatsgrenze zur BRD und zu Westberlin sowie Schlußfolgerungen für eine wirkungsvolle Grenzsicherung," p. 3, J IV 2/2A/1655 (Politbüro), SAPMO, the measures approved on 6 July 1971 went into effect on 1 September 1972. On this topic see also Peter Jochen Winters, "Wie souverän war die DDR?" *Deutschland Archiv* 2 (Mar./Apr. 1996): 170–72.

120. Author's interview with Bahr, 21 May 1996; and "NG über eine persönliche Unterredung mit Staatssekretär Bahr am Abend des 25. Oktober 1972," p. 2, in DC20-5596 (SeKo), BA-V. See also a memorandum from Bahr to Brandt on this topic: "Nur für den Bundeskanzler," 19 Oct. 1972, in 445, EBD, FES.

121. The Soviets had expressed a similar desire to Kissinger during his visit to Moscow in mid-September 1972; in particular, Moscow hoped to receive MFN (most favored nation) status. See document without title, handwritten note at top reads "Information des ZK der KPdSU," initialed by Erich Honecker on 18 Sept. 1972, p. 1, in J IV 2/202/571 (Allg. Abt.), SAPMO.

122. Garton Ash, *In Europe's Name*, 152.

123. Bundesministerium für innerdeutsche Beziehungen, *Zehn Jahre Deutschlandpolitik*, 28–29. For more details about the history of inner-German trade, see Haendcke-Hoppe-Arndt, "Interzonenhandel/Innerdeutscher Handel"; and Hartmut Zimmerman, *DDR Handbuch* (Cologne: Verlag Wissenschaft und Politik, 1985).

124. Quoted in Haendcke-Hoppe-Arndt, "Interzonenhandel/Innerdeutscher Handel," 1549.

125. "Information über die Haltung westdeutscher Regierungskreise zur weiteren Entwicklung des Handels DDR/BRD," 17 May 1972, p. 169, in HV A 383, ZA, BStU.

126. "Information über das Treffen der Partei- und Regierungsdelegationen der UdSSR und der DDR am 18. Mai 1971 in Moskau," p. 26, in J IV 2/2A/1.514 (Politbüro), SAPMO. Indeed, in April of 1972 the GDR had even needed to postpone repayment of credit given to it by the USSR. See Beschlußprotokoll from 4 Apr. 1972, in J IV 2/2A/1.585 (IntVer), SAPMO.

127. "Gespräch Bahr-Honecker am 7. September 1972 (Berlin-Ost)," p. 6, in 380A, EBD, FES.

128. Bundesministerium für innerdeutsche Beziehungen, *Zehn Jahre Deutschlandpolitik*, 28–29.

129. As explained in Zimmerman, *DDR Handbuch*, 645.

130. An internal West German note written by State Secretary Detlef Rohwedder also indicated that the FRG hoped to receive permission to construct new high-voltage power lines from Helmstedt to West Berlin. Note by Staatssekretär Dr. Rohwedder, 5 Nov. 1972, in HS privat Pz DDR 1966–74, Bd. I, HS PA.

131. "Anl. Direktive zum weiteren Vorgehen in der Verhandlung mit Staatssekretär Bahr am 2. und 3. November 1972," in J IV 2/2A/1.635 (Politbüro), SAPMO. The SED Politbüro recommended that certain concessions be made dependent thereupon, "daß unabhängig von den Verhandlungen über den Vertrag zur Regelung der Grundlagen der Beziehungen in den Verhandlungen zwischen Genossen Behrendt und Herrn Klein-

dienst im Verlauf der nächsten 8 Tage befriedigende langfristige Regelungen des Swings und der gegenseitigen Maschinenlieferungen erfolgen" ("that, independently of the Basic Treaty talks, in the course of the next 8 days the negotiations between Comrade Behrendt and Mr. Kleindienst should conclude satisfactory long-term agreements on swing credit and machinery deliveries on both parts").

132. First mentioned by Kohl to Bahr in "Vermerk über das persönliche Gespräch mit Staatssekretär Bahr am 27.9.1972," 4.

133. Michael Kohl, "Vermerk für Genossen Erich Honecker, Willi Stoph, Hermann Axen, Erich Mielke, Otto Winzer," 13 Oct. 1972, in Rechtsstelle 120/6, ZA, BStU.

134. Michael Kohl, "Vermerk über ein Gespräch mit Genossen Gorinowitsch am 14. Oktober 1972 um 18.30 in der sowjetischen Botschaft," p. 375, in SdM1837, ZA, BStU.

135. Ibid., 375.

136. Michael Kohl, "Vermerk für Genossen Erich Honecker, Willi Stoph, Paul Verner, Erich Mielke, Peter Florin, Betrifft: Ausschluß ehemaliger Republikflüchtiger von der Einreise in die DDR," 25 Oct. 1972, pp. 170–77, in Rechtsstelle 120/6, ZA, BStU.

137. "NG über eine persönliche Unterredung mit Staatssekretär Bahr am Abend des 25. Oktober 1972," p. 2–3, in DC20-5596 (SeKo), BA-V.

138. "Vermerk über persönliche Unterredungen mit Staatssekretär Bahr während der Verhandlungen vom 2. bis 4. November 1972," p. 4, in J IV 2/2J/4388 (IntVer), SAPMO. The German-language original of the discussion described above is as follows: "Bahr kam erneut auf das Thema der Zusammenführung von in der DDR lebenden Kindern mit ihren in der BRD lebenden Eltern zu sprechen. Wie vereinbart teilte ich ihm mit, daß nach der Paraphierung des Vertrages über die Grundlagen der Beziehungen 308 Kinder die Genehmigung zur Ausreise zu ihren in der BRD wohnenden Eltern erhalten würden. Ich gewährte ihm Einsicht in die entsprechende Liste, deren Übergabe ich für den Tag der Paraphierung zusagte."

139. This phrase appeared in Article 7 of the final treaty. See Bundesministerium für innerdeutsche Beziehungen, *Zehn Jahre Deutschlandpolitik*, 206.

140. See the "Briefwechsel vom 21. Dezember 1972 zur Familienzusammenführung, zu Reiseerleichterungen und Verbesserungen des nichtkommerziellen Warenverkehrs," appendix to the treaty, in Bundesministerium für innerdeutsche Beziehungen, *Zehn Jahre Deutschlandpolitik*, 208–9.

141. See Egon Bahr, "Vermerk," 4 Nov. 1972, p. 1, in 379, EBD, FES; and "NG über eine persönliche Unterredung von Genossen Kohl mit Staatssekretär Bahr in Bonn, 8.11.1972", p. 4, in J IV 2/2J/4392, (IntVer), SAPMO. Bahr even went so far as to pass the list on to the minister for inner-German affairs and tell him to notify the parents the same day that their minors would be leaving soon; see Bahr's note to Bundesminister Franke, 9 Nov. 1972, in 380A, EBD, FES. Ironically, at the same time that Kohl was getting involved in the most morally dubious aspect of dealing, he also received the distinction of a reception with Willy Brandt. Brandt wanted to convey his thanks for the work of the negotiators in reaching an agreement. See "Vermerk über einen Besuch bei Bundeskanzler Brandt am 8. November 1972," pp. 235–38 in Rechtsstelle 120/7, ZA, BStU.

142. See "Ergänzung zu dem Vermerk über das Gespräch mit Staatssekretär Bahr am 10. November 1972", p. 297, in Rechtsstelle 120/7, ZA, BStU. In other words, Bahr himself was personally involved in conversations about exchanging money for exit visas. Potthoff had criticized Bahr for only seeking to exchange partial recognition of the GDR for practical improvements in relations, thereby neglecting to use money as an incentive. Potthoff, "Zweite Etappe," 117. However these documents show that Potthoff's view

requires revision. SED files make it clear that while Bahr did indeed prefer to work on getting the GDR to accept manifestations of political recognition rather than money in exchange for humanitarian concessions, he was aware of the lure of, and indeed used, financial transfers as well.

143. See "Stenografische Niederschrift des Interviews des Ersten Sekretärs des ZK der SED, Erich Honecker, mit Mr. Sulzberger von der 'New York Times' am 22.11.1972," in J IV 2/201/1080 (Büro Honecker), SAPMO.

144. Karl Seidel, "Der Weg zum Grundlagenvertrag und zur Errichtung Ständiger Vertretungen. Erinnerungen eines Beteiligten," in *Deutschlandpolitiker der DDR erinnern sich*, edited by Detlef Nakath (Berlin: Fides, 1995), 203.

145. Technical talks for the signing indicate that, as late as the end of November, planners were working on the assumption that Brandt would visit the GDR. See "Kurzbericht über ein Gespräch zwischen Genossen Seidel und Herrn Sanne am 28.11.1972 über Fragen der Unterzeichnung des Vertrages über die Grundlagen der Beziehungen DDR/BRD," in DC20-5603 (SeKo), BA-V.

146. "3. Zur Haltung der Bevölkerung der DDR im Zusammenhang mit der Unterzeichnung des Vertrages in Berlin," no date but from context seems to be late November 1972, p. 6, in ZAIG 4636, ZA, BStU.

147. Document without title, handwritten date 11 December 1972, p. 1, in ZAIG 4638, ZA, BStU.

148. "Dank für Einladung einer DDR-Delegation zum 50. Jahrestag der Gründung der UdSSR nach Moskau," 12 Oct. 1972, in J IV 2/202/540 (Allg. Abt.), SAPMO.

149. "NG über persönliche Unterredungen mit Staatssekretär Bahr am 12. Dezember 1972," p. 1, in J IV 2/2J/4455 (IntVer), SAPMO.

150. Präsidium des Ministerrates, Vertrauliche Ministersache, "Beschluß zur Unterzeichnung des Vertrages über die Grundlagen der Beziehungen zwischen der Deutschen Demokratischen Republik und der Bundesrepublik Deutschland," 20 Dec. 1972, p. 256 in SdM 2399, ZA, BStU.

151. Isaacson, *Kissinger*, chap. 21.

152. As with the other German-German accords, the signing of the Basic Treaty was cause for an assessment of the practical implications of the accord for the work of the Ministry for State Security. See "Hinweise für die Kollegiumssitzung am 18.12.1972," pp. 1–7, in ZAIG 4640, ZA, BStU.

153. For a detailed analysis of the entire Basic Treaty, see Zündorf, *Die Ostverträge*, 211–319.

154. "NG über persönliche Unterredungen mit Staatssekretär Bahr am 12. Dezember 1972," 10–16.

155. See "Vermerk Gespräch mit Honecker am 7.9.1972 in seinem Büro," p. 6, in 380A, EBD, FES.

156. "NG über persönliche Unterrednungen mit Staatssekretär Bahr am 12. Dezember 1972," 16.

157. On the Kofferfälle, see Carsten Tessmer and Klaus Wiegrefe, "Deutschlandpolitik in der Krise: Herbert Wehners Besuch in der DDR 1973," *Deutschland Archiv* 6 (June 1994): 600–627.

158. Telegram from Horst Ehmke, head of the West German federal c1hancellery, to Michael Kohl, 30 Nov. 1972, pp. 43–45, in SdM 1837, ZA, BStU.

159. Bahr, *Zu meiner Zeit*, 436; see also Tessmer and Wiegrefe, "Krise," 603.

160. "Vermerk über ein Gespräch des Mitglieds des Politbüros des ZK der SED Genosse Paul Verner mit dem Bundesminister Egon Bahr am 21.12.72," 9. The SED transcript agrees in substance with Bahr's own summary of the meeting: "Vermerk über das

Gespräch von Bundesminister Bahr mit dem Sekretär des ZK der SED, Paul Verner, am 21. Dezember 1972 in Ostberlin," 21 Dec. 1972, in 445, EBD, FES.

161. "NG über persönliche Gespräche mit Minister Bahr am 21. Dezember 1972," p. 8, in J IV 2/2J/4483 (IntVer), SAPMO.

162. See, for example, "Gefangene des Friedens," *Der Spiegel*, 19 Feb. 1973, 30–31.

163. See Bahr's "Vermerk," 1 Mar. 1973, in 379, EBD, FES; and the East German "Bericht über das Gespräch zwischen Delegationen unter Leitung von Genossen Staatssekretär Dr. Kohl und Bundesminister Bahr am 28. Februar 1973," pp. 2–3, in J IV 2/2J/4572 (IntVer), SAPMO. Bahr noted that the atmosphere at the 28 February meeting was "frostig" (frosty) (p. 2).

164. See Bahr's "Vermerk," 1 Mar. 1973, 1; and the East German "NG über eine persönliche Unterredung mit Minister Bahr am 28. Februar 1973," p. 2, in J IV 2/2J/4580 (IntVer), SAPMO.

165. See both the West German summary (Chef BK, "Vermerk Betr.: Persönliches Gespräch mit Herrn Staatssekretär Kohl am 22. März 1973," 27 Mar. 1973, in 379, EBD, FES) and the East German "NG über persönliche Unterredungen mit Staatsekretär Horst Grabert am 22. März 1973", p. 8, in DC20-5613 (SeKo), BA-V; see also letter from Grabert to Kohl, 2 Apr. 1973, in DC20-5613 as well.

166. This was in keeping with the instructions given to him in "Direktive für das Gespräch zwischen Genossen Dr. Kohl und Bahr," in J IV 2/2A/1.663 (Politbüro), SAPMO.

167. See Chef BK, "Vermerk Betr.: Persönliches Gespräch mit Herrn Staatssekretär Kohl am 26. April 1973," 26 Apr. 1973, in 379, EBD, FES; and the East German "Bericht über das Gespräch zwischen Genossen Staatssekretär Kohl und Staatssekretär Grabert am 26. April 1973 im Bundeskanzleramt in Bonn" p. 6, in DC20-5614 (SeKo), BA-V.

168. Chef BK, "Vermerk Betr.," 27 Mar. 1973, 1.

169. As mentioned in the introduction, this is similar to the argument advanced in Robert H. Jackson and Carl Rosberg, "Why Africa's Weak States Persist: The Empirical and the Juridical in Statehood," *World Politics* 35 (1982): 1–24. This article makes the argument that African states sought international or juridicial recognition of their sovereignty to compensate for their lacking de facto, or empiricial, sovereignty (meaning the classic Weberian definition). This argument seems to apply well to the GDR as run by the SED, although it is difficult to document. The party was not given to saying in its documents that it, supposedly the party of the people, lacked legitimacy amongst the people.

170. "Niederschrift aus dem Gespräch über eine persönliche Unterredung mit Minister Bahr am 29. Juni 1973", p. 1, in J IV 2/2J/4785, (IntVer), SAPMO.

171. On the ratification process and the Bavarian legal challenge, see Bark and Gress, *Democracy and Its Discontents*, 218–21.

172. In an interview with the author in 1996, Egon Bahr said that he was of the opinion that Wehner did not play a role of much importance in top-level German-German politics before 1973. Potthoff, however, emphasizes the growing importance of the Honecker-Wehner channel after that time; see Potthoff, *Bonn und Ost-Berlin*, 39. See also Markus Wolf, *Spionagechef im geheimen Krieg* (Munich: List, 1997), 210–11.

173. On Wehner's visit, see Wehner's own summary of the event: Herbert Wehner, "Erster Bericht an den Parteivorstand der SPD" 1 June 1973, in Außenminister/Bundeskanzler 75, Willy Brandt Archive, FES. See also Baring, *Machtwechsel*, 608–14; and Tessmer and Wiegrefe, "Deutschlandpolitik in der Krise."

174. Potthoff, "Zweite Etappe," 120.

175. SED documents yielded no evidence for Bahr's suggestion that Wehner actually caused or initiated the "Kofferfälle" himself in some way, in order to play the hero by subsequently securing for them the right to exit. See Bahr, *Zu meiner Zeit*, 438.

176. Vogtmeier, "Sozialliberale Deutschlandpolitik," *Deutschland Archiv* 4 (July/Aug. 1997): 647.

177. "Information über das Gespräch des Genossen E. Honecker mit H. Wehner, 31. Mai 1973," p. 7, in J IV 2/2A/1688 (Politbüro), SAPMO . This document was published both in Wiegrefe und Tessmer, "Deutschlandpolitik in der Krise," 619–27; and in Potthoff, *Bonn und Ost-Berlin*, Document No. 14, 280–91.

178. "Information über das Gespräch des Genossen E. Honecker mit H. Wehner, 31. Mai 1973," 15.

179. This is the central argument of M. E. Sarotte, "Vor 25 Jahren: Verhandlungen über den Grundlagenvertrag. Zum internationalen Kontext der deutsch-deutschen Gespräche," *Deutschland Archiv* 6 (Nov/Dec. 1997): 901–11.

180. For further information on the Jackson-Vanik amendment, see Garthoff, *Détente and Confrontation*, 347–48.

181. See, for example, in the files of Hermann Axen, the Politbüro expert for foreign affairs, "Vermerk über ein Gespräch des Genossen O. B. Rachmanin, Mitglied der Zentralen Revisionskommission der KPdSU und stellvertretender Leiter einer Abteilung des ZK der KPdU, am 28. Februar in Moskau," pp. 28–29, in J IV 2/2.035/55 (Büro Axen), SAPMO.

182. "Niederschrift über ein Gespräch zwischen dem Generalsekretär des ZK der KPdSU, Genossen Leonid I. Breshnew, und dem Mitglied des Politbüros des ZK der SED und VdM der DDR, Genossen Willi Stoph, am 21.3.1973 im Kreml von 11.00–13.15 Uhr," p. 4, in DC20-4415 (Stoph), BA-V.

183. Ibid., 6.

184. Ibid., 3.

185. Ibid., 7.

186. Ibid.

187. "Vermerk über Gespräche des Genossen Winzer mit Genossen Gromyko am 12./13. Mai 1973," p. 123, in Rechtsstelle 128/2, ZA, BStU.

188. "Vermerk," (author unclear but probably Bahr), 7 May 1973, in 432, EBD, FES.

189. For a summary of Brezhnev's visit in the FRG, see document without title, dated 31 May 1973, from content seems to be Soviet summary of visit, in J IV 2/202/493 (Allg. Abt.), SAPMO.

190. "Stenografische Niederschrift der offiziellen Gespräche mit dem Generalsekretär des ZK der KPdSU, Genossen L. I. Breshnew, am 12. und 13.5.1973 in Berlin," identified in Findbuch as conversation with Honecker, pp. 24–25, in J IV 2/1/472 (ZK), SAPMO.

191. "Vorlage für das Politbüro," 1 June 1973, in J IV 2/2A/1692 (Politbüro), SAPMO.

192. "Sprechzettel für die Kabinettsitzung am 30. Mai 1973, Betr. Breschnew-Besuch," 29 May 1973, p. 2, notes under the heading "humanitäre Fragen" that the "Versicherung Bs. bei der Abreise, Sowjetunion werde Ausreien ermöglichen," in 435, EBD, FES. The notes from a conversation between Brandt and Brezhnev contain similar remarks; see "Aufzeichnung Vier Augen-Gespräch Bundeskanzler-Breschnjew, Freitag, 18. Mai 1973, 16.30–18.30," in 435, EBD, FES.

193. "Niederschrift aus dem Gespräch über eine persönliche Unterredung mit Minister Bahr am 29. Juni 1973," 1.

194. On the third Eastern treaty, the Prague treaty, see Bark and Gress, *Democracy and Its Discontents*, 222–23.

195. On UN membership, see Bark and Gress, *Democracy and Its Discontents*, 306–7.

196. Kohl, however, would return to the task by assuming the leadership of the GDR's permanent mission in the FRG.

Conclusion

1. Copy of letter from Egon Bahr to Axel Springer, 30 December 1969, in HS Privat-politisch 1970 Bd. 7, HS PA. The letter became public at the time; see Egon Bahr, *Zu meiner Zeit* (Munich: Blessing, 1996), 281.

2. A. James McAdams, *Germany Divided* (Princeton: Princeton University Press, 1993), 8.

3. Timothy Garton Ash, *In Europe's Name* (New York: Vintage, 1993). Political scientist Karl-Heinz Schmidt has argued in his study of German-German relations that the SED's main goal at all times was to achieve political recognition. While Schmidt has overstated his case, recognition was clearly the top priority on occasion. Karl-Heinz Schmidt, *Dialog über Deutschland: Studien zur Deutschlandpolitik von KPdSU und SED (1960–1979)* (Baden-Baden: Nomos, 1998), 338.

4. As mentioned in the Introduction, this conclusion challenges the hypothesis of Hope Harrison. See Hope M. Harrison, "Cold War International History Project: Ulbricht and the Concrete 'Rose': New Archival Evidence on the Dynamics of Soviet–East German Relations and the Berlin Crisis, 1958–1961" (Working Paper No. 5, Woodrow Wilson International Center for Scholars, Washington, D.C., May 1993), 7. Further details on specific documents are available in: H. M. Harrison, "Inside the SED Archives: A Researcher's Diary," *Cold War International History Project Bulletin* 2 (Fall 1992): 20, 28–32; and H. M. Harrison, "The Berlin Crisis and the Khrushchev-Ulbricht Summits in Moscow, 9 and 18 June 1959," *Cold War International History Project Bulletin* 11 (Winter 1998): 204–17.

5. In writings produced before archives were available, Edwina Moreton observed that the tight rein kept by the USSR on the GDR caused friction in Soviet–East German relations. See N. Edwina Moreton, ed., *Germany between East and West* (Cambridge: Cambridge University Press, 1987), 9. However, she argued that it was due to complete East German unwillingness to negotiate with FRG, which the analysis presented here shows not to have consistently been the case. See Moreton, *East Germany and the Warsaw Alliance: The Politics of Détente* (Boulder, Colo.: Westview, 1978), 201. Nonetheless, she was correct in identifying the strain that GDR-FRG negotiations placed on the relationship of the SED regime with the Soviet Union.

6. See the discussion of this issue in Chapter 3.

7. The most prominent among these is Monika Kaiser's biography of Ulbricht.

8. Jens Gieseke, *Die hauptamtlichen Mitarbeiter des Ministeriums für Staatssicherheit*, unnumbered volume, *MfS Handbuch: Anatomie der Staatssicherheit, Geschichte Struktur Methoden* (Berlin: BStU, Aug. 1995), 41.

9. Original phrasing in German (both quotes are contained in this statement): "Man muß sich hineindenken in diese Zeit. Wir wollten einen Beitrag zur Erhaltung des Friedens leisten. Was die DDR mit den Waren machte, war mir egal. Es ging doch um die Sache, und da hätte ich mit dem Teufel paktiert, um so ein paar arme Kerle aus dem Knast zu holen." Quoted in Thomas Kleine-Brockhoff and Oliver Schröm, "Das Kirchengeschäft B," *Die Zeit*, 28 Aug. 1992.

10. Author's interview with Egon Bahr, 21 May 1996.

11. For an overview of this literature, see Note on Sources.

12. There is a third alternative: to argue, as writers and philosophers such as Jean-Paul Sartre and Richard Rorty have, that "values and moral judgments are incommensurable between societies and epochs" and to then conclude, "As a result, we have no basis from which to assess the claims of innocence or guilt made in other places or in the past."

Quoted in Tony Judt, *Past Imperfect: French Intellectuals, 1944–1956* (Berkeley: University of California Press, 1992), 81.

13. Tony Judt, "Counsels on Foreign Relations," *New York Review of Books,* 13 Aug. 1998, 60.

14. Charles S. Maier, *Dissolution: The Crisis of Communism and the End of East Germany* (Princeton: Princeton University Press, 1997), 94.

15. John Lewis Gaddis predicted that scholars of the Cold War writing after the opening of Warsaw Pact archives would have to "take ideas seriously." John Lewis Gaddis, *We Now Know: Rethinking Cold War History* (Oxford: Clarendon, 1997), 283.

16. Gaddis, *We Now Know,* 290. On this topic, see also Nigel Gould-Davis, "Rethinking the Role of Ideology in International Politics during the Cold War," *Journal of Cold War Studies* (Winter 1999): 92.

17. As pointed out by Vojtech Mastny, the Soviets worried about the possibility of "a central European crisis in which deliberate or even casual Western instigation of political subversion might inadvertently provoke an armed clash leading to war." Vojtech Mastny, "Did NATO Win the Cold War? Looking Over the Wall," *Foreign Affairs* (May/ June 1999): 186.

18. Henry Kissinger, *WHY* (Boston: Little, Brown, 1979), 410.

19. Werner Link, "Vortrag," in Deutscher Bundestag, ed., *Deutschlandpolitik, innerdeutsche Beziehungen und internationale Rahmenbedingungen,* Vol. 5 of *Materialien der Enquete-Kommission "Aufarbeitung von Geschichte und Folgen der SED-Diktatur in Deutschland,"* (Baden-Baden/Frankfurt a.M.: Nomos Verlag/Suhrkamp Verlag, 1995), 437–39.

20. Raymond Garthoff, *Détente and Confrontation: American-Soviet Relations from Nixon to Reagan,* rev. ed. (Washington, D.C.: Brookings Institution, 1994), 24–25.

21. Heinrich August Winkler, "Rebuilding of a Nation: The Germans Before and After Unification," *Daedalus* 123 (Winter 1994): 111.

22. On the differences between Ostpolitik and détente, see Garthoff, *Détente,* 1171–74.

23. Wolfram Hanrieder, *Germany, America, Europe: Forty Years of German Foreign Policy* (New Haven: Yale University Press, 1989), passim.

24. Egon Bahr, *Zu meiner Zeit* (Munich: Blessing, 1996), 401.

25. Quoted in Chapter 2, note 21.

26. Garton Ash, *In Europe's Name,* chap. 8.

27. Quoted in Chapter 2.

28. Michael Sodaro, *Moscow, Germany and the West from Khrushchev to Gorbachev* (Ithaca: Cornell University Press, 1990).

29. Raymond Aron was one of the first contemporaries to publicize this insight. As explained by Tony Judt, "Raymond Aron was among the first in his generation to grasp the truth about post–World War II politics: that domestic and foreign conflicts were now intertwined and the traditional distinction between foreign policy and domestic policy had thus disappeared." Judt, *The Burden of Responsibility: Blum, Camus, Aron and the French Twentieth Century* (Chicago: University of Chicago Press, 1998), 156. Political scientist Heinrich End emphasized the importance of the international context in his *Zweimal Deutsche Außenpolitik* (Cologne: Verlag Wissenschaft und Politik, 1973). Wilhelm Bruns has discussed this phenomenon for the Schmidt era; see Bruns, *Deutschdeutsche Beziehungen* (Opladen, Ger.: Leske & Budrich Verlag, 1978), 18.

30. Indeed, Bundy has gone so far as to argue that the Soviets were actually in some regards in favor of the NATO presence in Europe, as long as it had strong U.S. leadership, because it "helped to restrain the weight and influence of West Germany." Bundy, *Tangled Web,* 113.

31. Kissinger, *WHY*, 821. Kissinger repeated this astonishment in his 1994 tome, *Diplomacy*: "That the Soviets should place such emphasis on West Germany's recognition of the borders established by Stalin in fact indicated weakness and insecurity. The Federal Republic, a rump state, was on the face of it in no position to challenge a nuclear superpower. At the same time, these treaties gave the Soviets a big incentive for restrained conduct at least while they were being negotiated and ratified. While the treaties were before the West German parliament, the Soviets were reluctant to do anything that could jeopardize their approval; afterward, they were careful not to drive Germany back toward the Adenauer policy. Thus, when Nixon decided to mine North Vietnamese harbors and resume the bombing of Hanoi, Moscow's response was muted." Henry Kissinger, *Diplomacy* (New York: Simon & Schuster, 1994), 736–37. Admittedly, Soviet "legalism," or confidence in the significance and viability of written accords, was not new. Externally, such legalism took the form of faith in such agreements as the Nazi-Soviet pact of non-aggression. Internally, examples of such legalism also emerged after Stalin's death, as Geoffrey Hosking has discussed, in an attempt to establish at least some minimal safeguards against a repeat of one-man terror. See Geoffrey Hosking, *The Awakening of the Soviet Union* (London: Heinemann, 1990), 143.

32. In 1975, Soviet specialist Robin Edmonds advanced the argument that the Moscow Treaty of 1970 should be considered the de facto peace treaty to World War II in Europe. This study finds that Edmond's assertion is an accurate description of how the Soviets viewed the USSR-FRG accord. Robin Edmonds, *Soviet Foreign Policy 1962–1973: The Paradox of Super Power* (London: Oxford University Press, 1975), 93.

Note on Sources

1. A minor problem is that SED documents do not always have page numbers. Sometimes there are page numbers, but they are not sequential (page 5 follows page 2), suggesting that editing has taken place. In this study, page numbers are given when they exist. Stasi documents have been numbered by the post-unification archive; these numbers are used instead of the original page numbers.

2. The archive of the Sozialistische Einheitspartei Deutschland is now an independent foundation within the German Federal Archive, called Stiftung/Archiv der Parteien und Massenorganisationen der DDR im Bundesarchiv, or SAPMO. Former GDR state documents have become part of the Federal Archive proper, called Bundesarchiv/Abteilung V, or BA-V. Stasi files are managed by the Bundesbeauftragte für die Unterlagen des Staatssicherheitsdienstes der ehemaligen Deutschen Demokratischen Republik, or BStU.

3. See my article about the discovery of these sources: M. E. Sarotte, "Wie der Osten es sah," *Die Zeit*, 24 Nov. 1995, 10.

4. An internal Bundesarchiv/SAPMO information sheet describes the office in the following way: "Die Allgemeine Abteilung war eine der wichtigsten Abteilungen im Parteivorstand/Zentralkomitee der SED gewesen. Sie war die Schaltstelle zum ZK der KPdSU, dessen Meinung seinerzeit für die SED absolut verbindlich war." ("The General Department was one of the most important departments in the party directorate/central committee of the SED. It was the crucial link to the central committee of the CPSU, whose opinions were at the time absolutely binding for the SED.")

5. Wilhelm Bruns, *Die Außenpolitik der DDR* (Berlin: Colloquium Verlag, 1985), 55.

6. Jonathan Haslam, "Russian Archival Revelations and Our Understanding of the Cold War," *Diplomatic History* 21 (Spring 1997): 217–28.

7. See list of interviews in the Bibliography.

8. The author thanks Egon Bahr, the board of directors of the Brandt Archive, and Frau Getrud Lenz for permission to use these sources, namely the Egon Bahr Depositorium (EBD) and the Willy Brandt Archiv (WBA), both in the Friedrich Ebert Stiftung (FES) in Bonn.

9. See Kissinger's own account of his dealings with Dobrynin in Henry Kissinger, *WHY* (Boston: Little, Brown, 1979), 112–14.

10. Some American documents seem to be open; according to Bill Burr of the National Security Archive, there are state department files available through 1969. However, the most important papers—the national security component of the Nixon papers, located in the National Archives, and Kissinger's own papers—were not open at the time of research. Theoretically, some American collections may switch to a 25-year delay, but as John Lewis Gaddis pointed out to the author, this switch will take some time to implement.

11. The most informative book on the German-German negotiations is not in fact a historical work but rather a careful summary by a participant. Antonius Eitel wrote a detailed account of the talks under the pen name Benno Zündorf: *Die Ostverträge* (Munich: C. H. Beck, 1979). The author thanks Dr. Eitel for the gift of a copy of this work, which is unfortunately out-of-print. See also the following scholarly works about the negotiations, listed in reverse chronological order: A. James McAdams, "The New Diplomacy of the West German *Ostpolitik*," in *The Diplomats, 1939–1979*, edited by Gordon A. Craig and Francis L. Loewenheim (Princeton: Princeton University Press, 1994), 537–63; Jack Snyder, "East-West Bargaining Over Germany: The Search for Synergy in a Two-Level Game," in *Double-Edged Diplomacy: International Bargaining and Domestic Politics*, edited by Peter B. Evans, Harold K. Jacobson, Robert D. Putnam (Berkeley: University of California Press, 1993), 104–27; Ernest D. Plock, *East German-West German Relations and the Fall of the GDR* (Boulder, Colo.: Westview, 1993); David M. Keithly, *Breakthrough in the Ostpolitik: The 1971 Quadripartite Agreement* (Boulder: Westview Press, 1986); and Ernest D. Plock, *The Basic Treaty and the Evolution of East-West German Relations* (Boulder, Colo.: Westview, 1986).

12. Klaus Hildebrand, *Von Erhard zur Großen Koalition 1963–1969* (Stuttgart: Deutsche Verlags-Anstalt, 1984), 462.

13. Ulrich Schröter, "Das leitende Interesse des Schreibenden als Bedingungsmerkmal der Verschriftung—Schwierigkeiten bei der Auswertung von MfS-Akten," in *Aktenlage: Die Bedeutung der Unterlagen des Staatssicherheitsdienstes für die Zeitgeschichtsforschung*, edited by Klaus-Dietmar Henke and Roger Engelmann (Berlin: Links, 1995), 40.

14. See Tagesordnungspunkt 3 at the meeting on 19 October 1971, in J IV 2/2A/1.547 (Politbüro), SAPMO. The entire meeting on 26 October 1971 was devoted to denouncing Ulbricht; in an unusual move, a "stenographic protocol" was produced. For an analysis of this meeting, see Jochen Stelkens, "Machtwechsel in Ost-Berlin: Der Sturz Walter Ulbrichts 1971," *Vierteljahrshefte für Zeitgeschichte* 4 (Oct. 1997).

15. See the various Bände of J IV 2/2/1360 (Politbüro), SAPMO. What seems to be Ulbricht's reply to the sharp criticism he was receiving appears in the Stasi archive. See "Antwort auf die Rede des Genossen Honecker im Politbüro vom 26. Oktober 1971," pp. 4–18, in SdM 1481, ZA, BStU.

16. "Stichwort-Protokoll über die Sitzung des Politbüros des ZKs am 26.10.1971," p. 49, in J IV 2/2/1360, Bd. 1 (Politbüro), SAPMO.

17. Heinrich Potthoff, *Bonn und Ost-Berlin 1969–1982: Dialog auf höchster Ebene und vertrauliche Kanäle Darstellung und Dokumente* (Bonn: Dietz, 1997), 16.

18. Roger Engelmann, "Zum Quellenwert der Unterlagen des Ministeriums für

Staatssicherheit," in Henke and Engelmann, *Aktenlage*, 23–39. In addition, Frank Petzold comes to a similar conclusion in "Zu einer elementaren MfS-Dienstvorschrift der achtziger Jahre für das Grenzregime," in Heiner Timmermann, ed., *Dikaturen in Europa im 20. Jahrhundert—Der Fall DDR* (Berlin: Duncker & Humblot, 1996), 328. He argues that relatively accurate reporting of events, not interpretation of them, was the task of the Stasi, and this reduced the arbitrariness of the reports.

19. On this practice of editing as documents were passed down the hierarchy, see Hans-Hermann Hertle and Gerd-Rüdiger Stephan, *Das Ende der SED* (Berlin: Links, 1997), 32 and fn. 26.

20. The author is indebted to Sylvia Gräfe, archivist at SAPMO, for this information.

21. At least three identical copies of the "calf-leather volume" have survived, all in SAPMO: J IV 2/2A/3195–6 (Politbüro), J NL 2/32 (Büro Ulbricht), and J IV A 158 (Büro Honecker).

22. Peter Przybylski, *Tatort Politbüro*, Vol. 1: *Die Akte Honecker* (Berlin: Rowohlt, 1991).

23. Czesław Miłosz, *The Captive Mind* (1953; reprint, London: Penguin, 1981).

24. Ibid., 54.

25. Ibid., 57.

26. Quoted in ibid., 57.

27. This system places the case workers in a difficult position between the upper level of the archive management, which wants to avoid any transgression against the law governing use of the Stasi archive, and users, who want as much material as possible released. Case workers also reportedly face difficulties in society at large; *Die Zeit* has reported that they often receive threats and are hesitant to give interviews in their own names. See *Die Zeit magazin*, 21 June 1996, 14–15.

28. The popular media carried reports of one such unexpected windfall: a computer specialist gained access to an electronic data bank. See "Das Pharaonengrab der Stasi," *Der Spiegel* (Mar. 1999), 32.

29. Siegfried Mampel, *Das Ministerium für Staatssicherheit der ehemaligen DDR als Ideologiepolizei: Zur Bedeutung einer Heilslehre als Mittel zum Griff auf das Bewußtsein für das Totalitarismusmodell.* (Berlin: Duncker & Humblot, 1996), 12.

30. For further discussion of this topic, see A. James McAdams, *Germany Divided* (Princeton: Princeton University Press, 1993), 11.

31. Put another way, this study focuses on elite decision-making. For a useful examination of elite decision-making, see Chalmers Johnson, *Revolutionary Change*, 2d ed. (Stanford: Stanford University Press, 1982). Johnson has rightly argued that elite intransigence, unwillingness to change, and inability to perceive changed external conditions play an important role in decision-making. For an application of Johnson's ideas to East Germany in 1989, see M. E. Sarotte, "Elite Intransigence and the End of the Berlin Wall," *German Politics* 2 (Aug. 1993): 270–87.

32. For readers' ease of reference, first references have been repeated in every chapter.

33. The following pre-1989 studies are especially worthwhile: Arnulf Baring, *Machtwechsel: Die Ära Brandt-Scheel* (Stuttgart: Deutsche Verlags-Anstalt, 1982); William E. Griffith, *The Ostpolitik of the Federal Republic of Germany* (Cambridge: MIT Press, 1978); P. C. Ludz, *Die DDR zwischen Ost und West* (Munich: Beck, 1977); N. Edwina Moreton, *East Germany and the Warsaw Alliance: The Politics of Détente* (Boulder, Colo.: Westview, 1978); Günther Schmid, *Die Deutschlandpolitik der Regierung Brandt/Scheel* (Munich: Tuduv Verlagsgesellschaft, 1975); Andreas Wilkens, *Der unstete Nachbar: Frankreich, die deutsche Ostpolitik und die Berliner Vier-Mächte-Verhandlungen, 1969–1974* (Munich:

Oldenbourg, 1990); and Vol. 5 of the multivolume K. D. Bracher, ed., *Geschichte der Bundesrepublik,* (Stuttgart: Deutsche Verlags-Anstalt; Mannheim: F. A. Brockhaus, 1986).

34. This essay focuses on works most useful in preparing this study, which was historical, archivally based research. However, I do not mean to convey the impression that the works discussed here in detail are the only ones worthwhile. Readers interested in the state of theoretical and political science scholarship on this era before (and shortly after) the archives opened should, to cite a few examples, seek out the following works: Karl Birnbaum, *Peace in Europe* (Oxford: Oxford University Press, 1970); Wilhelm Bruns, *Die Außenpolitik der DDR* (Berlin: Colloquium Verlag, 1985); Melvin Croan, *East Germany: The Soviet Connection* (Beverly Hills, Calif.: Sage, 1976); Heinrich End, *Zweimal deutsche Außenpolitik* (Cologne: Verlag Wissenschaft und Politik, 1973); Richard Löwenthal and Heinrich Vogel, eds., *Sowjetpolitik der 70er Jahre* (Stuttgart: Kohlhammer, 1972); Gert-Joachim Glaeßner, *Die DDR in der Ära Ostpolitik* (Opladen, Ger.: Westdeutscher Verlag, 1988); Richard Löwenthal, *Vom kalten Krieg zur Ostpolitik* (Stuttgart: Seewald Verlag, 1974); Martin McCauley, *The German Democratic Republic since 1945* (London: Macmillan, 1983); Hans-Peter Schwarz and Boris Meissner, eds., *Entspannungspolitik in Ost und West* (Cologne: Carl Heymanns, 1979); Peter Merkl, *German Foreign Policies, West & East* (Santa Barbara, Calif.: Clio, 1974).

35. Jens Hacker, *Deutsche Irrtümer: Schönfärber und Helfershelfer der SED-Diktatur im Westen* (Berlin: Ullstein, 1992), 453–54; and Konrad Löw, . . . *bis zum Verrat der Freiheit: Die Gesellschaft der Bundesrepublik und die "DDR"* (Munich: Langen Müller, 1993).

36. Timothy Garton Ash, *In Europe's Name: Germany and the Divided Continent* (New York: Vintage, 1993).

37. Ibid., 367.

38. Political scientist Manfred Wilke voiced regret about having done so in his testimony to the Enquete-Kommission, a committee set up by the unified German parliament to investigate the history of the GDR. As he testified: "Eins der beschämendsten Gespräche, das ich in diesem Zusammenhang erlebt habe, möchte ich zu Protokoll geben: Eine Kollegin an der Technischen Universität Berlin sagte mir 1979, sie wäre gestern in Ost-Berlin gewesen und hätte vergeblich versucht, ihren Bekannten zu erklären, wie glücklich sie doch sein müßten, daß sie diesen ganzen Konsumterror in der Bundesrepublik Deutschland nicht mitzumachen brauchten und nicht mit diesen Mallorca-Reisen behelligt würden. Das hat sie weder ironisch noch boshaft gemeint. Wie konnte es kommen, daß in vielen Kreisen der Bundesrepublik Deutschland so über die DDR-Verhältnisse diskutiert wurde?" ("I would like to put on the record one of the most shameful conversations that I have had concerning this context. In 1979, one of my colleagues at the Technical University of [West] Berlin told me that she had been in East Berlin the day before. She had tried, without success, to explain to her acquaintances there, how happy they must be to be spared the whole 'consumption terror' [pressure to consume] in the FRG. She had not meant that in an ironic or mean-spirited sense. How could it have come to pass, that in so many areas of the Federal Republic [of West Germany] this was how we discussed the conditions in the GDR?") Deutscher Bundestag, ed., *Deutschlandpolitik, innerdeutsche Beziehungen und internationale Rahmenbedingungen,* Vol. 5 of *Materialien der Enquete-Kommission "Aufarbeitung von Geschichte und Folgen der SED-Diktatur in Deutschland"* (Baden-/Frankfurt a.M.: Nomos Verlag/ Suhrkamp Verlag, 1995), 503.

39. Klaus Schroeder, ed., *Geschichte und Transformation des SED-Staates: Beiträge und Analysen* (Berlin: Akademie, 1994).

40. Peter Bender, *Die "Neue Ostpolitik" und Ihre Folgen: Vom Mauerbau bis zur Vereinigung* (Munich: dtv, 1995), 252.

41. Philip Zelikow and Condoleezza Rice, *Germany United and Europe Transformed: A Study in Statecraft* (Cambridge: Harvard University Press, 1995), 61. The author thanks Philip Zelikow for a conversation on this point.

42. One of the more useful works on an earlier time period is Norman Naimark, *The Russians in Germany: A History of the Soviet Zone of Occupation, 1945–1949* (Cambridge: Belknap Press of Harvard University Press, 1995).

43. On 1989, see, e.g., Manfred Görtemaker, *Unifying Germany 1989–1990* (New York: St. Martin's, 1994); Konrad Jarausch, *The Rush to German Unity* (New York: Oxford, 1994); Detlef Nakath and Gerd-Rüdiger Stephan, *Von Hubertusstock nach Bonn* (Berlin: Dietz, 1995) and *Countdown zur deutschen Einheit* (Berlin: Dietz, 1996); or Elizabeth Pond, *Beyond the Wall* (Washington, D.C.: Brookings, 1993). For a useful summary of literature on 1989, see Jost Dülffer, "Unification in the European Context," *German Historical Institute London Bulletin* 16 (Nov. 1994): 3–17.

44. Charles S. Maier, *Dissolution: The Crisis of Communism and the End of East Germany* (Princeton: Princeton University Press, 1997); McAdams, *Germany Divided*; and Hans-Hermann Hertle, *Der Fall der Mauer: Die unbeabsichtigte Selbstauflösung des SED-Staates* (Opladen, Ger.: Westdeutscher Verlag, 1996). A popular, illustrated version of the latter was published simultaneously: Hertle, *Chronik des Mauerfalls: Die dramatischen Ereignisse um den 9. November 1989* (Berlin: Links Verlag, 1996). See also Theo Pirker, M. Rainer Lepsius, Rainer Weinert, and Hans-Hermann Hertle, eds., *Der Plan als Befehl und Fiktion: Wirtschaftsführung in der DDR* (Opladen, Ger.: Westdeutscher Verlag, 1995), esp. the essay by Rainer Weinert, "Wirtschaftsführung unter dem Primat der Parteipolitik," 285–308.

45. Jeffrey Kopstein, *The Politics of Economic Decline in East Germany, 1945–1989* (Chapel Hill: University of North Carolina Press, 1997). See also Kopstein, "Ulbricht Embattled: The Quest for Socialist Modernity in the Light of New Sources," *Europe-Asia Studies* (formerly *Soviet Studies*) 46 (1994): 597–616.

46. Monika Kaiser, *Machtwechsel von Ulbricht zu Honecker: Funktionsmechanismen der SED-Diktatur in Konfliktsituationen 1962 bis 1972* (Berlin: Akademie, 1997).

47. Jochen Staadt, *Die geheime Westpolitik der SED 1960–1970: Von der Gesamtdeutschen Orientierung zur sozialistischen Nation* (Berlin: Akademie, 1993).

48. Heinrich Potthoff, ed., *Die Koalition der Vernunft: Deutschlandpolitik in den 80er Jahren* (München: dtv, June 1995), and Potthoff, *Bonn und Ost-Berlin*. See also Potthoff, "Im konspirativen Stil," *Spiegel*, 14 Oct. 1996, 60; and Potthoff, "Eine zweite Etappe der Deutschlandpolitik," *Deutschland Archiv* 1 (Jan./Feb. 1997): 116–24. For a review of Potthoff's ideas, see Andreas Vogtmeier, "Sozialliberale Deutschlandpolitik," *Deutschland Archiv* 4 (July/Aug. 1997): 645–47; and Gottfried Niedhart, "Motor der Entspannung," *Die Zeit*, 2 May 1997, 16.

49. Detlef Nakath, *Erfurt und Kassel: Zu den Gesprächen zwischen dem BRD-Bundeskanzler Willy Brandt und dem DDR-Ministerratsvorsitzenden Willi Stoph im Frühjahr 1970* (Berlin: Forscher- und Diskussionskreis DDR-Geschichte, 1995) and Nakath, *Die Verhandlungen zum deutsch-deutschen Grundlagenvertrag 1972: Zum Zusammenwirken von SED-Politbüro und DDR-Außenministerium bei den Gesprächen mit der BRD* (Berlin: Forscher- und Diskussionskreis DDR-Geschichte, 1993). See also Nakath, ed., *Deutschlandpolitiker der DDR erinnern sich* (Berlin: Fides, 1995), and Nakath, "Gewaltverzicht und Gleichberechtigung: Zur Parallelität der deutsch-sowjetischen Gespräche und der deutsch-deutschen Gipfeltreffen in Erfurt und Kassel im Frühjahr 1970," *Deutschland Archiv* 2 (Mar./Apr. 1998): 196–213.

50. William Bundy, *A Tangled Web: The Making of Foreign Policy in the Nixon Presidency* (New York: Hill and Wang, 1998); Raymond Garthoff, *Détente and Confrontation: American-Soviet Relations from Nixon to Reagan*, rev. ed. (Washington, D.C.: Brookings Institution, 1994); and W. R. Smyser, *From Yalta to Berlin* (New York: St. Martin's, 1999). Of works by Henry Kissinger, see *WHY*; *Years of Upheaval* (Boston: Little, Brown, 1982); and *Years of Renewal* (New York: Simon & Schuster, 1999). To name but three of the many works on Kissinger, I recommend William Burr, ed., *The Kissinger Transcripts: The Top-Secret Talks with Beijing & Moscow* (New York: New Press, 1998); Walter Isaacson, *Kissinger: A Biography* (New York: Simon & Schuster, 1992); and Robert Schulzinger, *Henry Kissinger: Doctor of Diplomacy* (New York: Columbia University Press, 1989).

51. John W. Young, *The Longman Companion to Cold War and Detente, 1941–1991* (London: Longman, 1993).

Bibliography

Primary Sources

Archival Collections

Bundesarchiv Abteilung V/I (BA-V), Potsdam
    Bestände der DDR
        Sekretariat Michael Kohl (SeKo)
        Ministerrat, including Sonderablage Stoph (Stoph)
        Staatliche Plankommission (SPK)
Since the conclusion of research for this project, this archive has moved to Berlin, to the same location as Stiftung/Archiv der Parteien und Massenorganisationen der DDR im Bundesarchiv, Berlin (see below).

Bundesarchiv, Koblenz
    Bildarchiv

Bundesbeauftragter für die Unterlagen des Ministeriums für Staatssicherheit (BStU)
    Zentrales Archiv Berlin (ZA), Berlin
Researchers are not allowed to view catalogues at this Stasi archive. Instead they must try, with the help of a case worker who is limited in what help he or she can offer, to guess which collections might exist and might be relevant to the topic at hand. The following departmental collections are those from which the author received documents. This list may nor may not reflect the organization of the currently inaccessible catalogues. In essence, what follows is an improvised catalogue produced from experience.

    The list below includes the department name, the abbreviation used in the endnotes (if any), and a departmental description. The departmental descriptions are summaries of information contained in BStU, ed., *Die Organisationsstruktur des Ministeriums für Staatssicherheit 1989* (Berlin: BStU, 1995), or *OMS*. This is the best guide currently available to the function of individual departments. Unfortunately (for this study), *OMS* primarily describes the status of the various departments as of 1989; however, the contents of files from the late 1960s and early 1970s suggest that the descriptions of departments from 1989 apply to the earlier time period as well.

    Abteilung 26 (Abt. 26): Telefonüberwachung, akustische Überwachung, optische und
        elektronische Beobachtung
    Befehle und Dokumente: Aktionen, Richtlinien, Reden
    Hauptabteilung VIII (HA VIII): Beobachtung, Ermittlung, Festnahme
    Hauptabteilung XVIII (HA XVIII): Sicherung der zentralen volkswirtschaftlichen
        Bereiche
    Hauptabteilung XIX (HA XIX): Verkehrswesen
    Hauptabteilung XX (HA XX): Aufdeckung und Verhinderung von "politisch-
        ideologischer Diversion" und "politischer Untergrundtätigkeit"
    Hauptamtliche Mitarbeiter (HM): Personalien
    Hauptverwaltung Aufklärung (HV A): Auslandsspionage
    Inoffizielle Mitarbeiter (IM): Personalien
    Juristische Hochschule (JHS): Ausbildung

Rechtsstelle (Rs): Mitwirkung an der Gestaltung von Gesetz- und Vertragsvorhaben
Sekretariat des Ministers (SdM): Persönliche Betreuung des Ministers
Zentrale Auswertungs- und Informationsgruppe (ZAIG): Erfassung, Auswertung
und Analysierung von Informationen

In addition to the sources listed above, the author also consulted the collection of duplicates of copies made for other researchers and the improvised "card catalogue" in the Popiolek office in Berlin.

Friedrich Ebert Stiftung (FES), Archiv der sozialen Demokratie, Bonn
Willy Brandt Archive (WBA)
Egon Bahr Depositorium (EBD)

Helmut Schmidt Privatarchiv (HS PA), Hamburg
HS privat (Panzerschrank) (Pz)
HS privat Pz Innenpolitisch
HS privat Pz UdSSR
Schriftwechsel
Presseecho

National Security Archive, Washington, D.C.
Nuclear History
Berlin Crisis Collection

*Stiftung / Archiv der Parteien und Massenorganisationen
der DDR im Bundesarchiv (SAPMO), Berlin*
SED-Parteiarchiv
Abteilung Internationale Politik und Wirtschaft
Abteilung Internationale Verbindungen (IntVer)
Abteilung Kaderfragen
Abteilung Parteiorgane
Abteilung Sicherheitsfragen
Allgemeine Abteilung (Allg. Abt.)
Außenpolitische Kommission
Büro Axen
Büro Honecker
Büro Mittag
Büro Norden
Büro Ulbricht
Nachlaß Ulbricht
Parteitage
Protokolle der Sitzungen des Politbüros, Arbeitsprotokolle and
    Reinschriftenprotokolle (Politbüro)
Sekretariat
Tagungen Parteivorstand/ZK ()

At the time this book was written, the GDR collections were still in the process of being catalogued and incorporated into the German archive system; hence, the Signaturen, or documentary call numbers, may be subject to change. For example, since research for this project was concluded, the call number "DY 30" has been added to the front of every call number for documents from the former SED archive. Hence, readers planning to use documents mentioned in this text should add "DY 30" to the beginning of every SAPMO call number. Similarly, when I reviewed them, certain documents had temporary numbers —for example, "vorl. SED 41656" ("vorl." being an abbreviation for "*vorläufig*" or "temporary")—which may have been changed.

Published Primary Sources

Auswärtiges Amt, ed. *Außenpolitik der Bundesrepublik Deutschland: Dokumente 1949 bis 1994*. Cologne: Verlag Wissenschaft und Politik, 1995.

Bundesministerium für innerdeutsche Beziehungen, ed. *Zehn Jahre Deutschlandpolitik: Die Entwicklung der Beziehungen zwischen der Bundesrepublik Deutschland und der Deutschen Demokratischen Republik 1969–1979*. Bonn: Bundesministerium, Feb. 1980.

Burr, William, ed. *The Kissinger Transcripts: The Top Secret Talks with Beijing and Moscow*. New York: New Press, 1998.

Crampton, Richard, and Ben Crampton. *Atlas of Eastern Europe in the Twentieth Century*. London: Routledge, 1996.

Deutscher Bundestag, 12. Wahlperiode, Enquete-Kommission. *Bericht der Enquete-Kommission "Aufarbeitung von Geschichte und Folgen der SED-Diktatur in Deutschland."* Bonn: Bundestag Drucksache 12/7820, 31 May 1994.

———, 13. Wahlperiode, Enquete-Kommission. *Bericht der Enquete-Kommission "Überwindung der Folgen der SED-Diktatur im Prozeß der deutschen Einheit."* Bonn: Bundestag Drucksache 13/11000, 10 June 1998.

"Dokumentation: Politbüro Prozeß." *Deutschland Archiv* 2 (Mar./Apr. 1996): 312–22.

Fischer, Horst, ed. *Schalck-Imperium: Ausgewählte Dokumente*. Bochum: Brockmeyer, 1993.

Grenville, J. A. S., and Bernard Wasserstein, eds. *The Major International Treaties since 1945: A History and Guide with Texts*. London: Methuen, 1987.

Mahnke, Hans-Heinrich, ed. *Dokumente zur Berlin-Frage 1967–1986*. Munich: R. Oldenbourg Verlag, 1987.

Mayall, James, and Cornelia Navari, eds. *The End of the Post-War Era: Documents on Great-Power Relations 1968–1975*. Cambridge: Cambridge University Press, 1980.

Министерство иностранных дел СССР, Министерство иностранных дел ГДР. *Четырехстороннее соглашение по Западному Берлину и его реализация 1971–1977 гг. Документы* (Москва: Издательство политической литературы, 1977.

Meissner, Boris, ed. *Die deutsche Ostpolitik 1961–1970 Kontinuität und Wandel Dokumentation*. Cologne: Verlag Wissenschaft und Politik, 1970.

———. *Moskau Bonn Die Beziehungen zwischen der Sowjetunion und der Bundesrepublik Deutschland 1955–1973 Dokumentation*. Cologne: Verlag Wissenschaft und Politik, 1975.

Mitter, Armin, and Stefan Wolle, eds. *Ich liebe euch doch alle! Befehle und Lageberichte des MfS Januar–November 1989*. Berlin: BasisDruck, 1990.

Public Papers of the Presidents of the United States: Richard Nixon. 5 vols., 1969–1973. Washington, D.C.: U.S. Government Printing Office, 1971–75.

Richard Nixon Library and Birthplace Foundation. "Transcripts of Newly Released White House Tapes." 25 Feb. 1999. Available on the Internet at www.nixonfoundation.org.

Schweitzer, C. C., et al., eds. *Politics and Government in the Federal Republic of Germany, Basic Documents*. Leamington Spa, Vt.: Berg, 1984.

Stasi-Unterlagen-Gesetz. Munich: C. H. Beck, Oct. 1993.

"Verurteilungen verstoßen nicht gegen das Rückwirkungsverbot: Beschluß des Bundesverfassungsgerichts." *Deutschland Archiv* 1 (Jan./Feb. 1997): 166–68.

Von Münch, Ingo, ed. *Dokumente des geteilten Deutschland*. 2 vols. Stuttgart: Kröner, 1976.

Weber, Hermann, ed. *DDR: Dokumente zur Geschichte der Deutschen Demokratischen Republik*. Munich: dtv, 1986.

Zimmerman, Hartmut. *DDR Handbuch*. Cologne: Verlag Wissenschaft und Politik, 1985.

Interviews and Conversations

Formal Interviews

Bahr, Egon. 21 May 1996, Bonn; 13–15 Nov. 1997, Vienna (conversation at Bruno Kreisky Forum conference on Ostpolitik)

Bräutigam, Hans-Otto. 7 Mar. 1996, Potsdam

Ehmke, Horst. 21 May 1996, by telephone

Eitel, Antonius. 20 Sept. 1996, New York City

Falin, Valentin. 17 May 1996, Tostedt; 13–15 Nov. 1997, Vienna (conversation at Bruno Kreisky Forum conference on Ostpolitik)

Gaus, Günter. 16 May 1996, Reinbek, near Hamburg

Görner, Gunter. 7 June 1996, Erfurt

Sahm, Ulrich. 12 July 1996, by telephone

Seidel, Karl. 25 Mar. 1996, Berlin

Wolf, Markus. 6 June 1996, Berlin

Informal Conversations

Bender, Peter. 18 Apr. 1996, Berlin

Leicht, Robert. 20 Dec. 1995, Hamburg

Leonhard, Wolfgang. 22 May 1996, by telephone

Schmidt, Helmut. 31 May 1997, Madison, Wisc.

Writings by or Published Interviews with Participants in Events

Абрасимов, П.А. *Западный Берлин вчера у сегодня*. Москва: Междунар. отношения, 1980.

Andert, Reinhold, and Wolfgang Herzberg, ed. *Der Sturz: Erich Honecker im Kreuzverhör*. Berlin: Aufbau-Verlag, 1990.

Axen, Hermann, with Harald Neubert. *Ich war ein Diener der Partei*. Berlin: Edition Ost, 1996.

Bahr, Egon. *Zu meiner Zeit*. Munich: Karl Blessing, 1996.

Barzel, Rainer. *Es ist noch nicht zu spät*. Munich: Droemer Knaur, 1976.

Brandt, Willy. *Begegnungen und Einsichten: Die Jahre 1960–1975*. Hamburg: Hoffmann & Campe, 1976.

——. *My Life in Politics*. Translated by Anthea Bell. New York: Viking, 1992.

——. *". . . was zusammengehört."* Bonn: Dietz, 1993.

Brezhnev, Zbigniew. *The Grand Failure: The Birth and Death of Communism in the Twentieth Century*. New York: Scribner and Sons, 1989.

Bundy, William. *A Tangled Web: The Making of Foreign Policy in the Nixon Presidency*. New York: Hill and Wang, 1998.

Cramer, Dettmar. *gefragt: Egon Bahr*. Bornheim, Ger.: Dagmar Zirngibl, 1974.

Dobrynin, Anatoly. *In Confidence: Moscow's Ambassador to America's Six Cold War Presidents (1962–1986)*. New York: Random House, 1995.

Ehmke, Horst. *Mittendrin*. Berlin: Rowohlt, 1994.

Ehmke, Horst, Karlheinz Koppe, and Herbert Wehner, eds. *Zwanzig Jahre Ostpolitik: Bilanz und Perspektiven*. Bonn: Neue Gesellschaft, 1986.

Falin, Valentin. *Politische Erinnerungen*. Munich: Knaur, 1995.

Gaus, Günter. *Wo Deutschland liegt*. Hamburg: Hoffmann & Campe, 1983.

Genscher, Hans-Dietrich. *Erinnerungen*. Berlin: Siedler, 1995. Abridged English translation: *Rebuilding a House Divided*. Translated by Thomas Thornton. New York: Broadway, 1998.

"Günter Mittags Rolle in der DDR-Wirtschaft: Fritz Schenk im Gespräch mit Gerhard Schürer." *Deutschland Archiv* 6 (1994): 633–37.

Громыко, А. А. *Памятное* Кн. 1.-2-е. Москва: издательство политической литературы, 1990. Abridged English translation: Gromyko, Andrei. *Memoirs*. Translated by Harold Shukman. New York: Doubleday, 1989.

Hager, Kurt. *Erinnerungen*. Leipzig: Faber & Faber, 1996.

Holdridge, John H. *Crossing the Divide: An Insider's Account of the Normalization of U.S.-China Relations*. Lanham, Md.: Rowman & Littlefield, 1997.

Institut für Marxismus-Leninismus beim ZK der SED, ed. *1949–1989 Vierzig Jahre*. Berlin: Institut für Marxismus-Leninismus, 1989.

Keworkow, Wjatscheslaw. *Der geheime Kanal*. Berlin: Rowohlt, Mar. 1995.

Kissinger, Henry. *Diplomacy*. New York: Simon & Schuster, 1994.

———. *White House Years* (first volume of memoirs). Boston: Little, Brown, 1979.

———. *Years of Renewal* (third volume of memoirs). New York: Simon & Schuster, 1999.

———. *Years of Upheaval* (second volume of memoirs). Boston: Little, Brown, 1982.

Leonhard, Wolfgang. *Die Revolution entläßt ihre Kinder*. Cologne/Berlin: Kiepenheuer & Witsch, 1955.

———. *Spurensuche*. Cologne: Kiepenheuer & Witsch, 1992.

Miłosz, Czesław. *The Captive Mind*. 1953. Reprint, London: Penguin, 1981.

Mlynář, Zdeněk. *Nachtfrost: Erfahrungen auf dem Weg vom realen zum menschlichen Sozialismus*. Cologne: Europäische Verlagsanstalt, 1978.

Modrow, Hans, ed. *Das Große Haus: Insider berichten aus dem ZK der SED*. Berlin: Edition Ost, 1994.

Najman, Maurice. *L'oeil de Berlin: Entretiens de Maurice Najman avec le patron des services secrets est-allemands*. Paris: Editions Balland, 1992.

Nixon, Richard. *The Memoirs of Richard Nixon*. New York: Grosset & Dunlap, 1978.

Przybylski, Peter. *Tatort Politbüro*. Vol. 1, *Die Akte Honecker*. Berlin: Rowohlt, Apr. 1991.

———. *Tatort Politbüro*. Vol. 2, *Honecker, Mittag und Schalck-Golodkowski*. Berlin: Rowohlt, 1992.

Rehlinger, Ludwig A. *Freikauf: Die Geschäfte der DDR mit politisch Verfolgten 1963–1989*. Frankfurt: Ullstein, 1991.

Runger, Irene, and Uwe Stelbrink. *Markus Wolf: "Ich bin kein SPION," Gespräche mit Markus Wolf*. Berlin: Dietz, 1990.

Sahm, Ulrich. *"Diplomaten taugen nichts": Aus dem Leben eines Staatsdieners*. Düsseldorf: Droste, 1994.

Schirdewan, Karl. *Aufstand gegen Ulbricht*. Berlin: Aufbau Taschenverlag, 1994.

Schürer, Gerhard. *Gewagt und Verloren*. Frankfurt/Oder: Frankfurt Oder Editionen, 1996.

Smith, Gerard. *Doubletalk: The Story of the First Strategic Arms Limitation Talks*. New York: Doubleday, 1980.

Stiller, Werner. *Im Zentrum der Spionage*. Mainz: von Hase & Koehler, 1986.

Uschner, Manfred. *Die Ostpolitik der SPD: Sieg und Niederlage einer Strategie*. Berlin: Dietz, 1991.

Wolf, Markus. *Die Troika*. Berlin/Weimar: Aufbau-Verlag, and Düsseldorf: Claassen Verlag, 1989.

——. *Im Eigenen Auftrag*. Munich: Schneekluth, 1991.

——. *Spionagechef im geheimen Krieg: Erinnerungen*. Munich: List, 1997.

Wolf, Markus, with Anne McElvoy. *Man without a Face: The Autobiography of Communism's Greatest Spymaster*. New York: Random House, 1997.

Zündorf, Benno [pseudonym for Antonius Eitel]. *Die Ostverträge: Die Verträge von Moskau, Warschau, Prag, das Berlin-Abkommen und die Verträge mit der DDR*. Munich: C. H. Beck, 1979.

Secondary Sources

Abteilung Bildung und Forschung, ed. *Wissenschaftliche Reihe des Bundesbeauftragten für die Unterlagen des Staatssicherheitsdienstes der ehemaligen Deutschen Demokratischen Republik*.

Vol. 1, Klaus-Dietmar Henke and Roger Engelmann. *Aktenlage: Die Bedeutung der Unterlagen des Staatssicherheitsdienstes für die Zeitgeschichtsforschung*. Berlin: Links Verlag, 1995.

Vol. 2, Karl Wilhelm Fricke. *Akten-Einsicht: Rekonstruktion einer politischen Verfolgung*. Berlin: Links Verlag, 1995.

Vol. 3, Helmut Müller-Enbergs, ed. *Inoffizielle Mitarbeiter des Ministeriums für Staaatssicherheit: Richtlinien und Durchführungsbestimmungen*. Berlin: Links Verlag, 1996.

Vol. 4, Matthias Braun. *Drama um eine Komödie: Das Ensemble von SED und Staatssicherheit, FDJ und Ministerium für Kultur gegen Heiner Müllers "Die Umsiedlerin oder Das Leben auf dem Lande" im Oktober 1961*. Berlin: Links Verlag, 1996.

Vol. 5, Siegfried Suckut, ed. *Das Wörterbuch der Staatssicherheit: Definitionen zur "politisch-operativen Arbeit."* Berlin: Links Verlag, 1996.

Vol. 6, Joachim Walter. *Sicherungsbereich Literatur: Schriftsteller und Staatssicherheit in der Deutschen Demokratischen Republik*. Berlin: Links Verlag, 1996.

Vol. 7, Clemens Vollnhals, ed. *Die Kirchenpolitik von SED und Staatssicherheit*. Berlin: Links Verlag, 1996.

Vol. 8, Siegfried Suckut and Walter Süß, eds. *Staatspartei und Staatssicherheit: Zum Verhältnis von SED und MfS*. Berlin: Links Verlag, 1997.

Vol. 9, Walter Süß. *Staatssicherheit am Ende. Warum es den Mächtigen nicht gelang, 1989 eine Revolution zu verhindern.*Berlin: Links Verlag, 1999.

Allin, Dana H. *Cold War Illusions: America, Europe, and Soviet Power, 1969–1989*. New York: St. Martin's, 1994.

Ambrose, Stephen E. *Nixon: The Triumph of a Politician, 1962–1972*. New York: Simon & Schuster, 1989.

Andrén, Nils, and Karl E. Birnbaum, eds. *Beyond Détente: Prospects for East-West Cooperation and Security in Europe*. The Netherlands: Sijthoff, 1976.

Andrew, Christopher, and Oleg Gordievsky. *KGB: The Inside Story of Its Foreign Operations from Lenin to Gorbachev*. New York: HarperCollins, 1990.

Asmus, Ronald D., J. F. Brown, and Keith Crane. *Soviet Foreign Policy and the Revolutions of 1989 in Eastern Europe*. Santa Monica, Calif.: RAND, 1991.

Arendt, Hannah. *The Origins of Totalitarianism*. New York: Harcourt Brace, 1973.

Baring, Arnulf. *Machtwechsel: Die Ära Brandt-Scheel.* Stuttgart: Deutsche Verlags-Anstalt, 1982.
———. *Der 17. Juni 1953.* 2d ed. Stuttgart: Deutsche Verlags-Anstalt, 1983.
Bark, Dennis L., and David R. Gress. *A History of West Germany.* 2 vols. 2d ed. Oxford: Blackwell, 1993.
Bauerkämpfer, Arnd. " 'Eliten' als Problem der historischen Forschung? Egalitärer Anspruch und gesellschaftliche Konstruktionspolitik." *Potsdamer Bulletin für Zeithistorische Studien* 7 (Aug. 1996): 48–53.
Bender, Peter. *Die "Neue Ostpolitik" und ihre Folgen: Vom Mauerbau bis zur Vereinigung.* 2d ed. Munich: dtv, Feb. 1995.
———. *Episode oder Epoche? Zur Geschichte des geteilten Deutschlands.* Munich: dtv, Apr. 1996.
Bessel, Richard, and Ralph Jessen, eds. *Die Grenzen der Diktatur: Staat und Gesellschaft in der DDR.* Göttingen: Vandenhoeck & Ruprecht, 1996.
Bideleux, Robert, and Ian Jeffries. *A History of Eastern Europe: Crisis and Change.* London: Routledge, 1998.
Birnbaum, Karl E. *East and West Germany: A Modus Vivendi.* Lexington, Mass.: Lexington Books, 1973.
———. *Peace in Europe: East-West Relations 1966–1968 and the Prospects for a European Settlement.* Oxford: Oxford University Press, 1970.
Bohnsack, Günter, and Herbert Brehmer. *Auftrag Irreführung. Wie die Stasi Politik im Westen machte.* Hamburg: Carlsen, 1992.
Boyle, Peter G. *American-Soviet Relations: From the Russian Revolution to the Fall of Communism.* London: Routledge, 1993.
Bracher, Karl Dietrich, Wolfgang Jäger, and Werner Link. *Republik im Wandel 1969–1974: Die Ära Brandt.* Vol. 5, *Geschichte der Bundesrepublik Deutschland,* edited by K. D. Bracher, Theodor Eschenburg, Joachim C. Fest, and Eberhard Jäckel. Stuttgart: Deutsche Verlags-Anstalt; and Mannheim: F. A. Brockhaus, 1986.
Bruns, Wilhelm. *Deutsch-deutsche Beziehungen.* Opladen, Ger.: Leske & Budrich Verlag, 1978.
———. *Die Außenpolitik der DDR.* Berlin: Colloquium Verlag, 1985.
———, ed. *Die Ost-West Beziehungen am Wendepunkt?* Bonn: Verlag Neue Gesellschaft, 1988.
———. *Die UNO-Politik der DDR.* Stuttgart: Verlag Bonn Aktuell, 1978.
Bundesbeauftragter für die Unterlagen des Staatssicherheitsdienstes der ehemaligen Deutschen Demokratischen Republik (BStU), ed. *Zweiter Tätigkeitsbericht des Bundesbeauftragten für die Unterlagen des Staatssicherheitsdienstes der ehemaligen Deutschen Demokratischen Republik.* Berlin: BStU, 1995.
Catudal, Honoré M. *A Balance Sheet of the Quadripartite Agreement on Berlin: Evaluation and Documentation.* Berlin: Berlin Verlag, 1978.
———. *The Diplomacy of the Quadripartite Agreement on Berlin: A New Era in East-West Politics.* Berlin: Berlin Verlag, 1978.
Childs, David. *The GDR: Moscow's German Ally.* 2d ed. London: Unwin Hyman, 1988.
———, ed. *Honecker's Germany.* London: Allen & Unwin, 1985.
Childs, David, and Richard Popplewell. *The Stasi: The East German Intelligence and Security Service.* London: Macmillan, 1996.
Childs, David, Thomas A. Baylis, and Marilyn Rueschemeyer, eds. *East Germany in Comparative Perspective.* London: Routledge, 1989.

Clemens, Clay. *Reluctant Realists: The Christian Democrats and West German Ostpolitik.* Durham, N.C.: Duke University Press, 1989.

Colitt, Leslie. *Spymaster: The Real-Life Karla, His Moles, and the East German Secret Police.* Reading: Addison-Wesley, 1995.

Courtois, Stéphane, et al. *Le livre noir du Communisme: Crimes, terreur, répression.* Paris: Laffont, 1997. Published in English as *The Black Book of Communism: Crimes, Terror, Repression.* Translated by Jonathan Murphy and Mark Kramer. Cambridge: Harvard University Press, 1999.

Craig, Gordon, and Alexander George. *Force and Statecraft: Diplomatic Problems of Our Time.* New York: Oxford University Press, 1983.

Craig, Gordon A., and Francis L. Loewenheim, eds. *The Diplomats, 1939–1979.* Princeton: Princeton University Press, 1994.

Croan, Melvin. *East Germany: The Soviet Connection.* Beverly Hills, Calif.: Sage, 1976.

Cronin, James E. *The World the Cold War Made: Order, Chaos, and the Return of History.* New York: Routledge, 1996.

Dau, Wolfgang, Helmut Bärwald, and Robert Becker. *Herbert Wehner: Zeit seines Lebens.* Wiesbaden: Ebner Ulm, 1986.

Daschitschew, Wjatscheslaw. "Die Wechselwirkung der gegenseitigen Beziehungen zwischen der Bundesrepublik Deutschland, der DDR und der Sowjetunion im Zeitraum 1970–1989." *Deutschland Archiv* 12 (Dec. 1993): 1460–88.

Dennis, Mike. *German Democratic Republic: Politics, Economics and Society.* London: Pinter, 1988.

Deutscher Bundestag, ed. *Materialien der Enquete-Kommission "Aufarbeitung von Geschichte und Folgen der SED-Diktatur in Deutschland."* 9 vols. Baden-Baden/Frankfurt a.M.: Nomos Verlag/Suhrkamp Verlag, 1995.
  Vol. 1, *Die Enquete-Kommission "Aufarbeitung von Geschichte und Folgen der SED-Diktatur in Deutschland."*
  Vol. 2, *Machtstrukturen und Entscheidungsmechanismen im SED-Staat und die Frage der Verantwortung.*
  Vol. 3, *Rolle und Bedeutung der Ideologie, integrativer Faktoren und disziplinierender Praktiken in Staat und Gesellschaft der DDR.*
  Vol. 4, *Recht, Justiz und Polizei im SED-Staat.*
  Vol. 5, *Deutschlandpolitik, innerdeutsche Beziehungen und internationale Rahmenbedingungen.*
  Vol. 6, *Rolle und Selbstverständnis der Kirchen in den verschiedenen Phasen der SED-Diktatur.*
  Vol. 7, *Möglichkeiten und Form abweichenden und widerständigen Verhaltens und oppositionellen Handelns, die friedliche Revolution im Herbst 1989, die Wiedervereinigung Deutschlands und Fortwirken von strukturen und Mechanismen der Diktatur.*
  Vol. 8, *Das Ministerium für Staatssicherheit-Seilschaften, Altkader, Regierungs- und Vereinigungskriminalität.*
  Vol. 9, *Formen und Ziele der Auseinandersetzung mit den beiden Diktaturen in Deutschland.*

Dülffer, Jost. "Unification in the European Context." *German Historical Institute London Bulletin* 16 (Nov. 1994): 3–17.

Dunbabin, J. P. D. *The Cold War: The Great Powers and Their Allies.* London: Longman, 1994.

Eberstadt, Nicholas. "Hastening Korean Reunification." *Foreign Affairs* (Mar./Apr. 1997): 77–92.

Edmonds, Robin. *Soviet Foreign Policy 1962–1973: The Paradox of Super Power*. London: Oxford University Press, 1975.

Eisenberg, Carolyn Woods. *Drawing the Line: The American Decision to Divide Germany: 1944–1949*. Cambridge: University Press, 1996.

End, Heinrich. *Zweimal deutsche Außenpolitik*. Cologne: Verlag Wissenschaft und Politik, 1973.

Engelmann, Roger, and Paul Erker. *Annäherung und Abgrenzung*. Munich: Oldenbourg, 1993.

Evans, Peter B., Harold K. Jacobson, and Robert D. Putnam, eds. *Double-Edged Diplomacy: International Bargaining and Domestic Politics*. Berkeley: University of California Press, 1993.

Fehér, Ferenc, Agnes Heller, and György Markus. *Dictatorship over Needs*. New York: St. Martin's, 1983.

Fink, Carole, Philipp Gassert, and Detlef Junker, eds. *1968: The World Transformed*. New York: Cambridge University Press, 1998.

Freeze, Gregory L., ed. *Russia: A History*. Oxford: Oxford University Press, 1997.

Freudenhammer, A., and K. Vater. *Herbert Wehner: Ein Leben mit der deutschen Frage*. Munich: Bertelsmann, 1978.

Fricke, Karl-Wilhelm. "Grundrechtsgarantie und DDR-Grenzregime: Zum Beschluß des Bundesverfassungsgerichts vom 24. Oktober 1996." *Deutschland Archiv* 1 (Jan./Feb. 1997): 4–6.

———. *MfS intern: Macht, Strukturen, Auflösung der DDR-Staatssicherheit. Analyse und Dokumentation*. Cologne: Wissenschaft und Politik, 1991.

———. "Ordinäre Abwehr—elitäre Aufklärung? Zur Rolle der Hauptverwaltung A im Ministerium für Staatssicherheit." *Aus Politik und Zeitgeschichte* 50 (5 Dec. 1997): 17–26.

———. "Wolfs Schuld." *Deutschland Archiv* 4 (July/Aug. 1997): 523–25.

Fricke, Karl Wilhelm, and Bernhard Marquardt. *DDR Staatssicherheit: Das Phänomen des Verrats Die Zusammenarbeit zwischen MfS und KGB*. Bochum: Brockmeyer, 1995.

Fuchs, Stephan. *"Dreiecksverhältnisse sind immer kompliziert": Kissinger, Bahr und die Ostpolitik*. Hamburg: Europäische Verlagsanstalt, 1999.

Fulbrook, Mary. *Anatomy of a Dictatorship: Inside the GDR 1949–1989*. Oxford: Oxford University Press, 1995.

———. *A Concise History of Germany*. 2d ed. Cambridge: Cambridge University Press, 1991.

———, ed. *German History since 1800*. New York: St. Martin's, 1997.

Furet, François. *The Passing of an Illusion: The Idea of Communism in the Twentieth Century*. Chicago: University of Chicago Press, 1999.

Fursenko, Aleksandr, and Timothy Naftali. *"One Hell of a Gamble": Khrushchev, Castro, and Kennedy, 1958–1964*. New York: Norton, 1997.

Gaddis, John Lewis. *Strategies of Containment: A Critical Appraisal of Postwar American National Security Policy* Oxford: Oxford University Press, 1982.

———. *We Now Know: Rethinking Cold War History*. Oxford: Clarendon, 1997.

Gaiduk, Ilya V. "The Vietnam War and Soviet-American Relations, 1964–1973: New Russian Evidence." *Cold War International History Project Bulletin* 6/7 (Winter 1995/1996): 232, 250–58.

Garthoff, Raymond L. *Détente and Confrontation: American-Soviet Relations from Nixon to Reagan*. Rev. ed. Washington, D.C.: Brookings Institution, 1994.

———. "Détente and Deterrence in the Cold War." *Diplomatic History* 22 (Winter 1998): 145–48.

Garton Ash, Timothy. *In Europe's Name: Germany and the Divided Continent*. New York: Vintage, 1993.

——. *We the People*. London: Granta, 1990.

Gasteyger, Curt. *Europa zwischen Spaltung und Einigung 1945 bis 1993*. Bonn: Bundeszentrale für politische Bildung, 1994.

"Germany and the Cold War." *Cold War International History Project Bulletin* 4 (Fall 1994): 34–49.

George, Alexander. "The 'Operational Code': A Neglected Approach to the Study of Political Decision-Making." *International Studies Quarterly* 12 (June 1969): 190–222.

Geyer, Martin H. "Deutscher Sport und die 'Hallstein Doktrin.' " *Vierteljahrshefte für Zeitgeschichte* 1 (1996): 55–86.

Gieseke, Jens. *Die hauptamtlichen Mitarbeiter des Ministeriums für Staatssicherheit*. Berlin: BStU, Aug. 1995.

Gildea, Robert. *France since 1945*. Oxford: Oxford University Press, 1996.

Gill, David, and Ulrich Schröter. *Das Ministerium für Staatssicherheit Anatomie des Mielke Imperiums*. Berlin: Rowohlt, 1991.

Gilles, Franz-Otto, and Hans-Hermann Hertle. "Sicherung der Volkswirtschaft." *Deutschland Archiv* 1 (Jan. 1996): 48–57.

Glaeßner, Gert-Joachim, ed. *Die DDR in der Ära Honecker*. Opladen, Ger.: Westdeutscher Verlag, 1988.

Glaeßner, Gert-Joachim, and Ian Wallace, eds. *The German Revolution of 1989: Causes and Consequences*. Oxford: Berg, 1992.

Glees, Anthony. *Reinventing Germany: German Political Development since 1945*. Oxford: Berg, 1996.

Golz, Hans-Georg. "Dem Alltag in der Diktatur gerecht werden: Internationales Kolloquium zur DDR- und Deutschlandforschung." *Deutschland Archiv* 2 (Mar./Apr. 1997): 277–79.

——. " 'Maßnahmen der Zersetzung.' Eine Ausstellung des BStU und neue Forschungsergebnisse." *Deutschland Archiv* 1 (Jan./Feb. 1997): 6–7.

Görtemaker, Manfred. *Unifying Germany 1989–1990*. New York: St. Martin's, 1994.

Gould-Davis, Nigel. "Rethinking the Role of Ideology in International Politics during the Cold War." *Journal of Cold War Studies* (Winter 1999): 90–109.

Grafe, Roman. " 'Niemals Zweifel gehabt': Der Prozeß gegen die Grenztruppen-Führung der DDR." *Deutschland Archiv* 6 (Nov./Dec. 1996): 862–71.

——. "Die Strafverfolgung von DDR-Grenzschützen und ihren Befehlsgebern: Eine vorläufige Bilanz." *Deutschland Archiv* 3 (May/June 1997): 377–80.

Griffith, William E. *The Ostpolitik of the Federal Republic of Germany*. Cambridge: MIT Press, 1978.

Grosser, Alfred. *Affaires Extérieures: La Politique de la France 1944–1989*. Saint-Amand, Fr.: Flammarion, 1989.

Hacker, Jens. *Deutsche Irrtümer: Schönfärber und Helfershelfer der SED-Diktatur im Westen*. Berlin: Ullstein, 1992.

Haendcke-Hoppe, Maria, and Erika Lieser-Triebnigg, eds. *40 Jahre innerdeutsche Beziehungen*. Berlin: Duncker & Humblot, 1990.

Hagen, Manfred. *DDR—Juni '53* Stuttgart: Steiner, 1992.

Hanrieder, Wolfram. *Germany, America, Europe: Forty Years of German Foreign Policy*. New Haven: Yale University Press, 1989.

Harrison, Hope M. "The Berlin Crisis and the Khrushchev-Ulbricht Summits in Moscow, 9 and 18 June 1959." *Cold War International History Project Bulletin* 11 (Winter 1998): 204–17.

——. "Cold War International History Project: Ulbricht and the Concrete 'Rose': New Archival Evidence on the Dynamics of Soviet–East German Relations and the Berlin Crisis, 1958–1961." Working Paper No. 5, Woodrow Wilson International Center for Scholars, Washington, D.C., May 1993.

——. "Inside the SED Archives: A Researcher's Diary." *Cold War International History Project Bulletin* 2 (Fall 1992): 20, 28–32.

Harrison, Selig S. "Promoting a Soft Landing in Korea." *Foreign Policy* (Spring 1997): 57–75.

Harsch, Donna. "Society, the State, and Abortion in East Germany, 1950–1972." *American Historical Review* 102 (Feb. 1997): 53–84.

Haslam, Jonathan. "Russian Archival Revelations and Our Understanding of the Cold War." *Diplomatic History* 21 (Spring 1997): 217–28.

——. *The Soviet Union and the Politics of Nuclear Weapons in Europe 1969–1987: The Problem of the SS-20.* London: Macmillan, 1989.

Held, Joseph, ed. *The Columbia History of Eastern Europe in the Twentieth Century.* New York: Columbia University Press, 1992.

Hendry, I. D., and M. C. Wood. *The Legal Status of Berlin. A Publication of the Research Centre for International Law, University of Cambridge.* Cambridge: Grotius, 1987.

Henke, Klaus-Dietmar. *Die amerikanische Besetzung Deutschlands.* Munich: Oldenbourg, 1995.

——, ed. *Wann bricht schon mal ein Staat zusammen! Die Debatte über die Stasi-Akten auf dem 39. Historikertag 1992.* Munich: dtv, June 1993.

Henke, Klaus-Dietmar, and Roger Engelmann, eds., *Aktenlage: Die Bedeutung der Unterlagen des Staatssicherheitsdienstes für die Zeitgeschichtsforschung.* Berlin: Links, 1995.

Herrmann, David. *The Arming of Europe and the Making of the First World War.* Princeton: Princeton University Press, 1996.

Hersh, Seymour. *The Price of Power: Kissinger in the Nixon White House.* New York: Summit, 1983.

Hertle, Hans-Hermann. *Chronik des Mauerfalls: Die dramatischen Ereignisse um den 9. November 1989.* Berlin: Links, 1996.

——. *Der Fall der Mauer: Die unbeabsichtigte Selbstauflösung des SED-Staates.* Opladen, Ger.: Westdeutscher Verlag, 1996.

Hertle, Hans-Hermann, and Igor F. Maximytschew. "Der Fall der Berliner Mauer." *Deutschland Archiv* 11 (Nov. 1994): 1145–58.

——. " 'Die Situation ist seit 1953 nie so ernst gewesen!' Wie die sowjetische Botschaft Unter den Linden die Wende in der DDR miterlebte." *Deutschland Archiv* 11 (Nov. 1994): 1137–44.

——. "Nach dem Fall der Mauer der Weg zur friedlichen Lösung: Anfang und Ende der Vorbereitung eines militärischen Einsatzes." *Deutschland Archiv* 12 (Dec. 1994): 1241–51.

Hertle, Hans-Hermann, and Gerd-Rüdiger Stephan, eds. *Das Ende der SED.* Berlin: Links, 1997.

Heydemann, Günther, and Christopher Beckmann. "Zwei Diktaturen in Deutschland: Möglichkeiten und Grenzen des historischen Diktaturenvergleichs." *Deutschland Archiv* 1 (Jan./Feb. 1997): 12–40.

Hildebrand, Klaus. *Von Erhard zur Großen Koalition 1963–1969.* Vol. 4, *Geschichte der Bundesrepublik Deutschland,* edited by K. D. Bracher, Theodor Eschenburg, Joachim C. Fest, and Eberhard Jäckel. Stuttgart: Deutsche Verlags-Anstalt, 1984.

Hirsch, Rudolf. *Der Markus Wolf Prozeß.* Berlin: Brandenburgisches Verlagshaus, 1994.

Hirschmann, Albert O. "Exit, Voice, and the Fate of the German Democratic Republic: An Essay in Conceptual History." *World Politics* 45 (Jan. 1993): 173–202.

Hogan, Michael J. *America in the World: The Historiography of American Foreign Relations since 1941.* New York: Cambridge University Press, 1995.

Holzweißig, Gunter. *Zensur ohne Zensor: Die SED-Informationsdiktatur.* Bonn: Bouvier Verlag, 1997.

Hosking, Geoffrey. *The Awakening of the Soviet Union.* London: Heinemann, 1990.

Huelshoff, Michael G., Andrei S. Markovits, and Simon Reich. *From Bundesrepublik to Deutschland: German Politics after Unification.* Ann Arbor: University of Michigan Press, 1993.

Isaacson, Walter. *Kissinger: A Biography.* New York: Simon & Schuster, 1992.

Jäckel, Eberhard. *Das deutsche Jahrhundert.* Stuttgart: Deutsche Verlags-Anstalt, 1996.

Jackson, Robert H. *Quasi-States: Sovereignty, International Relations, and the Third World.* New York: Cambridge University Press, 1990.

Jackson, Robert H., and Carl Rosberg. "Why Africa's Weak States Persist: The Empirical and the Juridical in Statehood." *World Politics* 35 (1982): 1–24.

Jacobsen, Hans-Adolf, Gert Leptin, Ulrich Scheuner, and Eberhard Schulz, eds. *Drei Jahrzehnte Außenpolitik der DDR.* Munich: R. Oldenbourg Verlag, 1979.

Jarausch, Konrad. *The Rush to German Unity.* New York: Oxford, 1994.

Joas, Hans, and Martin Kohli, eds. *Der Zusammenbruch der DDR.* Frankfurt: Suhrkamp, 1993.

Johnson, Chalmers. *Revolutionary Change.* 2d ed. Stanford: Stanford University Press, 1982.

Jowitt, Ken. *New World Disorder: The Leninist Extinction.* Berkeley: University of California Press, 1992.

Judt, Tony. *The Burden of Responsibility: Blum, Camus, Aron and the French Twentieth Century.* Chicago: University of Chicago Press, 1998.

——. *Past Imperfect: French Intellectuals, 1944–1956.* Berkeley: University of California Press, 1992.

Kaelble, Hartmut, Jürgen Kocka, and Hartmut Zwahr, eds. *Sozialgeschichte der DDR.* Stuttgart: Klett-Cotta, 1994.

Kaiser, Monika. *Machtwechsel von Ulbricht zu Honecker: Funktionsmechanismen der SED-Diktatur in Konfliktsituationen 1962 bis 1972.* Berlin: Akademie, 1997.

Keithly, David M. *Breakthrough in the Ostpolitik: The 1971 Quadripartite Agreement.* Boulder, Colo.: Westview, 1986.

Kershaw, Ian. *The "Hitler Myth": Image and Reality in the Third Reich* Oxford: Oxford University Press, 1987.

——. *The Nazi Dictatorship: Problems and Perspectives of Interpretation.* 3d ed. London: Edward Arnold, 1993.

——. *Popular Opinion and Political Dissent in the Third Reich: Bavaria 1933–1945.* Oxford: Clarendon Press, 1983.

Kimball, Jeffrey. *Nixon's Vietnam War.* Lawrence: University of Kansas Press, 1998.

Knabe, Hubertus. "Die Stasi als Problem des Westens. Zur Tätigkeit des MfS im 'Operationsgebiet.' " *Aus Politik und Zeitgeschichte* 50 (5 Dec. 1997): 3–16.

——. *Die "West-Arbeit" des MfS und ihre Wirkungen: Bericht des BStU an die Enquete-Kommission des Deutschen Bundestages "Überwindung der Folgen der SED-Diktatur im Prozeß der deutschen Einheit.* Berlin: BStU, 1998.

Koch, Peter-Ferdinand. *Das Schalck-Imperium lebt: Deutschland wird gekauft.* Munich: Piper, 1992.

Kocka, Jürgen, ed. *Historische DDR-Forschung: Aufsätze und Studien.* Berlin: Akademie, 1993.

Koop, Volker. *Ausgegrenzt: Der Fall der DDR-Grenztruppen.* Berlin: Brandenburgisches Verlagshaus, 1993.

Kopstein, Jeffrey. *The Politics of Economic Decline in East Germany, 1945–1989.* Chapel Hill: University of North Carolina Press, 1997.

——. "Ulbricht Embattled: The Quest for Socialist Modernity in the Light of New Sources." *Europe-Asia Studies* (formerly *Soviet Studies*) 46 (1994): 597–616.

Kowalczuk, Ilko-Sascha, Armin Mitter, and Stefan Wolle, eds. *Der Tag X 17. Juni 1953.* Berlin: Links, 1995.

Krasner, Stephen. "Compromising Westphalia." *International Security* 20 (Winter 1995/96): 115–51.

——. *Sovereignty: Organized Hypocrisy.* Princeton: Princeton University Press, 1999.

Kumanoff, Nicolas, ed. *Aspen Institute Berlin Conference on Germany and the Stasi Files: Between Justice and Reconciliation.* Berlin: Aspen Institute, 1995.

Küntzel, Matthias. *Bonn and the Bomb.* Boulder, Colo.: Pluto, 1995.

Kunz, Diane B. *Butter and Guns: America's Cold War Economic Diplomacy.* New York: Free Press, 1997.

Kwizinskij, Julij A. [Yuli Kvizinski]. *Vor dem Sturm: Erinnerungen eines Diplomaten.* Berlin: Siedler, 1993.

LaFeber, Walter. *America, Russia, and the Cold War: 1945–1992.* 7th ed. New York: McGraw Hill, 1993.

Larres, Klaus, ed. *Germany since Unification: The Domestic and External Consequences.* London: Macmillan, 1998.

Larres, Klaus, and Torsten Oppelland, eds. *Deutschland und die USA im 20. Jahrhundert: Geschichte der politischen Beziehungen.* Darmstadt, Ger.: Wissenschaftliche Buchgesellschaft, 1997.

Leffler, Melvyn P., and David S. Palmer, eds. *Origins of the Cold War: An International History.* New York: Routledge, 1994.

Lemke, Michael. *Die Berlinkrise 1958 bis 1963: Interessen und Handlungensspielräume der SED in Ost-West Konflikt.* Berlin: Akademie, 1996.

Lewytzkyj, Borys. *Sowjetische Entspannungspolitik heute.* Stuttgart: Seewald, 1976.

Löw, Konrad. *. . . bis zum Verrat der Freiheit: Die Gesellschaft der Bundesrepublik und die "DDR."* Munich: Langen Müller, 1993.

Löwenthal, Richard. *Vom kalten Krieg zur Ostpolitik.* Stuttgart: Seewald Verlag, 1974.

Löwenthal, Richard, and Heinrich Vogel, eds. *Sowjetpolitik der 70er Jahre.* Stuttgart: Kohlhammer, 1972.

Loth, Wilfried. *Stalins ungeliebtes Kind: Warum Moskau die DDR nicht wollte.* Berlin: Rowohlt, Mar. 1994.

Lundestad, Geir. *"Empire" by Integration: The United States and European Integration, 1945–1997.* New York: Oxford University Press, 1998.

Ludz, Peter Christian. *Die DDR zwischen Ost und West: Politische Analysen 1961 bis 1976.* Munich: Beck, 1977.

——, ed. *Gutachten zum Stand der DDR-und Vergleichenden Deutschlandforschung.* 4 vols. Bonn: Arbeitskreis für vergleichende Deutschlandforschung, 1978.

——. *Parteielite im Wandel: Funktionsaufbau, Sozialstruktur und Ideologie der SED-Führung.* Opladen, Ger.: Westdeutscher Verlag, 1968.

McAdams, A. James. *Germany Divided: From the Wall to Reunification.* Princeton: Princeton University Press, 1993.

McCauley, Martin. *The German Democratic Republic since 1945*. London: Macmillan, 1983.

McElvoy, Anne. *The Saddled Cow: East Germany's Life and Legacy*. London: Faber & Faber, 1992.

Mählert, Ulrich. *Die Freie Deutsche Jugend 1945–1949*. Paderborn, Ger.: Schöningh, 1995.

Maier, Charles S. *Dissolution: The Crisis of Communism and the End of East Germany*. Princeton: Princeton University Press, 1997.

———. "West Germany as Subject . . . and Object." *Central European History* 11 (Dec. 1978): 376–84.

Mampel, Siegfried. *Das Ministerium für Staatssicherheit der ehemaligen DDR als Ideologiepolizei: Zur Bedeutung einer Heilslehre als Mittel zum Griff auf das Bewußtsein für das Totalitarismusmodell*. Berlin: Duncker & Humblot, 1996.

Markovits, Inga. *Imperfect Justice: An East-West German Diary*. Oxford: Clarendon, 1995.

Marshall, Barbara. *Willy Brandt: A Political Biography*. Oxford: Macmillan, 1997.

Mastny, Vojtech. "Did NATO Win the Cold War? Looking Over the Wall." *Foreign Affairs* (May/June 1999): 176–89.

Meissner, Boris. *Sowjetische Kurkorrekturen: Breshnew und seine Erben*. Zurich: Edition Interfrom, 1984.

———. *Die Sowjetunion im Umbruch*. Stuttgart: Deutsche Verlags-Anstalt, 1988.

Merkl, Peter H. *German Foreign Policies, West & East*. Santa Barbara, Calif.: Clio, 1974.

———. *German Unification in the European Context*. University Park: Pennsylvania State University Press, 1993.

———, ed. *The Federal Republic of Germany at Forty*. New York: New York University Press, 1989.

Mitter, Armin, and Stefan Wolle. *Untergang auf Raten*. Munich: Bertelsmann, 1993.

Moreton, N. Edwina. *East Germany and the Warsaw Alliance: The Politics of Détente*. Boulder, Colo.: Westview, 1978.

———, ed. *Germany between East and West*. Cambridge: Cambridge University Press, 1987.

Morris, Stephen J. "The Soviet-Chinese-Vietnamese Triangle in the 1970s: The View from Moscow." Working Paper No. 25, Woodrow Wilson International Center for Scholars, Washington, D.C., Apr. 1999.

Morsey, Rudolf. *Die Bundesrepublik Deutschland: Entstehung und Entwicklung bis 1969*. Munich: Oldenbourg Verlag, 1990.

Müller, Reinhard. *Die Akte Wehner*. Berlin: Rowohlt, 1993.

Muron, Louis. *Pompidou*. Mesnil-sur-l'Estrée, Fr.: Flammarion, 1994.

Murphy, David E., Sergei A. Kondrashev, and George Bailey. *Battleground Berlin: CIA vs. KGB in the Cold War*. New Haven: Yale University Press, 1997.

Naimark, Norman M. *The Russians in Germany: A History of the Soviet Zone of Occupation, 1945–1949*. Cambridge: Belknap Press of Harvard University Press, 1995.

Nakath, Detlef, ed. *Deutschlandpolitiker der DDR erinnern sich*. Berlin: Fides, 1995.

———. *Erfurt und Kassel: Zu den Gesprächen zwischen dem BRD-Bundeskanzler Willy Brandt und dem DDR-Ministerratsvorsitzenden Willi Stoph im Frühjar 1970*. Berlin: Forscher- und Diskussionskreis DDR-Geschichte, 1995.

———. "Gewaltverzicht und Gleichberechtigung: Zur Parallelität der deutsch-sowjetischen Gespräche und der deutsch-deutschen Gipfeltreffen in Erfurt und Kassel im Frühjahr 1970." *Deutschland Archiv* 2 (Mar./Apr. 1998): 196–213.

———. *Die Verhandlungen zum deutsch-deutschen Grundlagenvertrag 1972: Zum Zusammenwirken von SED-Politbüro und DDR-Außenministerium bei den Gesprächen mit der BRD*. Berlin: Forscher- und Diskussionskreis DDR-Geschichte, 1993.

Nakath, Detlef, and Gerd-Rüdiger Stephan. *Countdown zur deutschen Einheit.* Berlin: Dietz, 1996.

——. *Von Hubertusstock nach Bonn.* Berlin: Dietz, 1995.

Nash, Philip. *The Other Missiles of October: Eisenhower, Kennedy, and the Jupiters, 1957–1963.* Chapel Hill: University of North Carolina Press, 1997.

Naumann, Gerhard, and Eckhard Trümpler. *Der Flop mit der DDR-Nation 1971.* Berlin: Dietz, 1991.

——. *Von Ulbricht zu Honecker: 1970 Krisenjahr.* Berlin: Dietz, Mar. 1990.

Nawrocki, Joachim. *Relations between Two States in Germany.* 2d ed. Bonn: Press and Information Office, 1988.

Nelson, Keith L. *The Making of Détente: Soviet-American Relations in the Shadow of Vietnam.* Baltimore: John Hopkins University Press, 1995.

Neubert, Ehrhart. *Geschichte der Opposition in der DDR 1949–1989.* Bonn: Bundeszentrale für politische Bildung, 1997.

Noland, Marcus. "Why North Korea Will Muddle Through." *Foreign Affairs* (July/Aug. 1997): 105–46.

Oberdorfer, Don. *The Turn: From the Cold War to a New Era: The United States and the Soviet Union 1983–1990.* New York: Simon & Schuster, 1991.

——. *The Two Koreas: A Contemporary History.* Reading, Mass.: Addison-Wesley, 1997.

Ostermann, Christian. "New Evidence on the Sino-Soviet Border Dispute, 1969–1971." *Cold War International History Project Bulletin* 6/7 (Winter 1995/96): 186–93.

——. " 'Die Ostdeutschen an einen langwierigen Kampf gewöhnen': Die Vereingten Staaten und der Aufstand vom 17. Juni 1953." *Deutschland Archiv* 3 (May/June 1997): 350–68.

Patton, David F. *Cold War Politics in Postwar Germany.* London: Macmillan, 1999.

Pauer, Jan. *Prag 1968: Der Einmarsch des Warschauer Paktes.* Bremen: Edition Temen, 1995.

Pirker, Theo, M. Rainer Lepsius, Rainer Weinert, and Hans-Hermann Hertle, eds. *Der Plan als Befehl und Fiktion: Wirtschaftsführung in der DDR.* Opladen, Ger.: Westdeutscher Verlag, 1995.

Plock, Ernest D. *The Basic Treaty and the Evolution of East-West German Relations.* Boulder, Colo.: Westview, 1986.

——. *East German-West German Relations and the Fall of the GDR.* Boulder, Colo.: Westview, 1993.

Podewin, Norbert. *". . . der Bitte des Genossen Walter Ulbricht zu entsprechen." Hintergründe und Modalitäten eines Führungswechsels.* Berlin: Forscher- und Diskussionskreis der DDR-Geschichte, 1996.

——. *Walter Ulbricht: Eine neue Biographie.* Berlin: Dietz, 1995.

Pollack, Detlef. *Kirche in der Organisationsgesellschaft: Zum Wandel der gesellschaftlichen Lage der evangelischen Kirchen in der DDR.* Cologne: Kohlhammer, 1994.

Pond, Elizabeth. *After the Wall.* New York: Priority, 1991.

——. *Beyond the Wall.* Washington: Brookings Institution, 1993.

——. "A Wall Destroyed." *International Security* 15 (Fall 1990): 35–66.

Potthoff, Heinrich. *Im Schatten der Mauer: Deutschlandpolitik 1961 bis 1990.* Hamburg: Propyläen, 1999.

——. "Eine zweite Etappe der Deutschlandpolitik." *Deutschland Archiv* 1 (Jan./Feb. 1997): 116–24.

Potthoff, Heinrich, ed. *Bonn und Ost-Berlin 1969–1982: Dialog auf höchster Ebene und vertrauliche Kanäle Darstellung und Dokumente.* Bonn: Dietz, 1997.

———. *Die Koalition der Vernunft: Deutschlandpolitik in den 8oer Jahren*. Munich: dtv, June 1995.

Prieß, Lutz, Vaclav Kural, and Manfred Wilke. *Die SED und der "Prager Frühling" 1968: Politik gegen einen "Sozialismus mit menschlichem Antlitz."* Berlin: Akademie, 1996.

Prokop, Siegfried. *Das SED-Politbüro Aufstieg und Ende (1949–1989)*. Berlin: Forscher- und Diskussionskreis DDR-Geschichte, 1996.

Pulzer, Peter. *German Politics, 1945–1995*. Oxford: Oxford University Press, 1995.

Rabinow, Paul, ed. *The Foucault Reader*. New York: Pantheon, 1984.

Raina, Peter, ed. *Internationale Politik in den siebziger Jahren*. Frankfurt: Fischer, 1973.

Rosenberg, Tina. *The Haunted Land: Facing Europe's Ghosts After Communism*. New York: Random House, 1995.

Salisbury, Harrison. *War between Russia and China*. New York: Norton, 1969.

Sarotte, M. E. "Elite Intransigence and the End of the Berlin Wall." *German Politics* 2 (Aug. 1993): 270–87.

———. "MfS-Dokumente zu den deutsch-deutschen Verhandlungen Anfang der siebziger Jahre." *Deutschland Archiv* 3 (May/June 1997): 407–11.

———. "Nicht nur Fremde ausspioniert: MfS-Dokumente zu den deutsch-deutschen Verhandlungen Anfang der siebziger Jahre," *Deutschland Archiv* 3 (May/June 1997): 409.1

———. "A Small Town in (East) Germany: The Erfurt Meeting of 1970 and the Dynamics of Cold War Détente." *Diplomatic History* (Winter 2001): in press.

———. "Spying Not Only on Strangers: Documenting Stasi Involvement in Cold War German-German Negotiations." *Intelligence and National Security* 11 (Oct. 1996): 765–79.

———. "Under Cover of Boredom: Review Article of Recent Publications on the East German Ministry for State Security, or Stasi." *Intelligence and National Security* 12 (Oct. 1997): 196–210

———. "Vor 25 Jahren: Verhandlungen über den Grundlagenvertrag. Zum internationalen Kontext der deutsch-deutschen Gespräche." *Deutschland Archiv* 6 (Nov./Dec. 1997): 901–11.

Schätzler, Johann-Georg. "Staatenfusion und Abrechnungsmentalität." *Deutschland Archiv* 1 (Jan./Feb. 1997): 105–15.

Schell, Jonathan. *The Time of Illusion*. New York: Vintage, 1976.

Schlomann, Friedrich. *Die Maulwürfe: Die Stasi-Helfer im Westen sind immer noch unter uns*. Frankfurt: Ullstein, 1994.

Schmid, Günther. *Die Deutschlandpolitik der Regierung Brandt/Scheel*. Munich: tuduv Verlagsgesellschaft, 1975.

Schmidt, Karl-Heinz. *Dialog über Deutschland: Studien zur Deutschlandpolitik von KPdSU und SED (1960–1979)*. Baden-Baden: Nomos, 1998.

Scholz, Günther. *Herbert Wehner*. Düsseldorf: ECON, 1986.

Schroeder, Klaus. *Der SED-Staat: Geschichte und Strukturen der DDR*. Munich: Bayerische Landeszentrale für Politische Bildungsarbeit, 1998.

———, ed. *Geschichte und Transformation des SED-Staates: Beiträge und Analysen*. Berlin: Akademie, 1994.

Schulzinger, Robert D. *American Diplomacy in the Twentieth Century*. New York: Oxford, 1984.

———. *Henry Kissinger: Doctor of Diplomacy*. New York: Columbia University Press, 1989.

Schwartz, Siegfried. "Die deutsche Frage-vielseitig betrachtet." *Deutschland Archiv* 6 (Nov./Dec. 1996): 966–69.

——. "Zäher Streiter für die Einheit." *Deutschland Archiv* 1 (Jan./Feb. 1997): 143–45.

Schwartz, Thomas A. "The Berlin Crisis and the Cold War." *Diplomatic History* 21 (Winter 1997): 139–48.

Schwarz, Hans-Peter, and Boris Meissner, eds. *Entspannungspolitik in Ost und West.* Cologne: Carl Heymanns, 1979.

Schwarze, Hanns Werner. *The GDR Today: Life in the Other Germany.* London: Wolff, 1973.

Seiffert, Wolfgang, and Norbert Treutwein. *Die Schalck-Papiere: DDR-Mafia zwischen Ost und West.* Munich: Quick Verlag, 1991.

Selvage, Douglas. "New Evidence on the Berlin Crisis, 1958–1962." *Cold War International History Project Bulletin* 11 (Winter 1998): 200–203, 218–29.

Sestanovich, Stephen Rockwell. "Nuclear Proliferation and Soviet Foreign Policy, 1957–1968: The Limits of Soviet-American Cooperation." Ph.D. diss., Harvard University, 1971.

Siebenmorgen, Peter. *Staatssicherheit der DDR: Der Westen im Fadenkreuz der Stasi.* Bonn: Bouvier, 1993.

Smyser, W. R. *From Yalta to Berlin.* New York: St. Martin's, 1999.

Sodaro, Michael J. *Moscow, Germany, and the West from Khrushchev to Gorbachev.* Ithaca: Cornell University Press, 1990.

Soutou, Georges-Henri. *L'alliance incertaine: Les rapports politico-stratégiques franco-allemands, 1954–1996.* Paris: Fayard, 1996.

Spittmann, Ilse. *Die DDR unter Honecker.* Cologne: Wissenschaft und Politik, 1990.

Staadt, Jochen. *Die geheime Westpolitik der SED 1960–1970: Von der gesamtdeutschen Orientierung zur sozialistischen Nation.* Berlin: Akademie, 1993.

——. "Walter Ulbrichts letzter Machtkampf." *Deutschland Archiv* 5 (Sept./Oct. 1996): 686–700.

Staritz, Dietrich. *Geschichte der DDR 1949–1989.* Frankfurt: Suhrkamp, 1996.

Stelkens, Jochen. "Machtwechsel in Ost-Berlin: Der Sturz Walter Ulbrichts 1971." *Vierteljahrshefte für Zeitgeschichte* 4 (Oct. 1997): 503–33.

Stent, Angela E. *Russia and Germany Reborn.* Princeton: Princeton University Press, 1999.

Stern, Carola. *Ulbricht: Eine politische Biografie.* Cologne: Kiepenheuer & Witsch, 1964.

Stöss, Richard, ed. *Parteienhandbuch: Die Parteien in der Bundesrepublik Deutschland, 1945–1980.* Opladen, Ger.: Westdeutscher Verlag, 1983.

"Symposium: Soviet Archives: Recent Revelations and Cold War Historiography." *Diplomatic History* 21 (Spring 1997): 215–81.

Szabo, Stephen. *The Diplomacy of German Unification.* New York: St. Martin's, 1992.

Thompson, Wayne C. *The Political Odyssey of Herbert Wehner.* Boulder, Colo.: Westview, 1993.

Timmermann, Heiner, ed. *Diktaturen in Europa im 20. Jahrhundert—Der Fall DDR.* Berlin: Duncker & Humblot, 1996.

Tessmer, Carsten, and Klaus Wiegrefe. "Deutschlandpolitik in der Krise: Herbert Wehners Besuch in der DDR 1973." *Deutschland Archiv* 6 (June 1994): 600–627.

Torpey, John C. *Intellectuals, Socialism, and Dissent: The East German Opposition and Its Legacy.* Minneapolis: University of Minnesota Press, 1995.

Towle, Philip. *Arms Control and East West Relations.* New York: St. Martin's, 1983.

Trachtenberg, Marc. *A Constructed Peace: The Making of the European Settlement 1945–1963.* Princeton: Princeton University Press, 1999.

Tucker, Robert C., ed. *The Marx-Engels Reader.* 2d ed. New York: Norton, 1978.

Turner, Henry Ashby, Jr. *Germany from Partition to Unification.* 2d ed. New Haven: Yale University Press, 1992.

Ulam, Adam B. *The Communists: The Story of Power and Lost Illusions: 1948–1991.* New York: Scribner's, 1992.

———. *Dangerous Relations: The Soviet Union in World Politics 1970–1982.* New York: Oxford, 1983.

———. *Expansion and Coexistence: Soviet Foreign Policy 1917–1973.* 2d ed. New York: Praeger, 1974.

Urwin, Derek W. *Western Europe since 1945: A Political History.* 4th ed. London: Longman, 1989.

Van Evera, Stephen. *Guide to Methodology for Students of Political Science.* Cambridge: MIT, 1996.

Vogtmeier, Andreas. *Egon Bahr und die Deutsche Frage: Zur Entwicklung des sozialdemokratischen Ost- und Deutschlandpolitik vom Kriegsende bis zur Vereinigung.* Bonn: Dietz, 1996.

———. "Sozialliberale Deutschlandpolitik." *Deutschland Archiv* 4 (July/Aug. 1997): 645–47.

Vollnhals, Clemens, ed. *Das Ministerium für Staatssicherheit: Ein Instrument totalitärer Herrschaftsausübung.* Berlin: BStU, 1995.

Volze, Armin. "Ein großer Bluff? Die Westverschuldung der DDR." *Deutschland Archiv* 5 (Sept./Oct. 1996): 701–13.

Voslensky, Michael S. *Sterbliche Götter: Die Lehrmeister der Nomenklatura.* Vienna: Straube, 1989.

Waltz, Kenneth N. *Theory of International Politics.* New York: Random House, 1979.

Wandycz, Piotr S. *The Price of Freedom.* London: Routledge, 1992.

Weber, Hermann. *Die DDR 1945–1990.* 2d ed. Munich: Oldenbourg, 1993.

———. *DDR: Grundriß der Geschichte.* New ed. Hannover, Ger.: Fackelträger, 1991.

Weber, Jürgen, ed. *Der SED-Staat: Neues über eine vergangene Diktatur.* Munich: Olzog-Verlag, 1994.

Weidenfeld, Werner, and Karl-Rudolf Korte, eds. *Handbuch zur deutschen Einheit.* Bonn: Bundeszentrale für politische Bildung, 1996.

Weitz, Eric D. *Creating German Communism, 1890–1990: From Popular Protests to Socialist State.* Princeton: Princeton University Press, 1997.

Wendt, Alexander, and Daniel Friedheim. "Hierarchy under Anarchy: Informal Empire and the East German State." *International Organization* 49 (Autumn 1995): 689–722.

Wenzke, Rüdiger. *Die NVA und der Prager Frühling 1968: Die Rolle Ulbrichts und der DDR-Streitkräfte bei der Niederschlagung der Tschechoslowakischen Reformbewegung.* Berlin: Links, 1995.

Westad, Odd Arne. "Secrets of the Second World: The Russian Archives and the Reinterpretation of Cold War History." *Diplomatic History* 21 (Spring 1997): 259–71.

———, ed. *Brothers in Arms: The Rise and Fall of the Sino-Soviet Alliance, 1945–1963.* Stanford: Stanford University Press, 1998.

Westad, Odd Arne, Sven Holtsmark, and Iver B. Neumann, eds. *The Soviet Union in Eastern Europe, 1945–89.* New York: St. Martin's, 1994.

Wettig, Gerhard. "Die sowjetische Politik während der Berlinkrise 1958 bis 1962." *Deutschland Archiv* 3 (May/June 1997): 383–98.

———. *Das Vier-Mächte-Abkommen in der Bewährungsprobe.* Berlin: Berlin Verlag, 1981.

Whitney, Craig R. *Spy Trader: Germany's Devil's Advocate and the Darkest Secrets of the Cold War.* New York: Random House, 1993.

Wiedmann, Roland, ed. *Die Organisationsstruktur des Ministeriums für Staatssicherheit 1989*. Berlin: BStU, 1995.

Wilkens, Andreas. *Der unstete Nachbar: Frankreich, die deutsche Ostpolitik und die Berliner Vier-Mächte-Verhandlungen, 1969–1974*. Munich: Oldenbourg, 1990.

Williams, Kieran. *The Prague Spring and Its Aftermath: Czechoslovak Politics 1968–1970*. Cambridge: Cambridge University Press, 1997.

Winkler, H. A. "Rebuilding of a Nation: The Germans Before and After Unification." *Daedalus* 123 (Winter 1994): 107–27.

Winkler, H. A., and Carola Stern, eds. *Wendepunkte deutscher Geschichte 1848–1990*. Frankfurt: Fischer, 1994.

Winters, Peter Jochen. "Wie souverän war die DDR?" *Deutschland Archiv* 2 (Mar./Apr. 1996): 170–72.

Wohlforth, William. "A Certain Idea of Science: How International Relations Theory Avoids the New Cold War History." *Journal of Cold War Studies* 1 (Spring 1999): 39–60.

———. "New Evidence on Moscow's Cold War." *Diplomatic History* 21 (Spring 1997): 229–42.

Wolfe, Thomas W. *Soviet Military Power and European Security*. Los Angeles: RAND Corporation, 1966.

Young, John W. *Cold War Europe, 1945–1991: A Political History*. 2d ed. London: Arnold, 1996.

———. *The Longman Companion to Cold War and Detente, 1941–1991*. London: Longman, 1993.

Zatlin, Jonathan R. "Hard Marks and Soft Revolutionaries: The Economics of Entitlement and the Debate about German Monetary Union, November 9, 1989–March 18, 1990." *German Politics and Society* 33 (Fall 1994): 1–28.

Zelikow, Philip, and Condoleezza Rice. *Germany Unified and Europe Transformed: A Study in Statecraft*. Cambridge: Harvard University Press, 1995.

Zubok, Vladislav, and Constantine Pleshakov. *Inside the Kremlin's Cold War: From Stalin to Khrushchev*. Cambridge: Harvard University Press, 1996.

Index

Treaty, 69–71, 97–98; and quadripartite talks, 71–77, 123, 127
—relations with SED: oil deliveries, 19; and ouster of Ulbricht, 77–84, 98–101, 107–11, 168, 174; and question of "linkage," 97–98, 177; and Basic Treaty, 143–44; pressures SED to cooperate with West Germany, 159–60
Brezhnev Doctrine, 17, 32–35, 43
Brezhnev-Nixon summit. *See* Moscow Summit
Buchenwald: Brandt visit to, 49–50
Bundesrat, 102
Bundestag, 102, 131, 136
Bundy, William, 136, 187, 238 (n. 52)

Cambodia: invasion of, 56
CDU (Christlich-Demokratische Union/ Christian-Democratic Union), 13, 26, 27, 96, 130, 132, 136; loss in election of 1972, 153. *See also* Barzel, Rainer; Kohl, Helmut
Checkpoint Charlie, 11
Chemical weapons, 49
"Child support" payments, 155–56, 172. *See also* Emigration from East Germany
China. *See* PRC
Cienfuegos Bay incident, 73, 77
Citizenship: question of German, 140, 146–47, 169
Clay, Lucius, 57
Conference on European Security. *See* CSCE
Constitution (East German), 13, 141
"Consumption Terror," 266 (n. 38)
Council of Ministers (East German), 154
CPSU (Communist Party of the Soviet Union), 2, 31, 64, 66, 80, 82, 94, 108, 136, 148, 167, 181, 185. *See also* Brezhnev, Leonid; Soviet Union
CSCE (Conference on Security and Cooperation in Europe), 122, 148, 153, 160, 195 (n. 32)
CSSR (Czechoslovak Socialist Republic), 81. *See also* Prague Spring of 1968
CSU (Christlich-Soziale Union/ Christian-Social Union), 26, 130, 132, 136; loss in election of 1972, 153. *See also* CDU

Cuba, 73–74. *See also* Cienfuegos Bay incident

Damansky Island, 21
Dayton Accord, 122
Dean, Jonathan, 76
De Gaulle, Charles, 16, 70
Détente, 4–7, 10, 30, 57, 166–67, 174, 179
Deutsche Bank, 33
Deutschlandpolitik, xvi
Divergence: between East German and Soviet interests, 168–69
Division of Germany, 5, 8
Dobrynin, Anatoly, xvii, 25, 75, 104, 107, 117, 136
Dubček, Alexander, 16
Dresden, 84

East German Revolt of 1953, 10, 16
East Germany. *See* German Democratic Republic; SED
Eastern Treaties. *See* Moscow Treaty; Warsaw Treaty
"East Sea Week," 80
Ehmke, Horst, xii, 86, 155
Eitel, Antonius, xii, 70, 72, 92–93, 95
Elections: 1969 U.S. and West German, 23; 1972 West German, 150, 153
Emigration from East Germany, 140; of children and minors, 152–53, 178; blockage of, 155–60; from Soviet Union, 158
Erfurt, 84; "summit" meeting, 38; planning for meeting, 42–46; Brandt's arrival, 46–48; negotiations at, 48–51; "optical impression" of, 51–53; consequences of, 53–54; subsequent impact of, 58, 65, 67, 95, 170, 173–74, 187
Erhard, Ludwig, 151
Essen agreement of 1970, 33, 70
European Community, 136
European Security Conference. *See* CSCE

Falin, Valentin, xii, 38, 41, 71, 119, 129, 167; and Erfurt, 42; and Bertsch Delegation, 84–85; and Soviet fear of PRC, 102–3
FBS (Forward-Based Systems), 119
FDJ (Freie Deutsche Jugend/Free German Youth), 30

Nuclear Non-Proliferation Treaty, 16, 27
Nuclear weapons. *See* Atomic weapons
NVA (Nationale Volksarmee/National
People's Army), 17

Oder-Neiße line, 69
Oil trade, 19
Olympic Games, Munich 1972, 140–42,
172
"Optical impression" of Erfurt, 51–54
Ostpolitik, xvi, 3, 10, 27, 28, 30, 53, 57,
68, 99, 166, 173, 176, 179, 182, 185,
187, 201 (n. 109); importance of, 4–7;
Ulbricht's attitude toward, 77–78, 110–
11, 171; and Stasi, 170; comparison to
détente, 174–75. *See also* Basic Treaty;
Moscow Treaty; Warsaw Treaty

Pakistan, 38
"Pass-Agreement," 12, 86, 88, 194 (n. 20)
Peace Notes, 13
Peking. *See* PRC
Pentagon, 119
Permanent representations, 154
Poland, 69, 82, 97–99
Politburo, East German. *See* Honecker,
Erich; SED; Ulbricht, Walter
Politburo, Soviet. *See* Brezhnev, Leonid;
CPSU
Pompidou, Georges, 58, 75
Postal agreement of 1970, 60
Prague Spring of 1968, 8, 11, 16–17, 29,
53–54, 81, 197 (n. 56)
Prague Treaty, 160
Pravda, 82, 108, 109
PRC (People's Republic of China), 38, 41,
64, 74–76, 118, 120, 131, 134–35; Sino-
Soviet antagonism, 4, 21–24, 43, 103,
108–9, 124, 138, 144, 159–60, 167, 169,
177–78; Sino-Soviet border skirmishes
begin, 21–23. *See also* Lin Biao; Mao
Zedong; Zhou En-lai
Public opinion: impact on Soviet Bloc, 45,
171, 192 (n. 13)

Quadripartite Accord. *See* Quadripartite
Agreement
Quadripartite Agreement, 114–24, 127,
131, 135; enters into force, 137. *See also*
Quadripartite talks

Quadripartite talks, 35, 38, 43–44, 59, 66,
71–77, 86, 87, 97, 102, 111, 114–23,
148. *See also* Kissinger, Henry; Rush,
Kenneth

Revanchism: fear of German, 145
Revolution of 1989, xi, 11
RIAS (Radio im amerikanischen Sektor/
Radio in the American Sector), 27
Rogers, William, 138
Rush, Kenneth, 25, 35, 72, 76, 104, 106–7,
116–17, 129; finalizes Quadripartite
Agreement, 120–21

Sahm, Ulrich, xii, 45, 92–93, 130
SALT (Strategic Arms Limitation Talks),
33, 56, 71, 104, 114, 124, 132, 137, 178,
182; linkage to quadripartite talks, 76–
77, 118–20
Sauvagnargues, Jean, 74, 121
Scheel, Walter, 13, 34, 39, 68, 134, 144
Schmidt, Helmut, xii, 13, 21, 54, 142, 182,
186
Schnitzler, Karl Eduard von, 51
Schröder, Gerhard, 12
Schumann, Maurice, 74
Second World War. *See* World War II
SED (Sozialistische Einheitspartei
Deutschlands/Socialist Unity Party of
Germany,), 1–2
—early history: formation of, 8–9; and
Berlin Wall, 10–11; and churches, 11
—at beginning of Ostpolitik era: unnerves
Moscow, 3; seeks international legitimization, 3, 136; and secret police, 4; as
economic "model," 8, 17–21, 82; faces
revolt of 1953, 10; and Sino-Soviet
rivalry, 21; negotiations with West, 23;
cooperation with Warsaw Pact, 31–32
—begins contact with West Germany:
sends draft treaty to West Germany,
32–33; Erfurt meeting, 42, 44–46, 48–
49, 51–54, 56; Kassel meeting, 60, 63–
64
—in context of superpower relations: and
détente, 65–66; and Moscow Treaty, 67,
69; and Brezhnev's "double game," 80–
82, 98; and Valentin Falin, 84–85
—begins negotiations with West Germany: Bahr-Kohl talks commence, 88;